More praise for *Lincoln's Generals' Wives*

"Candice Hooper's vivid new look at the lives of these Union generals' wives reveals a hidden chapter of Civil War history. Brimming with rich detail, Hooper's brisk and beguiling narrative weaves together the military and the personal to introduce a fascinating cast of characters: John Charles Frémont and Jessie Benton, George McClellan and his wife Nelly, Ellen and William T. Sherman, and Ulysses Grant and Julia Dent. These Union women emerge from the shadows and take their rightful place in the forefront of Civil War women's history."
    —**Catherine Clinton**, author of *Mrs. Lincoln: A Life*

"Cliches ought to be avoided like, well, cliches, yet occasionally one has substance, and none more than the old adage about there being a good woman behind every successful man. It is almost always true, and demonstrated nowhere better than in Candice Hooper's fine new work *Lincoln's Generals' Wives*. No women gave their husbands greater entree into high political and military circles than Jessie Benton Frémont, 'Nelly' Marcy McClellan, and Ellen Ewing Sherman. None acted as a greater stabilizing force and safe haven from the pressure of command than Julia Dent Grant. Among them they reveal the full gamut of a spouse's potential influence on her husband's career, from the harm to be done by Jessie's too strong an advocacy to the damage done by Nelly's ego boosting, to Ellen's unflinching faith and loyalty that sustained her 'Cump,' and perhaps most of all in Julia, whom Hooper aptly summarizes in three perfect words: 'center of gravity.' This is a fine book, imaginatively conceived, deeply researched, and ably written. Our hats should be off to all five of the women involved."—**William C. Davis Jr.**, author of *Crucible of Command: Ulysses S. Grant and Robert E. Lee—The War They Fought, the Peace They Forged*

"Candice Shy Hooper's *Lincoln's Generals' Wives* offers unprecedented opportunities to appreciate heretofore unheard voices in the strategic debates that shaped wartime polices in the Civil War North. The four generals whose spouses are profiled in this work all benefited from both the overt and subtle input of their closest confidante who might serve as a moral compass, calm doubts, or rein in overconfidence, or quietly and simply provide a secure sounding board for important decisions. As the author clearly shows, the wives of Generals Frémont, McClellan, Sherman, and Grant each tried to meet these challenges, and Hooper's evaluation of their methods and priorities—as well as their successes and failures—merits our attention."—**Carol Reardon**, George Winfree Professor of American History, Penn State University

"For those who think they know everything about the Civil War, here are fresh, revealing, well-crafted portraits of women who not only helped propel their husbands to major military careers but established themselves, for better or worse, as formidable battlers in their own right. Yet this is even more than behind-the-scenes history. For in turning the spotlight on the generals' wives, the author invariably shines humanity on chieftains we have heretofore imagined only in tents, not homes; in the company of fellow officers, not families. Candy Hooper's research and analysis helps us better understand what inspired—or inhibited—these generals and how their spouses helped shape them into heroes—or failures."—**Harold Holzer**, author of *Lincoln and the Power of the Press: The War for Public Opinion* (winner of the Lincoln Prize)

"Hooper's book is unique in the annals of Civil War history. Here I found Julia Grant, wife of Ulysses S. Grant, and my great-great-grandmother, as I'd never known her before. Thoroughly researched and readable, the book is remarkably moving."—**Ulysses Grant Dietz**, board member and Vice President, the Ulysses S. Grant Association and Presidential Library

"In this insightful study, Candice Shy Hooper reminds us of the important role played by the wives of several key players in the Union high command. Even as they served as sounding boards and personal advisers for their husbands, these women took it upon themselves to protect their men's interests and advocate on their behalf; at times they became subjects of controversy. Essential reading for those who want to understand these men, the war they waged, and the women who stood beside them."—**Brooks D. Simpson**, Arizona State University

"With *Lincoln's Generals' Wives,* Candice Shy Hooper has opened a new door in Civil War scholarship. Her invaluable book sheds light not only on the lives of these four remarkable women and their marriages but on the broader theme of Civil War era politics, of both the national and gender varieties."—**Clay Risen**, coeditor of *Disunion,* the *New York Times*'s series on the Civil War

"If ever there has been a need for a particular book, it is certainly for this one. Candy Hooper has studied the wives of four Civil War generals and demonstrated the essential roles they played in their husbands' lives and the life of the nation. She presents important insights into military history, the Civil War, and gender history. Scholars and the general public will find this book well-written and intriguing. It is a must read."—**John F. Marszalek**, executive director of the Ulysses S. Grant Association's Ulysses S. Presidential Library, Mississippi State University, and the author of important books on Grant, Sherman, and the Civil War

"Hooper's book gives us a fresh look at some of the most famous military men in American history—through the prism of their marriages. *Lincoln's Generals' Wives* proves the old adage that the toughest job in the military is that of a military spouse."—**General Paul Kern**, U.S. Army (retired)

Lincoln's Generals' Wives

Clockwise from upper left: Jessie Frémont, Ellen Sherman, Julia Grant, and Nelly McClellan—circa 1865.

LINCOLN'S GENERALS' WIVES

Four Women Who Influenced the Civil War—for Better and for Worse

Candice Shy Hooper

The Kent State University Press • Kent, Ohio

Excerpts from *The Civil War Papers of George B. McClellan: Selected Correspondence, 1860–1865,* edited Stephen W. Sears. Copyright © 1989 by Stephen W. Sears. Reprinted by permission of Houghton Mifflin Harcourt Publishing Company. All rights reserved. Excerpts from *The Personal Memoirs of Julia Dent Grant (Mrs. Ulysses S. Grant)* by John Y. Simon. Copyright © 1975 by the Ulysses S. Grant Association. Reproduced by permission of the publisher and Ulysses S. Grant Presidential Library. Excerpts from The Papers of Ulysses S. Grant appear courtesy of the Ulysses S. Grant Presidential Library. Excerpts from the William T. Sherman Family Papers are reproduced courtesy of the University of Notre Dame Archives.

Library of Congress Catalog Card Number 2015036101
ISBN 978-1-60635-278-6
Manufactured in the United States of America

LIBRARY OF CONGRESS CATALOGING-IN-PUBLICATION DATA
Hooper, Candice Shy, author.
 Lincoln's generals' wives : four women who influenced the Civil War—for better and for worse / Candice Shy Hooper.
   pages cm. — (Civil War in the North)
 Includes bibliographical references and index.
 ISBN 978-1-60635-278-6 (hardcover : alk. paper) ∞
   1. United States—History—Civil War, 1861–1865—Women. 2. Frémont, Jessie Benton, 1824–1902. 3. McClellan, Mary Ellen Marcy, 1835–1915. 4. Sherman, Ellen Ewing, 1824–1888. 5. Grant, Julia Dent, 1826–1902. 6. Generals' spouses—United States—Biography. 7. United States—History—Civil War, 1861–1865—Biography. I. Title.
 E628.H66 2016
 973.7082—dc23
                          2015036101
20 19 18 17 16   5 4 3 2 1

 for Lindsay

Contents

Notes to Readers

The original spelling and grammar have been preserved in quoting from the letters, journals, and memoirs of the women and men who fill these pages.

Many of the illustrations are reproductions of photographic cards popular in the nineteenth century, called "cartes de visite."

Introduction

This is the story of four remarkable women whose marriages placed them in positions to influence the course of history and whose personalities ensured they would. Jessie Frémont, Nelly McClellan, Ellen Sherman, and Julia Grant were all strong, smart, resilient women. They had to be. If not, they would not have attracted the men who wooed and married them, nor could they have endured the humiliation and heartbreak that the Civil War held in store for them. None of the women was a principal actor on the stage of the Civil War, but each one's family, education, character, perception of Abraham Lincoln, and relationship with her husband uniquely fitted her to play a strong supporting role. The story of the Civil War is not complete without them.

In the middle of the nineteenth century, in the midst of a terrible civil war, American women who had been nurtured and educated to supervise household staff and adorn society found themselves wrenched from their traditional roles. They were thrust into a wholly unfamiliar social and political landscape. While brother fought brother on the battlefield, sisters were torn from each other's arms by their husbands' call to duty. The choice of which side to favor, North or South, was almost never the wife's. Jefferson Davis's wife, Varina, spoke for women on both sides of the conflict when she retreated from Washington to the first capital of the Confederacy, in Montgomery, Alabama, declaring, "My husband is my country." During the Civil War, women's struggles to raise children and keep hearth and home intact were titanic, their adaptability Darwinian.[1]

Compared to the extensive literature on Confederate women, relatively little has been written about wives of Union soldiers. Some historians have provided valuable insight into how Northern women faced twin challenges of coping with the war's impact on their lives and with often unfavorable public comparisons to the aggressive patriotism of their threadbare, fire-eating sisters in the South. Wives of senior Union generals, who were by and large from the middle class, suffered relatively fewer deprivations than their Southern sisters. But their lives were not easy, and their choices were fraught with difficulties. If they sought to stay near their husbands, they traveled vast distances through dangerous country to set up housekeeping, often in tents or crude shacks. They brought, and sometimes bore, children on the way. They constantly improvised to deal with the poor quality of food, furniture, clothing, and shelter. They risked disease, capture, and death to provide comforts of home in the field. If they stayed at home, the women endured lengthy separations from their husbands as they struggled on their own to maintain their households, care for children and parents, and juggle complex financial transactions to keep financially afloat. Letters, which could be infrequent, might be a couple's only form of communication for months at a time.[2]

Wives eagerly read newspapers to keep informed of war news, but also, to be sure, to track their husbands' welfare. A wife's attention in that regard was as much for battlefield casualty reports as for news from Washington, where Congress and the Administration micromanaged the war, especially in the early years. While her first concern was for his safety, a general's wife knew that her husband had as much chance of losing his command from a political misstep or malicious gossip as from a military defeat. The nineteenth century was the high watermark of the Victorian-era culture, which valued separate "spheres" for men (public) and for women (private). But the challenges of the Civil War began to erode that division. Women not only sought more opportunities for themselves, but on occasion during the war, wives stepped into the public sphere to help their husbands. When opportunity arose or disaster struck, some bravely hurled themselves into the very vortex of the war to save the Union: they stormed the office of President Abraham Lincoln.[3]

That was one aspect of his job that Lincoln apparently enjoyed. "Selecting generals was a galling, dull business, and [President Lincoln] seized every chance he had to get some fun out of it," wrote historian T. Harry Williams, in the first modern study of Lincoln as commander in chief.

> He liked to have attractive wives of officers besiege him for promotions for their husbands. In the Lincoln Papers is a list he made in 1861 of officers he wanted to remember when he made appointments. After the name of Lieutenant Slemmer is the notation: "His pretty wife says a Major, or first Captain." Of another wife who wanted him to make her husband a brigadier general,

Lincoln wrote: "She is a saucy woman and I am afraid she will keep torment-
ing me until I may have do it."[4]

Lincoln did, in fact, make Lieutenant Slemmer a captain, owing, perhaps,
in part to his pretty wife's pleading, but no doubt also to the young man's
courageous defense of Fort Pickens early in the war. Mrs. Gabriel Paul also
saw her husband promoted—to brigadier general, as she wished—less than a
month after that "saucy woman" visited the president.[5]

The hordes of office seekers who hounded Abraham Lincoln at all hours of
the day and night are a staple of any history of his presidency, but some of the
most memorable tales are those of desperate wives within that throng begging
presidential passes to the front lines to care for wounded husbands or par-
dons for husbands accused of desertion or dereliction of duty. Less familiar,
though, are tales of ambitious military officers sending their wives to petition
the president for promotion.

Lincoln's search for a successful general-in-chief spanned three of the
war's four terrible years. Many men auditioned for the role, recommended
to Lincoln by their experience in earlier wars or their powerful political connections, which sometimes included their wives' families. Even when women
had no hand in their husbands' promotions, however, the president's appointments were in some instances a prelude to historically significant connections
between Lincoln and his generals' wives.

This was particularly true with respect to the wives of four of Lincoln's most
famous generals. Jessie Frémont, Nelly McClellan, Ellen Sherman, and Julia
Grant each met with Lincoln. Although none of the women asked Lincoln to
promote her husband, two of those women did, in fact, personally appeal to
the president when their husbands' careers were in trouble during the war. The
most famous of those encounters occurred late in the evening of September
10, 1861, when Jessie Frémont's effort to convince Lincoln to revoke his order
to her husband quickly escalated into a hostile confrontation with the president. Ellen Sherman's visit to the White House early the following year was far
less dramatic but far more gratifying to her and her family. Though Nelly Mc-
Clellan and Julia Grant each met Lincoln on more than one occasion, neither
woman ever sought an audience with the president to plead for help or forbearance, even when their husbands suffered serious disfavor in Washington.
But Nelly and Julia expressed their very different opinions of Lincoln to their
husbands. Nelly's negative view of Lincoln fed her husband's disdain for him,

which was a factor in the general's failure. Julia's respect and affection for the president, on the other hand, resonated with her husband and his commander in chief and was reflected in the upward trajectory of Grant's wartime career.

Jessie Benton Frémont, Mary Ellen "Nelly" Marcy McClellan, Ellen Ewing Sherman, and Julia Dent Grant were all tough, fearless women—like so many military wives of the era—who provided more than merely a domestic backdrop for their husbands' military ventures. As will be shown, they were quite different from each other. In two respects, though, they were alike. First, perhaps owing to the fashion of the times, likenesses of the women taken at roughly the same time show them to be strikingly similar. Except for Julia Grant, who, though tiny, had a strong, athletic build, they were petite, brunette, and they all dressed for portraits demurely in dark dresses with white collars. The photographs of Jessie Frémont and Nelly McClellan probably do not do them justice, since daguerreotype technology required stiff, unsmiling poses. In paintings of Jessie Frémont, Ellen Sherman, and Julia Grant, on the other hand, the artists may have taken pains to flatter, and they reveal a bit more spirit in their eyes. In that respect, their paintings are more accurate than the photographs, revealing the second similarity they shared: these women had spunk.

Jessie Ann Benton Frémont stirred up a storm all of her life, almost from the day she was born and given a man's name. Thomas Hart Benton, one of the most powerful politicians in the United States, had planned to name a son for his father Jesse. When his wife presented him with a girl, he merely altered the spelling of the child's name. Benton proceeded to educate her like a man, too, and by the time she was a teen, Jessie spoke three languages and read Latin and Greek. Vivacious, opinionated, and talkative, she rebuffed her parents' efforts to marry her to respectable, successful, elderly suitors, like former President Martin Van Buren. By that time, she had already found the heart into which she would pour her endless love. To his everlasting regret, when Jessie was fifteen years old, Benton introduced his beloved daughter to the strikingly handsome, glamorous, famous Western explorer John Charles Frémont.

The marriage of Jessie and John Frémont has long been celebrated as a "modern" marriage, based largely on Jessie's zealous tendency toward action in the traditionally male worlds of politics and war. During the twenty years preceding the Civil War, Frémont had crossed the Rockies and mapped trails for Americans to follow, he helped to seize California in the Mexican War, and he was chosen to run as the first Republican candidate for president. Jessie played a pivotal role in each of those feats. When Lincoln selected Frémont major general in May of 1861, the dashing forty-eight-year-old's career reached its zenith. Jessie would be intimately involved in his military command during the Civil War as his unofficial chief of staff. In the words of one historian, they were a nineteenth-century "power couple." From the inside, however, the Frémonts' marriage looked more traditional, quite nineteenth-, if not eighteenth-, century, in the wife's unquestioning devotion to the husband. If her marriage was old-fashioned, though, Jessie's personal angst was utterly modern. Her frustration at society's strict gender roles only made her strive harder to seize and exercise power she could have easily won and confidently wielded were she a man. When she claimed roles as her husband's ghostwriter and later his military chief of staff, Jessie brilliantly exploited opportunities for influence and power rare in Victorian society. By the time the Civil War began, all three parts of her famous name—Jessie and Benton and Frémont—carried nearly equal weight in the public mind.[6]

Famous Jessie stands in stark contrast to obscure Nelly McClellan. Nelly wrote her husband every day they were apart, but only a clutch of her letters survived, and her postwar diaries sit in the Library of Congress, rarely viewed. She has no biographer; very little has been published about her at all. We do know that she died in 1915—the *New York Times* carried her obituary, although it misspelled her name—but for more than one hundred years, Nelly has been seen only dimly through the fog of her husband's celebrity.

Born to a distinguished army officer and his refined but adventurous wife in 1835 near present-day Green Bay, Wisconsin, one of Nelly Marcy's first nannies was reportedly an Indian squaw who carried the baby girl on her back. Educated at the best schools in Philadelphia and Connecticut, blue-eyed Nelly was a celebrated beauty, strong-willed and confident of her charms. After her parents forced her to break her secret engagement to a young army officer of whom they disapproved, Nelly rejected more than half a dozen marriage proposals, including one from handsome and successful Captain McClellan, whom her parents adored. His persistence eventually overcame her obstinacy, and he seemed to quell her rebellious spirit, too. The second time McClellan proposed proved to be a charm, and they married in May 1860. Spirited Nelly dutifully assumed all of the trappings of deference and obedience to her husband.[7]

McClellan had resigned from the army in 1857; he was president of a major railroad on his wedding day. A year and a half later, the thirty-four-year-old was general-in-chief of the United States Army in the midst of the nation's most severe crisis. His rise was nothing short of meteoric, and he reveled in

the power and fame it brought him. Nelly thoroughly enjoyed the elevated social stature of the wife of the nation's senior military commander, but there are
signs that the young wife chafed at the price of popularity. She did not openly
support efforts to aid wounded soldiers that were the hallmarks of women's
activities during the war. She fled from society's criticism of her husband. She
even encouraged him to resign from the army on more than one occasion.

Notwithstanding her reluctance to actively engage with his career, Nelly
played a central role in crafting McClellan's famous but controversial legacy.
McClellan doted on his beautiful bride, and he wrote her daily letters, filled
with love for her, conceit about himself, and venom for others. Nelly dutifully
fed his boundless arrogance and paranoia. He often urged her to keep their
correspondence secret, but after his death in 1885, she did something that is almost inexplicable: she allowed his letters to be published. While he was alive,
McClellan's critics attacked the general's actions—and inaction—to damage
his reputation. But even they could not inflict the injury that McClellan's own
words dealt to his character when extensive excerpts from his personal correspondence were published in 1887. The mystery of Nelly McClellan is whether
she fully embraced her husband's warped worldview, or whether she spent
twenty-five years in an unrelenting struggle to repress her rebellious inner
nature in order to do what a Victorian wife was supposed to do—provide
unquestioning support to her husband.

There is no such mystery about Ellen Ewing Sherman. Her strong-minded,
independent nature is a pronounced feature of every biography of her husband, where she is most often depicted as a negative influence upon him. His
biographers typically highlight her zealous Catholicism. Or her nagging. Or
both. Such generalizations, though true, fail to acknowledge how much her
fierce and undivided loyalty to God and country and family contributed to her
husband's success during the Civil War.

The Ewings of Ohio were wealthy, well educated, politically powerful. Their
patriarch was Thomas Ewing, one of the most influential politicians and successful lawyers in the United States. He served as U.S. senator from Ohio, as
secretary of the treasury under Presidents William Henry Harrison and John
Tyler, and as the nation's first secretary of the interior. Thomas Ewing believed
his daughter had a superb mind, and he educated her as well as Thomas Hart
Benton educated Jessie. Although Ellen had a lifelong interest in politics, it
was Catholicism, inspired and nurtured by her mother, that became the focus of her energies and sustained Ellen and her family through innumerable
sorrows. Along with her fierce patriotism, her faith fed her hatred of slave-

holding secessionists, inciting her enthusiastic endorsement of Sherman's "hard war" against the rebels, their women, and their homes. Ellen did not encourage Sherman's every instinct, however. Indeed, she disputed his decisions—military and personal—as often as not. Ellen's great value to Sherman lay as much in her blunt, candid appraisals of his failings as in her intelligent, steadfast support for his virtues, all of which were apparent in her intelligent appeals to Lincoln early in the war, when the national press labeled Sherman "insane." Ellen and Sherman grew up together as children. Their relationship was an intimate blend of sturdy friendship and romantic love shared by two strong personalities. Theirs was truly a marriage of equals.

Like the Frémonts, McClellans, and Shermans, the Grants experienced highs and lows throughout their lives together, and it can be argued that they reached the highest high and the lowest low of the four couples. The most striking aspect of their relationship was their utter devotion to each other, which was often noted by those who knew them personally and by countless historians who have studied them. Theirs is one of the greatest love stories in the history of the United States.

To look at them, though, they were nothing special. Ulysses was not as dashing as Frémont or as handsome as McClellan, nor as striking a figure as the tall, red-haired Sherman. Of average height for the day (five feet seven inches), chronically underweight, with brown hair and a retiring nature, only Ulysses's bright blue eyes merited notice on meeting him. He was a quiet man all his life, given to small talk on occasion, but was most comfortable around his horses and his children. Nor was Julia as beautiful as Nelly, as accomplished as Jessie, or as self-assured as Ellen. When she was young, Julia had a trim, tiny frame and beautiful hair and hands. Sadly, she was born with a defect that made her appear cross-eyed. The condition, called strabismus, also impaired her vision, making it difficult for her to read and write. It also, understandably, made her self-conscious all of her life. Nor were the Grants as wealthy as the Frémonts or the McClellans; the Grants were barely financially self-sufficient in the years before the war. Army pay in the antebellum years was meager, and most of Grant's attempts at civilian enterprises scarcely fed his family. A snapshot of the Grants in the run up to the Civil War would reveal a couple slightly below average in wealth and social status.

They were special to each other, though, and in that simple statement is one of the most important ingredients to Grant's success. He adored Julia; more than that, he needed her. He thrived when they were together and pined for her when they were not. So apparent was his need for her and so obvious, too, was her love for him that she battled her fears and disability to travel more than ten thousand miles during the war to be with him. Like her husband and his soldiers, she risked death, disease, and capture to be by his side. She risked those dangers, too, on behalf of their children, who so often accompanied her. Julia's bravery, devotion, and tenacity provided Ulysses the emotional support he needed. She made it possible for that gentle man to make terrible war.

In the four years from 1861 to 1865, each of these four couples celebrated great successes and experienced great failures, even tragedies. Some were military, some political, some personal. Their stories have reverberated through history because of the consequential nature of their lives in that consequential time for our nation. Historians who have told their stories have, by and large, focused on the generals, but more recently, the influence that the wives had on those men has begun to see the light. Modern biographies of Sherman by John Marszalek and of Grant by Brooks Simpson provide sensitive portraits of the relationships between those generals and their wives. Notably, Carol Bleser and Lesley Gordon edited a collection of studies of Northern and Southern couples by prominent historians, called *Intimate Strategies of the Civil War*, which includes the Frémonts, Shermans, and Grants. Carol Berkin's *Civil War Wives* provides a nuanced and perceptive examination of Julia Grant's efforts to cope with the many changes the war wrought on her life. Until now, however, no author has examined, compared, and contrasted the marriages of these four couples and the influence that the wives had on their generals, nor factored Abraham Lincoln into their stories.[8]

Abraham Lincoln's personality provided an opening unique in American military history for resourceful and fearless women to affect their husbands' careers. No president before or after Lincoln made himself as accessible to his fellow Americans, exercised such power over individual military appointments in wartime, and had such curious relationships with women.[9]

Lincoln was famously accessible, almost infamously so in the eyes of his wife and his secretaries, who tried many times and in many ways to limit his exposure to public favor seekers. Proof that they failed can be found in the volumes written about Lincoln penned by the steady succession of visitors to the president's house or to his summer cottage at the Soldiers' Home, north of the White House. Whether during daylight office hours or late at night, Lincoln was portrayed as almost unfailingly gracious, even if he answered the call in his nightshirt and slippers with a book in his hand. Journalist Noah Brooks, who became a good friend of President and Mrs. Lincoln, described in late 1863, a typical day of the president in the midst of the Civil War:

[B]y nine o'clock, he has directed that the gate which lets in the people shall be opened upon him, and then the multitude of cards, notes and messages which are in the hands of his usher come in upon him. It is very much of a lottery as to who shall get in first. . . . The President sits at his table and kindly greets whoever comes. To the stranger he addresses his expectant "Well?" and to the familiar acquaintance he says, "And how are you to-day, Mr.—?" When we recollect that every day, except Sunday, is occupied in the manner thus described, from nine o'clock until three o'clock in the afternoon, and that during the sessions of Congress several hours of the evening are also thus taken up, it is a matter of surprise that the President can find time to do so wisely and so well the various work which comes from his hands.[10]

Like his accessibility to the public, Lincoln's involvement in military appointments absorbed much of his time. For four years, Lincoln embraced the responsibility of selecting military officers up and down the grades. Lincoln unabashedly chose and promoted officers as much for political purposes as on the basis of merit and seniority. Lincoln's preoccupation with the serious side of finding competent commanders was leavened by his inherent tendency to find humor in the task. When he was told that a brigadier general and a number of horses had been captured, Lincoln retorted, "I don't care so much for brigadiers. I can make them. But horses and mules cost money." He was always focused on winning, though, and there were times that Lincoln reluctantly but dispassionately chose men he did not like, because they were the best tools at hand. Lincoln thoroughly enjoyed visits in the field to meet with officers and soldiers and sailors alike. Despite his lifelong avoidance of alcohol and tobacco—the usual lubricants of male society—Lincoln had a knack for storytelling and a repertoire of bawdy humor that helped mark him as truly a man's man.[11]

A ladies' man he most certainly was not. Throughout his life, his reputation was that of a bumbling suitor, an awkward guest in mixed society, and a husband harassed by a harridan of a wife. In the South during the Civil War, his reputation was much worse. Harsh Confederate views of Lincoln echoed across the Atlantic, where London newspapers reprinted Southern journals' inflamed and inaccurate accusations of Lincoln's cruelty toward Confederate women. None of these perspectives provides a complete picture of Lincoln's relationships with women, though. Lincoln had great respect for women, beginning with his mother and stepmother, whose toughness and sacrifices he often recalled. He was relatively comfortable around married women, especially wives and mothers of his close friends, including his best friend Joshua Speed's mother and Illinois Sen. Orville Browning's wife. Relationships with single women were more problematic. His appearance and manners were never likely to sweep a young belle off her feet. His were virtues that revealed themselves over time, in conversation. With women (as with men) who were excessively impressed with their own importance, Lincoln rarely got a chance to make a better second impression.[12]

Mary Todd, the belle of Springfield, Illinois, was willing to take Lincoln as he was in order to mold him into what she realized he could be. She was nearly as ambitious in the political sphere as Lincoln, and he respected her political instincts and skills throughout their marriage. Of course, Mary's political ambitions, like those of other women of her era, including Jessie Frémont, were limited by nineteenth-century society to finding and supporting a husband who would achieve political distinction. That she perceived the jewel beneath Lincoln's rough exterior is considered by her biographers—and many of his— as a sign of her political acuity. That she treasured her diamond in the rough could not be doubted; Mary Lincoln was a jealous woman. Although some historians undoubtedly exaggerate the extent and violence of her jealousy, so many tales in this genre have been recorded that a fair number of them must be true. As a result, her husband's innate awkwardness around women was likely compounded by the knowledge that Mary would react with fury to reports of his interactions with most ladies.[13]

There were, however, three categories of women whose company he could keep while risking minimal marital consequences: most Cabinet officers' wives and daughters; most military officers' wives; and the widows, wives, daughters, and mothers who streamed through the White House as supplicants for presidential favors. Particularly in those brief, singular encounters with female strangers, Lincoln could freely demonstrate his deep compassion or his playful sense of humor with little fear of Mary's wrath. Yet, he rarely allowed his respect or sympathy for women to affect his evaluation of their requests. "President Lincoln was a soft touch for women with a genuine case," according to one historian, "but was a hard case when it came to those women who sought to manipulate him." In dealing with the Frémonts, McClellans, Shermans, and Grants, Lincoln had ample opportunity to demonstrate both aspects of his nature.[14]

What Lincoln endured at the hands of the Frémonts and McClellans was nothing less than friendly fire—damaging attacks on the president and his policies by his own forces. The generals even fought Lincoln in the civilian

Left: Carte de visite of Abraham Lincoln, c. 1860. (*Author's collection*). *Right:* Carte de visite of Mary Lincoln, 1861. (*Courtesy of the Library of Congress*)

arena, when they both ran against him in the presidential election of 1864. While Lincoln fully recovered from his injuries at their hands, the reputations of the Frémonts and McClellans continue to suffer from their self-inflicted wounds. Lincoln's repugnance at Jessie Frémont's efforts to manipulate him is palpable in every account of their meeting, whether written by his partisans or hers. Their meeting provides one of the most human portraits of the president, struggling to gain control of the war and of himself. The McClellans disdained Lincoln's repeated offers of friendship and support; like her husband, Nelly McClellan never amended her first negative impression of Abraham Lincoln. Captured in their letters, their tragic self-absorption has echoed through the years. It is cruel irony for Nelly and George that the president's virtues and military insights are so fully revealed through their correspondence, which, amazingly, Nelly allowed to be published. Without that record, the history of the Civil War would be much less accurate and far less astonishing.

In contrast, the Shermans and the Grants shared common cause with Lincoln in prosecuting the war. The generals publicly and privately disavowed political ambition during Lincoln's lifetime. While they often took a dim view of politicians as a breed, they and their wives were respectful and often admiring of President Lincoln. They were astute in their judgment of his character (Sherman soon revised his first negative impression of Lincoln) and proper in their respect for civilian control of the military, even when they chafed against it. Generals Sherman and Grant never sought to undercut Lincoln. Their wives also had common cause with Lincoln in their efforts to keep the generals in fighting form. When Ellen Sherman and her father visited Lincoln in the wake of newspaper attacks on the general's sanity, Lincoln clearly recognized the important political connections of William Tecumseh Sherman. Lincoln also acknowledged "a genuine case" in the general's depression and his wife's suffering, and the president advised them on how to help Sherman recover his mental strength and his military career. Julia Grant's is the most tender of the four stories. Julia related to Lincoln simply, honestly, kindly, as did his many married women friends, and he returned the favor by accepting her visits to her husband, which were widely acknowledged to be beneficial to his peace of mind. Ellen, Julia, and the president shared a common interest in supporting Sherman and Grant, and the mutuality of support among Lincoln, those generals, and their wives was an important element in winning the war.

❦

The seeds of the Civil War were sown in the Constitution's recognition of slavery, but the vast territory acquired by the United States at the end of the Mexican War in 1848 exacerbated the question central to the nation's future: Would new territories come into the Union as slave states or free? The Civil War was as much about the West as it was about North and South. For more than a decade, while the fabric of American society ripped apart, skilled politicians forged delicate compromises that merely delayed the inevitable. The final straw, from the South's point of view, was Lincoln's election as president in November 1860. That sparked a series of political detonations, as South Carolina led six other states out of the Union and into a proud and belligerent confederacy. After the South fired the first shots on the U.S. Army's Fort Sumter in Charleston Harbor on April 12, 1861, the slave-holding states viewed with alarm President Lincoln's call for 75,000 men to enlist for three months to put down the rebellion. To them, it was a vile act of naked aggression. In quick succession, four more slave states seceded. By July 1861, Confederate troops were marching toward Washington, D.C. They stopped just thirty miles west of the U.S. Capitol, on the banks of Bull Run, near a railroad crossing called Manassas Junction.

At that point, Frémont, McClellan, Sherman, and Grant—all of whom had left the U.S. Army after the Mexican War—were in the army again. John Charles Frémont and George Brinton McClellan were two of Lincoln's first appointments to the grade of major general in May 1861. By the end of 1862, though, neither man commanded any troops at all. Their rise to power was only slightly swifter than their fall from grace. On the eve of the Battle of Bull Run, the other two men were colonels. By 1865, though, their names were on every tongue, North and South. In four years, with Lincoln's support, William Tecumseh Sherman and Ulysses S. Grant rose from obscurity to national, even international, fame.

Over the past century and a half, historians have examined the childhoods, parents, education, friendships, rivalries, religions, philosophies, and the physical and mental health of these four generals, all in an effort to understand them and explain why their lives unfolded as they did. In nearly every study, the wives of those men make at least a cameo appearance, but their influence on their husbands' careers is rarely examined in any detail, and the women themselves are buried under the weight of "his story." For the most part, the wives are, in the words of Henry Adams, "known only through a man." Sometimes they are portrayed as their husbands' unfailingly lovely and helpful companions. Sometimes they look like meddling nags. The reality is, of course, far more complex.[15]

More than seventy thousand books relating to the Civil War have been published since 1865, but it has really only been within the past two decades that accounts of the experience of women during the war have begun to attract scholars and readers that the more traditional tales of soldiers, generals, and battles have long educated and entertained. They are attracting new readers, too. This study is meant to add fresh insight and perspective to the many books about Lincoln and his generals and to the relatively few about his generals' wives. It is a sort of "layered biography," in which each of the four wives' tales builds upon the previous one, enabling us to better understand the women and the men as individuals, as couples, and as important historical figures. Each tale begins with a vignette—a window into the couple's unique relationship with each other or with Lincoln—then proceeds to a brief account of their courtship, marriage, and family before the war began, providing a basis for understanding the dynamics of their union. Once shots were fired on Fort Sumter, the women were launched out of their "sphere" into a wholly different universe— one where Jessie acted as General Frémont's chief of staff, Nelly encouraged her husband to disobey orders, Ellen's fighting spirit exceeded Sherman's, and

Julia sent her young son off to war with her husband. In that universe, their private relationships with their husbands and their personal opinions of the president of the United States affected their husbands' careers and had national and historical consequences.[16]

This is the story of the very different ways in which these remarkable women responded to the unique challenges of being Lincoln's generals' wives.

PART ONE

Friendly Fire

Jessie Benton Frémont

JESSIE FRÉMONT'S CIVIL WAR

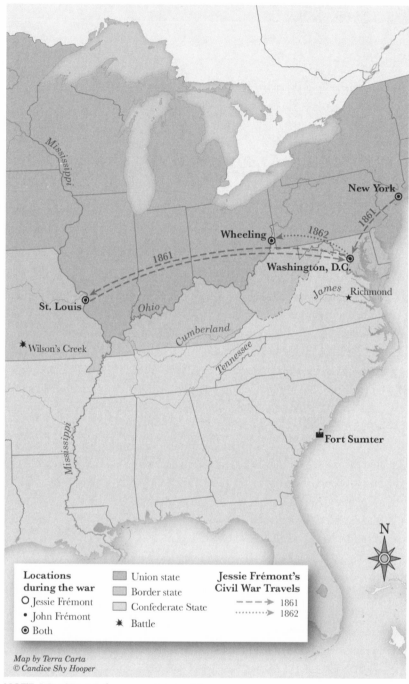

Map by Terra Carta
© Candice Shy Hooper

NOTE: West Virginia became a state in 1863.

"the place a son would have had"

Jessie Benton Frémont gaped as a "swarm" of dugout canoes, manned by "naked, screaming, barbarous negroes and Indians," approached her over-crowded steamboat in the mouth of Panama's Chagres River. It was almost exactly the midpoint of the nineteenth century, and travel from the East Coast of America to the west was not for the faint of heart. After more than a week of rough Atlantic seas aboard the SS *Crescent City* from New York around Florida to the east coast of Panama, twenty-five-year-old Jessie and her fel-low passengers faced an even more arduous trip by river and land across the slender, rugged isthmus to Panama City on the Pacific coast. Before the pas-sengers could recover from the river trip, she recalled, a horde of native entre-preneurs descended on them, claiming exorbitant prices to rent "small, badly fed, ungroomed, wretched" mules for the two-day trip along steep, narrow "mule staircases" over the mountains.[1]

Once in Panama City, Jessie and her six-year-old daughter Lily eagerly an-ticipated the last leg of their trip to San Francisco on the SS *California*. But the *California* was not there; nor was there any idea when it would appear. Nearly two more months would pass before Jessie heard the boom-boom of the can-non that signaled the arrival of another vessel, the *Panama*. "It could only be conjectured why the *California* did not return," Jessie wrote thirty years later, "and it was supposed, as was afterwards proved, that all her crew had deserted to go to the mines, and no men could be induced to take their places. The mad-ness of the gold fever was upon everybody. . . ." It was April 1849, and Jessie was riding a tidal wave of humanity to the goldfields of California.

By the standards of the day, Jessie's journey to that point, though daunting, was unremarkable. But during those seven weeks of unplanned "detention," she—and thousands of other Americans stranded mid-journey in Panama City—contracted an array of illnesses. Many died. Jessie came down with what she called "brain fever," which left her bedridden and utterly dispirited. Two doctors prescribed wildly conflicting remedies for her illness, but both agreed her survival depended upon returning to New York. Jessie refused. She believed her survival depended on reaching San Francisco. Despite her illness and frailty, Jessie never lost her nerve or her hallmark stubbornness. She was determined to continue to California, no matter what the cost. Unlike the Argonauts, as the hordes of gold-seekers were called, Jessie's goal was not the yellow metal. It was something much more precious: it was her heart's desire, her husband, John Charles Frémont.[2]

When she began her journey to California from New York that March 15, Jessie felt she was "launched literally on an unknown sea . . . towards an unknown country." Although she had been married for eight years by that time, her husband's "long absences had taken him from home more than five years." When the prospect of another of Frémont's "long absences" loomed in late 1848, in the form of yet another survey expedition to California, Jessie would not remain behind. She decided they should make California their home; while he traveled overland, she and Lily would venture by ship. This trip to California was yet another of Jessie's many journeys to be by her husband's side. She made them in rich times and poor, in sickness and health, in fame and infamy. Hers were not only geographical trips, nor did she merely follow Frémont's lead. She rushed with him—sometimes ahead of him—into the worlds of politics and war as eagerly as she set out from that New York pier on the Ides of March in 1849 to meet her husband on the other side of America. Jessie's lifelong love for John Charles Frémont fueled her passion to overcome the many obstacles that geography and society raised between them.

While Jessie moved in upper-middle-class circles of society from her birth, Frémont grew up in very different conditions. He was the illegitimate son of Anne Pryor, the desperately unhappy wife of a wealthy Virginian nearly thirty years her senior, and her impoverished French tutor, Charles Fremon. Born in Savannah, Georgia, in 1813, John Charles later reclaimed his father's real surname, Frémont, which Charles had altered when he fled Canadian authorities and entered the United States. Frémont was a bright child, who became a clever, ambitious young man. He attended the College of Charleston, where he excelled in drawing and math, two skills that would help make his fortune. Beginning early in his life, Frémont attracted the help of a succession of mentors, including, most importantly, Joel Poinsett, first United States minister to Mexico and secretary of war in the late 1830s. With Poinsett's help in 1838, Frémont obtained a commission in the U.S. Corps of Topographical Engineers, although he had no formal military education. The Corps was charged with, among other things, exploring and mapping the United States. It was part of the U.S. Army and one of the most indispensable bureaus of the nation's government during this era of rapid American expansion. Even though the phrase was not in vogue until the 1840s, the concept of Manifest Destiny was, in fact, manifest by the second decade of the 1800s. The push to develop road, rail, and river transportation in order to populate the continent required a dedicated corps of explorers, engineers, surveyors, and mapmakers. Frémont found his calling in the exciting, exacting, lonely work.[3]

Loneliness never seemed to be a problem for Frémont; he appeared to prefer mountains to men. Frémont was a very private man who lived a very public life. Sensitive about his illegitimacy and his lack of West Point credentials, he longed for respect and recognition, encouraged adulation, and was intolerant of slights. His strong sense of personal reserve and equally strong belief in his infallibility combined to project an imperial nature, which led to problems wherever Frémont was placed in a chain of command. If introverted and prickly, Frémont was also remarkably handsome and charming. He captivated women with his flattering attentions and men with his quiet composure. He was a good-looking man all of his life. As a young man, Frémont's curly black hair, brilliant blue eyes, and slim figure appeared to equal advantage in crisp military uniforms or rough Western garb. When his hair began to turn gray in his thirties, Frémont was, if possible, even more attractive. The adjective "dashing" seems to have been invented for the man who became known in American history as the Pathfinder.

Second Lieutenant Frémont arrived in Washington, D.C., in September 1839. As part of a team led by the brilliant but frail Joseph Nicollet, a French scientist who had been assigned to the U.S. Army Corps of Topographical Engineers, Frémont had spent the previous fifteen months exploring and surveying the Mississippi River basin from southern Minnesota to Iowa. The two men settled into a small townhouse a few blocks from the U.S. Capitol to prepare a report and detailed maps for publication by Congress, the first accurate guide to that vast, fertile territory. News of their work traveled quickly in the capital city, and inquisitive Washingtonians stopped in to meet the explorers and hear firsthand accounts of their travels. Among the most interested and persistent visitors was a Capitol Hill neighbor, Missouri Sen. Thomas Hart Benton.[4]

Benton was one of the first two senators to represent Missouri when it entered the Union in 1821. By 1839, he was a dynamic and influential fifty-seven-year-old politician in the fourth of five terms he would serve in the Senate. As a young man, Benton had managed his widowed mother's landholdings and slaves in Tennessee before abandoning farming for the law. He was a big, powerfully built, regal-looking man, who never shied away from a fight. When Andrew Jackson entered the Senate in 1823, he and Sen. Tom Benton together waged unrelenting legislative war in favor of "hard money" (gold coin or gold bullion) against paper money backed by gold. In the course of that decades-long battle, Benton was dubbed "Old Bullion," the nickname by which he was known to generations of politicians, including Abraham Lincoln.[5]

Benton's special passion was America's westward expansion. His keen interest in the geography, geology, and natural wonders of the American West led the senator to spend many hours in Frémont's garret, as the second lieutenant labored over the task of transforming field notes and calculations into accurate maps and detailed botanical descriptions. The elder statesman craved validation of his belief in the vast potential of the continent. The young explorer was flattered and pampered by the wealthy and influential national political figure, who invited him to elegant dinners at his home with leading politicians, scientists, and artists of the day. Sometime in 1839, Benton also invited Frémont to attend a concert at the senator's daughters' boarding school. There, to his everlasting regret, Benton introduced Frémont to his fifteen-year-old daughter, Jessie Ann.[6]

Jessie Ann was inseparable from her father's world from the day she was born: "He made me a companion and a friend from the time almost that I could begin to understand. We were a succession of girls at first, with the boys coming last, and my father gave me early the place a son would have had," Jessie recalled. Old Bullion may have instinctively recognized his own strong character in his infant daughter. Apparently others saw the resemblance, too. In President James Buchanan's memorable phrase, Jessie was "the square root of Tom Benton."[7]

Jessie's education was not merely excellent, it was superlative, owing to her father's vast knowledge and love of books. The best library west of the Mississippi was reputed to be in the Benton home in St. Louis, where he regularly debriefed those travelers from the West he could trap before they headed east. The best library east of the Mississippi was a close call between the Library of Congress, where Senator Benton "pastured" Jessie daily on his walks to work in the U.S. Capitol, and his own study in the Benton house nearby on C Street. In both places, Senator Benton supplemented Jessie's education at ladies' schools with sterner stuff from his own shelves. Jessie assisted her father in his work by researching and taking dictation for his letters and speeches. She spoke fluent

Spanish and French (and read Greek and Latin) and often played hostess at dinner to the many distinguished American and international guests whom Benton entertained. If Senator Benton deliberately cultivated Jessie's intelligence, he likely regretted that she inherited his streak of stubborn independence. Raised like a son, Jessie flailed against society's restrictions on women's conventional roles in nineteenth-century American society.[8]

In a century and a half of literature on women of the Civil War, only Mary Todd Lincoln has eclipsed Jessie Benton Frémont's combination of celebrity and notoriety. Jessie's partisans are fierce and her detractors equally ferocious. She has inspired numerous books, including Irving Stone's "biographical novel," *Immortal Wife*, a paean to a paragon of absolute perfection. Jessie's early biographers were generally only slightly less fawning, beginning with Catherine Coffin Phillips's 1935 volume. A recent biography portrays Jessie as the flawless female half of a power couple who "shaped nineteenth-century America." Jessie's approach to shaping history—and her husband—was aggressive: she fought fiercely and publicly, though perhaps not always wisely, for everything she loved. When Jessie rebuffed her parents and married Frémont, Senator Benton became merely the first in a series of powerful men whom Jessie challenged on behalf of the husband she not merely loved, she worshipped.[9]

Some of Jessie's rebellion against Victorian society's rules for women may have been the product of her ambivalent relationship with her mother, who was in many respects the perfect image of a nineteenth-century woman. Elizabeth McDowell was the beautiful, refined daughter of a wealthy planter. She lived and traveled in style—with maids and footmen and her own bright yellow carriage lined with red leather that had been made in London. Raised at Cherry Grove, a magnificent estate in southwestern Virginia (where Jessie Ann was born in 1824), Elizabeth loved every aspect of luxurious plantation life, except for the engine of her father's wealth, slavery. Jessie later told abolitionist Lydia Maria Child that her mother "brought us up to think it good fortune to be free from owning slaves. She urged upon us many reasons why we ought never to own them. She dwelt especially on the evil influence of slavery on the temper of children, making them domineering, passionate, and arbitrary."[10]

Benton courted Elizabeth for six years, gradually wearing down her opposition to his army commission (many friends still referred to the senator as Colonel Benton), his Democratic politics, and his red hair—all of which she cited as insurmountable barriers to her happiness. Benton gave up the first for her, but pleaded that his principles and his heritage prevented him from doing more. Though she finally married him, Elizabeth never felt at ease in the frontier town of St. Louis, where famed explorer Gen. William Clark was still a fixture of society, or in Washington's rough-and-tumble political atmosphere. Even before a stroke in 1844 rendered her nearly mute and immobile, Elizabeth suffered unidentified chronic illnesses, and she withdrew from the mainstream of her husband's life. Jessie recalled that when she was a young girl, she regularly dined with her father and her siblings and an array of fascinating guests. Then she would go upstairs to her mother's room to entertain the recluse with amusing anecdotes from the evening. In contrast to the many words that Jessie wrote about her father and her husband, she wrote relatively little about her mother. "My mother's long illness deprived my father of her companionship to a great extent, and made him turn to me still more," Jessie wrote in 1878. "How great a loss this was to him and to us can only be known to those who knew her; but I do not speak of that life, for it is not, like mine, in a manner public property." Such veiled references speak to a sense of competition for her father's love, perhaps even scorn for the woman who would not fully share his life. Jessie's marriage would be different.[11]

The difference began the moment Jessie and John met. She was swept off her feet by Frémont's good looks and elegant manners. After the concert, she told her sister that Frémont was the handsomest man she had ever met. "I'm so glad I wore the pink candy-stripe with the rose sash instead of the dotted muslin with the blue," she said, "It made me look much older." She hoped she had made an impression on the young lieutenant. She had. Frémont's roommate, Nicollet, recalled that when he returned to their townhouse that evening, the young man told him he was in love.[12]

Was Frémont smitten with Jessie's looks? It is difficult to determine how pretty Jessie was. In her memoirs, Jessie was unhappy with her appearance, criticizing the long "Roman nose" that she had inherited from her father, which she felt would have been more attractive in a son than a daughter. An early drawing by artist John Wood Dodge shows a round-faced Jessie with plain features, but the artist Thomas Buchanan Read later created a cameo of the young woman that reveals a striking oval face with regular features, lovely dark eyes, and long dark hair parted down the middle and knotted at the back of her neck. A white blouse open at the throat and a pale blue scarf emphasize her youth and beauty. It is a very flattering portrait, and if accurate, there is no wonder that Frémont was immediately attracted to Jessie. But when he wrote about their first meeting late in his life, his compliments were indirect, almost ambivalent. "She made the effect that a rose of rare color or beautiful picture would have done," according to his *Memoirs*. "Her beauty had come

Portrait of Jessie when she was thirty-two years old, painted by Thomas Buchanan Read for the 1856 presidential campaign. According to Jessie, it was "barely founded on fact." (*Braun Research Library Collection, Autry National Center, Los Angeles; photo 81.G.2*)

far enough down from English ancestry to be now in her that American kind which is made up largely of mind expressed in the face; but it still showed Saxon descent."[13]

Not many fifteen-year-old girls want to hear they are admired for their minds, but Frémont's backhanded compliments may be closer to the mark. The earliest photographs of Jessie, taken in her twenties, are not flattering. In a photograph at her home on San Francisco Bay in 1861, she is a plain, almost unattractive woman, her hair parted down the middle and severely pulled back from a decidedly round face, her mouth sternly set. She is sitting, almost squatting, on a low chair, enveloped in a voluminous black dress. Her eyes are the eyes one sees in the photographs of so many pioneer women: hard, focused, penetrating. It is likely that a decade of arduous travel and often primitive living conditions had taken its toll on her looks by then. But daguerreotypes cannot reveal how those eyes might have sparkled or how her smile might have lit her face as she conversed about literature, history, or current events with her distinguished guests.

Whether the beautiful portrait or the harsh daguerreotype was the more accurate likeness of Jessie, it is not too much of a stretch to imagine that Frémont's early infatuation with her was aided, even predestined, by his desire to

remain close to her powerful father. Benton's affection, admiration, and support for the young man whose work would promote his dream of settling the
West was unbounded—until the senator realized, with a shock, that the beloved daughter he had raised to reign over Washington society was in love with
a penniless, bastard adventurer.

CHAPTER 2

"Be sure you're right and then go ahead"

As soon as they grasped what was happening, both Bentons leaped into action to prevent Jessie's marriage to a man of no pedigree. Some reports credit the senator with pulling the levers of government to derail the budding love affair. Jessie later claimed that her mother roused herself to seek help from her friend, the wife of Secretary of War Joel Poinsett. This one-two punch sent Frémont reeling more than a thousand miles away, to Iowa, on an expedition to survey the Des Moines River basin in June 1841. The two young lovers barely had time to say good-bye. But if the Bentons thought that throwing obstacles in the couple's path would weaken their resolve, they had obviously forgotten Tom's relentless courtship of Elizabeth. On Frémont's return two months later, he and Jessie were as much in love as ever.

Many years later, Galusha A. Grow, who was a Speaker of the House of Representatives during the Civil War, remembered how Jessie and her father both lived "by the creed handed down by David Crockett, 'Be sure you're right and then go ahead.'" Jessie lived her life by her own version of Crockett's doctrine: she always charged ahead because she knew she was always right. At that moment, and for the rest of her life, Jessie was certain that Frémont was the right man for her.[1]

Although the Bentons labored to keep the two apart, the couple's friends aided their clandestine romance. Shortly after he returned from the expedition, John and Jessie were secretly married on October 19, 1841. None of the Protestant clergy in Washington would risk Benton's displeasure, but Jessie's ally, Maria Crittenden, wife of the Kentucky senator, found a Catholic priest who was willing to conduct the ceremony in her home. Afterwards, Jessie returned to her parents' house and Frémont to his garret. Although they kept the marriage secret for a short time, Frémont finally decided the formidable Senator Benton had to be told, and Jessie insisted on accompanying him to break the news to her father. As her mother wept, her father roared his displeasure and ordered John out of Jessie's life forever. With full knowledge of the depth of her father's love for her, Jessie later recalled, she turned from Benton to Frémont and quoted the Book of Ruth: "Whither thou goest, I goest. . . ." Shortly thereafter, at her parents' insistence, the newlyweds took up residence in the Bentons' home. Benton could not countenance the loss of his daughter.[2]

On November 27, the *Washington Globe* newspaper carried a highly unusual wedding announcement: "On the 19th ult., in this city, by the Rev. Mr. Van Horseigh, Miss Jessie Ann Benton, second daughter of Col. Benton, to Mr. J. C. Frémont of the United States Army." Twenty-first-century eyes are not likely to recognize the shocking nature of that notice, but Francis Preston Blair's did. Blair, one of Benton's best friends and the editor of the *Globe,* saw the problem the moment Benton "handed him the notice announcing the marriage of Jessie Benton to John C. Frémont." Victorian etiquette and editorial practice insisted that the man married the woman, not the other way around. When Benton's "attention was called to the fact that he had reversed the usual form, he banged his fist down and cried: 'Damn it sir. It will go in that way or not at all. John C. Frémont did not marry my daughter. She married him!'" Blair obligingly accommodated his friend's demand, which may have been prompted by Benton's desire to avoid further scandal: Jessie was then only seventeen years old. Frémont, twelve years her senior, had married an underage woman. As Washington society eagerly lapped up details of the daring elopement and Senator Benton's discomfort, the newlyweds were a titillating addition to the capital city's holiday gatherings that winter.[3]

But Jessie wanted more than her husband's arm at White House parties. Just as she helped to engineer their wedding, Jessie immediately began to seize opportunities to play a significant role in her husband's work. From the first time she saw Frémont bent over the large scrolls of paper, carefully noting longitude and latitude, sketching rivers, grass plains, and mountains, Jessie grasped that his work was the tangible key to unlocking the vast potential of the West. Although Frémont could make maps on his own, according to Jessie, he seemed nearly helpless to convert his journal entries into written reports, as required by the Congress that funded his expeditions. When he finally expressed his agony in trying to translate his fascinating, informative tales into a readable report, Jessie assumed the role of scribe and collaborator.[4]

Over the course of his five Western surveying expeditions in more than a decade, Jessie's skill and diligence helped transform Frémont's field notes and oral recollections into coherent, popular volumes that seized the public imagination and inspired a boom in westward migration. Frémont's report on his 1838 expedition, submitted to Congress in Jessie's handwriting, was the first milestone in what became Jessie's lifelong effort to make a myth of a man. In doing so, she achieved nearly mythic stature herself.

Shortly after the couple married, Senator Benton, as chairman of the Senate Military Affairs Committee, authorized funding for a mapping expedition to the Rocky Mountains in 1842. The expectation was that Nicollet would lead the team, with Frémont second in command. It soon became apparent, however, that Nicollet's health was failing, and Benton's son-in-law got the nod to lead the expedition. The stated mission was to map a trail to the Rocky Mountains, measure the highest peak, and return promptly. But night after night at the dinner table, Benton, John, and Jessie all spoke of the need to find, mark, and advertise safe routes over the mountains to spur western migration; simply locating the highest peak in the Rockies was not enough. They believed that a flood of American settlers would bolster the United States' case in its ongoing diplomatic and possible military efforts to gain a large part of the Oregon Territory from Great Britain and an even larger portion of land from Mexico, including California, Arizona, and New Mexico.[5]

The 1842 expedition was Frémont's first experience in command of a major topographical survey, and he planned and provisioned for it with care. Sometimes, though, it is better to be lucky than to be smart. By pure chance, on a riverboat near St. Louis, Frémont met "Kit" Carson, and after a brief conversation, hired him to guide the expedition (at the exorbitant price of $100 per day). Frémont could not have found a better man for the job, even though Christopher Carson was then known only within a relatively small circle of mountain men, trappers, and guides. Kit was a small, soft-spoken man who barely learned to read and write English, but was, by some accounts, fluent in more than a dozen Indian languages. His third wife was an elegant Mexican woman who lived in Taos with their children. Carson doted on his family, and over the years, he became close to Frémont and Jessie, too. Much of Carson's later fame grew out of the first attention they gave him in their expedition reports. If Carson owed Frémont his fame, Carson repaid the debt many times over; on more than one occasion, Carson saved Frémont's life.[6]

Frémont returned to Jessie from that first arduous expedition on October 29. Two weeks later, she gave birth to their first child, a daughter named Elizabeth, but always called Lily. Almost immediately, Jessie returned to work as her husband's secretary and collaborator on his report to Congress. With Jessie's help, but without formal acknowledgment of it, the account of Frémont's

1842 expedition became an exciting, informative, inspiring best seller, spiced with anecdotes about Carson, information about soils and game, details about flowers, birds, and even a famous little bee that Frémont clasped in his fist at the peak of the Wind River Mountain range in Wyoming. Henry Wadsworth Longfellow, in far-off Massachusetts, wrote that Frémont had "particularly touched my imagination," while hundreds of hopeful men and women bought his report as a practical guide to finding a new home in the West.[7]

Even as Jessie and Frémont prepared the report, another expedition was in the works. The new head of the Topographical Corps, Col. John James Abert, instructed Frémont to lead a surveying party into the Oregon Territory and return via the relatively well-known Oregon Trail. Jessie wanted to be near her husband as long as possible, so she and Lily accompanied Frémont from Washington to St. Louis that spring, where he undertook final preparations for the journey. This time, in addition to the usual supplies he requisitioned through the army post in St. Louis, Frémont requested a mountain howitzer, a small, short-barreled, heavy cannon, mounted on a carriage. He also wanted five hundred pounds of ammunition for it.[8]

Col. Stephen Watts Kearny, who commanded the Third Military Department near St. Louis, expressed concern that Frémont's peaceful survey was taking on the trappings of a military expedition as it headed into territory contested by Great Britain. But Frémont insisted he would need the howitzer to deal with hostile Indians. With reluctance, since there was no time to secure proper authorization from Washington, Kearny ordered the army's arsenal to provide the howitzer. The officer at the arsenal who supplied it was markedly unhappy by the flouting of army regulations. Though he turned over the field gun to Frémont, Capt. William Bell sent a letter to the War Department, noting his personal disapproval of the matter.[9]

Shortly after Frémont left on May 13 for the first leg of his journey to present-day Kansas City, a letter arrived for him in St. Louis. Jessie, who had been "directed to open all mail and forward only what related to the expedition," was shocked to read a message from Colonel Abert, containing what Jessie characterized as "*an order* directing Mr. Frémont to 'return to Washington . . . [and news that] meantime another officer would be sent out to take charge of his men.'" The woman who lived by her version of Crockett's creed "felt the whole situation in a flash, and met it—as *I* saw right."[10]

Jessie correctly suspected that a copy of Abert's letter was on its way to Frémont in Kansas, and she feared her husband might actually obey his superior officer. She felt she had to prevent Frémont from reading Abert's letter; if not, "the grand plan [for western expansion] ripening and expanding from Jefferson's time . . . would have fallen before petty official routine." Jessie knew that one of Frémont's men had remained in St. Louis, planning to catch up with the group later, and Jessie sent for him. Swearing him to secrecy and urging all possible speed, she gave him a note to deliver to her husband: "*Only trust me and Go.*" The Canadian mountain man, Baptiste Derosier, and his brother raced west and placed the note in Frémont's hands. Derosier went on with the party, but his brother soon returned to Jessie with Frémont's reassuring reply: "I trust and GO."[11]

In going, Frémont left General Kearny to bear the brunt of the army's severe disapproval of the breach in regulations. No disciplinary action was taken against the general, but Kearny suffered embarrassment and humiliation excruciating to one steeped in military protocol. At the time, Jessie shrugged off the general's displeasure, but the Frémonts' handling of the howitzer incident—and of Kearny—would return to haunt them less than five years later.

"Jessie wrote several accounts of the incident during her lifetime," according to Pamela Herr, the biographer who best balances Jessie's virtues with her vices, "each more dramatic than the last. They reveal much about her character . . . in exaggerating the threat to the expedition and her own part in averting it, Jessie revealed herself to be not only a fiercely devoted daughter and wife but a woman . . . who relished the moments when she felt she had played a real part in the masculine world . . . Jessie, John, and Thomas Benton had formed a powerful alliance . . . such power bred arrogance."[12]

They would display their arrogance and disdain for conventional limits on their actions again and again. John's brash disregard for authority became manifest once again on this expedition, when he ignored Abert's instructions to confine his exploration to Oregon Territory and return via the Oregon Trail. Instead, he acted in concert with Jessie's and Benton's and his own superior comprehension of the nation's need for a southern passage through the Rockies that pioneers could follow. When he reached the site of present-day Portland, Oregon, in November, Frémont turned not east but south, toward California. His unauthorized trek through the Sierra Nevada Mountains toward the end of 1843 required all of Carson's skills to avert disaster. As fall turned to winter in the rugged mountains, Frémont divided his team several times, allowing any who wished to return to civilization. By early 1844, the weakened explorers had abandoned the controversial howitzer in the heavy mountain snows. They avoided starvation by eating some of their horses and at least one of their dogs. Even with Carson's expertise, the group got lost on several occasions, but the guide finally led them out of the mountains to safety in northern California. Back in St. Louis, Jessie was wild with anxiety until August, when the Frémonts were reunited and quickly made their way to Washington, D.C., to prepare another report and another expedition.

During this time, the nation's politics were splintering over the issue of Texas annexation, which raised the question of the expansion of slavery into new territories in the West and Southwest. Anticipating the possibility of acquiring lands from Britain and Mexico (without reference to how they would be acquired), proponents and opponents of expansionism and of the spread of slavery created schisms in the Democratic Party of Jackson and Benton and in the Whig Party of Lincoln and Clay and Webster. Benton's expansionist passion had no room for slaves in it. The same was true of his friend, *Washington Globe* editor Francis Preston Blair. Blair owned slaves and never apologized for doing so, but he believed that slavery should not spread beyond those states in which it already existed. In this, he matched Benton's fervor.[13]

Blair was a fixture in Washington society, where the elegant, diminutive, keenly observant man lived in a large townhouse across the street from the White House. In 1840, he bought an estate in Maryland just north of Washington, which he called Silver Spring, and often rented out his city house. Like Benton, Blair was a protégé of Andrew Jackson, and though he never held elective public office, Blair wielded enormous influence in Washington. Benton and Blair fought many political battles together, and the two families became close, too. For many years, Jessie looked upon Blair as almost a second father. Blair's daughter Elizabeth, or Lizzie, was one of Jessie's most intimate friends.

While Blair and Benton represented the growing antislavery wing of the Democratic Party, James K. Polk of Tennessee and Pennsylvanian James Buchanan were the party's standard bearers for allowing slavery in new territories. In 1844, when Polk was elected president, he appointed Buchanan, close friend of the Bentons and, briefly, one of Jessie's suitors, secretary of state. The Frémonts and Benton could rejoice that their expansionist views were reflected at the very top of the government, though it made no difference in how they acted. When Frémont received orders from Colonel Abert in early 1845, to survey the Great Basin area, he decided he could exceed those orders and head to California, as he had done before. No doubt he thought it worth the risk. The last time he disregarded authority, he had embarrassed a general but won himself a brevet promotion to the grade of captain. This time, the consequences to the Frémonts would be anything but benign.

Frémont's third expedition followed much the same arduous route as his previous one, ending again near Sutter's Fort in the Sacramento/Sonoma Valley area. It coincided with the outbreak of the Mexican War, which led to the United States' acquisition of a vast swath of the Southwest and California. In fact, Frémont is often credited with "the conquest of California," one of the most complicated and consequential series of events during that complicated and consequential war. What began with great promise ended badly for Frémont. Many years later, Frémont defended his actions when he wrote: "The distance was too great for timely communication, but failing this, I was given discretion to act."[14]

Act he did, encouraging a small band of about thirty Americans near present-day Sonoma to revolt against Mexican Gen. Mariano G. Vallejo, who, surprised in his bed, offered no resistance. The revolutionaries declared California's independence from Mexico on July 4, 1846, establishing what they called the Bear Flag Republic. Up to that point, Frémont and his topographical engineers had remained in the background. U.S. Navy Commodore Robert Stockton arrived shortly thereafter, under orders to seize all California ports in the event of war. As the ranking U.S. military officer in California at that moment, Stockton assumed military command of all U.S. forces there and appointed Frémont lieutenant colonel of an assembly of engineers and militia, called the California Battalion. When the Treaty of Cahuenga incorporated California as a territory of the United States in January 1847, Frémont accepted Stockton's assignment as military governor of California. During this time, Frémont had received a letter from Jessie, informing him of his fame and promotion on the other side of the continent: "So your merit has advanced you in eight years from an unknown second lieutenant, to the most talked of and admired lieutenant-colonel in the army. . . . As for your Report, its popularity astonished even me, your most confirmed and oldest worshipper."[15]

His moment of triumph quickly shattered. In what must have seemed to Frémont a bad dream, Gen. Stephen Kearny materialized with orders from Washington to assume the post of California's military governor. Kearny had marched at the head of a regiment from St. Louis, and once he stepped onto California soil, he became the ranking U.S. Army officer in the territory. Kearny ordered Frémont to relinquish the governorship. Caught between a Navy officer who gave him power and authority and an Army officer who wanted to take it from him, everything in Frémont's life up to that point combined to produce a predictable result: Army officer Frémont sided with the Navy. He refused to step down. Kearny was furious, and by the time Frémont finally realized he ought to yield to his superior officer, it was too late. Kearny finally forced him to return east in the spring of 1847. When he and Frémont arrived in Ft. Leavenworth, Kansas, on August 22, Kearny arrested Frémont on charges of mutiny, disobedience, and military misconduct, and ordered him to Washington to face a court-martial.[16]

During this expedition, Jessie and Lily lived with her parents in Washington, and she did not learn of her husband's difficulties right away. She had been keeping herself busy in his absence by translating confidential papers for Secretary of State James Buchanan. The man who once had been a suitor for Jessie's affections had messengers deliver to her purloined Mexican and Spanish government documents, reports from spies, and newspapers from Mexico and Spain that he did not trust his own staff to translate. One day in the spring of 1847, she pulled from the diplomatic pouch a Mexican newspaper and read with shock that her husband had been expelled from California by an American general. When she confronted her father with the news, he admitted he had contrived to keep the story from her; Benton had been maneuvering politically for months to extract Frémont from his predicament.[17]

Shortly thereafter, Kit Carson arrived in Washington, carrying a letter written by Frémont explaining his conduct, and Jessie sprang into action. She insisted that she and Carson should go together to the White House with the letter. According to Frémont family lore, the fearless mountain man replied that he would be pleased to "meet Mr. Polk under her protection." Apparently, President Polk also considered her the more formidable of the two, for according to his diary, he avoided disagreeing with her directly: "Mrs. Frémont seemed anxious to elicit from me some expression of approbation of her husband's conduct, but I evaded [making any]. In truth, I consider that Colonel Frémont was greatly in the wrong when he refused to obey the orders issued to him by General Kearny. . . . It was unnecessary, however, that I should say so to Colonel Frémont's wife, and I evaded giving her an answer." Unhappy with his evasions, Jessie determined to get satisfaction from the president, but her second meeting with him that week, at her insistence, resulted only in further equivocation.[18]

Confronting the president of the United States did not produce the results she wanted, so Jessie aimed her sights slightly lower and called on Kearny. Beginning with a modest, tearful plea that he drop the charges, Jessie's temper quickly got the better of her, and she began attacking him for persecuting her husband. The general was adamant in his outrage at Frémont's refusal to obey his orders and would not give ground. In the midst of the heated exchange, Kearny likened Frémont's insubordination in California to their flouting of authority in the incident involving the long-lost howitzer. Jessie was stunned. She feared then, she later said, that her husband would not have a fair chance to clear his name in the army trial. And when key military witnesses to the dispute between Stockton, Kearny, and Frémont were ordered west just ahead of the court-martial, Jessie protested to Polk. "Do not suppose Sir," twenty-three-year-old Jessie Benton Frémont wrote to the president on September 21, 1847, "that I lightly interfere in a matter properly belonging to men." But she received no satisfactory response to her request that the witnesses be recalled to Washington or the trial postponed.[19]

The court-martial, which began in November, was in session six days a week, five hours a day, for three months. It was a wrenching experience for Jessie, who sat each day in the crowded courtroom. Every evening, she worked until late on Frémont's defense with her husband, her father, and her sister Eliza's new husband, attorney William Carey Jones. Jessie soon realized she was pregnant and tried to keep the news from her family, fearing they would forbid her participation in the trial. Her pregnancy soon became obvious, and Frémont's concern for her was yet another burden. Frémont benefited from Benton's counsel in mounting his defense, but at the end of January, the court reached a verdict of guilty on all counts and stripped Frémont of his military rank. Many thought the sentence too harsh; in fact, seven of the thirteen judges urged the president to ameliorate the sentence. Polk offered Frémont a full pardon and reinstatement, but though his father-in-law urged him to accept it, Frémont refused. Accepting the pardon was tantamount to admitting his guilt, he declared, and he would not do it.[20]

The Frémonts assumed a proud, disdainful attitude toward all who had brought him down, blaming much of it on West Pointers' jealousy. No matter how good a face they put on in public, Jessie, John, and Benton were mortified by the trial and its outcome. Even though in many respects Frémont became more popular with the public, particularly as interest in California grew, he had added the shame of dismissal from the army to his trove of personal humiliations. As they began to plan a new life, Frémont's thoughts turned to some land in California that he had asked a friend, Thomas Larkin, to acquire for him. Larkin had indeed bought some land from the man to whom Frémont had sent him, but not the property south of Yerba Buena (now San Francisco) that Frémont had in mind. Instead, Larkin had applied Frémont's $3,000 to the purchase of more than forty thousand acres in a remote part of the state near Yosemite Valley. Once again, Frémont would prove luckier than smart. His court-martial and the subsequent expedition delayed his efforts to undo Larkin's error. In the meantime, Frémont's love affair with California and his desire to escape Washington impelled him west.[21]

Jessie would not be left behind this time. The Frémonts decided that they would move to California and live there for seven years (though it is not clear why they chose that number). Thanks to Senator Benton's success in finding funding from some St. Louis businessmen, Frémont traveled west at the head of an expedition to plot the route for a railroad roughly following the thirty-eighth parallel. This route, linking St. Louis to San Francisco, was the central route that Benton and the Frémonts had always favored. Seeking to prove that it was an all-weather path to California, Frémont was determined to make the trip in winter. Once again, Frémont plunged into preparations for an expedition, but with a difference—he would have to make the difficult westward trek this time without Kit Carson, who was ill in Taos.[22]

Though Jessie was in the latter stages of pregnancy, she threw herself into plans for the move. In the midst of making the arrangements, on July 24, 1848, her second child, Benton Frémont, was born in the Bentons' Washington, D.C., home. He was a tiny baby whose very name seemed to weigh him down. Jessie had been sick through much of her pregnancy. She blamed her illness on the trial and Polk's refusal to avert it, but most specifically, she blamed General Kearny. When the baby proved sickly and frail, she blamed him for that, too. It was a daunting prospect to travel with two small children, one a feeble infant, across the continent. In some respects, Jessie's own expedition promised to rival Frémont's. First, she and the children would accompany Frémont from Washington to St. Louis and see him off on his overland expedition. Then she, Lily, and Benton would return east to New York, and make the trip to California by steamship and mule.

Two life-changing events occurred before Jessie set sail. The first happened in California—gold was discovered in enormous quantities near the Yosemite Valley property that Frémont had accidentally acquired and fortunately not relinquished. The second happened in St. Louis—fragile little baby Benton died. Once again, Jessie blamed Kearny. Her hatred was so implacable that when Kearny lay on his deathbed near St. Louis shortly thereafter and sent word he wanted to see her, she dismissed his messenger, saying that a "little grave lay between them."[23]

CHAPTER 3

"Frémont and Our Jessie"

While Jessie and Lily battled tropical dangers on their way to California in early 1849, Frémont made the hazardous overland journey, through scorching deserts and freezing mountain snows. This expedition proved an almost total disaster. Frémont barely survived; ten of his men did not. When they found the remains of a small group that had split from the main party, one of the bodies bore unmistakable signs of cannibalism. Jessie's "brain fever" in Panama City began, she later claimed, when she learned of Frémont's peril in a newspaper account that reached the isthmus. Frémont's substitute guide, "Old Bill" Williams, somehow dragged the weak, starving remnants of the expedition into Taos, where Carson nursed Frémont back to health.[1]

The Frémonts reunited in chaotic San Francisco and focused their energies more than one hundred miles east, in Las Mariposas, "The Butterflies," the name given to Frémont's property by its previous Spanish owner. Ownership of the vast Spanish land grant was something that bedeviled Frémont from the beginning. Although the property eventually produced prodigious amounts of gold, Frémont spent enormous sums to defend his claim to the land and finance the development of mines on the property to extract the ore. In the view of historian Allan Nevins, Frémont's land of gold was a "sinister impersonal force," a "malignant stroke of Fate," but Frémont's decisions had as much to do with its destructive impact on his life as did the ore it contained. He surrounded himself with men who always seemed to operate over the ethical edge, with the result that Frémont was as often cheated as were his investors. Las Mariposas boomed as often as it busted, and the Frémonts never seemed to be able to smooth the bumps in the trajectory of their prosperity. When times were good, they spent money with abandon, no doubt Jessie remembering her mother's London-built yellow carriage and Frémont his mother's poverty. When times were bad, they relied on the kindness of others, and in later years,

Jessie turned to writing articles and books for money. The butterfly was an apt metaphor for the fortune that flitted in and out of the Frémonts' lives beginning in 1849.[2]

At the same time the Frémonts were establishing their new life and extracting gold in the valley, efforts to secure statehood for California were underway. The Frémonts were in the middle of that, too. Before California could be admitted to the Union, the biggest political issue had to be resolved: Would it be admitted as a free state or a slave state? Forty-eight delegates were appointed from across the territory to meet in September 1849 to write a constitution required for California's admission as a state. Although Frémont was not a delegate, both he and Jessie were part of the deliberations on the question of slavery. At one point, fifteen delegates traveled to their home to hear Jessie's views on the question, including her mother's admonition against it, and to marvel at a Virginia-born lady's ability to keep house without slaves. There was growing support for slavery, particularly in southern California, but the convention delegates outlawed it in the state constitution. The ultimate decision, they knew, would rest with the U.S. Congress, which was then also wrestling with the slavery question.[3]

Senate debate over the Compromise of 1850 showcased a string of distinguished orators, including Henry Clay, Daniel Webster, John C. Calhoun, Stephen Douglas, and Thomas Hart Benton (Lt. William Tecumseh Sherman watched the debate from the gallery). At one point, while Benton was in the midst of an impassioned speech, Mississippi Sen. Henry S. Foote lunged toward him, brandishing a pistol. Benton dramatically pulled open his coat and dared the assassin to do his worst, but a host of other senators wrestled Foote to the floor before he could fire. Passage of the Compromise, a package of bills, was often in doubt, but by September 20, all five were signed into law. Benton's support of the Compromise, which brought California into the Union as a free state and staved off secession, was one of his last legislative battles in the Senate. Missouri would no longer accept his strident antislavery stance; after the election of 1850, Benton was not returned to the Senate. Benton's record thirty-year term in that body was marked by such devotion to principle that two men who later became president wrote biographies of him: Theodore Roosevelt Jr. penned a tribute in 1887, and Sen. John F. Kennedy included Benton in his 1957 Pulitzer Prize–winning *Profiles in Courage*.[4]

Back in California, a host of politicians was pondering the question of who would fill the various federal and state government positions when California was admitted to the Union. "Mr. Frémont could have been either Governor or first senator from the state," according to Jessie. "As Governor he could have overlooked his private interests to greatest advantage . . . but on the other hand, as Senator he could defend the interests of the state in Congress." Those factors surely went into Frémont's calculations, but equally important was the obvious fact that a seat in the United States Senate would enable the Frémonts to return to Washington in triumph—with power and wealth beyond imagination—little more than a year after they had departed the city under a cloud of shame. It is hard to imagine the Frémonts could resist such an opportunity. He chose to become a senator and was in turn chosen for the post by the delegates. Frémont would represent the antislavery interests in the state; the other senator, William Gwin, was an avowed pro-slavery advocate. Even though Frémont had drawn the short straw between the two new California senators' terms and would have to seek reelection within months, when the current session of Congress ended, the Frémonts were confident he had a sinecure.[5]

Jessie's trip to Washington retraced her outbound isthmus journey with Lily. This time, though, they were accompanied by Frémont (who wondered at Jessie's fortitude in facing the hardships and dangers involved). They arrived at the Bentons' home in Washington in the spring of 1850, almost exactly a year from the day Jessie and Lily had left to join her husband in California. With Benton's help, Frémont worked to complete California's entry to statehood. When that was accomplished on September 9, Jessie watched from the gallery as he was sworn in. Senator Frémont's consistent antislavery votes (for abolition of the slave trade in the District of Columbia; against stronger penalties for refusing to return runaway slaves) quickly cost him his Senate seat. Frémont's first term in the Senate was also his last.[6]

During this time, Benton attempted to resolve the Frémonts' financial problems—the California property required staggering amounts of capital investment, exceeding current gold production, in order to continue producing gold—by finding a buyer for Las Mariposas. Offered $1 million—including a significant earnest money deposit—Frémont backed away from the sale at the last minute. A major new vein of gold had just been discovered on the property, making him scornful of the $1 million price tag. Apparently, he did not move to return the erstwhile buyer's earnest money promptly either. The whole transaction was clouded in the usual Frémont-Mariposas fog of poor judgment and questionable ethics. Benton was furious as he watched Frémont fritter away the chance to extract his beloved Jessie from the financial instability that marked her husband's management of the property. With pain, Jessie realized that a new chasm was opening between her father and her husband.

Soon the Frémonts were back again in California, where politics were quickly forgotten in the face of the challenges posed by Las Mariposas. Their early days there were consumed in finding financing for the expensive equipment needed to fully exploit the gold deposits and in protecting the property from squatters and claim jumpers. One bright spot in their lives was the birth of John Charles Frémont Jr., or Charley, on April 19, 1851.[7]

Seeking a new source of funding to develop the Mariposas mines and a respite from the privations of California, the Frémonts sailed for Europe in late 1851. They traveled in imperial style, projecting an aura of affluence and sophistication designed to assure potential investors of the Mariposas's vast gold reserves and encourage them to help finance the extraction of ore from the mountains. In London, they settled into a vast suite at luxurious Clarendon House, and Jessie was presented to Queen Victoria. One evening in April 1852, as they were stepping into a carriage to go to dinner, several policemen interrupted them and hauled Frémont off to jail. His arrest had nothing to do with the Mariposas. It was the result of an unpaid U.S. government debt to an arms supplier that Frémont had incurred in the Bear Flag expedition. Frémont was released from jail the next morning, and the U.S. government eventually paid the debt, but the incident understandably dampened enthusiasm among potential gold mine investors. Those who backed away from the project were lucky; as usual, the vast quantities of gold that the Mariposas mines produced did not keep pace with the massive capital investment they required. Though disappointed with the financial results of their European sojourn, the Frémonts thoroughly enjoyed their visit. While in Paris, Jessie gave birth to their second daughter, Anne Beverly Frémont, on February 1, 1853.[8]

Shortly thereafter, the family returned to America, in order to attend to Mariposas business and to boost Frémont's chances to lead another expedition. The U.S. government had announced in 1852 it would finance five expeditions to survey possible routes for a transcontinental railroad, and Frémont hoped he would be chosen to lead one of them. Benton once again pulled all the strings he could for his son-in-law, but there were lingering resentments in the War Department over Frémont's actions, and Benton's political influence had waned. When the survey teams were announced, Frémont was not on the list (though future Union generals George McClellan and John Pope were), nor was the St. Louis-to-San Francisco route that he and Benton favored. With tremendous effort, Benton again organized a group of prominent St. Louis businessmen to fund Frémont's private survey of the route.[9]

As Frémont prepared for the expedition, tragedy struck the family again. Little Anne suddenly wilted in the stifling heat of the capital city's summer. Hoping that cooler air would help revive the child's health, Jessie hurried with her to Francis Preston Blair's Silver Spring mansion, where he and his daughter Lizzie welcomed them with every possible attention. But baby Anne faced daunting odds. In 1850, the first year for which there are reliable statistics, 218 of every one thousand children born in the United States died in infancy. Anne became part of that tragic 20 percent. As Jessie's best friend and her "second father" looked on helplessly, Anne died in her mother's arms. Frémont later told Benton, "it was she who remained dry eyed to comfort me, for I was unmanned over the cruelty of this bereavement."[10]

Frémont did not hire a guide for this fifth expedition, since he was essentially retracing the route he had taken on his previous mission. Again, Frémont wanted to prove the journey could be made in the winter, and again weather, geography, and some highly questionable decisions by Frémont wrought hardships and suffering that brought the party to the brink of disaster. This trip proved to be Frémont's last expedition, and though it did not decide the route of the transcontinental railroad, in combination with the other surveys, it did contribute to the momentum for its construction.[11]

By the time Frémont and his men arrived in San Francisco in April 1854, the country was not focused on what could unite East and West but on what divided North and South. The presidential election of 1856 would be about slavery. Illinois Sen. Stephen Douglas had introduced the Kansas–Nebraska Act in the Senate in early 1854, which would carve the territories of Kansas and Nebraska out of the heartland of the country and would allow the residents of those territories to determine whether they would be free states or slave states. In effect, it repealed the Missouri Compromise of 1820, for the first time allowing slavery into territory from which it had been banned for more than thirty years. Amid howls of anger from antislavery legislators, it passed in the Senate with the votes of a large majority of slave state senators.

Then it went to the House, where newly elected U.S. Rep. Thomas Hart Benton roared back to life. He railed against the act's destruction of the Missouri Compromise in a memorable speech on April 25: "What is the excuse for all this turmoil and mischief? We are told it is to keep the question of slavery out of Congress! Great God! It was out of Congress, completely, entirely, and forever out of Congress, unless Congress dragged it in by breaking down the sacred laws which settled it."[12]

Benton's dedication to public service had survived his Senate defeat, and he had won a seat in the House in 1854, with the help of the son of his old friend, Francis Blair Sr. Young Frank Blair had been Benton's protégé and was an up-and-coming Missouri state representative at the time. Though seventy-one-year-old Benton had lost none of his passion, he was on the losing side of history this time. President Franklin Pierce signed the Kansas–Nebraska Act into law on May 30, 1854. That year, Benton also lost his wife. His beloved Elizabeth, barely able to speak or walk, died in September, just two months before Benton's stand against the Kansas–Nebraska Act cost him his seat in the House of Representatives. Jessie wrote movingly about her mother's death, perhaps realizing by then just how difficult it was to be wife and mother.[13]

At the age of thirty-one, Jessie became a mother for the fifth time on May 17, 1855. Francis Preston Blair Frémont carried a weighty name, but Frank, as he was known, was better able to bear it than had his late brother Benton. Francis Blair Sr. and his wife stood godparents to this child, and when little Frank was christened that spring in Washington, the Frémonts and Blairs could hardly have been closer. However, even a new baby could not push the political turmoil in Washington from Jessie's mind. "Before my baby was a month old, the bitterness of the coming strife invaded even my guarded room," she wrote. "I felt I was no longer in my place—it was certainly too hard on Mr. Frémont, and as soon as I could be moved, New York became our city of refuge."[14]

While she rested, the nation exploded in violence. As pro-slavery and anti-slavery forces flooded into the territories to secure a majority of voters for their position, bloody conflicts erupted, especially in Kansas. What was meant to be a prescription for democracy produced a bloodbath. The traditional political parties—Whigs and Democrats—splintered over the issue, and a new party was born. Democrats who opposed the act and any extension of slavery into the territories, like Francis Blair Sr. and Salmon Chase, joined with former Whigs, like Charles Sumner and later Abraham Lincoln, to form the Republican Party. With the presidency at stake, every faction sought a candidate who could capture the public's imagination. They all considered the Pathfinder an obvious contender. Frémont began receiving overtures to run for president in autumn. The first solid offer came from the Democratic Party, which wanted the glamorous man of action on its ticket, but insisted that he agree to support extension of slavery into the territories.[15]

That summer, Jessie rented a cottage on Nantucket in search of sunshine for the children and quiet for herself. Frémont came to the island to confer with her about the Democrats' offer, and there the man who had been a Democrat all his life told her that he could not carry the party's pro-slavery standard as president. Jessie agreed with him completely but thought her husband still had a role to play on the national scene. She was well aware of Blair's maneuverings to create a party opposed to slavery and quickly wrote the Maryland politician a sly note, telling of the Democrats' pursuit of her husband and suggesting that Blair confer with Frémont about his political future. That was quickly done, and Jessie, Frémont, and Blair easily agreed that the Pathfinder would make a splendid Republican nominee for president.[16]

They also believed that old Tom Benton could be persuaded to turn his back on his Democratic Party roots, as Blair and Frémont had done. Benton's support of Frémont's candidacy would be a big boost for his son-in-law and the new party, and after all, the Democratic Party had deserted Benton twice. But Benton would not desert the Democratic Party. Jessie later blamed much of Benton's animosity toward Frémont and the Republicans on the rift over the aborted sale of Las Mariposas, but Benton's motivating force was his abiding love for the party to which he had devoted his talents all his life.[17]

The leading candidate for the fledgling Republican Party's nomination, the Pathfinder, trumped more rabid antislavery candidates for the nomination at the party's first national convention in Philadelphia in June. In the vice presidential balloting, William Dayton of New Jersey bested a little-known, one-term former U.S. congressman from Illinois named Abraham Lincoln. The ticket was set, but there were a number of obstacles to success at the polls. The Republican Party was brand new, and it was competing for anti-Democrat votes against the American Party, often called the Know Nothing Party. A diverse group of anti-everythings (anti-Catholic, antislavery, anti-immigrant), the American Party nominated former President Millard Fillmore in February 1856, giving the party an early start toward collecting voters who would oppose the pro-slavery Democratic nominee. A deeply fractured Democratic Party met in Cincinnati, Ohio, where current President Franklin Pierce, Sen. Stephen Douglas, and former Secretary of State James Buchanan all vied for the nomination. For the first time in the history of the United States, a sitting president was denied his party's nomination for reelection. After seventeen ballots, James Buchanan finally received the nod.

The election of 1856 was historic in many respects—the first Republican candidate for president, the first sitting president denied his party's nomination, the first presidential election openly about slavery, and the first presidential election in which a candidate's wife was prominently featured in a positive manner. While the catchiest slogan of the Republican Party wrote itself—"Free

Soil, Free Men, Frémont"—men and women also sported campaign ribbons declaring, "Frémont and Our Jessie," and "Jessie's Choice." Of course, women did not have the right to vote, but that did not prevent them from demonstrating their support for Jessie and her husband. In New York, the *Tribune* noted "a new feature—four hundred women" at one gathering of Frémont supporters on June 10, 1856. According to the *Boston Liberator,* Needham, Massachusetts, was the site of a huge rally in August, which included "a multitude of the sisters of Jessie, who by their presence, inaugurated a new and happy era in the history of out-door political meetings in this section." Abraham Lincoln, who campaigned for Frémont, noted more than fifty young mothers in a crowd. The *Washington Union* wrote of banners for "John and Jessie" and one for "Jessie for the White House."[18]

Tales of Jessie's role in the howitzer incident were widely and approvingly recounted, and at an enormous rally in Cleveland, there were "three thunderous cheers 'for the gallant wife of a gallant man.'" Baby girls were named Jessie Ann. Jessie projected the image of an intelligent and devoted wife and mother who inspired early suffragettes, like Elizabeth Cady Stanton and Lucretia Mott. Similarly, activist women abolitionists looked to the Republican Party. It was then that Jessie penned the letter about her mother's antislavery views in an effort to attract more votes to Frémont. Upon reading the letter, abolitionist Lydia Maria Child told another friend, "Our hopes . . . rest on Frémont."[19]

Jessie welcomed—even exploited—the public interest in her for the attention it brought to her husband's candidacy. It is clear, too, that she relished the chance to step out from her husband's shadow. In one letter to Lizzie Blair Lee, Jessie wrote: "Just here & just now I am quite the fashion—5th Avenue asks itself, 'Have we a Presidentress among us—' and as I wear fine lace and purple I am in their eyes capable of filling the place. So I go out nightly—sometimes to dinner & a party both the same night and three times a week to the opera where I hold a levee in my box." Indeed, the nascent Republican Party seized upon Jessie's popularity and her talents to attract attention to it.[20]

Jessie acted as campaign manager, strategist, and secretary. With John Bigelow, editor of the *New York Evening Post,* she crafted a campaign biography of Frémont. It was a sensitive but important assignment, since there was much in Frémont's past that required the attention of skilled wordsmiths. As soon as he was nominated, ugly stories began to surface, charging Frémont with being a bastard, a Catholic (because of their wedding ceremony), and a womanizer, in addition to claiming eyewitness accounts of atrocities against Indians during his surveying expeditions. Most devastating to Jessie, though, was the fact that she and Francis Preston Blair Sr. had completely misread her father. Not only would Benton not support Frémont, but Old Bullion endorsed Buchanan's nomination and actively campaigned for him. The seventy-four-year-old statesman was caught in a political squeeze play between his family, his party, and his principles, but "I am above family and above self when the good of the Union is concerned," Benton declared to crowds who gathered to hear him.[21]

Benton's irritation with and distrust of Frémont became an open sore within the family, and he stopped all communication with Jessie for months. Even before Frémont was formally nominated by the Republican Party, Jessie wrote Lizzie Blair Lee: "I have written constantly to Father . . . but for four months I have not had a line from him. . . ." Benton felt Frémont's decision to run as a Republican was a direct slap in the face. He feared the consequences of sectional politics: "We are treading upon a volcano that is liable at any moment to burst forth and overwhelm the nation."[22]

That was, in fact, the most damning charge of all—that Frémont's election would lead to war, secession, and rebellion. Buchanan charged that a Republican victory would mean "immediate and inevitable" disunion. Republicans countered that their party represented the last chance to avert civil war, but a majority of men who went to the polls that November believed otherwise. Buchanan won with about half a million more votes than Frémont, which translated into 174 electoral votes for the Democrat and 114 for the Republican. Fillmore received eight. The Republican Party had made a respectable showing for its first time in the presidential field, but that was little comfort to those who had worked so hard for victory.[23]

Frémont appeared to take the loss philosophically, as befit his personal sense of reserve. Jessie was devastated. Her dashed hopes of becoming "Presidentress," her husband's public failure, her father's role in it, all combined to depress her spirits. Even worse, some of the allegations of her husband's infidelity continued to surface after the election (which she called "a trial by mud"). Her collaborator John Bigelow severed connections with Frémont because the newspaperman believed that Frémont had fathered a child with one of his own housemaids. While Frémont soon returned to Las Mariposas, where continuing legal and financial problems could divert his attention, thirty-two-year-old Jessie escaped her demons in Paris. Jessie's thoughts continually strayed across the ocean and the continent, though; she still loved her husband. She worried that Frémont was no longer attracted to her, so she dieted and exercised. "I am trying to make the sun go from west to east," she wrote to him, "—that is trying to look young and pretty . . . I am trying in my old age to please you."[24]

At the end of 1857, learning that Jessie's father was sick, both Frémonts returned to Washington. Thomas Hart Benton was, in fact, dying of cancer, though he hid it from his daughter during their stay. Soon, the Mariposas's problems demanded the couple's presence on the West Coast, and though she did not know it then, when Jessie bid her father good-bye in February, it was for the last time; he died two months later. In California, Frémont devoted himself to developing and operating the mines, while Jessie set about making a home on the property out of crude shacks. To the astonishment of the workmen she supervised, she had them attach several structures and whitewash the lot, creating a large home of comfortable proportions that she dubbed "The White House." Jessie always strove to create a sophisticated, welcoming home, one that was also a stage worthy of the Frémonts' ambitions, whether in the cities of St. Louis, San Francisco, Washington, or in the middle of nowhere, such as Las Mariposas. That she brilliantly achieved her aim was evident in *New York Tribune* editor Horace Greeley's glowing praise during his 1859 trip to their home: "I expected to see Jessie Anne a worn if not a resigned little recluse, living on bacon and greens. What I see is French frills and blue sash ribbons." Jessie's memoirs reveal that the charming outfits she and the children wore to welcome Greeley had been hastily fashioned, on three days' notice, by her own hands from well-worn Parisian frocks and table linens.[25]

The Frémonts were still in California in November 1860, when Abraham Lincoln was elected president and a steady stream of Southern states began seceding. In February 1861, the Mariposas's insatiable appetite for cash sent Frémont to Europe again to find more investors, but this time, Jessie and the children did not make the trip. Frémont took with him his lawyer, Frederick Billings, and according to Billings, Frémont also took a mistress and her child. Frémont was still dealing with the seemingly endless investment problems relating to his gold mine two months later, when the Confederates fired on Fort Sumter, and Congress authorized the appointment of four major generals.[26]

The Blairs supported the appointment of Frémont to one of those posts, although Lincoln probably needed little encouragement from the venerable senior Blair or from his politically powerful sons, U.S. Rep. Frank Blair and Postmaster General Montgomery Blair, whom Lincoln had just brought into his Cabinet. Despite Frémont's less than routine separation from the U.S. Army fifteen years earlier, he retained the image of the dashing military officer and explorer. His antislavery stance still resonated, and even though he lost the 1856 election, many Americans recalled the excitement of his campaign. Lincoln needed generals who could inspire as well as those who could fight. In 1861,

Carte de visite of Jessie in California in 1860, when she was thirty-six years old. (*Author's collection*)

Frémont's popularity and a shortage of experienced military officers combined to make him an obvious choice for a senior military command. He received word of Lincoln's offer of a command while he was in Europe. His responsibility would be the vast, newly created Western Department, which stretched roughly from the Rocky Mountains to the Mississippi River and included the strategically valuable and politically sensitive border state of Missouri. Lincoln hoped, of course, that the Pathfinder could quickly find a path to Union success in that very large, very volatile, and very critical area. But Frémont did not move quickly. He stayed in Europe for a time to purchase guns and munitions for his new post before he sailed back to the United States.[27]

During her husband's European venture, Jessie had remained in California with the children. When Frémont sent word for her to meet him in New York on May 30, she was elated. Despite the prospect of another lengthy, strenuous cross-country trip with three children, she threw herself into the move. Jessie was thrilled at the rank and responsibility given her husband, and she looked forward to ending their long separation. In her mind, his summons may have also signaled the end of his philandering. It certainly offered the opportunity to renew the partnership they had previously enjoyed. In a letter to a friend on June 10, Jessie wrote: "We will go to join him on the 21st, and I will keep with him when I get there . . . this is a worthy cause to labor for." Her active participation in his expeditions, in his brief Senate career, and in his campaign for president must have reassured her that she could reprise her starring role as Frémont's closest aide, even in a major military command in the middle of a civil war. She was correct.[28]

"quite a female politician"

Once reunited in New York, the Frémonts did not proceed immediately to his new post. They stayed in the city for two more weeks, in part attending to personal matters (again, relating to the mine). Only then did they travel to Washington, where Frémont met with Lincoln on July 2. At that meeting, the two men discussed briefly—in retrospect, perhaps too briefly—Frémont's mission to bring order to the Western Department. Frémont emerged from that meeting declaring that the president had granted him "*carte blanche*" to act in Missouri, a description that echoes the broad grant of "discretion" he claimed from the Polk Administration in his ill-fated Mexican War adventure.[1]

During their short stay in Washington, Jessie visited the Blairs in Silver Spring, and they tried to convince her not to accompany her husband to St. Louis. Frank Blair was then commanding militia troops in Missouri, and his letters were filled with reports that St. Louis had become hostile and dangerous. Jessie rejected their advice. She knew she was right, and she went ahead. By the time the Frémonts finally arrived in St. Louis in July, nearly two months had elapsed since he had been offered the command. Frémont was shocked—by many accounts, frankly overwhelmed—by the task before him. Particularly daunting were the blatant and often violent anti-Union activities of the pro-slavery, pro-secession faction in Missouri; the earliest bloody guerrilla activities of the war tore apart that volatile state.

Jessie immediately set about organizing quarters for her husband's use and for her family. From her cousin, she secured a mansion for the general's military headquarters at the cost of $5,000 per year, considered a princely sum by his detractors. A large and adoring staff, composed mostly of Germans and Hungarians, transformed Frémont's innate personal reserve into imperial isolation. Decades later, Ulysses Grant commented about Frémont's command style during that period of the war. "Frémont had as much state as a sovereign, and was as difficult to approach," he told journalist John Russell Young in 1878. "I was under his command a part of the time, and remember how imposing was his manner of doing business. You left without the least idea of what he meant or what he wanted you to do." The general's isolation was even parodied nationally, when a correspondent for the *New York Times* wrote the following colorfully wry description:

> Let me say here that Gen. FRÉMONT is supposed to be in St. Louis. I say "supposed"—no one that I have heard of knows him to be here to a certainty. . . . To gain Heaven (here in St. Louis, especially); to gain speech with the man in the moon; to make love to the favorite of a Turkish harem; to wean a believer in Allah from predestination, or to instill maternal instincts into the bosom of a mule, are all thought to be difficult—yet in view of all these difficulties, that of obtaining audience with FRÉMONT sinks into utter insignificance.[2]

While Frémont's staff kept nearly everyone—military and civilian, important or not—away from the general, Jessie assumed the role of his secretary and installed herself in an office next to his. With her help, Frémont began his Western campaign by bombarding President Lincoln with requests for more men and more supplies. That came to naught, since rebel forces were gathering west of Washington, and the War Department's scarce resources were spread painfully thin. Just two days after her arrival in St. Louis, Jessie had sized up the situation and described it graphically in a letter to her best friend, Lizzie Lee: "It's making bricks without straw out here and mere human power can't draw order out of chaos by force of will only."[3]

Frémont, who had risen in the ranks of the U.S Army as an officer in the Topographical Service and had virtually no combat experience, confronted a tough command decision almost at once. Two of his subordinates, facing independent Confederate threats more than 250 miles apart, demanded immediate, substantial reinforcements, far beyond the capacity of headquarters to supply. Frémont correctly determined that Gen. B. M. Prentiss, who held the strategic junction of the Mississippi and Ohio Rivers at Cairo, Illinois, was the more urgent case for reserves. Frémont ordered the other commander, Gen. Nathaniel Lyon, to retreat from his precarious position at Springfield toward the nearest railroad head at Rolla, Missouri. Fearing a slaughter if he retreated, though, Lyon rejected the order of his superior. Despite being outnumbered at least two to one, Lyon ordered an attack. The Battle of Wilson's Creek, on August 10, 1861, with more than twelve hundred casualties on each side, was

Carte de visite of Maj. Gen. John
C. Frémont, c. 1861, when he was
forty-eight years old. (*Author's
collection*)

MAJ. GEN. FREMONT.
ELIAS DEXTER 562 BROADWAY

the tragic consequence of Lyon's decision. Lyon displayed conspicuous courage in leading his doomed troops against overwhelming odds before he was
killed during the battle. He had been a close friend of the Blairs, particularly of
Frank Blair, who blamed his death on Frémont's refusal to reinforce him. The
Blairs' disenchantment with Frémont began during this time. Frank's steadily
deteriorating evaluations of Frémont and the situation in Missouri made their
way to Silver Spring in a continuous stream of critical letters.[4]

In an effort to quell the mounting civilian and military disorder, Frémont
grasped a tool that perfectly fit his politics. He drafted an order for martial law
throughout Missouri, which gave him administrative control of the state and
included an order that armed guerrillas would be tried and, if convicted, shot.
The truly controversial provision that "fell upon the country like a thunderbolt," in Allan Nevins's memorable words, was his proclamation of immediate emancipation of slaves belonging to "all persons in the state of Missouri
directly proven to have taken an active part with their enemies in the field."[5]

Frémont wielded the weapon of emancipation as a means of resolving the immediate military crisis in his department. He believed that, faced with the prospect of losing their valuable human property, rebels would lay down their arms and return to their homes. This was an argument that found support in many quarters, particularly among the most ardent abolitionists. Lincoln disagreed. He feared such a move would push Unionist slaveholders in the border states to secede and tilt the geographic and economic equation to the benefit of the South. "I hope to have God on my side, but I must have Kentucky," Lincoln had said. He was not ready to risk the wrath of loyal slaveholders to the detriment of the entire country.

But Frémont focused only on his own situation and was still ardent in his antislavery beliefs. He was convinced that Lincoln had given him carte blanche to deal with the military situation in the Western Department, and he consulted no one before crafting his order. Furthermore, Frémont previewed the proclamation to only two people early on the morning he intended to issue it: Jessie and a prominent Quaker abolitionist, Edward Davis of Philadelphia. The former had earlier expressed her support of such a move by Frémont, and in this instance, her natural inclination to agree with her husband was fully in accord with her own personal antipathy toward slavery. "I would as soon place my children in the midst of small pox, as rear them under the influences of slavery," she once wrote. In advising Frémont to issue the emancipation order he had drafted, Jessie acted from the very highest of motives—loyalty to her husband and absolute abhorrence of slavery. Unfortunately, those laudable motives likely prevented her from offering her husband the best possible counsel at that point in his life.[6]

Instead it was the abolitionist—the man whose singular focus was freeing slaves—who offered Frémont the best advice for the general's own career. After reviewing the proclamation at Frémont's request (and, of course, agreeing with the principle it embodied), the Quaker expressed grave concerns about its timing, its scope, Frémont's authority to issue it, and (presciently) the political blowback from Washington against Frémont should it be issued. According to her memoirs, Jessie pressed Frémont to proceed. Frémont issued the order on August 30, 1861, making it public through wide dissemination in newspapers.

That is how the president of the United States learned of it. Hoping that what he read was inaccurate, Lincoln requested an official copy of the order through regular military channels. When it arrived, it confirmed his worst fears. Frémont had, in fact, assumed the power to free slaves forever. Almost immediately, reports of major political and military fallout from the proclamation reached Washington. Intended by Frémont to calm the roiled atmosphere in Missouri by inducing rebels to stop fighting, his order had the opposite result. Union loyalists protested Frémont's martial grab for power and, according to reports, Union soldiers laid aside their weapons more readily than did the enemy; their fight was not for the slaves, but for the Union. Within days, a letter from Lincoln's longtime friend and Kentucky confidant, Joshua Speed, reached Washington with the warning that "[Frémont's order] will hurt us in Ky.—If a Military Commander can turn [slaves] loose by the thousand by mere proclamation—It will be a most difficult matter to get our people to submit to it. . . ." Speed then voiced the gravest concern: "All of us who live in Slave states whether loyal or not have great fear of insurrection . . . [Frémont's proclamation] will crush out every vestige of a union party in the state. . . ." Robert Anderson, commander of the Department of the Cumberland, reported to Lincoln he had learned that "[o]n the day that one company in Missouri heard the proclamation, a company which was ready to be sworn into the service was disbanded." Anderson cautioned Lincoln, "[I]t is the opinion of many of our wisest and soundest men that if this is not immediately disavowed, and annulled, Kentucky will be lost to the Union."[7]

Frémont's proclamation also raised substantial legal and constitutional problems. A military officer's ability to seize combatants' property in war (contraband) was limited both in type and in time. The seizure of property—or liberation, in the case of human property—could only be justified if the enemy were using the property as part of its military operations. In addition, the seizure could last no longer than the conflict, at which time it would become the subject of final negotiations between the parties at war. Gen. Benjamin Butler had earlier designated as "contraband" those slaves used by Confederates in noncombat support roles and who had been either captured or had sought refuge behind Union lines. It was clear to all (especially to the contrabands, as they were called) that they were free only as long as they remained in Union-controlled areas, and that their ultimate fate awaited the outcome of the war. Congress passed the First Confiscation Act in August 1861, embodying Butler's solution, and Lincoln signed the bill.[8]

What Lincoln could not accept, however, was the action of one military officer in the most volatile theater of the war declaring that slaves of absent rebels would be freed for all time. That was a power that Lincoln believed belonged only to the president, if it existed at all. At that point, he was not sure that it did. It took another year of battles and thousands of deaths, during which the value of the South's slaves to the Confederacy's military effort became apparent, before Lincoln resolved in his lawyer's mind that emancipation could be justified under the president's war powers. But in September 1861, Lincoln continued to vow that reunion was the aim of the war, not emancipation, and he told an abolitionist who expressed his support for Frémont's measure, "*This thunderbolt will keep.*"[9]

General Frémont had aimed his blow at the enemy, but it had landed squarely on his commander in chief instead. Lincoln wrote an amazingly restrained reply to Frémont's insubordinate action. In it, the president requested that the general cancel the portions of his order that provided for immediate emancipation of slaves and required the execution of captured Confederates. Lincoln wrote that his letter was "written in a spirit of caution, and not of censure. I send it by special messenger in order that it may certainly and speedily reach you." The messenger was indeed special—one of Lincoln's personal secretaries, John Hay. Hay described meeting the Frémonts in his diary: "I went west, and passed several days in St. Louis. Saw very much of Frémont and his wife. He was quiet earnest industrious, imperious. She very much like him though talking more and louder."[10]

Frémont refused to take Lincoln's polite and private "no" for an answer, even when delivered by the president's personal secretary. On September 8, Frémont wrote a letter in which he rejected Lincoln's request and instead asked the president to publicly withdraw the emancipation order himself. If the president would not change his mind, Frémont wrote, then the president should take full responsibility for revoking the order by doing so publicly, thereby sparing Frémont the embarrassment of appearing to have changed his mind. Frémont also declined to withdraw his orders to shoot captured Confederates, despite a direct order by Lincoln, who expressed deep concern that it would invite retaliation against Union prisoners of war. Frémont's letter was drafted, sealed, and sent on its way to Washington.

At that point, however, even Frémont's rather insensitive political antennae finally began to vibrate with concern for his future. On that same day, September 8, Frémont also produced a detailed letter to the president outlining the specifics of his military strategy for winning the war in his department. But fate, in the form of Jessie, stepped into Frémont's effort to salvage his career. Jessie insisted upon personally carrying to Washington that strategy letter as well as a copy of the letter containing Frémont's refusal to withdraw his proclamation. She intended to personally place them in the president's hands, in a reprise of her earlier mission to deliver one of John's letters to President Polk.

Although she told Lincoln that she made the journey at Frémont's request (and many of her biographers state this as fact), it is at least likely that Frémont was powerless to stop her. "Doubtless the general knew that it would be better to keep the fiery Jessie at home," wrote Nevins, "but she would suffer no restraint." Jessie herself later wrote that she had become concerned that her husband had enemies within Lincoln's circle who might prevent her husband's letters from reaching the president. Quite possibly she believed her powers of persuasion and her political name could be of greater value to Frémont's future than his letter on its own.[11]

In fact, she had urged her husband from nearly their first day in Missouri to allow her to travel to Washington to educate the president about the desperate situation facing the Western Department. In the "bricks without straw" letter to her friend Lizzie Lee on July 27—just two days after the Frémonts had finally reached St. Louis—Jessie had also written that

> It is not safe to say on paper all that should be said at Washington. The President is a western man and not grown in red tape. If he knew the true defenceless condition of the west it would not remain so. I have begged Mr. Frémont to let me go on & tell him how things are here. But he says I'm tired with the sea voyage—that I shan't expose my health any more & that he can't do without me. . . . Don't be surprised if you see me some day in Silver Spring. I will obey a higher law than my dear chief's and open out the view to the M[ississi]ppi. It seems to stop now at the Potomac.[12]

Just five weeks later, on September 8, apparently, "a higher law" directed Jessie to make that trip. Taking her maid with her, she boarded an eastbound train.

Many years after the meeting, Jessie wrote at least three accounts of her audience with Lincoln, but she never published them, in order "to avoid controversy." She wrote the first, "a skimpy report," in 1888, the second in 1890, and the third a year later. Just as with her three accounts of the howitzer incident, Jessie's three accounts of the meeting with Lincoln do not contradict each other; rather, each successive version adds detail and drama to the previous one. Her decision to write them may have been sparked by publication of a description of the meeting by Nicolay and Hay, which Jessie had just read in its serialized version in *Century* magazine.[13]

In their narrative, the two men took Jessie to task for her accusations, her demands, and her "impetuous earnestness." They portrayed Lincoln's calmness in the face of this female fury as "no light task" but claimed he was successful in being "at once patient, polite, and just." And they included an excerpt from Hay's diary of 1863, in which was recorded Lincoln's recollection of the visit, told that year "in a confidential evening conversation with a few friends." According to the diary entry (the earliest extant written recollection of the meeting, albeit a secondhand account), the focus of the president's conversation was not the Frémonts but the Blair family and its gradual disenchantment with Frémont's military, political, and management skills. Lincoln recounted to his friends how he had encouraged Montgomery Blair to go to Missouri to discuss Frémont's problems with the general. According to Lincoln, Montgomery Blair "went as the friend of Frémont. He passed, on the way, Mrs. Frémont, coming to see me. She sought an audience with me at midnight, and taxed me so violently with many things that I had to exercise all the awkward tact I have to avoid quarreling with her. She surprised me by asking why their enemy, Montgomery Blair, had been sent to Missouri. She more than once intimated that if General Frémont should decide to try conclusions with me, he could set up for himself."[14]

Probably nothing in that description more infuriated Jessie—nor has since drawn more fire from her devotees—than the reference to her request for a meeting "at midnight." Abraham Lincoln's papers in the Library of Congress contain her written request to the president:

[September 10, 1861]

Mrs. Frémont brings to the President, from Genl. Frémont, a letter and some verbal communications, which she would be very glad to deliver with as little delay as possible.

If it suits the President's convenience will he name a time this evening to receive them—or at some early hour tomorrow.

Tuesday night, 8 o'clock
Willard's Hotel.[15]

The president's succinct reply is contained in Mrs. Frémont's papers:

A. Lincoln
Now.[16]

In her recollection of that evening, Jessie wrote: "As I had not been able to undress or lie down since leaving St. Louis I had intended taking a bath and going to bed at once," a statement decidedly at odds with her request for meeting "this evening," "with as little delay as possible." According to Jessie, she proceeded with an escort to the White House at about nine o'clock in the evening, still in her crumpled traveling clothes. There, she encountered Abraham Lincoln at his most inhospitable, an attitude that surprised her. Not only was Lincoln's reputation for bonhomie well known, but Lincoln had supported her husband for president in 1856, speaking forcefully for his election at more than two dozen political rallies in Illinois. Jessie had anticipated a much friendlier reception.[17]

Without a doubt, Lincoln was not as polite to Jessie as a nineteenth-century gentleman ought to have been to a female guest in his home. As she repeatedly emphasized in her written accounts, she was an exhausted woman who had just arrived late in the evening in Washington, after two days' and two nights' travel from St. Louis. She wrote that the president did not offer her a seat when she entered the room in the presidential mansion, "trembling from fatigue and recent illness." She considered him rude: he greeted her only with "Well?" (a phrase that journalist Noah Brooks had noted was Lincoln's standard inquiry of a petitioner).[18]

Nor is there room for doubt that in writing her versions of the meeting— and perhaps during the meeting, too—Jessie was trying to have it both ways. According to her earliest biographer, she had chosen to approach Lincoln as a peer in political and military terms, "thinking of herself not as the wife of an ill-treated officer approaching the President to protest in his behalf, but as a messenger from a man of unimpeachable integrity." When she began to explain that the proclamation could forestall European support of the Confederacy, "The President said, 'You are quite a female politician.' I felt the sneering tone and saw there was foregone decision against all listening." That should have been the end of the meeting, but before she left, she warned Lincoln that the Blairs were enemies of her husband, and she demanded copies of the president's correspondence with the Blairs.[19]

Had General Frémont sent his letters and the messages they contained via a military aide or even a male civilian adviser, no doubt Lincoln's response would have been the same. He would have again ordered that Frémont revoke his order, and under such circumstances, Lincoln's manner of rejecting his subordinate's unauthorized decree likely would have been as relatively unremarked upon as it was in later similar instances. It is Jessie's description of Lincoln's "sneer" and his phrase, "female politician," that made her meeting the grist of many historical mills. Lincoln was not merely impolite; according to her account, he was discounting her message solely because she was a woman.[20]

In the context of the nineteenth century, however, Lincoln was much more liberal regarding women's rights than many of those around him, including Jessie herself. Although Jessie was certainly one of the most famously independent women of her day, she never supported women's suffrage. When approached by Elizabeth Cady Stanton in 1866 to support a suffrage petition, Jessie refused, saying, "Oh, no. I do not believe in suffrage for women. I think women in their present position manage men better." She later sent Miss Stanton a small donation for the cause as a tribute to their friendship, but reiterated in the accompanying letter that "I cannot see the subject as you do." By the time of his meeting with Jessie, though, Lincoln had been on record for more than two decades in support of women's suffrage. As president, he interacted with women of all stations in his professional capacity every day; and socially, he especially appreciated women of learning and letters. When Lincoln called Jessie "quite a female politician," he was reacting to a particular woman at a particular moment.[21]

If she had truly been a "female politician," she would not have been surprised by Lincoln's behavior toward her. If, from the moment Lincoln appointed Frémont to command the Western Department, the Frémonts had intended to produce the worst possible reception for Jessie at the White House that evening, she and her husband could not have planned a better campaign from the point of view of Lincoln and his secretaries. Frémont had delayed his formal acceptance of the coveted grade of major general and command of the Western Department; delayed in proceeding from New York to St. Louis to take up the post; and he failed to respond to Lincoln's telegraphed inquiries about progress while repeatedly petitioning him for more men and more supplies. According to one observer, he allowed his wife to appear to act as "the real chief of staff" in St. Louis, and her license to act on her husband's behalf led Jessie to be called, albeit affectionately by some, "General Jessie." Another observer of the couple remarked that she was "the better man of the two." Those reports had circulated widely in the West, and in the East, too.[22]

Most damning, of course, Frémont had unilaterally issued an emancipation order, deciding within one military department a major national issue of the terrible civil conflict, without prior consultation with the nation's ultimate civilian and military leader. And he had done so in a manner calculated to test even Lincoln's famous good humor—he forced Lincoln to learn about it just as Jefferson Davis did—in the newspapers. It might be argued that Jessie had worked harder over three days to impress Horace Greeley in California than she and John had done in three months to earn his commander in chief's goodwill.

Patriotic envelopes were in vogue during the Civil War. Testifying to the fame of both of the Frémonts, their names were not thought necessary to print on this one. (*Author's collection*)

Moreover, if Jessie had been a politician—or at least, if she had been a good one—her note might not have urged Lincoln to see her late in the evening, as the plain meaning of its language clearly did ("with as little delay as possible"; "name a time this evening"). Late evening, whether eight o'clock, nine o'clock, or midnight, was a time when she—and also, presumably, the president of a nation in the midst of a civil war—might well have been tired, irritable, and impatient after a long day. While every historian's account of the meeting emphasizes Jessie's long, arduous trip from St. Louis to see the president, none has offered a corresponding description of Lincoln's activities that day.

The president began that morning by authorizing General Butler to "raise . . . a Volunteer force for the War," then rode across town to attend a meeting of the navy board about "building of ironclad vessels," then met "a delegation of prominent Kentuckians." Traveling "north of Georgetown," he observed the presentation of colors to Pennsylvania troops, followed by a "public review of General George McCall's Division." From there he rode with General McClellan to "tour fortifications on [the] Virginia side of Potomac and return[ed] at 7pm." No doubt there was a throng of petitioners awaiting his return to the White House. That is not an extraordinarily busy day by Lincoln standards, but it is a full one, with travel on horseback or in a carriage during the usually sticky month of September, when the average high temperature in the District of Columbia is 80 degrees Fahrenheit and average humidity is 80 percent.

If Jessie had been a good politician, she would have recognized and tried to counteract the possible downside of requesting the favor of a late meeting from such a busy man.[23]

Jessie seems not to have acknowledged that she was a supplicant at all. During the meeting, even according to her own written accounts, she spoke as if she had made the forty-eight-hour trip from St. Louis as a favor to Lincoln, to help the naive president comprehend the desperate military and political situation her husband had so brilliantly resolved with his proclamation, and to transmit his new and equally brilliant military plan for winning the war in the West. In point of fact, Jessie was neither a good politician nor a good judge of character. Her opinions of people were determined solely by how quickly and completely they bent to her will. Jessie's early positive view of Lincoln, after he had made her husband a general, was wholly forgotten when he repudiated her husband's emancipation proclamation and removed her husband from command. Then, she wrote, Lincoln revealed his "tenderness toward slavery" and his "sly, slimy nature."[24]

Because her father had taken pains to place her on intimate terms of friendship with so many presidents—as a child she sat in Andrew Jackson's lap—she felt as at home in the White House in Washington as she did in the "White House" she and her husband had built (and she had so pointedly named) in the mountains of California after he lost the 1856 presidential election. It was during that election, when she had been cheered as lustily as her husband and greatness seemed tantalizingly within her grasp, that she quoted Shakespeare's *Julius Caesar* in a letter. "I can say as Portia did to Brutus," she wrote, "'Should I not be stronger than my sex, Being so Fathered and so Husbanded.'" Perhaps Jessie simply could not countenance Mary and Abraham Lincoln as occupants of the Executive Mansion, an honor denied the Frémonts.[25]

Most obviously, though, Jessie was not a good judge of her own abilities, or she would not have tried with Lincoln what had not worked with Polk. Not surprisingly, the outcome of the meeting was not favorable to her cause. She did not convince the president to allow her husband's emancipation edict to stand, nor did she secure approval of Frémont's military strategy outlined in the letter she delivered to the president. More significantly, though, Jessie's outburst severely taxed the patience of Abraham Lincoln, by all accounts the most patient man in the entire United States in late 1861, certainly where his generals were involved. Though the president's biographers claimed he was calm during the meeting with Jessie, there is third-party testimony to the turbulence she left in her wake. The meeting with Jessie was not Lincoln's last meeting that evening. Iowa Rep. Josiah Bushnell Grinnell wrote in his memoirs in 1891 about a meeting of his own with the president that same evening:

> General Frémont's proclamation was, as I had good occasion to know, a severe trial to Mr. Lincoln. On the opening of a budget of my grievances, he said, "Don't mention them. I meet insults, standing between two fires, and the constant blazes of anger. Why, not an hour ago, a woman, a lady of high blood, came here, opening her case with mild expostulation, but left in anger flaunting her handkerchief before my face, and saying, 'Sir, the general will try titles with you. He is a man and I am his wife.' I will tell you before you guess. It was Jessie, the daughter of old Bullion, and how her eye flashed!"[26]

In this short reminiscence there is substantiation for aspects of both the Nicolay-Hay and the Frémont accounts. That Grinnell's meeting was an hour after Jessie's makes it more likely that hers was earlier than midnight, as she claimed. The vow to "try titles," as reported by Grinnell, like "try conclusions" in the Nicolay-Hay account, speaks to Jessie's rash language, even of a challenge to Lincoln's authority. Nevins favors Jessie's interpretation of the meeting over the Nicolay-Hay version, arguing, "Her narrative is probably more accurate than Lincoln's casual conversation, some two years after the event, casually jotted down later by John Hay, for the interview must have been burned deep into her retentive memory." But Grinnell's account of Lincoln's heated description of the meeting and the fact that even two years later, as recounted by Hay, Lincoln recalled the meeting with such vivid language ("insults," "blazes of anger," "violently taxed me," "avoid quarreling," "surprised me") and as having been at the very late hour of midnight testify that the meeting's emotions had burned equally deeply into the president's own memory.[27]

Jessie's escort to the White House meeting, Judge Edward Cowles, who had remained just outside the open door of the room where it took place, recognized the negative import of the meeting almost immediately. As he and Jessie walked back to the Willard Hotel, he told Jessie that her husband's career was over as a result of the Frémonts' attacks on the Blairs. Jessie was undeterred. Over the course of the next week, she persisted in communicating with the president via a series of letters, exactly as she had with President Polk. Her pleas met a similar fate. Two days later, Lincoln sent a letter to her at the Willard Hotel in which he declined to share with her his personal correspondence with the

Blairs. His pique at her assault had still not abated; he concluded the letter by insisting, "No impression has been made on my mind against the honor or integrity of Gen. Frémont; and I now enter my protest against being understood as acting in any hostility towards him. Your Obt. Servt A. Lincoln."[28]

CHAPTER 5

"It is your Lerida"

As Jessie parried with the president, she kept her husband informed through telegrams. Some were in a secret code the Frémonts had devised and often used, containing references to history and literature they both knew and to family details that others would not know. Feeling surrounded by enemies of her husband, she used it in the earliest extant message she sent to her husband during her visit to Washington. An undated telegram, which the editors of Jessie's letters date September 11, the morning after her meeting, reads:

> Genl. Meigs and Postmaster Genl. Blair leave this morning for St. Louis to investigate that Department. See New York Times of Tuesday. It is true and sent by the Cabinet Things evidently prejudged. Collateral issues and compromises will be attempted but the true contest is on the proclamation. It is your Lerida. Listen but remember our Salem witch. Remember and by note about General Washington. Guard originals and have copies ready. Some true active friends here and the heart of the country with you everywhere. I will wait for Billings. Will repeat this dispatch until you answer. That I may rely on the answer sign the name you gave one of Bronte's puppies.
> I am really well and Dr. Van Buren has just sent up his card.[1]

The one point of information in the telegram that is completely intelligible without a secret decoder ring is that on September 10, the *New York Times* carried an item, datelined September 9, which read in its entirety: "GOING TO ST. LOUIS. Postmaster-General BLAIR and Quartermaster-General MEIGS leave Washington for St. Louis in the morning. They go for the purpose of personally examining the condition of the Western Division." It contained no mention of the Cabinet, so Jessie must have deduced that from other sources.[2]

The editors of her papers have deciphered most of the code phrases in the telegram, including "Lerida," which is the site in Spain of Julius Caesar's great military victory in 49 B.C. over Pompey, his former co-consul turned political rival. Jessie's caution to "guard originals" and "have copies ready" almost certainly refers to Frémont's emancipation order. It is unclear why she would insist that he "have copies ready," since Lincoln had twice ordered it revoked by then, but those instructions to her husband may help explain a heretofore inexplicably insubordinate military order issued by Frémont nearly two weeks later.[3]

Whether or not this telegram was the first information about the meeting that Frémont received—there is an oblique reference in Jessie's papers to a message she sent that has never been found—this communication is hardly a model of succinct, dispassionate reporting, analysis, or advice during arguably the most critical decision point in Frémont's military career. Most notably, if it were sent the day after Jessie's meeting with Lincoln, it does not reference the president at all or her efforts to extract from him his correspondence with the Blairs. That Frémont's proclamation was in serious disfavor with Lincoln and his men may be inferred from the message. But the telegram gave him no useful news, except that Blair and his brother-in-law were on their way to investigate his Department. Jessie's fear was misplaced. The Blairs were not their worst enemy; the Frémonts were.

Word of the meeting reached Francis Blair Sr. the next morning, and he journeyed the few blocks from his townhouse to the Willard Hotel to see Jessie. He reminded her that he had begged her not to go to St. Louis. He lamented over her husband's insubordination and her verbal assault on the president. They launched into a three-hour verbal fistfight. A week later, in a letter to her husband, Lizzie Blair Lee quoted her father's account of that meeting, which Blair had written right after he left the hotel:

In a word [the Frémonts] hate & fear Frank [Blair] & are also hostile to everybody in the administration who is supposed to stand between them & imperial power which is they think to be clutched as easily as martial law by proclamation. . . . I then stated what Frank had done to give [Frémont] his command—what I & Montgomery had done to elevate him in the public eye—what we had done to advance his private fortune . . . & as She bridled up at this & put on a very *high* look . . . I told [her] she was to play the part of Empress Catherine. "Not Catherine but Josephine" she said—I said you are too imperious for her & too ungrateful for me. . . . [4]

The break between the Frémonts and Blairs was nearly complete.

While General Frémont's popularity instantly soared among fervent abolitionists across the country with the publication of his emancipation order, his
stock within the Administration and the military command plummeted. Jessie
and John alternated between periods of buoyant optimism and deep depression. During this time, Lincoln told all who asked that he would not remove
Frémont from office solely because of the emancipation order, but Frémont's
relatively smaller sins soon caught up with him. Management of men and materiel in St. Louis was atrocious and alleged to be thoroughly corrupt. Jessie,
however, may have added the final straw. Shortly after her meeting in Washington, Frémont arrested Col. Frank Blair, blaming him for malicious press
reports, "insidious & dishonorable efforts to bring my authority into contempt
with the Govt & to undermine my influence as an officer." Thoroughly outraged, Montgomery Blair laid the blame at Jessie's feet, saying Frank's arrest
had been "General Jessie's doing." The break was now complete.[5]

Lincoln was more patient with General Frémont during this time than he
had been with the general's wife. But even calm and patient Lincoln finally
determined that Frémont's tenure as a senior commander of the war had to
end. Secretary of War Simon Cameron and Adjutant-General Lorenzo Thomas
journeyed to St. Louis and interviewed a host of military and civilian officials
on a confidential basis about the management of the Western Department.
When Thomas's report was leaked from the War Department and published
in a number of major newspapers on October 31, 1861, the world read the worst
of what could be alleged against Frémont (and an unfavorable report about
General Sherman, too). In addition to the report's charges of the Pathfinder's
isolation, incompetence, and corruption, readers would have been astounded
to see a copy of an order sent from General Frémont to his adjutant general,
Justus McKinstry, twelve days after the president had publicly revoked Frémont's emancipation proclamation:

> Adjutant-general will have 200 copies of proclamation of commanding gen-
> eral, dated 30th August, together with address to the army of same date, sent
> immediately to Ironton [Missouri], for use of Major Gavitt, Indiana cavalry.
> Major Gavitt will distribute it through the country.
> J. C. F., Commanding General   September 23, 1861[6]

If Frémont's original publication of the proclamation without the president's
approval and his subsequent refusal to withdraw it had been insubordination,

Frémont compounded the offense by ordering production of copies of the proclamation and distribution of it well after he learned of Lincoln's direct order to rescind it. Frémont's motive for distributing the proclamation in defiance of Lincoln's direct command remains unclear, but his fatal lack of judgment in doing so was obvious.

If Frémont's order stemmed from or was encouraged by Jessie's earlier insistence that he "have copies ready," then Jessie may have done him even more harm after her meeting with Lincoln than during it. Thomas first presented his report in a Cabinet session on October 22. It was in that setting that Lincoln read Frémont's directive of September 23, which was reprinted in the report. According to Attorney General Edward Bates, Lincoln told his senior advisers in that meeting he believed it "clear that Frémont was not fit for the command." The next day, he issued an order that Gen. David Hunter replace Frémont. Testifying to Frémont's well-known desire for seclusion, senior officials carefully planned a subterfuge to insure delivery of the letter relieving him of command.[7]

When Jessie returned to St. Louis after her meeting with Lincoln in mid-September, Frémont moved quickly to demonstrate determination and leadership to his superiors in Washington. Spurred, no doubt, by Lincoln's implacable opposition to his use of martial law to suppress dissent in Missouri, Frémont launched the military plan that he had outlined to the president in the letter Jessie had delivered. Still smoldering with resentment against Lincoln and his Cabinet, both Frémonts applied themselves in a frenzy of action to assemble the men, arms, and rations needed for a major military offensive. As he prepared to lead troops from St. Louis in search of Confederate forces under Gen. Sterling Price, fresh encouragement arrived in the form of a poem by John Greenleaf Whittier, an admirer of both Frémonts since the 1856 election and a summer neighbor in Nahant, Massachusetts. Two years later, Jessie described the scene in a letter to Whittier: "[Frémont] was smarting under some fresh proof of the determination of the powers at Washington to make him fail . . . when one of the staff officers came up to me with an Evening Post containing your lines. . . . I read the words to the General and it was like David's harp of old. . . . His natural serenity came back & the whole tone of his mind was altered. Thanks to your true brave words. For it was brave at that time to believe well of the General. . . ."[8]

The famous opening lines of the poem praised Frémont's issuance of the emancipation order in a stirring condemnation of Lincoln and his council:

Thy error, Frémont, simply was to act
A brave man's part, without the statesman's tact,
And taking counsel but of common sense,
To strike at cause as well as consequence.[9]

As Frémont and his army marched from St. Louis, Jessie's concern for her husband escalated when she heard from a confidential source that some traitorous Missourians had given Confederate General Price information about her husband's troop strength and movements. Her panic for Frémont's safety spurred her to send him a warning by fast messenger. It also literally turned her hair white overnight. At dinner that evening, her cousin observed with surprise, "We have had such a rain today that I can't understand why your hair is all dusty." But it wasn't until her maid later combed her hair that Jessie became aware that "every hair was marked with an alternating white patch about an inch apart, giving an odd look of mottle gray to the whole." Thirty-eight-year-old Jessie noted wistfully that just a day before, "It had been a chestnut brown."[10]

By November 1, Frémont and his men were more than 150 miles west of St. Louis. The president had instructed Hunter to delay replacing Frémont if the general was in the act of engaging the enemy, but the enemy was still well beyond Frémont's reach that evening. Time ran out for the Pathfinder. When a U.S. Army corporal, disguised as a farmer claiming knowledge of enemy movements, was ushered into Frémont's presence, the general's first reaction was not focused on the content of the president's order but on its process. Angry that his security had been breached, he demanded of the messenger, "How did you get here?" He did not need to ask why.[11]

The next day, Frémont advised Jessie of his dismissal and asked her to "prepare for an immediate departure from St. Louis." Sad and dejected, they packed to return to Washington, where Frémont was already scheduled to defend himself against Thomas's allegations before the Congressional Joint Committee on the Conduct of the War.

Most historians agree that Jessie's meeting with Lincoln did harm, even perhaps "irreparable harm," to Frémont's military career. Although Jessie's frantic White House antics damaged her husband's career, in the end, Frémont deserves the blame for his own failure. After all, Lincoln (whose own wife was often uncontrollable) was unlikely to punish a general for the sins of his wife when he was so often reluctant to punish generals for their own sins. Yet, Jessie's actions deprived Frémont of his best opportunity to plead his own case through his letter to the president. The imperious manner of her visit and reports of her management of so much of her husband's business in his Department also likely made Lincoln less sure of Frémont's judgment and management skills and less tolerant of the continuing chaos and mismanagement that marked Frémont's administration of the strategically vital Western Department. And to the extent that she pressed her husband to flout Lincoln's order to revoke the emancipation order and "make copies," Jessie did her beloved husband a grave disservice. His proclamation was his Lerida, his greatest battle, as she fantasized in more than one of her ciphered telegrams to him. Largely through his own efforts, but with Jessie's encouragement every step of the way, however, Frémont played the role of the defeated Pompey.[12]

The next time Jessie saw Lincoln was in the White House in February 1862. The Frémonts were among five hundred privileged guests at an elaborate reception organized by Mary Lincoln to display her expensive redecoration of the White House. Jessie did not enjoy the evening. Like some of the other guests, she thought the celebration in poor taste during a war, and even less appropriate because of Willie Lincoln's illness (he died eighteen days later). Three months had passed since their host had removed General Frémont from command of the Western Department, and Frémont continued to languish without a significant military assignment. According to Jessie, "So many [of the guests] criticized the conduct of the war and there was so much feeling of sorrow that Gen. Frémont's policy of emancipation was not to be carried out, that it became embarrassing."[13]

The Frémonts prepared to leave the ball early, but before they reached the door, Sen. Charles Sumner intercepted them and dragged them back upstairs at the express wish of the president, who had learned that Generals Frémont and McClellan had never met. On the McClellan side, there is no extant record of the meeting at all, not even of the White House reception. On the Frémont side, Jessie's postmortem of the encounter with the president and the McClellans was predictably biting, even thirty years after the event:

> As we crossed the long East Room, the President came forward to meet the General; took him by the arm leading him to Gen. McClellan who was at the upper end of the room, and introduced them to each other, then introducing Mrs. McClellan and myself. We bowed, but as each seemed to wait for the other, neither of us spoke a single word. One look showed me she was dressed in the Secession colors. A band of scarlet velvet crossed her white dress from shoulder to waist, and in her hair were three feathers of scarlet and white. If

this was intentional, it was unpardonable in the wife of the commander-in-chief of the Union armies, and yet it seemed impossible to have been quite an accident. After a few minutes' talk between the President, Gen. McClellan, and Gen. Frémont we left.[14]

Jessie never saw Lincoln again.

Lincoln had not heard the last from the Frémonts, though. If the Frémont emancipation order had been an instance of friendly fire—an unintentional blow at an unintended target—the Frémonts soon mounted a direct assault on the commander in chief. This time, their weapon was the ballot box.

◦◦◦ CHAPTER 6 ◦◦◦

"There is a time to do and a time to stand aside"

Shortly after Mary Lincoln's cheerless reception in February 1862 (but not soon enough to placate the Frémonts), Lincoln gave Frémont another command. Frémont had defended himself so well before the Joint Committee on the Conduct of the War that the president acceded to the pleadings of the Pathfinder's many political supporters. In late March 1862, Jessie, the general, and their children headed to the town of Wheeling, then still technically in the state of Virginia. Frémont's newly created Mountain Department encompassed western Virginia (which had split from the Confederate eastern Virginia, but did not become a state until 1863), the eastern part of Kentucky, and a large portion of eastern Tennessee. Jessie set up housekeeping for the family in the same hotel where Frémont established his headquarters. As in Missouri, she claimed a small anteroom to his office for her own, and proceeded as usual to handle his correspondence and screen visitors. Unlike his unhurried approach to command of the Western Department less than a year earlier, General Frémont quickly prepared to engage the enemy. With Jessie's assistance, he organized a campaign to move troops westward, across the mountainous western Virginia highlands to Tennessee to aid Unionists there by capturing the vital railroad in Knoxville.[1]

Frémont had no hand in crafting the challenging plan he was about to execute. Lincoln himself had designed and ordered the strategy. It was a "pet idea of the President's," whose interest in aiding Union supporters in eastern Tennessee never flagged. The plan was destined for failure from the outset. Moving even the small army under Frémont's command (many fewer than the 25,000 troops allocated to him on paper) westward from Wheeling posed substantial difficulties unappreciated in Washington. West Virginia's motto is "the Mountain State" for good reason. The area lies wholly within the Appalachian mountain range, a series of steep ridges running roughly southwest to northeast, interrupted by two large "plateau" areas of rugged, stony plains. Poorly mapped in the nineteenth century, dense forests and river rapids rendered western Virginia a nearly impenetrable wilderness. Ironically, Frémont, who made his mark by making maps, was hampered from the start by the lack of any good ones. Frémont also struggled against a chronic shortage of men and materiel.[2]

No doubt the Frémonts felt an ominous sense of déjà vu in their Mountain Department experience. Once again, Lincoln sent Frémont west to rescue a border "state." Once again, Frémont complained—this time, with substantial justification—that Lincoln did not send the support he needed. Once again, Frémont failed. This time, to be sure, the failure was not his alone. In what was uniformly hailed as Thomas "Stonewall" Jackson's "brilliant and spectacular Valley campaign," Union generals Nathaniel P. Banks, Irwin McDowell, and Frémont all failed to prevent Jackson from ranging over nearly the entire Shenandoah Valley, threatening the outskirts of Washington itself and returning south with "substantial spoils and thousands of prisoners." Frustrated that his plan to secure eastern Tennessee had failed and stunned by the major military and psychological defeat wrought by Jackson, Lincoln combined the three generals' commands into a new entity, the Army of Virginia, and placed Gen. John Pope in charge. Frémont indignantly refused to subordinate himself to Pope, who had led one of the survey teams he thought he should have led, who he believed had conspired against him in Missouri, and whom he (and many other military officers) simply hated. Rather than report to Pope, Frémont resigned his command in June 1862, but not his commission. Writing to a friend, Jessie expressed her complete agreement with her husband's decision: "If he had stayed, they (the Administration) would have prepared defeats & destroyed his reputation." The Frémonts moved to New York.[3]

Frémont once again turned his energies to Las Mariposas, and in January 1863, he was finally rewarded for his years of work and worry when he sold it for $4 million. The Frémonts were rich, fabulously rich. But he was no longer dashing, and the only fire that burned in Jessie was one of anger against a host of enemies, especially the Blairs, who had sabotaged his generalship and denied them the presidency. Jessie turned to writing to vent her frustrations and finished a book that she had begun in 1861 to defend her husband. *The Story of the Guard* was published at Christmas in 1862. It garnered acceptable reviews, with critics stepping delicately around Jessie's apparently well-known tendency to the melodramatic and emphasizing instead her ladylike approach to her subject. "Mrs. Frémont is a true woman and has written a true woman's book," read part of the *Atlantic Monthly*'s review. "Instead of being a labored and exhaustive defense of General Frémont by the fair Jessie, while her Benton blood was up," wrote the *Hesperian*'s reviewer, "it is as mild and gentle as the heart of a woman."[4]

Jessie also turned to charitable work, particularly for the U.S. Sanitary Commission. Still a major general in the U.S. Army, Frémont very publicly donated his military pay to such soldiers' welfare organizations. Jessie had helped to organize the Western Sanitary Commission during Frémont's command in St. Louis, and she continued to support its work. Similarly, the U.S. Sanitary Commission collected and distributed medical supplies and arranged for treatment of sick and wounded soldiers and sailors. Men dominated the business side of the organization, but women were its public face and busy hands. Towns and cities held "Sanitary Fairs," in which women collected items for raffles and sales to raise money for the Commission. Some cities held more than one during the war. New York had hosted one in 1862, but the 1864 New York Sanitary Fair was the biggest of all. It featured the sale of tiny pieces of stone chipped from Plymouth Rock, demonstrations of Mr. Singer's revolutionary new sewing machine, and opportunities to pay to gaze upon a "hairy eagle," crafted from flowers and bits of hair donated by Abraham Lincoln. In all, the fair raised more than $2 million for soldiers' care. Jessie was one of the most prominent of the fair's organizers. She encouraged famous authors to write short books and memoirs to be sold (and she wrote one herself); she produced a memorably costumed "Cinderella" pageant, starring her son Charley and 250 children, all of whose parents paid to attend; and she even charitably cochaired the "Arms & Trophies" Committee with General McClellan's wife. Jessie wrote a friend: "On opening night we shall all be in full bloom with generals attached."[5]

Not so privately, the Frémonts continued to nurse their anger against those in Washington who, they believed, had wronged them. It was not surprising that Lincoln's political enemies would seek out their company, including the hard-line abolitionists of the radical wing of the Republican Party. These "Radical Republicans," or "Radicals," had judged Lincoln's prosecution of the war incompetent and insufficiently antislavery from the start. As the war dragged on, the Radicals also grew increasingly frustrated with Lincoln's apparent lack of zeal to punish the Confederacy after the war. With the approach of the election of 1864, they determined to elect a president more in tune with their punitive reconstruction philosophy.[6]

Casting about for a candidate to replace Lincoln, they seized upon Frémont, still the abolitionists' darling. They urged him to run for president in order to save the country from Lincoln, who was almost certain to be nominated by the mainstream Republican Party, or from worse—a Democrat, who would do the South's bidding on the slavery issue. The Frémonts' deep sense of injustice and persecution by Lincoln, Stanton, and especially the Blairs, along with their strong pro-emancipation, anti-Democrat stand, made them amenable to the political stratagems of the Radicals. Meeting in Cleveland on May 31, a group of about four hundred delegates, styling themselves the Radical Democracy Party, nominated Frémont. With Jessie's blessing, Frémont accepted the nomination, and he resigned from the army.

The Republican Party, still a major political organization despite the Radicals' defections, would not appear on 1864 ballots by that name. Two years earlier, Frank Blair had urged party fathers to adopt a new name in an effort to attract votes from Democrats. So it was that Abraham Lincoln sought the nomination of the "National Union Party" when it convened in Baltimore on June 6, 1864. "Don't Change Horses in the Middle of the Stream," his supporters warned. With some deft maneuvering by Lincoln's political operatives, the delegates overwhelmingly nominated the president.

The fractious Democratic Party (which did not change its name) opened its nominating convention in Chicago at the end of August. Split between factions that wanted peace at any price and those who wanted to continue to vigorously prosecute the war, party organizers had delayed the convention in order to capitalize on what were expected to be further defeats for the Union Army. Waging their own internal civil war, delegates finally produced a platform that favored immediate peace talks with the Confederacy. It put peace ahead of all other goals, including maintaining the Union and ending slavery. The party chose as its candidate a man personally and publicly committed to continuing the war. Gen. George McClellan accepted the nomination in absentia, remaining at his home in Orange, New Jersey, through the election. The Democrats did not require that McClellan resign from the army to pursue the presidency, and he did not choose to do it. McClellan had no qualms about remaining on active duty in the U.S. Army during his campaign against his commander in chief.[7]

It is unlikely that any president has ever felt as betrayed by his generals as Lincoln must have felt in mid-1864. In 1861, Lincoln had given Frémont and McClellan the military man's opportunity of a lifetime—senior command in the most important war ever fought by the United States. Three years later, they returned the favor by seeking to replace him as president and commander in chief. This was the first time in history that a democracy held a national election in the middle of a civil war. The fact that it was a three-way electoral contest between a president and two of his generals seems almost beyond comprehension. Radical Democracy Party candidate John Frémont, National Union Party candidate Abraham Lincoln, and Democratic Party candidate George McClellan waged one of the most consequential presidential campaigns in history. Would the Union be preserved? Would slavery be abolished? There were times in 1864 when Lincoln despaired of reelection. At one point, John Nicolay wrote his fiancée that the National Union Party was in the throes of "disastrous panic—a sort of political Bull Run." Lincoln's political advisers, who had initially scoffed at Frémont's candidacy, soon feared the Pathfinder's ability to siphon off antislavery votes from Lincoln. Such a split might possibly produce a McClellan victory.[8]

By this time, Lincoln and Frémont were in agreement on the issue of emancipation. During the summer of 1862, Lincoln the lawyer had finally convinced Lincoln the president that his constitutional war powers conferred authority to free slaves, a widely acknowledged vital resource for the Confederate military. Shortly after the Battle of Antietam in September 1862, Lincoln issued his Preliminary Emancipation Proclamation, signaling his intent to issue a final proclamation of emancipation, which he did on January 1, 1863. By proclaiming slaves free only in states in active rebellion against the Union, however, Lincoln defied the wishes of ardent abolitionists, who denounced him bitterly and flirted with Frémont's Radical Democracy Party. Additionally, the lack of clear, consistent, major Union military victories from August 1863 until August 1864 played into the hands of the Radicals.

Lincoln's advisers knew Frémont still claimed the hearts—and votes—of many abolitionists in the Northeast, as well as of the sizable Midwestern German population. They wanted to leave nothing to chance. So began serious efforts to convince Frémont to withdraw. Michigan Sen. Zachariah Chandler assumed the role of principal intermediary between Frémont's advisers and Lincoln's. Chandler deftly maneuvered behind the scenes, appealing to Frémont's strong antipathy toward McClellan, who had consistently opposed emancipation. In a face-to-face meeting with Frémont, Chandler offered to sweeten the deal. He proffered a senior military command for Frémont or senior administration posts for him and his friends, and he pledged Montgomery Blair's dismissal from the Cabinet if Frémont would drop out of the race. While the last prospect must have been nearly as tantalizing to Frémont as the presidency itself, there is no evidence that he accepted the deal (nor any solid evidence that Lincoln had specifically agreed to it). Indeed, Jessie, who did not play an active, public role during this presidential election campaign, scorned the insult to her husband that such a deal implied.[9]

Nonetheless, in a surprising move, Frémont soon did abandon the race. In doing so, he made it clear that he did not endorse Lincoln's candidacy. His withdrawal statement, published in newspapers on September 22, was as harsh toward Lincoln personally as it was toward all that McClellan and the Democrats represented. Shortly thereafter, Lincoln asked for Montgomery Blair's resignation from the Cabinet. Although Lincoln and Blair had previously discussed such a move, its timing—on the heels of Frémont's withdrawal—was undoubtedly aimed at bringing former Frémont supporters to the polls on Lincoln's behalf.[10]

That Frémont withdrew reluctantly is evident. That he withdrew at all was surprising. It was not in Frémont's character to allow himself to appear indecisive: his demand that Lincoln revoke the Missouri emancipation proclamation was case in point. Frémont was not motivated to withdraw from the race by his own judgment that his chances of victory were slim while his potential as catalyst for disastrous political change was great. Attractive offers of political position and income had not swayed him. Even the greatest seduction of all—revenge on the Blairs—did not entice him to renounce his chance for the presidency. Why, then, did he do it?

Jessie had not initially grasped the potentially terrible implications of the split in the Republican Party. Then, according to her earliest biographer, Catharine Coffin Phillips, she saw a cartoon in *Harper's Weekly* depicting McClellan dressed as Hamlet, holding Lincoln's skull in his hand and quoting, "I knew him, Horatio, a fellow of infinite jest. . . . Where be your gibes now?" The graphic possibility that McClellan, foe of emancipation and friend of pro-slavery Democrats, might become president stunned Jessie. From that moment, she began to think more like Old Bullion's daughter than like the Pathfinder's wife. According to her memoirs, she recalled her father's rage in 1844 when a third-party candidate nearly derailed a Democratic victory. It is also likely that Jessie recalled her father's opposition to Frémont's Republican candidacy in the 1856 race as well.[11]

Time and again throughout his life, Frémont had stubbornly rebuffed good advice from wise men when his wife sided with him against them. This time, though, was different. This time, Jessie took a stand with a wise man who advised Frémont to withdraw. As she desperately tried to determine the best course of action in 1864, Jessie later wrote: "[n]ever since my father's passing had I so longed for him. Yet even as I grieved, it was as though he had spoken,

"I KNEW HIM, HORATIO: A FELLOW OF INFINITE JEST. * * * WHERE BE YOUR GIBES NOW!"—*Hamlet, Act IV, Scene 1*

The political cartoon that startled Jessie into orchestrating her husband's withdrawal from the 1864 presidential election: McClellan as Hamlet, holding Lincoln's head and saying, "I knew him, Horatio, a fellow of infinite jest. . . . Where be your gibes now?" (*Courtesy of the Library of Congress*)

for I thought of that other man of clear vision and courage, John Whittier." Notwithstanding John Greenleaf Whittier's earlier admiration for Frémont's emancipation order, the poet believed firmly in 1864 that Lincoln must be reelected. Although Whittier's views on the election were generally known, Jessie grasped the power that a personal appeal from Whittier to Frémont would hold. Twenty-five years later, in a letter to Whittier, Jessie wrote of those days: "Among the words I remember from you are: 'There is a time to do and a time to stand aside.' I never forget your saying this to me at our Nahant cottage in 1864 when you had come to say them to Mr. Frémont. . . . Do you not remember it too? It was a deciding word, coming from you."[12]

Virtually all historians of the 1864 election cite Jessie's reference to Whittier's "deciding word," and in so doing, they acknowledge the role that Whittier, along with Chandler and other "Lincoln men," played in convincing Frémont to withdraw. If Whittier's was a deciding word in Frémont's decision, then Jessie is owed at least as much credit. Other than Jessie's first biographer, however, no other historian gives her the credit she is due. For Jessie did not merely agree with Whittier during his noteworthy visit to Frémont. She had, in fact, arranged it.[13]

Without her husband's knowledge, Jessie met earlier with the poet in his nearby home. During their visit, according to Jessie, they "reviewed the devious paths this country had taken since 1856, the great influence of his poems, articles, and speeches in the cause of freedom. . . . I laid my questionings, my perplexities, my convictions open to those earnest, kindly eyes. He agreed with me and promised to come to Nahant, and if possible, not betraying our previous consultation, to lay before Mr. Frémont his own convictions as to the best course to follow. He agreed to come when I should give the signal."[14]

In late August, Jessie coyly gave the signal. "Dear Mr. Whittier," she wrote, "The General will be here on Wednesday and will be glad to talk with you." At that meeting, Whittier advised Frémont to "stand aside," and Jessie agreed with him. On the heels of that meeting, Frémont issued his carefully crafted withdrawal letter.[15]

Lincoln swept to victory at the polls, aided in large measure by Sherman's capture of Atlanta, Gen. Philip Sheridan's signal victories in the Shenandoah Valley, and Adm. David G. Farragut's triumph in Mobile Bay. Lincoln won the Electoral College vote overwhelmingly and swamped McClellan in the soldier vote. Gross numbers are misleading, however. Lincoln won by slim margins in several of the most important states, where Frémont might have siphoned off votes: New York, Pennsylvania, and Connecticut. While it is not probable that Frémont would have made McClellan president had he stayed in the race, his withdrawal guaranteed Lincoln's victory. It takes only a moment's contemplation of a McClellan presidency to appreciate the incalculable gift that Whittier's advice and Jessie's arrangement and endorsement of it were to Frémont—and to the United States. After twenty-three years of steadfast but often ill-advised support for Frémont's every wish, Jessie made her most valuable contribution to her husband by finally disavowing blind allegiance to him. The Frémonts' time on the national scene ended with their well-advised retreat from the presidential contest.

Even after Lincoln's death, Jessie never overcame her dislike of him. Lincoln is conspicuously absent from Jessie's 1887 book, *Souvenirs of My Time,* which contains chatty, informative tales about important people whose paths she had crossed, including Andrew Jackson, Dolley Madison, Elizabeth Schuyler Hamilton, and Prince de Joinville. The published letters of Jessie Benton Frémont do not include any from the time of Lincoln's assassination, and the major biographies of the couple do not contain reflections by either of them upon Lincoln's death or his legacy.[16]

The woman who would not visit General Kearny on his deathbed never did speak kindly of Lincoln. That her bitterness against Lincoln never faded can be deduced from lines in two letters she wrote after the war. In them, Jessie implied that if Lincoln had died other than by assassination, she would willingly speak ill of him. In 1877, she told the publisher of the *Philadelphia Times:* "On that subject [emancipation] I have a tale to tell, but the manner of Mr. Lincoln's death bars the truth at present." Years later, she wrote Whittier's literary executor: "Mr. Lincoln's cruel death silenced much truth."[17]

By then, Jessie desperately needed the income she could produce with her pen. The Frémonts' postwar years continued as unstable as their lives to that point, if not more so. At first, their fortune allowed them to try to bury their disappointment under an avalanche of costly possessions. They bought a literal castle on the banks of the Hudson River and gave it an Indian name, Pocaho. There, Jessie created a world of luxury that recalled Elizabeth Benton's youth at Cherry Grove Plantation. An army of servants maintained their museum-quality collection of books and art, including Albert Bierstadt's magnificent painting of San Francisco's Golden Gate. The Frémonts entertained in style, but they were no longer at the center of the life of the nation.

Soon they were no longer wealthy, either. In a move that almost defies belief, Frémont invested nearly every cent of his Mariposas profit in a railroad project that soon failed. Again he pursued investors in Paris with less-than-honest agents. Although Jessie was present with him in Paris, he was smitten by a stunning, sexy young sculptress named Vinnie Ream. Frémont's investment sortie failed, forcing the Frémonts to liquidate their considerable estate. By 1873 everything, including Pocaho itself, was sold at auction, with the exception of three portraits (of Jessie, Frémont, and Thomas Hart Benton) and the remnants of the ragged United States flag that Frémont had raised at the summit of the Wind River Mountains in 1842.[18]

Desperate for money, they traveled to Washington to redeem the chit Senator Chandler had offered Frémont to drop out of the 1864 election. Frémont accepted appointment as military governor of the Territory of Arizona. He promptly began using that office to do what Jessie said he scorned to do in California in 1850—to "overlook his private interests." But even in that, Frémont failed. He spent so much time in New York raising money for his new mining interests that the secretary of state for Arizona called for his resignation. Frémont resigned as governor on October 11, 1881. Through it all, Jessie supported the man who was always her hero. She had been writing all along, making small amounts of money from articles she penned for a wide array of magazines. Some of her sketches were gathered together and published as books, including the vivid description of her 1849 journey with little Lily by ship and mules to California, which became *A Year of American Travel.*[19]

After the Arizona debacle, the Frémonts moved to a small home in the booming little southern California town of Los Angeles. Frémont spent the rest of his life trying to secure a government pension. In 1890, he traveled to Washington to lobby Congress, which finally restored him to the grade of major general (retired) at a salary of $6,000 per year. From Washington he went to New York to begin the trip West. There, Frémont fell ill with peritonitis and rapidly failed. His son Charley, a U.S. Navy officer on duty nearby, rushed to his bedside. On July 13, 1891, the man who once conquered mountains died in a tenement flat in New York City. Jessie had remained in Los Angeles because they could not afford for her to go with him to the East Coast. Her children feared for her life once she learned of Frémont's death, but Jessie was made of sterner stuff than even they knew. When it became apparent the family could not afford to ship his body back West for burial, Charley arranged for his father to be buried at a cemetery near Pocaho, overlooking the Hudson River. More than ten years later, Jessie's ashes would be sent to the same place.

Frémont's pension stopped upon his death. For the rest of their lives, Jessie and Lily (who never married) began relying on the kindness of strangers, although Charley and Frank protested that they could care for their mother. Congress later granted her a small widow's pension, but as soon as her plight became known, the women of Los Angeles paid tribute to the famous widow in their community. They gathered funds and bought a small house for her and Lily. The city gave them lifetime passes on the streetcars. Jessie's world had become very small indeed. The only constant was her writing, but when offered money for an article about her husband's emancipation order, she refused. She could not bring herself to write admiringly of Lincoln, and she knew the public did not want to hear anything negative about him.

Before Lincoln died—indeed, in the very middle of the war—he found it within himself to praise Frémont for making a signal contribution to emancipation, despite the troubles he had suffered at the hands of the general and his wife. In late January 1863, a group of prominent abolitionists, including friends of the Frémonts, such as Wendell Phillips, visited Lincoln to complain that the limitations of the president's Emancipation Proclamation prevented it from striking the blow against slavery they had sought. During the meeting, they also expressed continuing admiration for General Frémont and their desire that Lincoln give him yet another command. The president declined to make any promises, although he told them solemnly that he had "great respect for General Frémont and his abilities." Lincoln then went on to speculate that Frémont's fate was not unexpected, at least not if history were a guide. "[T]he fact is that the pioneer in any movement is not generally the best man to carry that movement to a successful issue. It was so in old times, wasn't it?" he mused. "Moses began the emancipation of the Jews, but didn't take Israel to the Promised Land after all." Lincoln continued thoughtfully in words that seem eerily prophetic regarding his own fate. "It looks as if the first reformer of a thing has to meet with such a hard opposition and gets so battered and bespattered that afterward, when people find they have to accept his reform, they will accept it more easily from another man."[20]

Jessie, who likely heard of Lincoln's philosophical observation from her friends in the meeting, probably did not find Lincoln's perspective on her husband's pioneer status comforting. She may, though, have taken grim satisfaction in Lincoln's acknowledgment of her husband's contribution to the elimination of slavery, even though she forever blamed Lincoln for robbing Frémont of full credit for it. Until her death in 1902 at the age of seventy-eight, Jessie never stopped defending the man who had been her life since her seventeenth year, never stopped fighting for him.

Perhaps the Frémonts would have fared better had she fought less.

PART TWO

Self-Inflicted Wounds

Mary Ellen Marcy McClellan

NELLY MCCLELLAN'S CIVIL WAR

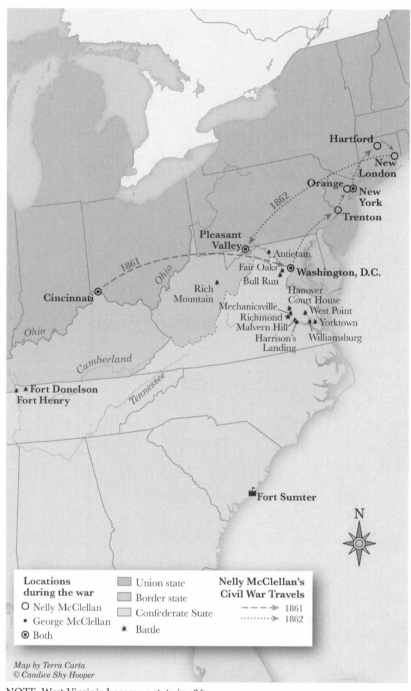

Hartford

New
London

Orange
New
York

1862

Trenton

Pleasant
Valley

Antietam

Fair Oaks

Washington, D.C.

Bull Run

1861

Ohio

Rich
Mountain

Hanover
Court House

Cincinnati

Mechanicsville

West Point

Ohio

Richmond

Yorktown

Malvern Hill

Williamsburg

Cumberland

Harrison's
Landing

Tennessee

Fort Donelson
Fort Henry

Fort Sumter

N

**Locations
during the war**

○ Nelly McClellan

• George McClellan

◉ Both

Union state

Border state

Confederate State

★ Battle

**Nelly McClellan's
Civil War Travels**

– – –▸ 1861

·········▸ 1862

Map by Terra Carta
© Candice Shy Hooper

NOTE: West Virginia became a state in 1863.

"you are fond of attention and gaiety"

Jessie Frémont was not the only one who noticed the striking dress Nelly Mc-Clellan wore to Mary Lincoln's reception in February 1862. Several days after the event, *Frank Leslie's Illustrated Newspaper* carried an engraving of prominent, fashionably dressed women at the event, including Nelly and Mary Lincoln. The newspaper made no comment on Nelly's red-and-white color scheme, even though, as Jessie scathingly observed, the war had made women's fashions fair game for partisan criticism. Following Lincoln's inauguration, Marylanders who flagrantly displayed red and white were prosecuted in that state for showing "secession colors." Apparently, that color combination was suspect in the national capital as well. It is almost impossible to imagine, however, that Mary Ellen Marcy McClellan would have chosen to wear that color scheme in the White House as a means of telegraphing sympathy for the Confederacy. She was not only the wife of the newly appointed Union general-in-chief, she was also the daughter of highly respected U.S. Army officer and legendary Western explorer Randolph Marcy.[1]

In the surviving correspondence she exchanged with her husband, Nelly never expressed favor toward the Confederate cause, although she was openly contemptuous of the Lincoln Administration. Her contempt reached such heights, in fact, that in one letter she wrote to her husband: "I almost wish you *would* march up to Washington & frighten those people a little." In such spectacularly self-absorbed thinking, she and Jessie Frémont were remarkably similar. In the eyes of those who knew them, they did not merely love their husbands; they worshipped them. Nonetheless, the women expressed their devotion quite differently. Jessie tackled those she believed were her husband's foes; Nelly nurtured her husband's delusions while remaining detached from his world. Despite her submissiveness, or rather because of it, Nelly had an

Mrs. McClellan.   Mrs. Lincoln.   Mrs. Senator Crittenden.

Nelly McClellan (*left*) and First Lady Mary Lincoln (*center*) shown in their ball gowns at Mary's grand reception in February 1862. Nelly's dress was described as "white with bands of cherry velvet"—the red and white "secession colors" that drew bitter words from Jessie Benton Frémont in her memoirs. (Frank Leslie's Weekly, *February 22, 1862*)

equally decisive impact on her husband's career, on his relationship with Lincoln, and on history's judgment of the president and of her husband.[2]

The McClellans' marriage has always been portrayed as a nearly iconic Victorian union, with the strong, public husband and the meek, adoring, private wife. Based on the surviving written record, historians conclude that Nelly and George loved each other deeply all their lives. From all of the available evidence, it is apparent that Nelly parroted McClellan's fantasies in her daily letters to him when they were apart and matched his every ill-advised social step when they were together. After his death, however, she failed to adopt the widow's conventional role as guardian of her husband's reputation. Indeed, if Jessie Frémont fought too hard for her husband, Nelly McClellan fought not at all.

Nelly and George were born in different worlds. Capt. Randolph Marcy was a line officer in the U.S. Army, deployed to the Wisconsin Territory during the Black Hawk War in the early 1830s. His wife, Mary Amelia Mann, followed him to the frontier and to life in the shelter of a fort near the little village of Astor (now Green Bay). On May 17, 1835, Mary Marcy gave birth to their first child, Mary Ellen. According to one account, an Oneida Indian "squaw" served as little Nelly's nurse and often carried her charge in a papoose, strapped to her back. Some of Nelly's earliest words were in the Oneida language. The Marcys had strong ambitions for their children, and they looked forward to moving back east to realize them.[3]

Half a continent away in Philadelphia, nine-year-old George Brinton Mc-Clellan was living the upper-middle-class lifestyle that the Marcys sought to emulate. His surgeon father founded the Jefferson Medical College, his mother was an elegant and refined hostess, and they emphasized languages, arts, and letters in their children's education. The McClellans, whose social circle included Daniel Webster, were of the "best society" in Philadelphia, precisely the class to which the Marcys aspired. It was not society, however, but the U.S. Army that brought the two families together.[4]

As Randolph Marcy had done many years earlier, McClellan attended the U.S. Military Academy at West Point, New York. Graduating in 1846, McClellan served with distinction in the Mexican War. He was a favorite of Secretary of War Jefferson Davis, who gave him a plum assignment in the spring of 1852 as a member of the army's expedition to discover the source of the Red River. McClellan first saw a photograph of beautiful sixteen-year-old Nelly Marcy that year, just after he had been assigned as second in command to the expedition's chief, Captain Marcy. By that time, Mrs. Marcy and the children were "back east," and Nelly was attending boarding school in Connecticut. Taken with her beauty, McClellan communicated his feelings to his mother. Two years later, Elizabeth McClellan wrote to her son that she had been socializing with Captain Marcy's wife and daughters (who then lived in Philadelphia), and that as a result of the many good things said about him by her and by the general, "Miss Nelly . . . was just ready to fall in love with you."[5]

McClellan finally met Miss Nelly in the last week of April 1854. It was, indeed, love at first sight—for McClellan. His mother's breathless hope notwithstanding, Nelly was far from smitten. In fact, when McClellan proposed to Nelly two months later, she turned him down, to the distress of McClellan and the chagrin of her parents, who adored him. Stoically, McClellan refused to accept her rejection as final. According to his biographer, McClellan determined that "the only way to [Nelly's] heart was through her mother," and for more than four years, McClellan corresponded assiduously with Mrs. Marcy. During that time, he also wrote to Nelly, but she did not answer any of his letters until 1858. In the meantime, she nearly slipped from his grasp.

Ambrose Powell Hill captured her heart. Nelly met him in Washington during her father's posting there in the mid-1850s, and she fell deeply in love. At the age of twenty-one, she accepted a ring from the young army officer, inscribed "je t'aime," as a token of their engagement. Known to his friends as A. P. or Powell, the Virginian had been McClellan's onetime roommate at West Point and continued as friend and confidant even during their concurrent courtship of Nelly. Hill was tall, handsome, and romantic, imbued with a strong sense of honor and a Southern passion to defend it. He loved to be in love and was unashamed to admit it. In a letter to his sister Lucy, he once confessed, "You know that I am so constituted that to be in love with some one is as necessary to me as my dinner. . . ."[6]

Nelly's parents violently opposed her engagement to Hill because they emphatically insisted they had not raised their daughter for the nomadic, penurious life of a military wife. Her parents were certain she could find a better match than Hill because Nelly Marcy never lacked for suitors. At least eight other men proposed marriage to Nelly. Their letters to Nelly reveal desperate, burning passions that her charms inflamed and her indifference failed to dampen. They were all military men, like her father, and understandably so. As an "army brat," Nelly would naturally have come into constant contact with army officers who knew Marcy, or who could invent an excuse to meet his daughter. Just like Marcy, generations of military men have pleaded with and even ordered their daughters not to marry military men like themselves. Wanting more for their daughters than can be found in a marriage to a soldier—low income, often poor living conditions, separation, isolation from the larger society, a life largely tedious but sometimes highly dangerous—even today military men urge their daughters to marry into the ranks of civilians, where they perceive the good life to be.

It should not have come as a surprise to her parents therefore that Nelly accepted a proposal from a young army officer. Nor should it have surprised Nelly that Captain Marcy exploded in anger in late May 1856, when news of her engagement reached him at his posting in distant Laredo, Texas. He immediately wrote his daughter a lengthy, harsh letter, which reflected not only his intense ambition for Nelly but revealed much about her character as well:

> In regard to Mr. Hill I know but little of him, he seemed to be a gentlemanly man, and if he was not in the army but engaged in some business that would insure you a comfortable home I should not have so much objection, but I should suppose you would have more ambition. . . . You say you are not ambi-

tious but you are fond of attention and gaiety, and you certainly never have these in the army. . . . I shall expect that you at once abandon all communication with Mr. Hill. If you do not comply with my wishes in this respect I . . . fear that my ardent affection would turn to hate. Do nothing therefore my dear child without choosing between me and him.[7]

Nelly apparently weathered that blast of parental censure as easily as Jessie had withstood Senator Benton's opposition to Frémont. Her swift retort reflected a spirited personality and fierce determination. She countered with a reminder that Marcy had not objected to Captain McClellan's proposal, even though he was also a soldier. Then she took the additional step of urging Hill to send Captain Marcy a letter disclosing his financial situation. Neither missive swayed Marcy, who responded to his daughter in June 1856:

I received a letter from Mr. Hill in which he says he is worth about $10,000. This is something but not much. I have not yet answered his letter. Although I should not have objected to your marrying Captain McClellan, yet I had no great desire for it after he went into the line of the army, as the same hard fate would have awaited you as with other officers. His talents and well known high character with the warm friendship which exists between us would have caused me to discard all other considerations and given you to him.[8]

Even that was not enough to discourage Nelly. Unlike Jessie Benton, however, Nelly McClellan did not react to her father's desire for her to choose a more suitable husband by secretly marrying her own favorite. Nelly's impudence went only so far. She threw facts and logic at her father from a distance, but she did not irrevocably oppose him. A month after her father's letter, she decided to seek Captain McClellan's advice on the matter of defying her parents to marry his former roommate, rather cold-blooded treatment of the spurned yet still determined suitor. Even in responding to Nelly's rare letter to him, McClellan refused to take sides in the battle between the woman he loved and her parents who loved him. He wrote Nelly that she should "govern [her]self by the dictates of [her] good sense & true woman's feeling."[9]

While Captain Marcy restricted his campaign to straightforward objections based on Hill's finances and occupation, Mrs. Marcy's tactics were personal and poisonous. She told her daughter that a friend had reliably informed her that Hill had a venereal disease that would promise despair, debilitation, and shame to any woman who would marry him. Although her attraction to Hill was strong, Nelly had no choice but to retreat in the face of such an insurmountable barrier. Tearfully but dutifully, Nelly ended her relationship with A. P., returning Hill's engagement ring without informing him of her mother's charge. In return, she received a joyous expression of love from her father. "[I] . . . found your letter in which you express a determination to be governed by our wishes in regard to Mr. Hill," he gushed. "You are the pride of my heart and a dear good girl!"[10]

Nearly a year later, Mrs. Marcy's charge reached Hill's ears, and his sense of honor demanded that he seek redress. Etiquette prevented the young man from confronting a lady, but he sought satisfaction, man to man, in an extraordinary letter to Captain Marcy. Mrs. Marcy's slander was not merely untrue, according to Hill, but her willingness to spread the rumor was fatal to any prospect he might have of marriage or future happiness:

> I have heard from truthful lips and with delicacy, that Mrs. Marcy's objections (one at least and the only one to which I reply), as stated to me, is that from certain early imprudences (youthful indiscretions I suppose), my health and constitution had become so impaired, so weakened, that no mother could yield her daughter to me, unless to certain unhappiness. . . . I ask it of you as one gentleman from another, as one officer who has been wronged, from a brother officer, who can right him, that you put this matter right in the proper quarter, and that your wife correct this false impression with whomever she may have had any agency in hearing it—I think too that in justice both to herself and myself she should make known the name of her informant to be used by me as I see fit.[11]

Hill's letter stunned Marcy and inflamed his sense of honor. Not only did he reply to Hill that he was convinced his wife's accusation was a "base fabrication." He also immediately wrote to his wife that if what Hill said was true, "I should insist upon Ellen's marrying Mr. Hill at once as a just reparation." Somehow Mrs. Marcy sidestepped both her husband's belief in Hill's innocence and Hill's demand that she expose the informant.[12]

No one has ever determined the source of Mrs. Marcy's information. Hill was never robust, even as a young man, and his sickly disposition gave rise to questions about his health, even by those not privy to his West Point medical records, which indicated he had been treated for venereal disease. Gonorrhea was a common enough ailment among military men of that era to have been a convenient charge for a desperate mother to wield against a young officer of whom she disapproved. Furthermore, every kind of gossip ran rampant through the military community, so Mrs. Marcy could have heard it from any number of sources. One may even wonder if McClellan were the source of Mrs. Marcy's information about Hill's gonorrhea. He would have known of Hill's illness through his close association with him at West Point; he was still in love with Nelly; he was in regular correspondence with Mrs. Marcy as part of his determined effort to win her daughter's hand; and, as he would later demonstrate, he was far more ruthless in pursuit of personal victories than military ones. Although he had the weapon and the motive to eliminate his rival, he did not do it. Instead, McClellan soon found himself in a most bewildering situation. He had to defend his honor against attacks by Mrs. Marcy.[13]

Mrs. Marcy had not only spewed venom against Hill to Nelly, she had also maligned Hill in more than one letter to her longtime pen pal, McClellan. When Captain Marcy confronted his wife with Hill's letter, Mrs. Marcy concluded that McClellan had revealed her role in the affair to his former roommate. Mrs. Marcy fired off a furious, slanderous letter to McClellan, accusing him of revealing her appalling gossip to Hill. McClellan sharply disabused her of that notion. "As a matter of course," he retorted, "I transmitted to Hill *none* of the remarks you made; I thought that you would regret what you had written before the letter reached me ... So I shall destroy your letter & never allude to its contents to any human being." Although the events surrounding Nelly's broken engagement are remarkable, perhaps the most astonishing aspect of this sad episode is the fact that so many of these intimate and inflammatory letters were saved for posterity.[14]

Whatever the source of Mrs. Marcy's information about Hill, her cutthroat tactics eliminated him from the queue of Nelly's suitors. Yet, Mrs. Marcy's triumph was incomplete. Even after Nelly ended her engagement with Hill, she did not warm to McClellan, and that angered her mother. Mrs. Marcy feared that, as part of the fallout over the Hill affair, McClellan had completely given up his pursuit of Nelly, and her wrath spilled over in letters to her daughter. "[T]he time is coming sooner or later just as sure as you live when you will regret it—if ever a woman did," she blasted her Nelly. "Mark my word, I see it, I know it! Yet your perverseness will in the end make you miserable. I have done all that is in the power of a mother to do, and now whatever your fate may be hereafter, I cannot reproach myself." Nelly had given up her heart's desire, but that was not enough to prevent her mother's withering condemnation. Captain

Marcy might have been content that his daughter was not going to marry Hill, but Mrs. Marcy was more distraught that Nelly had thrown away her chance with McClellan.[15]

In 1858, McClellan resigned from the army to pursue a more lucrative career with the Illinois Central Railroad. Such a career move would have further enhanced his attractiveness as a son-in-law to the Marcys. It is also likely that the snail-like pace of promotions in the peacetime army frustrated McClellan's ambitions, as it did so many other young officers. In any event, Nelly continued to ignore McClellan's persistent letters until later that year, when she deigned to reply to one of them, and an intermittent correspondence between the two began. About the same time, Marcy was appointed to a command in the West. As the family prepared to move to the Minnesota Territory, McClellan invited Nelly and her family to visit him in Chicago on their way west to their new home. The patient, persistent suitor seized the opportunity to renew his proposal to Nelly. To his eternal delight, this time she accepted his offer.

We have none of her letters or any diary entries from this time in her life to help us understand her reason for changing her mind about marrying McClellan. In fact, very little in Nelly's voice has survived at all. In the George Brinton McClellan Papers in the Library of Congress, there are only five letters and three telegrams she sent to her husband between July and October 1862, and there are three small diaries written after the Civil War. On the other hand, she saved hundreds of letters he wrote to her. Lacking documentation from her, while swimming in it from him, most historians have described Nelly's acceptance of McClellan's proposal and their ensuing twenty-five years of marital felicity from McClellan's point of view. He was positively gleeful. "I can't tell you how happy & *proud* I am that you are mine & all mine, *mine forever*," he wrote during their engagement as he urged her to name an early date for the wedding. "I *may* yet play my part on the stage of the world's affairs and leave a name in history, but Nelly whatever the future may have in store for me *you* will be the chief actor in the play. . . ." His diary describes his wedding day with exclamation. "!!May 22!! Le jour de ma vie," and he wrote his mother, "I believe I am the happiest man that ever lived. . . ."[16]

Although we do not have her version of the events, it is possible to imagine what might have been in the thoughts of Nelly Marcy on that day in 1859 as she arrived at the door of George McClellan's home in the bustling metropolis of Chicago, on her way to life in Indian country. She was approaching twenty-five in an era when a Northern woman of that age was on the threshold of being considered a spinster (in the South, that word was applied at least two years earlier). In company with her mother, father, and brother, she was leaving the heavily populated East Coast, heading to the wilds of the Minnesota Territory, where the odds against finding an acceptable suitor (particularly given her parents' high standards), much less a soul mate, escalated with each mile westward. McClellan was then a senior officer at the Illinois Central Railroad. As such, he held one of the nation's most powerful and prestigious civilian jobs, with an excellent salary. The railroad provided him with a beautiful home. His appearance was dashing, his manners impeccable. He had won the hearts of both of her parents, and he had ardently sought hers for years. He had never wavered in his affections. He was, in short, a very good match, in an age where that was society's principal goal for a marriageable female. Nelly was nearly five years older—and presumably wiser—than when she rejected his first proposal. McClellan was, perhaps, the last suitor standing when Nelly decided it was time to marry, but that was good enough for him. This time, when McClellan proposed, the scales tipped in his favor. Nelly and George were married in New York City on May 22, 1860, in a wedding packed with military luminaries, including future Civil War commanders G. W. Smith, Cadmus Wilcox, Joseph Johnston, and General-in-Chief Winfield Scott.[17]

Like the Frémonts, the McClellans shared many of the same traits, some positive, some decidedly negative, and, also like the Frémonts, they often reflected and reinforced those traits in each other. They were both attractive, and in their photographs together, they present a handsome couple. Standing five-feet eight-inches tall, McClellan was of average height for American men during the mid-nineteenth century. He was a strong man, with a broad chest that tended to make him look shorter than he was. In one of the most iconic photographs of the Civil War, taken after the Battle of Antietam in 1862, McClellan appears Lilliputian as he faces the six-foot four-inch Lincoln. Auburn-haired, blue-eyed McClellan was a handsome man, fastidious in his dress and conscious of his appearance. According to one astute Washington observer, "McClellan liked pomp and circumstance. . . . When he dashed through the streets on his black horse—stocky, with close-cropped hair, high color and bright blue eyes, he seemed a whirlwind of controlled power."[18]

Nelly attracted as much favorable notice as did McClellan. As her many suitors attested, Nelly was beautiful, and her personality sparkled, too. More than one observer described her as "vivacious." She was of a delicate build, with a tiny waist, smoothly coifed light brown hair and heavy-lidded, soft, hazel eyes. In most photographs, Nelly is staring in the distance, an unfocused, impassive expression on her face. In those where her gaze is fixed on the camera,

MRS. GEN. MC CLELLAN.

GEN. MC CLELLAN.

Left: Carte de visite of "Mrs. Gen. McClellan," c. 1861, when she was twenty-six years old. (*Author's collection*). *Right:* Carte de visite of "Gen. McClellan," c. 1861, when he was thirty-five years old. (*Author's collection*)

however, her broad forehead, raised chin, and bare hint of a smile evoke an enigmatic mid-nineteenth-century Mona Lisa.

McClellan and Nelly were both bright and well educated, certainly by nineteenth-century standards. As a very young man, the precocious McClellan had expressed an interest in a military career, choosing not to follow his father, a well-respected surgeon, into the medical profession. Instead, at the age of thirteen, he began his studies at the University of Pennsylvania. Two years later, McClellan entered West Point by special waiver, since the minimum age for cadets was seventeen. Recognized as a brilliant student, a true leader, and a genial companion by his peers, McClellan graduated second in the famed Class of '46. That class provided many of the senior officers who fought the Civil War: twelve future U.S. generals and ten future Confederate generals, among them Thomas "Stonewall" Jackson, John Gibbon, Darius Couch, Ambrose Powell Hill, George Pickett, Jesse Reno, George Stoneman, and Cadmus Wilcox. McClellan excelled in the engineering studies that were the focus of West Point's educational system. He entered the elite Corps of Engineers upon graduation and was awarded two field promotions in the Mexican War for his exemplary service as an engineer, and a fighting one at that. He was fluent in several languages and at one point taught himself Russian in order to translate a military treatise from that language. His native intelligence combined with a deep vein of inventiveness as well. McClellan designed a saddle that bore his name, which became the U.S. Army standard for more than a century.[19]

Nelly, too, had an excellent education. Testifying to their ambitions for her, Nelly's parents sent her to one of the nation's most prominent private schools for women. Founded by Catharine Beecher, Harriet Beecher Stowe's oldest sister, the Hartford Female Seminary enrolled more than one hundred students in the early nineteenth century and dedicated itself to "moral, physical, and intellectual development of women." Nelly could converse easily in French, and she and McClellan often sprinkled French phrases in their correspondence. Of course, Nelly also was skilled in the conventional womanly arts of the era, from needlework to household management. Nelly appeared the very epitome of feminine perfection to all who met her. But the coolness with which she dismissed the entreaties of her father and the ardor of her many suitors—not to mention her request for McClellan's advice in deciding whether to marry his rival—hint at an icy autonomy within.[20]

After his lengthy and hard-fought effort to win Nelly's hand, McClellan bound himself more closely to her by conforming to her upbringing in two important matters. Turning his back again on his own family traditions, he embraced the medical and religious beliefs that grounded Nelly and her family. Although McClellan's family boasted several distinguished men of medicine, including most notably his own father, McClellan joined the Marcys in rejecting conventional medicine. They favored homeopathy, and one of Nelly's uncles was, in fact, a leading homeopathic doctor. Homeopathy is an alternative practice of medicine in which illnesses are treated by administering diluted remedies that mimic weak versions of the patient's symptoms. It got its start in the late eighteenth century, but reached its widest acceptance in the 1800s. Considering the poor survival rate of patients who endured the nineteenth century's ill-informed, aggressive conventional treatments, homeopathic patients likely benefited in relative terms because their doctors did less harm.

Nelly was in residence in Washington with McClellan when he contracted typhoid fever late in December 1861. In short order, her uncle, Erasmus E. Marcy, and another homeopathic doctor from New York arrived in Washington and began treating the general and his similarly ailing father-in-law. Homeopathy was not held in high regard in the military medical community

as evidenced a month later, when the Army Medical Board forbade homeopathic doctors from serving in military hospitals, so as to discourage requests
"from all types of 'quacks' and 'charlatans' claiming medical expertise." Nor
was homeopathy generally accepted in the non-medical portion of the military community. Gen. George Meade made that clear in a letter to his wife,
in which he wrote that McClellan's reliance on homeopathy "has astonished
all his friends, and very much shaken the opinion of many in his claimed extraordinary judgment."[21]

Similar comments were voiced as far away as London, where the humor
magazine *Punch* quoted a report of the generals' reliance on homeopathy.
Headlined "Insanity in the Federal Camp," the January 26, 1862, edition carried
this commentary: "If GENERAL McCLELLAN and GENERAL MARCY have
been 'undergoing homeopathy,' they will never be strong enough for their situations. It will be all gone goose with the Federal cause unless such geese as they
must be are sent about their business: which might be that of carrying placards
for BARNUM instead of hoisting the star-spangled banner."[22]

Historian Ethan Rafuse postulates that "McClellan's use of a homeopathic
doctor . . . may have contributed to growing public skepticism toward the
general in chief" during the winter of 1861–62.

If adopting Nelly's preference in medical treatments changed the way people thought about McClellan, adopting her religion changed the way McClellan thought about everything, especially about himself. More than one historian has commented on McClellan's "messianic" vision of himself, and such
a conclusion is inescapable from reading his letters to Nelly. Three months
before his designation as general-in-chief—before he had actual responsibility for all the armies of the United States—an adoring reception in the Senate
chamber prompted McClellan to muse to Nelly: "Who would have thought,
when we were married, that I should so soon be called upon to save the country?" Nelly played a key role in enlarging his sense of destiny through her
Presbyterian faith, which McClellan enthusiastically embraced before their
wedding (he had been raised in the Episcopal Church). In letters written to her
during that time, McClellan's language is that of the newly converted zealot: "I
believe we are to be united *forever* & that our union *on this earth is only a state
of preparation for our union through eternity in a higher & better state.*"[23]

From the time he adopted Presbyterianism, McClellan seized upon its doctrine of predestination to explain everything that happened in his life, good
and bad: Nelly's ultimate acceptance of his marriage proposal, his selection as
general-in-chief, his failure to capture Richmond, his defeat as a presidential

candidate. He gloried in their shared belief in God. "We feel alike about these trials," he wrote to her on July 27, 1862, as Lincoln pressured him to move before he felt his army was ready. "I do feel that God does what is right. . . ." As he internalized it, "God's will," the Calvinist credo, meant that God, not Lincoln, had placed the mantle of deliverer on his shoulders. With God guiding his destiny, McClellan expressed unbounded self-confidence. Addressing the president's apprehension about the enormity of the task ahead of him, he reassured Lincoln, "I can do it all." Soon after he became commander of the Army of the Potomac, he wrote: "I feel that God has placed a great work in my hands. I have not sought it." The day before he assumed General Scott's responsibilities as general-in-chief of all the Union armies, McClellan told Nelly, "I do not feel that I am an instrument worthy of the great task, but I *do* feel that I did not seek it. It was thrust upon me. I was called to it; my previous life seems to have been unwittingly directed to this great end. . . ."[24]

Combined with his own high opinion of himself and low opinion of others, McClellan's belief in his divine mission made him unwilling to listen to the president, General Scott, or the secretary of war, and he was often unwilling to even talk to them. In most strategy meetings, he rarely uttered a word. In one such council, which took place while he was "still pale and weak" from typhoid fever, McClellan bluntly refused to tell Lincoln his military plans. McClellan whispered to Gen. Montgomery Meigs, seated next to him, that "if he revealed his plans now, they would be in the *New York Herald* the next day. The president could not keep military secrets; he even told them to Tad, his eight-year-old son." Ensuring the accuracy of his prophecy, McClellan himself briefed a reporter for that newspaper for three hours the very next day. Less than two weeks after Lincoln appointed him commander of all the Union armies, McClellan even refused to see the president, who traveled to McClellan's house and waited patiently for more than an hour. McClellan's natural hubris was inflated by the sense that his status was divinely ordained, a belief that his version of Nelly's faith infused in him.[25]

The same God who brought him early success and fame, however, also occasionally inflicted defeats. While he often willingly appropriated to himself some of the credit otherwise due to God for his victories ("to have it recognized that I have saved the lives of my men & won success by my own efforts is to me the height of glory . . ."), McClellan was far less eager to share God's responsibility for any loss. To McClellan, a defeat not only was not his fault but was divinely ordained for some greater purpose. When he failed to capture the Confederate capital, he wrote Nelly in July 1862: "I think I begin to see his wise purpose in all this. . . . If I had succeeded in taking Richmond now the fanatics of the North might have been too powerful & reunion impossible. However that may be I am sure that it is all for the best."[26]

Stern Calvinist doctrine sustained and inspired generations of Americans who fought first for their survival in a hostile new world and then for their independence. Confederate Gen. Thomas "Stonewall" Jackson was a famously devout Presbyterian, but his interpretation of the doctrine inspired a fighting style almost completely the opposite of McClellan's. The Almighty might decide a setback was in store for Jackson, but He would not find Stonewall crouched on the defensive when He delivered it. When processed through McClellan's mind, however, the doctrine of predestination held grave dangers for his country. A general who contemplates victory and defeat with equal complacency is unfit for service in any war in any era. Such a commander learns nothing from either loss or gain. He does not—need not—cannot—change his understanding of the enemy or alter his own behavior. McClellan's inflexible mind, reinforced by his sense of divine destiny and his encouraging wife, could not bend.

Military historians who have searched for the cause of McClellan's failed career almost always point to the rapidity of his rise to general-in-chief as one of the major factors. Bruce Catton called it the "dazzling, too-lucky stroke that had lifted him from the Western Virginia mountains to the top command in Washington." Even McClellan conceded that "It would probably have been better for me personally had my promotion been delayed a year or more." His rapid advancement deprived McClellan of more experience in smaller military units and engagements that would have afforded him chances to learn from his mistakes. Sherman and Grant had opportunities early in the war to fail in more limited roles—and often did—yet went on to succeed in larger commands. Those generals' careers, and Lincoln's rise to greatness as commander in chief, are examples of men learning from their mistakes over time. Unlike Sherman, Grant, and Lincoln, who consistently learned on the job, McClellan ended his service in the war with the same mental toolbox he brought to it. But McClellan faced a singular obstacle in learning from his mistakes: he never believed he made any.[27]

McClellan's flaws were not apparent at first glance, though. When first summoned to Washington in July 1861, McClellan impressed Lincoln with his confidence and modesty. The president was not alone in mistaking the handsome, successful, highly intelligent, and well-spoken general for a brilliant young man and, possibly, a genuine military genius. Quite the reverse of Lincoln, McClellan almost always made an excellent first impression, particularly on those whom he wished to impress. One's initial positive encounter with McClellan, however, often gave way to a sort of buyer's remorse, as on successive meetings he proved to be little more than an excessively self-important, self-absorbed dandy, who thrived on cheering crowds and adoration. Even that critique of his shortcomings, though, is wide of the mark. To put it bluntly, McClellan was paranoid.

In his fascinating essay, "McClellan's Tragic Flaws in the Light of Modern Psychology," Joseph Glatthaar aligned McClellan's documented behavior with traits now associated with paranoid personality disorder: mistrust, suspicion of others' motives, extreme secretiveness, need to dominate in any situation, inability to defer to others or to accept blame or criticism while highly critical of others. And Glatthaar noted that a paranoid personality is often associated with narcissistic personality disorder, whose sufferers "hold majestic views of their own talents and accomplishments . . . [and] convert minor successes or even failures into sensational accomplishments." Glatthaar described in detail McClellan's lifelong inability to get along with any of his superiors, from a teacher he had at the age of twelve through President Abraham Lincoln. The only exception, according to Glatthaar, was his service under Capt. Randolph Marcy in 1851. During their exploration of the Red River, Glatthaar observed, the two men "worked well together."[28]

"Interestingly," wrote Glatthaar in the only reference to Nelly in his essay, "McClellan courted Marcy's daughter Ellen for several years and eventually won her hand." Glatthaar's observation is much more than merely interesting, especially when examined through the psychological lens he provides. Given McClellan's innate dislike of authority figures, he may have intuitively viewed the amiable Marcy as the only possible father-in-law for him. McClellan's father had died suddenly when George was twenty-one years old; Marcy might also have represented the father he lost too early. McClellan's single-minded pursuit of Nelly could have been unconsciously linked to his desire to stay close to her father. The fact that McClellan arranged Marcy's appointment as his chief of staff as soon as he had an opportunity is also noteworthy. Certainly Marcy was a respected, experienced officer who could be relied upon to offer sage counsel and administrative efficiency to the young and inexperienced commanding general. Additionally, his choice of Marcy, who was thereby promoted, further ingratiated himself with his beloved wife and her parents. Nevertheless, it is also significant that in promoting his father-in-law to that senior military position, McClellan ensured Marcy's daily deference to McClellan in his professional life, thus resolving in McClellan's favor any lingering authority figure issues he might have had with his father-in-law.[29]

A complete understanding of the complex McClellan's patient but relentless five-year campaign for Nelly's hand is only slightly more difficult than comprehending Nelly's change of heart—or her change of mind—about marrying him. Whether Nelly's decision to marry McClellan was made for practical reasons yet she grew to love him over the years, or whether she forever nurtured a frozen core of bitterness in her soul against a world that thwarted her heart's desire for A. P. Hill, or both, can never be known. Love for McClellan or lack of it transformed the spirited young woman of those impertinent letters to her father into an outwardly submissive, apparently wholly supportive, unquestioning wife.

In any case, Nelly's relationship with McClellan—his peculiar embrace of her religion, her conduct when they were together, their correspondence while they were apart—helped to reinforce McClellan's worst traits. Like Frémont, McClellan was certainly the architect of his own downfall. Similarly, his wife provided critical support for his flawed judgments and actions. Nelly might have realized she had married a complex and idiosyncratic young man, but she could not have imagined the consequences to the nation of his flawed character or of her unquestioning support for him. In psychology, there is a term for a person whose actions make it easier for another to persist in self-destructive behavior: Nelly was Little Mac's enabler.

CHAPTER 8

"Flora McFlimsey"

As different as Frémont and McClellan were, the Civil War careers of the two men followed roughly the same dizzying and dismal trajectories, providing Jessie and Nelly nearly identical opportunities to revel in their successes and to endure their failures. Frémont soared and plummeted to earth in the space of a year; McClellan took seven months more to do the same. Frémont's initial grade was higher than McClellan's—Lincoln appointed him major general in May 1861—but that was Frémont's zenith as well. McClellan started lower on the military horizon, as commander of Ohio's militia in April 1861, before Lincoln appointed him major general in the regular army the next month. But McClellan rocketed higher, to general-in-chief of the U.S. Army in six months and, thus, ultimately fell further. In all, it took only nineteen months from his reentry into military service in April 1861 for McClellan to win and lose the full spectrum of authority within the U.S. Army.

The opening shots of the Civil War, fired in Charleston Harbor on April 12, 1861, found the McClellans living in Cincinnati. The recent offer of a position leading to presidency of a division of the Ohio & Mississippi Railroad had attracted McClellan away from Chicago. He had chafed under his superiors at the Illinois Central and, as usual, sought independence and absolute authority. The position's salary made the prospect even more attractive; at $10,000 per year, McClellan was one of the most highly compensated men in the country. During their brief time in Cincinnati, Nelly and George enjoyed a comfortable lifestyle, and they were expecting their first child in the autumn of the year.

The war changed everything.

McClellan was anxious to join the fight, confident that military promotions would occur far more quickly in wartime than in the antebellum years. With his brilliant record in the army and managerial skills acquired in the railroad industry, he easily gained a command. On April 23, 1861, McClellan accepted the Ohio Legislature's commission as major general of the state's volunteers (McClellan did not resign his railroad position until late 1862). From that point, his ascent was more rapid than even the narcissistic McClellan could have anticipated. He assumed command of the Department of the Ohio of the U.S. Army on May 3. Less than two weeks later, with the support of Army General-in-Chief Winfield Scott, President Lincoln appointed him major general in the regular army, which placed McClellan second in rank only to Scott himself. As the Department's lines expanded over the following months, Major General McClellan's responsibilities grew to include Missouri and western parts of Pennsylvania and Virginia.[1]

McClellan soon turned his attention to western Virginia. Immediately upon approval of Virginia's secession ordinance in May, Confederate troops raced from Richmond to the northwestern corner of Virginia, which had voted overwhelmingly not to secede. In a series of skirmishes and small engagements, troops under McClellan's authority, though never under his direct command, compelled rebel forces to surrender or retreat from the area. In the context of Civil War battles, McClellan's forces had achieved only a minor military victory in a part of Virginia that had few slaves and little sympathy for rebellion. Politically, however, the action paved the way for establishment of the State of West Virginia, which happened two years later. McClellan also guaranteed that his military success would translate into public relations success. He insisted on stringing telegraph wire behind him, and, as he no doubt hoped, most of his dispatches to the War Department quickly appeared in newspapers. Their content and tone captured Northerners' imagination and boosted civilian and military morale; McClellan was always better at writing than fighting. None of his dispatches was more satisfying than McClellan's signed telegram on July 14 to the War Department, which appeared verbatim in the *New York Times* the next day: "We have annihilated the enemy in Western Virginia. . . . Our success is complete, and secession is killed in this country." McClellan's success boosted the fortunes of the Lincoln Administration at a critical early point in the war.[2]

It was also during this time that McClellan earned the undying hostility of abolitionists. He did not approve of slavery, but he did not believe that the war or the warriors should play any role in slavery's demise (he favored a long-term program of compensated emancipation). Without consulting the Lincoln Administration, on May 26, 1861, McClellan issued a proclamation "*To the Union Men of Western Virginia*," which pledged that "All your rights shall be religiously respected . . . not only will we abstain from all interference [with your slaves], but we will, on the contrary, with an iron hand crush any attempt at insurrection on their part." McClellan's pledge to protect slavery in western Virginia would return to haunt him at the ballot box three years later.[3]

The western Virginia military campaign's immediate impact, though, was on McClellan's career. Less than two weeks after the *Times* carried news of McClellan's "annihilation" of Confederate forces in western Virginia, Federal troops suffered a shocking defeat in the Battle of Bull Run, less than thirty miles from the U.S. Capitol. Demoralized soldiers and terrified civilians, who had foolishly carried picnic lunches to watch the battle, streamed back into Washington from Manassas Junction on July 21, with tales of slaughter and mayhem. Lincoln desperately needed to install a charismatic, winning general at the head of Union forces to quell the rising panic, and McClellan uniquely fit the bill. Two days later, Lincoln appointed McClellan to command of what was then named the Military Division of the Potomac. From that point, it was only a matter of months before McClellan's inability to tolerate supervision and his ability to manipulate others led General Scott to retire and Lincoln to appoint McClellan general-in-chief of the U.S. Army. By the time he assumed the post of the nation's senior commander on November 1, 1861, McClellan had impressed many with his reorganization of several eastern armies into the Army of the Potomac. He was already beginning to dismay Lincoln and his Cabinet, however, by his reluctance to use that army. Confederate forces still occupied strategically valuable positions near the Capitol in and around Manassas Junction, and McClellan wrongly feared the enemy had vastly overwhelming forces there. So, in what was quickly to become the trademark of his command style, McClellan settled in at headquarters, demanding more troops, more training, more materiel, and more time.

As McClellan prepared for victory and glory (some might say in reverse order), Nelly remained in Cincinnati, pregnant with their first child. Buoyed by McClellan's success, she was nonetheless suffering from the heat, poor health, and her husband's absence. She wrote to McClellan's mother in June that she was "in wretched spirits most of the time, and generally disquieted." On October 12, 1861, baby "May," Mary McClellan, was born. As she slowly recovered from childbirth, Nelly began preparations to join her husband at his new headquarters in Washington. There, she knew, her status as the general-in-chief's wife would place her near the very top of the social pyramid in the wartime capital.[4]

McClellan's life also changed dramatically from the time he arrived in Washington in July. He set a brutal pace for himself and his aides. He oversaw construction of a circle of more than sixty forts to defend the national capital and continued to strengthen and perfect "his" Army of the Potomac. When he became general-in-chief, McClellan fashioned national military strategy. Mc-Clellan drove himself relentlessly ("Had to work until nearly three this morning," he wrote Nelly), but he did not want for entertainments. Invitations piled up, he told his wife, but he had little time for them. "Refused invitations to dine to-day from Gen. Scott and four secretaries." There were some invitations he could not refuse. The Young Napoleon, as he had been dubbed by the press, dined with Prince Napoleon "at the President's," he wrote Nelly in August. He was unimpressed. "The dinner was not especially interesting; rather long, and rather tedious, as such things generally are." McClellan was the toast of the nation, and his activities were routinely reported in the press. In late November 1861, as Lincoln hoped that McClellan would launch his army west to Manassas to push out the Confederate victors of Bull Run or south to Richmond, McClellan instead traveled north. The *New York Times* reported on November 25 that "MEYERBEER'S new opera, 'Dinorah,' was produced here last evening. . . . The house was crowded to its greatest capacity. Among the visitors was Gen. GEORGE B. McCLELLAN, who, being recognized, was greeted with cheers and honored with National anthems."[5]

Back in Washington, it seemed that preparations for the Army of the Potomac would never end. The summer after the Battle of Bull Run passed into an autumn of unsurpassed beauty and dry roads, but McClellan refused to move. He claimed his army was not ready. On October 31, McClellan blandly recapped his progress and his prognosis to Secretary of War Cameron: "So much time has passed & the winter is approaching so rapidly that but two courses are left to the Government, viz: Either to go into winter quarters, or to assume the offensive with forces greatly inferior in numbers to the army [I desire.]" Mc-Clellan's army went into winter quarters. It was not yet ready.[6]

In early December, thirty-five-year-old McClellan met Nelly, baby May, and his mother-in-law at the train station in Baltimore and brought them to Washington. At the age of twenty-six, the new mother entered the capital of the United States as the wife of the nation's cherished young military savior-to-be. Lionized wherever they went, the McClellans saw no reason to avoid an active social life in Washington during the first winter of the war, even though many citizens found the lavish entertainments available in the nation's capital disrespectful to the men fighting and dying in the field. Unlike most generals' wives who joined their husbands in the field during the war, Nelly enjoyed a comfortable home, surrounded by family. McClellan had found "a very good house" for them at Fifteenth and H Streets, right around the corner from the White House, and one that could accommodate quite a crowd. Before the baby was born, McClellan had written his mother to come to Washington and bring one of his sisters with her "just as soon as Nell is well & established here . . . I have plenty of room here for you—& I *rather* think that you will enjoy services etc as much as anyone else." By the time Nelly, Mrs. Marcy, and two-month-old May joined him there, his father-in-law, Chief of Staff General Marcy, and his brother, Capt. Arthur McClellan (whom McClellan also made part of his staff), were already in residence, running interference with annoying politicians who came to call on the general. It was hardly hardship duty for Nelly or for McClellan.[7]

While McClellan housed himself and his family in comfort, the rest of his officers camped with their soldiers in the forts hastily erected around the capital. One was Fort Corcoran, on the Virginia side of the Potomac River opposite Georgetown, "a kind of western suburb of the Capital," according to Lincoln's secretary William O. Stoddard. The Federals had seized that part of Virginia nearest Washington when Virginia seceded. While the physical distance between the residence of the general-in-chief on H Street in Washington and the camps of his troops across the Potomac was less than five miles, the psychological distance was significant in the eyes of at least one of his subordinates. Col. William Tecumseh Sherman, posted to Fort Corcoran, observed the general's preference for town over camp, and many years later recalled in his memoirs:

> General McClellan arrived, and, on assuming command, . . . [i]nstead of coming over the river, as we expected, he took a house in Washington, and only came over from time to time to have a review or inspection. . . . August was passing, and troops were pouring in from all quarters, . . . and I still hoped he would come on our side of the Potomac, pitch his tent, and prepare for real hard work, but his headquarters still remained in a house in Washington City. I then thought, and still think, that was a fatal mistake.[8]

In addition to dining with a prince at the president's house, McClellan hosted fellow officers and Democratic politicians to sumptuous nightly dinners at Wormley's Restaurant. Operated by a free black man, the restaurant stood two blocks from the Executive Mansion, where Lincoln and his Cabinet anxiously waited in vain for signs of movement by McClellan and his army. The beautiful and politically savvy Kate Chase, daughter of Treasury Secretary Salmon P. Chase and her ambitious father's most fervent political supporter, carefully noted McClellan's gatherings at Wormley's in her diary, as did McClellan's other critics and admirers. In late January, Secretary of War Stanton pointedly thundered, in one of the most memorable depictions of McClellan's extravagant immobility, "This army has got to fight or run away . . . the champagne and oysters on the Potomac must be stopped." But McClellan remained in Washington and continued his patronage of Wormley's, where both champagne and oysters could be found in abundance.[9]

McClellan's luxurious wartime lifestyle set the tone for Nelly's appearance on the public stage. Mrs. General McClellan, as she was known in society, mirrored her husband's insensitivity to the war's subdued social conventions. Indeed, she joined enthusiastically with him in the entertainments that were available. Nelly's activities on the Washington social scene during that first winter of the war validated her father's appraisal that she was "fond of attention and gaiety," but defied his prediction that army life would be devoid of amusement. Nelly held herself available "at home" one morning of the week for her friends and for admirers of her husband to visit, as was the nineteenth-century custom. When Ellen Sherman traveled to Washington in late January, for example, she visited Nelly on one of her "reception days." In a letter that Ellen Sherman wrote to her husband after Mary Lincoln's reception in February, she referenced the McClellans. "People criticise Mr Lincoln's party," she wrote. "McClellan attended several parties while I was in Washington. Genl. Rosecrans waited there two weeks & could not see him and during all that time the correspondants of the New York Herald were seeing him every day & when I was there immediately after he was attending parties constantly. I know of three he attended. . . ." McClellan had only recently recovered from his bout with typhoid in January 1862, so they might have been making up for lost social time.[10]

That seems to have delighted Nelly. Apparently, she attended so many parties in her first six weeks in Washington that she ran out of suitable evening wear—at least, in her opinion. On January 23, 1862, McClellan wrote to his mother-in-law: "Poor Nell wanted to go out to a party this evng & found that she was absolutely in the condition of Flora McFlimsey! [a fictional character with hundreds of dresses who had "nothing to wear"]. . . . So please get her *at least one* very handsome silk for an evening dress—some color that will become her—red (not brick dust) is my favorite, but she has one already—get her a *very* handsome one." As McClellan penned that sentence, Nelly apparently chimed in with a very specific request of her own, since McClellan's next sentence asked his wife's mother to "Please get the young woman also a *wreath of rose color* to match the white (trimmed with pink) dress she had made here— she says you will know the color & had better go to Haldimans. . . ." He concluded, "Poor Nell—bears her disappointment tonight like a young angel."[11]

That letter reveals an intimate portrait of Nelly even as it provides a plausible explanation for the red-and-white ensemble she wore to Mary Lincoln's reception in the Executive Mansion the following month. Had Jessie Frémont condemned Nelly to her face for wearing "secession colors," Nelly's defense would have been that red was her husband's favorite hue, that it was mere coincidence her colors were also those under which A. P. Hill was fighting. For a woman as conscious of fashion and of her lofty social position as the general-in-chief's wife, however, it should have been obvious that a different color scheme might have been a wiser choice that particular evening. One of Lincoln's private secretaries, William Stoddard, sagely observed after one of Mary Lincoln's receptions that "Somehow or other, the best of women make too much of dress...." Nelly would have been aware of the hypercritical attention that would be paid to her, but she nonetheless sailed into that storm flying the colors of her country's foes.[12]

Nelly's love of soirées was not limited to attending them. In the wake of the Lincolns' tragic loss of their son, McClellan attended the boy's funeral and took time to write a touching letter to the president offering sympathy on the death of young Willie, who likely died of the same disease from which McClellan had just recovered. At the same time, Nelly planned a party splendid enough to eclipse grieving Mary's one short-lived social triumph. According to Kate Chase's biographer, "Kate, who circulated freely and had friends in every camp, came home with tale after tale of the social doings of the General and his wife, of the fine fare at their dinners, of his bay horses and splendid carriages, of the extravagant party given in February by Mrs. McClellan soon after Mrs. Lincoln's ill-starred venture." Gen. George Meade, who attended one of Nelly's receptions, wrote to his wife: "Her manners are delightful; full of life and vivacity, great affability, and very ready in conversation." The grand military parades and reviews that so fully occupied McClellan's days also thrilled his wife. Nelly wrote to her sister-in-law about one that McClellan arranged to honor her: "I had a Maj. Genl's salute of seventeen guns given as we drove in to the grounds & altogether we had a very exciting & merry day."[13]

All winter, official Washington looked for signs that the general's military movements would match the pace of his social ones. That did not appear to be a near-term possibility. When typhoid fever struck McClellan and his father-in-law in late December, a frustrated Lincoln attempted to find consensus among the healthy generals to act in McClellan's absence. Even typhoid did not prevent McClellan from preventing his army's advance. He rose from his sickbed to chastise the president and the generals for their audacity. The dawn of 1862 found his army still camped around Washington.

For more than seven months, McClellan held his army close to the national capital, preparing for the one great battle south of Washington that would capture Richmond and (in concert with operations in the West) win the war for the Union. At least, that was his plan. No matter that Confederate Gen. Joseph Johnston and his army could be found in force from July to March thirty miles west of the U.S. Capitol, near Manassas Junction. McClellan's strategy was to sail his army down the Potomac, through the Chesapeake Bay to the Rappahannock River, disembark and march northwest, and occupy Richmond. To obtain information about Confederate forces and movements, McClellan contracted with private detective Allan Pinkerton, whose intelligence he trusted more than his own army's sources. From "Mr. Allen" (Pinkerton's startlingly straightforward code name), McClellan learned variously over the winter that Johnston had 100,000, then 140,000 men camped there. As Johnston's army multiplied in "Mr. Allen's" calculations (the Confederate general never had more than forty thousand men at Manassas at any one time), McClellan flatly rejected the idea of a direct assault on so massive a force. Instead, he resolved even more firmly on his amphibious plan, which he believed would divert Johnston away from Washington. To execute his plan, he requisitioned nearly four hundred steamers, schooners, and barges to transport more than 120,000 men, fifteen thousand horses, more than four thousand wagons, forty-four batteries, seventy-four ambulances, plus pontoon bridges, telegraph materials, and an "enormous quantity of equipage."[14]

Months passed. While McClellan fine-tuned his plan, Lincoln and Stanton fumed. Indiana Rep. George H. Julian, a member of the Committee on the Conduct of the War, later wrote: "[I]t seemed like a betrayal of the country itself to allow him to hold our grand armies for weeks and months in unexplained idleness, on the naked assumption of his superior wisdom." Horace Greeley, publisher of the *New York Tribune*, urged the army "On to Richmond!"—to no avail. While the Army of the Potomac continued its preparations, winter turned to spring, and other Union armies were on the march. On February 6, a combined force, led by Brig. Gen. Ulysses S. Grant, captured Fort Henry, on the Tennessee River. Ten days later, nearby Fort Donelson fell to Grant on the only terms he would accept—unconditional surrender. His brilliant operation at that strategic location forced the Confederacy to cede southern Kentucky and much of middle and west Tennessee, and it opened the Tennessee and Cumberland Rivers to transportation by Union forces.[15]

Successful military action in the West underscored its lack in the eastern theater. McClellan finally moved, but only because of Lincoln. On January 31, the president had issued a Special War Order No. 1, which *"Ordered* That all the disposable force of the Army of the Potomac, after providing safely for the defense of Washington, be formed into an expedition for the immediate object of seizing and occupying a point upon the railroad southwestward of what is known as Manassas Junction; all details to be in the discretion of the General in Chief, and the expedition to move before or on the 22d day of February next." Two days before that deadline, McClellan did make a move west, but only to the opposite bank of the Potomac River. Even that feint was newsworthy, though, in the opinion of *Harper's Weekly:* "GENERAL McCLELLAN ACROSS THE RIVER."

> General McClellan rode across the river on 20th, for the first time in a long interval, visiting the head-quarters of the different commanders of divisions and brigades. The camps are represented to be in splendid order, both as regards health and discipline. All that the men now require is a fair chance to relieve the quietude of camp life by the activity of the battle-field.[16]

McClellan finally set March 9 as his own deadline for a detached force to head toward Manassas (in grudging deference to Lincoln), prior to the transportation of his army by water south to attack Richmond. Johnston moved first, however. Before McClellan's deadline, Johnston and his army melted away from Manassas Junction, leaving behind logs painted to look like cannon. Johnston's "Quaker guns" were mute but powerful testimony to the general-in-chief's extraordinarily faulty military intelligence. They were also tribute to McClellan's persistent, war-long belief that Confederates would wait for his attack, no matter how long he delayed. Most importantly, the episode marked the loss of a priceless opportunity to engage the enemy decisively. While some newspapers defended McClellan, others had a field day with the embarrassing misadventure. Lincoln might have personally shared McClellan's mortification, but politically he could no longer accommodate the general's stubborn reluctance to attack the enemy.[17]

While her husband hesitated to engage the enemy, Nelly seemed equally disinclined to engage in the women's work of the war, principally charitable activities designed to aid wounded soldiers and their families. Such work was of supreme importance during the Civil War, which began without a robust military medical system. Ad hoc community groups, largely composed of women, made and supplied bandages, uniforms, and other items to troops, and neighbors cared for widows and orphans. In the first months of the war, prominent

Northerners, including Frederick Law Olmsted, organized the U.S. Sanitary Commission in New York City, designed to "do what the government could not do" for the soldiers, counterpart to the Western Sanitary Commission in St. Louis. Caring for soldiers, particularly in wartime, has long been regarded by the military "family" at large as a labor of love, respect, and duty that most military wives accepted as part of their marriage vows. Women, especially military wives who learned of specific frontline needs in letters from their husbands, had a vast number of ways to assist the war effort. In their letters and memoirs, Jessie and Ellen Ewing Sherman refer in a most routine manner to their efforts to provide aid to wounded soldiers and comfort to families of those injured or killed. Jessie was always in motion, sewing clothing, making bandages, writing petitions, organizing military hospitals and fund-raisers for them. Ellen's extensive charitable work was mostly done through her church. Julia Grant's memoirs include a self-mocking account of a failed attempt to become part of a wartime sewing circle before she learned that her best contribution to the war effort was to travel with her husband in the field as much as possible. Even Mary Lincoln spent hours visiting wounded soldiers in the hospitals near Washington; she brought them oranges and wrote letters to their loved ones for them.

Nelly was a new military wife when the war began, but she was a lifelong military daughter. Amazingly, though, there is no evidence that Nelly herself actively aided the cause that her husband led. Nelly knew the other officers and their wives, to be sure. She socialized with them and passed along their gossip in letters to her husband, but there is little evidence that she tried to help the soldiers, the men in ranks, who so loved her husband they would follow him to the death. Evidence in this regard comes from a letter to Nelly in mid-January 1862, about two weeks before "Flora McFlimsey's" request for a new ball gown. The letter was written on the stationery of the Metropolitan Fair for the U.S. Sanitary Commission, the New York branch that was planning a major fund-raiser. The correspondent was a formidable arbiter of etiquette (and later author of *Manners and Social Usages*), Mrs. John Sherwood. Her tone was as frosty and insistent as good manners would permit:

> My dear Mrs. McClellan,
> I have written you several official notes, which I fear like many others have miscarried. The ladies are exceedingly anxious to have you on the Board of Managers. The name of McClellan certainly ought to be in anything connected with the soldiers. Will you accept? We do not ask you to *work* only to

give us as one circular says "the influence of the name, example, and position." Please come and see us any day at 2 Great Jones St. or write to us, and believe me very truly and respectfully yours,
M. E. W. Sherwood[18]

There is no record of Nelly's response to Mrs. Sherwood, nor does Nelly's name appear in connection with the Sanitary Commission during her husband's tenure as commanding general. The few details we have of her activities during this time reinforce a view of Nelly as detached from that important part of her role as the general-in-chief's wife.

As spring flowers burst to life in the nation's capital, her husband's ambitious amphibious campaign continued to soak up men, materiel, and time, but seemed no nearer to execution. In utter frustration, the president decided on a measure to help McClellan focus on the massive operation that the general vowed would bring a swift end to the war. On March 11, Lincoln removed McClellan as commander of all armies. Little Mac remained commanding general of the Army of the Potomac, but he was no longer general-in-chief. Lincoln publicly sought to preserve McClellan's dignity by noting that while McClellan was leading an army in the field, he might be cut off from communications with the rest of Union armies, and that he should not be distracted by military demands spread across the continent. Though Lincoln also left the post of general-in-chief unfilled, as if McClellan could return to it later, it was a rebuff nevertheless, and particularly because McClellan first learned of it when Marcy telegraphed he had read it in a newspaper. Still harboring some hope that the news might be false, McClellan wrote to Nelly on the day of Marcy's telegram: "Do not be at all worried by what has occurred & say nothing about it. I have meant well for my country—& God will not desert me." The Army of the Potomac was a major command to be sure, but quite a comedown from general-in-chief of the U.S. Army. McClellan burned with resentment against the men in Washington whom he perceived to be his personal enemies, but he finally did move. Beginning on March 17, 1862, the Army of the Potomac sailed down the Potomac River and landed at Fort Monroe at the tip of the peninsula. McClellan sailed from the capital on April 1 to lead his Peninsula Campaign.[19]

Rather than stay in Washington in his absence, Nelly stored her silver in a trunk at Corcoran & Riggs bank, and she and May traveled for the next seven months to New Jersey, New York, and Connecticut, staying with friends and family. The McClellans had no plans to establish a permanent residence for themselves, at least not until Nelly and her husband were reunited in Washington upon his triumphal return from capturing Richmond. When the McClellans were separated during the war, her letters speak of her loneliness without him, but she enjoyed the comfort and entertainment in cities and seaside

MAJOR GEN'L. GEO. B. McCLELLAN:
WIFE : MOTHER, Mrs.Gen Marcy : CHILD : NURSE.
HEADQUARTERS AT CAMP SEMINARY, NEAR ALEXANDRIA, VA., TAKEN AT THE MOMENT OF EMBARKING FOR FORTRESS MONROE, APRIL 3, 1862.

This drawing captures McClellan leaving his wife, mother, child (and nurse) in April 1862, as he finally launched his massive campaign toward Richmond. (*Courtesy of the Library of Congress*)

resorts that she would not have found at her husband's side in the field. On March 27, the *New York Times* reported that "Mrs. MCCLELLAN, wife of Gen. GEORGE B. MCCLELLAN, intends to take up her residence in Trenton, N.J., for the Summer, and . . . apartments have already been engaged for her accommodation." Six weeks later, on May 13, the *New York Times*'s "Amusements" correspondent spotted Nelly in that city: "The neighborhood of the Fifth-avenue Hotel was densely crowded last evening with an expectant throng, who has assembled to hear the promised serenade to Mrs. Gen. MCCLELLAN. . . . Mrs. MCCLELLAN appeared on the balcony and gracefully bowed her thanks for the compliment paid to her, but intended for her gallant husband. It was long after midnight before the crowd departed."[20]

McClellan's letter to his sister-in-law during the Peninsula Campaign reveals more about Nelly's activities in Connecticut than perhaps did her own letters to him. On June 9, 1862, McClellan protested, "My dear Maria . . . You are mistaken about Nelly & the baby holding levees in Hartford—they are there to rest and are resting most quietly." Surely, that is what Nelly told her husband.[21]

As troops gathered on the Virginia Peninsula and McClellan began the march toward Richmond, it became apparent that his magnificent army had been designed for power, not speed. A series of sieges and engagements against smaller Confederate forces delayed progress and increased McClellan's paranoia about the size of the army he faced. McClellan's first target was Yorktown, which his army approached on April 5. McClellan halted outside the town, where he established a headquarters and spent nearly a month preparing sophisticated siege works and installing batteries with stupendous firepower. He ordered a massive bombardment of Yorktown to commence on May 5.[22]

Once again, though, Johnston moved more quickly. He evacuated the city on May 3, retreating toward Richmond. Aerial reconnaissance by the U.S. Army's state-of-the-art balloon corps confirmed that the Confederates had fled. McClellan's initial reaction was astonishment and disappointment, but also—uncharacteristically—swift pursuit. In this instance, McClellan ordered that the enemy be intercepted with haste, sending cavalry on land and a larger force by transports. They collided with Johnston's troops in the Battle of Williamsburg, which McClellan characterized as a "brilliant victory" against much greater forces. He was wrong on both counts. In fact, Johnston had mounted a successful delaying action, buying time for a stronger defense of Richmond. The Army of the Potomac continued to lumber northwestward, fighting smaller forces stretched from the southeast to the northwest of Richmond—at West Point,

Mechanicsville, Hanover Court House, and Fair Oaks. McClellan claimed all as major victories for his troops against greater numbers of Confederates, but in reality, they were all slim successes against smaller forces.

The Army of the Potomac's victory in the Battle of Fair Oaks on May 31, proved in the long run more costly than was immediately apparent. Gen. Joseph Johnston was severely wounded in that engagement, and Jefferson Davis replaced him with Gen. Robert E. Lee. A month earlier, McClellan had commented on the two Confederate generals to his commander in chief. "I prefer Lee to Johnston," McClellan had confided to Lincoln on April 20. "[T]he former is *too* cautious & weak under grave responsibility—personally brave & energetic to a fault, he yet is wanting in more firmness when pressed by heavy responsibility & is likely to be timid & irresolute in action." McClellan's evaluation of Confederate leaders proved to be as faulty as his judgment of his own superiors.[23]

McClellan led his army to within eight miles of Richmond; his men could hear the city's church bells. That proved to be the high watermark of his Peninsula Campaign. McClellan never launched an all-out assault on Richmond that would have justified the men, the months, and the money spent in its preparation. After the Battle of Fair Oaks, the Army of the Potomac lost the strategic initiative. Lee nimbly maneuvered his troops and outfought McClellan's forces, driving them farther and farther away from the Confederate capital in a series of brilliantly improvised and fiercely fought counterattacks, known as the Seven Days' Battles. McClellan and the Army of the Potomac backed down the peninsula in the face of bitter fighting led by Lee and "Stonewall" Jackson. This campaign ended in what was actually a Federal victory at Malvern Hill on July 1, but by then McClellan was not present on the field at Malvern Hill or anywhere on land nearby. He was safely on a steamer in the James River and in a panic. He decamped at Harrison's Landing on the James River and stalled for more than two months. Lincoln and his newly appointed general-in-chief, Henry Halleck, initially urged him forward, but they soon recognized the impossibility of forcing McClellan to action.

The five surviving letters Nelly wrote her husband all come from this period of the war, the summer and fall of 1862. They give us tantalizing glimpses of her personality. The first was written on July 31, from a hotel in New London, Connecticut. She had traveled there with her mother and baby May from Orange, New Jersey, where they had been visiting family. Her letter that day to her husband was a long, chatty one, which began: "My own precious George, Now I *am* going to have a nice time I trust with you alone." She wrote about her visit in Orange and her one-day stopover in New York City, where Mr. and Mrs. Joseph Alsop (he was the president of the Ohio & Mississippi Railroad, which was still paying McClellan a huge salary) met them at the ferryboat. What woman could resist shopping in New York City? "Mother & I got into Mrs. A's carriage & rode up with her & I stopped on the way at several places to do shopping. . . . I bought your locket & left some of my hair to be put into it & will send it to you when it comes. I also bought a little silver [nosegay] basket for Henry Robinson's bride—& don't whisper it but I bought some false fronts. I am obliged to take to the artificial again since baby has deserted me! Are you not ashamed of your wife?!"[24]

It was nearly a year since baby May had been born, and Nelly's figure was adjusting to the fact that she was no longer breast-feeding. McClellan's biographers all remark on his penchant for telling his wife everything that crossed his mind. At times, Nelly did the same.

Later in the same letter, reacting to his complaints about the hazards of tent camping in the hot, sticky Virginia summer, she wrote: "what a perfect nuisance those flies must be. . . . There is a kind of sticky paper that is used to attach them & when they are once in it I believe they never get off. Why do you not get some?" Five days later, she became quite coy: "I think I shall take a bath to-night again & *some pills*. Don't you envy me? I wish you were here to take some too! I think you might keep me company you dear darling fellow." On August 6, Nelly wrote another long letter, ending, "This is a lovely place— so tranquil & peaceful you [cannot] imagine there was a war going on."[25]

But there was a war going on, although by that time, McClellan was busy sending his soldiers to another general. Halleck had ordered McClellan to send all available troops to Gen. John Pope, whom Halleck and Lincoln had brought from the western theater to command the defense of Washington. As he reluctantly dispatched troops to Pope's command, McClellan was soon left with little more than his personal staff. On August 31, he wailed to Nelly: "I am left in command of *nothing*. . . ."[26]

Neither the fates nor Lincoln were quite through with McClellan, though. At nearly the same time McClellan was writing Nelly, Pope was crushed at the Second Battle of Bull Run, and the surviving troops under his command retreated from the field completely demoralized. In one of the most controversial military decisions of his presidency, the very next day Lincoln defied his Cabinet and restored the Army of the Potomac to the man who was still its nominal commander. The president had no greater faith in McClellan as a combat general on September 1 than he had a month earlier. As commander in chief, though, he knew that the first order of business was to restore the soldiers' faith in themselves. That was the one thing—perhaps the only thing—he knew McClellan could be relied upon to do.

Despite the fact that McClellan's orders were to defend the capital and included no language authorizing expeditions beyond its immediate perimeter, McClellan determined (correctly) that Lee would approach Washington on an arc through the western Maryland countryside. He planned to fight him there. In what was perhaps the luckiest break of any general in any campaign, Lee's battle plans fell into McClellan's hands four days before the two armies faced each other near Antietam Creek. Even so, McClellan's lethargic movements nearly snatched defeat from the jaws of victory, and the subsequent battle ended in little more than a draw. Lee's withdrawal after one of the fiercest days of fighting in the Civil War, however, reinforced McClellan's delusion that he had achieved a tremendous victory in "driving the enemy from the field." Satisfied, he rested his army while Lee crossed the Potomac and returned south. While Lincoln seized upon that fragile victory to provide a more confident context in which to issue his Preliminary Emancipation Proclamation, he never was content with merely retaining Union territory that the enemy had invaded. Destruction of the Confederate Army was the president's goal. When McClellan did not appear to share it, Lincoln traveled to Antietam to urge him forward. The president returned to Washington unsatisfied. There, he sought to stimulate McClellan to action through the military chain of command. On October 6, Halleck telegraphed McClellan: "The President directs that you cross the Potomac and give battle to the enemy or drive him south. Your army must move now while the roads are good." The general did not move.[27]

The next day, Lincoln sent McClellan a letter in reply to the general's ill-timed request that he be allowed to spend time with his family after his recent exertions. "You wish to see your family, and I wish to oblige you," Lincoln reassured McClellan, as he suggested a win-win solution for the general and for the defense of the Union: McClellan should move south. "It might be left to your own discretion," Lincoln wrote, "certainly so, if Mrs. M. could meet you here at Washington." But McClellan had other ideas. In an arrangement that held twin advantages for him, he sent for Nelly and May to visit the battlefield instead. That allowed his family to view the site of what he forever believed to be his greatest victory. Remaining near the battlefield also enabled McClellan to avoid Washington and thus to avoid also as much as possible President Lincoln's continued entreaties to pursue the Confederate Army.[28]

It is not clear precisely when Nelly joined McClellan in camp near Antietam, but daily letters from McClellan to Nelly stopped abruptly on October 8 and did not begin again until October 26. If she were with him during that entire period, then Nelly was present not only at the location of his self-described greatest triumph but also during a reprise of McClellan's greatest embarrassment. The latter was at the hands of Confederate cavalry commander Gen. J. E. B. Stuart. From October 10 to 12, "Stuart's Second Ride Around McClellan," by which name the maneuver is referenced in the history books, took place. As he had done so brilliantly in June during the Peninsula Campaign, the dashing Stuart and his cavalry again tore a trail entirely around the bulk of McClellan's troops. During Stuart's "First Ride Around McClellan," he had been on Confederate soil, as McClellan hesitated in front of Richmond. The second time, however, Stuart cut right through Union territory. With nearly two thousand men, he traced a circle northeast from Leesburg, Virginia, through Maryland, into Pennsylvania, and then southwest through western Virginia, completely around McClellan's army, ending the ride less than thirty miles west of the house the Union general was then sharing with his wife and daughter. Stuart's orders from General Lee forbade him to engage the enemy or unnecessarily destroy civilian property, but as his men scrambled for much-needed clothing, stores of ammunition, and provisions, they sparked terror among civilians and desperate pleas for help to McClellan from the governor of Pennsylvania.

By this time, however, McClellan's skill in ignoring politicians' pleas for action was unsurpassed, and his chief response to Stuart's rampage was to move his family swiftly to a safer site. On October 16, the *New York Times* noted that accommodations were being prepared for the general and his family near Harpers Ferry. "Orders have also been issued to begin the work of restoring a fine residence near by. Rumor has it that this building is being fitted up for Gen. McClellan, who will soon occupy it with Mrs. McClellan and the boy." Though the correspondent was wrong about the sex of the McClellan child, his wry analysis of the general's embarrassment was on target: "If rebel raids are to become the order of the day, such a strategical movement is certainly demanded, for should our Commander-in-Chief remain at his former quarters, Gen. STUART will certainly carry him off on his next visit—camp equipage and all."[29]

The move to Harpers Ferry never happened; Halleck forbade the time and cost for such an effort. That merely encouraged McClellan to stay where he was. The day after the *Times* article, McClellan wrote to his close friend, confidant, and financial adviser, Samuel Barlow, from a very tranquil "Head-Quarters of the Army of the Potomac" in Pleasant Valley, Maryland. "My wife is with me here—in a quiet old fashioned little farm house near my camp," he wrote. "Mrs. Marcy is also here & we are having a very quiet & pleasant time all by ourselves." McClellan concluded the letter with a typically McClellan view of the present, of the future, and of the Confederate general he consistently underestimated. "Lee is still near Winchester & will probably remain there until I am prepared to move upon him," he predicted. "I hope for still further success when I next advance." Neither advance nor success was in McClellan's future, however. Lee did not wait for McClellan, nor did McClellan pursue Lee. The Confederate general made a rapid march south, leaving a passive McClellan and a seething Lincoln in his wake.[30]

In the wake of Stuart's second ride, on October 13, Lincoln had written McClellan again to press for movement, this time in a lengthy letter that noted Lee's rapid movement to the south and referenced their conversation at Antietam two weeks earlier. "You remember my speaking to you of what I called your over-cautiousness," Lincoln wrote. "Are you not over-cautious when you assume that you can not do what the enemy is constantly doing?" Two days later, the *New York Times* reported that Nelly was still with McClellan near Antietam. Neither McClellan nor his army had moved.[31]

During her October stay with her husband, it is highly unlikely that Nelly was unaware of Lincoln's orders to her husband or Stuart's potential threat to her and her child. McClellan's habit of communicating to her everything that crossed his mind when they were apart surely continued when they were together. There is no indication, though, that she ever questioned either her husband's failure to pursue Lee or her continued presence with their child so close to Confederate forces. The fact that her mother was also with her in Pleasant Valley indicates that Chief of Staff General Marcy either felt no fear for his family or he, too, was unwilling to confront his son-in-law and superior officer.

On October 25 (likely the day that Nelly left Maryland), Lincoln's irritation flashed to anger. He telegraphed McClellan: "I have just received your despatch about sore-tongued and fatigued horses. Will you pardon me for asking what the horses of your army have done since the battle of Antietam that fatigues anything?" McClellan's tone-deaf, mind-numbing, detailed reply explaining his request—and the subsequent flurry of other similar messages he quickly forwarded—were not calculated to satisfy the president.[32]

In one of the many coincidences of the war, McClellan's removal from command came under circumstances strikingly similar to Frémont's. Two weeks after Lincoln's query about fatigued horses, unscheduled visitors interrupted McClellan as he sat in his tent, penning his nightly letter to his wife. After they left, he resumed the letter: "11.30p.m.—Another interruption—this time more important. It was in the shape of [General Ambrose] Burnside, accompanied by Gen. [Catharinus] Buckingham, the secretary's adjutant-general. They brought with them the order relieving me from the command of the Army of the Potomac, and assigning Burnside to the command."

If anyone who has followed McClellan's career ever needed more justification for his removal, it can be found in the next sentence of his letter: "No cause is given."[33]

Leaving his beloved Army of the Potomac was among the most difficult duties McClellan performed during the Civil War, but he did so with dignity. Truly dispirited himself, he nonetheless rode through ranks of tearful men, urging them to obey Burnside as they had obeyed him. They loved him, and he knew it. Almost two years to the day he was interrupted in his tent, however, McClellan would learn that his army's love for him could not survive his politics.

❧ CHAPTER 9 ❧

"don't send any politicians out here"

When Lincoln relieved McClellan of command, the general was directed to take his few remaining staff to a new posting in Trenton, New Jersey, but he was never again given military responsibilities. In short order, McClellan decamped to New York, where Nelly joined him. They stayed at the Fifth Avenue Hotel while deciding on their next move, attending public and private entertainments in the company of the most politically conservative Democrats in the city. All their actions were noted carefully in the newspapers. Still a commissioned officer in the army, he soon found civilian employment in his first profession, that of engineer. His friends sought to help him even more, and on January 20, 1863, McClellan wrote to Samuel Barlow that "Mrs. McClellan desires me to acknowledge the receipt of your kind letter of yesterday, accompanying the title papers & insurance policies of the house No 22 West 31st Street."[1]

Except for a trip to Boston for an enormous reception in the general's honor, attended by ten thousand admirers, the McClellans remained in New York until February 1863. The Joint Committee on the Conduct of the War, led by Radical Republicans Ben Wade and Zachariah Chandler, called McClellan to Washington and grilled him on his leadership of the Army of the Potomac. He handled himself well, but it was a grueling ordeal for a man accustomed to deference, and he missed his wife, who had not accompanied him. From the Willard Hotel at midnight on the 28th, he wrote to Nelly: "I am very sorry that I did not bring you on, for I find that I have no chance in Wash without you ! . . . I sincerely believe, you little scamp, that you are far more popular in Wash today than your husband is." His playful observation was validated more than half a century later. Nelly's obituary in the *New York Times* on February 14, 1915, candidly said more about him than about her: "She had lived a retired life since the death of her famous husband in 1885, but before that time she took an active part in social life in this city and in Washington. . . . *Her exceptional tact, it was said before the General's death, was of vast assistance to him on many occasions . . ."* (emphasis added).[2]

About the only extant example of Nelly's exceptional tact happened as the presidential election year of 1864 opened, when both McClellan and Frémont were already being touted as possible opponents to Lincoln in November. Although nineteenth-century campaigning almost never involved appearances by the candidates and certainly not by their wives (Jessie's involvement in 1856 was the exception that proved that rule), it appears that a singular event in April 1864 made Nelly a proxy for her husband in the upcoming presidential election. Nelly appeared at the New York Sanitary Fair on at least one day during which she and Jessie Frémont and Julia Grant faced off on behalf of their husbands in a contest to see which general would win a magnificent Tiffany sword, to be awarded to the general who received the most votes from patrons paying $1 per vote. Mrs. August Belmont, wife of the Democratic Party chairman who was then championing McClellan's run for the presidency, served on the fair's Executive Committee, and Nelly may have been unable to decline an invitation from her. Perhaps the opportunity to further her husband's political future made a more compelling case than did the opportunity to aid her husband's soldiers in 1862.

Jessie Frémont provided evidence of Nelly's participation in that fair in a letter to her friend, Rev. Thomas Starr King, when she admonished him "'that it will pay' to be kind to the Sanitary Comm. now. . . . Mrs. McClellan & Mrs. Frémont work together on a committee for 'Arms & Trophies.' After that let your lambs & lions go to work together too." Mrs. McClellan is listed on the official program of the fair under the "Arms and Trophies Committee." It is not clear just how actively Nelly participated because in March 1864, McClellan wrote to his mother, "New York is quite busy at present with preparations for the Sanitary Fair—how it will turn out I have no means of knowing, but people expect a great success." If his wife were actively involved, he surely would have remarked upon that to his mother.[3]

By the time Nelly appeared at the fair, the Democratic Party had been wooing McClellan for more than a year. He fit their needs precisely: he was not invested in Lincoln's program of emancipation, and despite his glacial military pace, he retained an aura of vigor and leadership and continued popularity. With the Republican Party split between the Pathfinder and the Railsplitter, the prospect of Little Mac as the Democratic candidate excited both the "peace" and the "war" wings of the Democratic Party, who could find little else to agree upon. Even before the Democratic Party's convention in Chicago in August

1864, Lincoln had predicted that its deep divisions would force his opponents to run either a war candidate on a peace platform or a peace candidate on a war platform. They chose the first option, nominating the former general-in-chief for president, then saddling McClellan with a platform that deemed the war "a failure" and called for "immediate efforts" to initiate peace talks with the Confederacy. The delegates then proceeded to do even worse damage to their cause. They chose as his running mate Ohio Rep. George Hunt Pendleton, one of the most notorious Peace Democrats, or Copperheads, in the country.

Pendleton's views were as well known on the field of battle as off it. "The nomination of McClellan is not well received in the army," wrote an officer in the Army of the Potomac to his wife shortly after McClellan's nomination, "from the fact that they put that abominable traitor, Pendleton, on as Vice President." Soldiers in the western theater, who had never served directly under Little Mac, were even less enthusiastic. "I would hide my head with shame sooner than vote for any man nominated under the Chicago banner," wrote one. A soldier serving in Sherman's army eloquently justified his support for Lincoln. "[W]e must have the man who dares to say: the Nation must live," he wrote. "We can trust ourselves to no other pilot."[4]

Pro-McClellan poster for the 1864 presidential campaign. The electorate generally, and soldiers in particular, did not find this persuasive. (*Courtesy of the Library of Congress*)

McClellan was a quiet candidate. The general had built a house, which he named Maywood, for his family in Orange, New Jersey, and he remained there during the campaign—in seclusion from politics and politicians. While all presidential candidates in that era expressed their desire to appear aloof from the frenzy of electoral politics, McClellan actually was. He despised the entire process; if God wanted him to be president, it would happen without the help of any human being. Time and again, he refused to meet supporters at his home or appear at rallies. He discouraged any political visitors. He did maintain a correspondence with his closest political deputies, such as Samuel L. M. Barlow and William Cowper Prime, forwarding to them suggestions he received in letters from admirers and discouraging them from sending potential supporters to see him. "[D]on't send any politicians out here—I'll snub them if they come—confound them!" he wrote to Prime on August 10. Democratic politicians fought over whether the party should demand peace at all costs. They finally did, in the "Chicago" platform, adopted on August 30. The next day, the Democrats nominated McClellan for president. According to a letter Lincoln received from a friend visiting New York on September 3, Nelly told one of her longtime friends that morning: "her husband *would not accept the nomination on the Chicago platform.*" Five days later, McClellan accepted the nomination but protested that preservation of the Union was paramount to immediate peace.[5]

On the other hand, Lincoln involved himself intimately in the design of political strategy and tactics. Mary Lincoln followed the election closely, too, even if, as some biographers have charged, her primary interest was staying in the White House in order to avoid revealing the massive debts she incurred in redecorating the Executive Mansion. Similarly, the Frémonts privately paid close attention to all aspects of the race, while the general publicly distanced himself from the fray. During Frémont's short candidacy in 1864, Jessie rarely stepped outside the conventional bounds of behavior for a candidate's wife, but as recounted earlier, she played a significant role in the denouement of Frémont's run for the country's highest office.

Lack of Union victories in the first half of 1864 boosted McClellan's popularity and weakened Lincoln's. As summer turned to fall, however, the political landscape changed dramatically. Within a month of McClellan's nomination, Jessie's maneuvering helped to end Frémont's shaky candidacy. That left the abolitionists—who had never forgiven McClellan for his order protecting slavery three years before in western Virginia or for his well-known antipathy to the Emancipation Proclamation—with no one to support but Lincoln. Union victories late in the summer improved Lincoln's popularity. Adm. David Glasgow

Farragut's decisive victory at Mobile denied that strategic port to the Confederates. Gen. Philip Sheridan, charged by Grant to "Give the enemy no rest," finally drove Confederate forces out of the Shenandoah Valley, from which they had launched numerous attacks on Washington. General Sherman's telegram to Lincoln on September 3, saying that "Atlanta is ours and fairly won," electrified citizens North and South. By mid-September, Lincoln's fortunes were looking up.

Three weeks before the election, an officer in the Army of the Potomac reported to his wife that a straw vote in his corps was ten to one in favor of Lincoln. As for McClellan, the colonel flatly stated, "He can't win at all." McClellan remained optimistic, though, particularly about "the soldier vote." On October 13, he wrote, from his home in New Jersey, to August Belmont, chairman of the Democratic Party: "I hear but little out here—but my letters from the Army are encouraging."[6] Perhaps he heard little of the soldiers' disenchantment with him because McClellan's political intelligence operation was no better than his military intelligence operation had been. The reason for that was simple: Pinkerton was still on his payroll.[7]

McClellan submitted his resignation from the army on the morning of Election Day, November 8, 1864. By then, he was certain that a government-wide conspiracy (aided by General Grant) would deprive him of votes from many soldiers, but he still nurtured hope of becoming president that day. That proved to be the only time in McClellan's career that he underestimated the number of men who opposed him. The popular vote went 55 percent to 45 percent for Lincoln, but the electoral count was a walkaway victory, 212 votes to McClellan's 21. Most impressive was Lincoln's margin among soldiers. Overall, 78 percent of the soldiers who voted cast their ballots for Lincoln. The Army of the Potomac, which had wept at McClellan's departure, cast fewer than 30 percent of their votes for Little Mac. They supported instead the man he scorned and whose friendship he never trusted. McClellan did not see it coming, although he later claimed he did. Three days after the election, he wrote to his mother: "The smoke has cleared away and we are beaten!"[8]

The McClellans were together on Election Day, so Nelly would have shared fully in her husband's humiliating repudiation by civilian and military voters alike. Comforting letters of condolence poured in from his supporters, including a heartfelt and flattering one from Barlow. McClellan replied that he had been "fully prepared for the result," that he hoped that "our poor country may not be ruined in the course of proving that we were right," and that "Mrs. McC . . . says that she appreciated your letter more than she can express."

Nonetheless, he was ready to flee the political and personal wreckage that surrounded them. "I should be delighted if a miracle should occur which would give me something to do that would take me to Europe for a few months," he wrote in a transparent but unsuccessful effort to obtain Barlow's assistance.[9]

Shaken and humiliated, George, twenty-nine-year-old Nelly, and May sailed for Europe in January 1865. The *New York Times* reported their departure on the Cunard steamer *China,* noting that relatively few family and friends saw them off at the pier. Later that year, their son George B. McClellan Jr. (Max) was born in Dresden, Germany. The McClellans traveled in Europe for three years, learning from afar of Sherman's march to the sea and Lee's surrender to Grant. Understandably, McClellan retained his bitterness toward Lincoln and his administration, which he poured forth in letters to his friends that echoed the worst and most delusional of the sentiments that he had expressed to Nelly in their correspondence two years earlier. On November 28, he wrote to Manton Marble, one of his most vigorous supporters and editor of the *New York World,* in language that echoed his twisted accounts of every one of his military failures: "We have aided in 'making history' and that too a history which some yet unborn Homer or Milton will some day clothe in verse. As I look back upon it it seems to me a subject replete with dignity—a struggle of honor patriotism & truth against deceit selfishness & fanaticism, and I think that we have well played our parts. The mistakes made were not of our making. . . ."[10]

Lincoln's death so soon after the election chastened McClellan. Word of the assassination reached the McClellans in early May 1865, when they also probably learned of the death of A. P. Hill, who was killed in Petersburg, Virginia, one week before the surrender at Appomattox. From Sorrento, Italy, McClellan wrote to a friend, using "wonderful" in its nineteenth-century sense of "amazing": "while we have been enjoying ourselves among these magnificent scenes, you at home have passed through the most wonderful transition of which history bears record. How strange it is that the military death of the rebellion should have been followed with such tragic quickness by the atrocious murder of Mr Lincoln! Now I cannot but forget all that had been unpleasant between us, & remember only the brighter parts of our intercourse."[11]

McClellan probably meant what he wrote, but there is no record of whether Nelly's contempt for Lincoln ever dimmed.

CHAPTER 10

"you have quite enough else to attend to"

In 1887, excerpts from over two hundred letters from McClellan to Nelly were made public as part of *McClellan's Own Story,* which was represented as the general's autobiography. Although Lincoln did not live long enough to learn why his expressions of friendship and his exhortations were utterly futile, readers of those letters, including many of Lincoln's and McClellan's contemporaries, easily solved the mystery that had plagued Lincoln about his relationship with the general. For one so conscious of his public persona, it is ironic that McClellan's own words provide the most shocking portrait of the man. In 1952, T. Harry Williams wrote: "Of these missives it has been said that it was remarkable that he ever wrote them in the first place and even more re- markable that he published them in his autobiography for all the world to see." Williams was mistaken on two counts. McClellan did not publish his letters; he did not even write the "autobiography," which bears his name as its author. McClellan was dead when the book was compiled and rushed into print. The journey of those letters from Nelly's private cache to publication is a story that has not yet been fully explored.[1]

McClellan and Nelly wrote to each other at least once a day every day they were apart; he had extracted that promise from her when they became en- gaged. Fortunately, he withheld nothing from Nelly in his letters. Most fortu- nately of all, the bulk of the letters has survived, albeit in edited form. What McClellan wrote about his contemporaries still has the power to stagger the modern reader. His wildly flawed judgments are almost comic were they not equally tragic, coming from a man who held so vital a position for defense of the Union. Secretary of State Seward was "a meddling, officious, incompetent little puppy." He believed Stanton "the most depraved hypocrite & villain that I have ever had the bad fortune to meet with." His evaluation of Lincoln was also tragically wrong. In McClellan's letters, Abraham Lincoln was "the original gorilla," and "nothing more than a well-meaning baboon." McClellan had formed an immutably low opinion of the president during Lincoln's time as a lawyer for the railroad that employed McClellan, and more than a decade later, McClellan's opinion of Lincoln remained unchanged. In 1862, he wrote his wife that he could "never regard [Lincoln] with other feelings than those of thorough contempt—for his mind, heart & morality." Lincoln's frequent anecdotes were "ever unworthy of one holding his high position."[2]

On the day in 1861 before the thirty-five-year-old officer assumed command of the armies of the United States, McClellan lambasted the men who made his rapid rise to power and fame possible. In a letter to his wife, he confided: "I have not been home for some 3 hrs, but am 'concealed' at Stanton's to dodge all enemies in shape of 'browsing' Presdt. etc. . . . It is perfectly sickening to have to work with such people & to see the fate of the nation in such hands . . . it is terrible to stand by & see the cowardice of the Presdt, the vileness of Seward, & the rascality of Cameron—Welles is an old woman—Bates an old fool. The only man of courage & sense in the Cabinet is Blair, & I do not altogether fancy him!"[3]

McClellan had initially viewed Stanton as a friend and was delighted when Stanton replaced Cameron as secretary of war. Stanton swiftly grasped McClellan's flaws, however, and the new secretary of war just as swiftly incurred the general's severest wrath. Shortly after Halleck assumed the command of all the U.S. armies, placing him over McClellan, Nelly learned from her husband that "Halleck has begun to show the cloven foot already. . . ."[4]

"Enemy" is a word sprinkled liberally throughout McClellan's letters, but McClellan rarely used it to refer to the Confederate Army. Those whom he faced in battle were usually termed "the Secesh" (slang for "Secessionist") or "rebels." "Enemy" was a term largely reserved for his personal foes within the political and military establishment on his own side. He also used "friend" with heavy sarcasm. "[E]ven now when doing the best I can for my country in the field I know that my enemies are pursuing me more remorselessly than ever," he wrote. "[And] 'kind *friends*' are constantly making themselves agreeable by informing me of the pleasant predicament in which I am—the rebels on one side, & the abolitionists, other scoundrels on the other. . . ." Nelly followed his lead. "What does it mean that you don't hear *some* thing from Washington?" she wrote in August 1862. "They are all crazy there—or perfect scoundrels."[5]

So omnipresent were his foes that, at times, clarification was needed. On April 23, 1862, for example, he took pains to clear up any confusion. "You will have learned ere this that Yorktown is ours . . . ," he wrote. "The villains (secesh) have scattered torpedoes [land mines] everywhere. . . ." Two months later, he wrote Nelly that "By an arrival from Washn today [Pinkerton] I learn that Stanton & Chase have fallen out. . . . That Seward & Blair stand firmly by me—that Honest A has again fallen into the hands of my enemies & he is no longer a cordial friend of mine!"[6]

Four months after that, at the end of August 1862, as McClellan agonized over losing his army to Pope and prayed for a chance to command it again, the views of both McClellans on the possibility of his restoration to senior command assumed an Alice-in-Wonderland quality. A letter from Nelly dated August 30 encouraged a most perverse perspective, particularly considering that all her life she had been part of a military family. "Why *don't* you behave in a *human* manner & trouble old Halleck as much as you can by *not* helping him," she suggested tartly. "You are a perfect angel darling . . . [Lincoln & Halleck & Stanton] will be glad enough to have you help them out of their perplexities & I think you are mighty good to be willing to do it you dear darling unselfish fellow!!"[7]

Even her remarkably myopic characterization of a military officer's duty cannot prepare readers for McClellan's calculation of what was at stake in his next military encounter. Shortly after that letter from Nelly and a week before the Battle of Antietam, he wrote her with satisfaction: "It is something of a triumph that my enemies have been put down so completely & if to that I can add the defeat of secesh I think I ought to be entitled to fall back into private life. . . ." If his language hints that McClellan valued his personal victories slightly more than those of his country, his evaluation of the results of the Battle of Antietam supports that judgment. In a letter to Nelly three days after the battle, McClellan crowed: "I feel some little pride in having with a beaten and demoralized army defeated Lee so utterly, & saved the North so completely. . . . Thank Heaven for one thing—my military reputation is cleared—I have shown that I can fight battles & *win* them! I think my enemies are pretty effectively killed by this time! May they remain so!!"[8]

It is nearly impossible to square any part of McClellan's interpretation of the Battle of Antietam with reality, except perhaps that he had started with a demoralized army. Despite the fact that Lee's plan of battle had fallen into his hands on September 13, McClellan fumbled every opportunity to defeat the Army of Northern Virginia decisively. In fact, Antietam could only be cast as a victory because Lee withdrew across the Potomac. McClellan's failure to pursue Lee reinforced the hollowness of the Federal "victory" but did not dim McClellan's perception of his triumph. McClellan's verdict, as expressed to Nelly, is nearer blasphemy than self-aggrandizement. September 17, 1862, has long been remembered in the United States as the single bloodiest day of battle in history. That McClellan could survey the field where the smell of decaying corpses still filled the air and find solace in having figuratively "killed" his "enemies" in Washington is beyond comprehension.[9]

One history of the couple portrays the McClellans as living in their own world of paranoia and conspiracy, oddly detached from the grim reality of war that engulfed the world around them. That characterization finds strong support in his letters. Beyond their shared detachment from reality, however, there is also evidence in Nelly's few surviving letters of her detachment from her husband's work and the national life-and-death struggle surrounding her. It was on same day in August 1862, when he wrote Nelly with palpable despair that he had been "left in command of *nothing*," that Nelly recalled the silver she had left for safekeeping in Washington. She wrote to him: "I really do feel a little [anxious] about the silver & don't know what had better be done about it. It is in a trunk in Corcoran & Riggs Bank [but it is] not packed for traveling [and] would be jammed were it to go anywhere at a distance. . . ." With a broad hint for his personal attention to the matter, she continued, "I should be afraid to have any servant pack it for they might steal some of it." Then, perhaps, she recalled that she was writing to a man who had just suffered a tremendous professional setback and was struggling to regain his prestige, and she cut him some slack. "Don't attempt though to pack any of the furniture or clothes," she lovingly cautioned, "for you have quite enough else to attend to you darling fellow without having to take care of me."[10]

There are also echoes of her detachment from McClellan's world in letters that he wrote to her during the Peninsula Campaign, when the value of the Sanitary Commission became apparent. Thousands of Northern men transported south to fight a human enemy encountered one even more deadly. In the Civil War, two men died of disease for every one who died as a result of combat. As men fell in battle up and down the peninsula, malaria, yellow fever, and typhoid took an even greater toll, and the combination overwhelmed the government's ability to treat and evacuate the men. The Sanitary Commission applied to the secretary of war for use of idle military transports, and Stanton agreed. In addition to ships that could accommodate one thousand men, he approved the retrofitting of one of the ships, the steamship McClellan named *Daniel Webster,* as a hospital. With surgeons, nurses, and officials of the Sanitary Commission aboard, it accommodated wounded officers and provided medical care to all.[11]

McClellan's daily letters of July 26, 27, and 28 to Nelly recounted his visits "among the sick and wounded," where he saw wounded officers being treated on the "steam-hospital" ship. On the 26th, he spent more than nine hours with the wounded, and late that evening wrote Nelly: "If you could have seen how the poor, maimed, brave fellows, some at the point of death, brightened up when they saw me and caught my hand, it would have repaid you for much of our common grief and anxiety." Obviously deeply affected by what he saw, he wrote that it had "been the most harrowing day I ever passed, yet a proud one for me, too." The next day, as he prepared himself to meet another incoming group of wounded soldiers, he told her solemnly that "I regard it as a duty I owe the poor fellows—rather a hard one to perform, but still one that cannot be neglected...."[12]

Less than two weeks later, McClellan wrote to Nelly: "I am so glad you visited that hospital. I thank you for it from the bottom of my heart. I know it did them infinite good, and I am sure that you will never meet one of the Army of the Potomac without a kind word and your brightest smile." Praise of Nelly is not rare in McClellan's letters, but in this instance, his praise reads as if he is noting an unusual occurrence in her visit to soldiers in a hospital. It was the only time during the war that he mentioned such a visit. Military hospitals in the Civil War were terrible places, and visits to them were not to be undertaken lightly. But more than a year after the firing on Fort Sumter, such a visit should not have been an unusual one for the wife of General McClellan.[13]

While stray passages in his letters allow us to glean bits of Nelly's personality, the couple's correspondence is awash in clues to McClellan's. McClellan praised few men in his letters and damned many, but what he wrote about himself was even more damning than what he wrote about others. Time and again in his letters to Nelly he fervently expressed his belief that he was called by God to be the Savior of the Union. One such reference can be found not long after he had been relieved of command of the Army of the Potomac after his failed Peninsula Campaign. At nine o'clock on the morning of September 2, 1862, Lincoln and Halleck called upon McClellan at his home at Fifteenth and H Streets in Washington. Unlike the presidential visit to his home in Washington nearly a year earlier, McClellan had the sense to see his visitors this time. The Confederate Army threatened Washington, and despite misgivings on the part of both visitors (which were reflected in furious Cabinet reaction later that day), Lincoln and Halleck asked him to return to command and defend the city. Shortly after Lincoln and Halleck left, McClellan wrote one of his most messianic letters to Nelly: "Again I have been called upon to save the country—the case is desperate, but with God's help I will try unselfishly to do my best & if he wills it accomplish the salvation of the nation...." McClellan transformed standard military orders into holy crusades.[14]

Many generals in the war perceived value in sending detailed letters home for "archives," as McClellan called his—records of their actions for future use, if questioned by the authorities, to aid in constructing a memoir, or just to share their experiences with their families. McClellan's letters, though, have a different feel to them. When he is writing about his actions and his thoughts, his letters read as if he were speaking to himself. In fact, he admitted as much. In the letter he wrote to Nelly in 1859, just after their engagement—the one in which he imposed the daily letter-writing requirement—he said, "In talking or writing to you it is exactly as if I'm communing with myself—you *are* my alter ego, darling." It is clear that he loved his wife, and there are many loving expressions in his letters to her, yet the highest compliment that McClellan could pay the woman he had pursued for five years was that *she* was *he*.[15]

No evidence has ever surfaced, however, that Nelly ever shied away from that characterization of her. In fact, there is scarce firsthand evidence of Nelly at all—apart from her husband's letters to her, a clutch of her letters to him, and several postwar diaries, which relate her activities but never her thoughts. Nelly carefully guarded his letters to her for more than thirty years, but only a handful of her letters have survived. This was not unusual; more soldiers' letters survived the war than did those from home to the front lines. In some cases, the letters were destroyed in order to prevent the enemy from obtaining intelligence about the home front; in others, women's letters were destroyed for reasons of privacy (as when Lily Frémont destroyed most of her parents' correspondence upon her mother's death).[16]

In the few but lengthy letters from Nelly to George that we can read, she is parroting her husband's visions of glory. For example, in the summer of 1862, while McClellan was pursuing his doomed Peninsula strategy, Nelly traveled from Washington to New York and then to the beaches of New Jersey and Connecticut. In one letter, she told him that everywhere she went, "the better class of people" enthusiastically praised him, thus reinforcing McClellan's belief that he was a hero to the nation. She shared, too, his aggravation and anger at the civilian superiors who frustrated him. In another letter that same summer she wrote: "I am tired of you having to wait on the pleasure of fools & idiots. How *galling* it *must* be to you & how *bravely* you bear every thing," she fumed. "I don't believe there was *ever* such a man as you are George, and there is no flattery in *that*."[17]

Because the language of her letters so readily mirrored his, her expressions of support for him were often based on less than perfect knowledge. Such was the case in early August 1862, when she chastised his superiors for holding him back. "It seems to me that the *North* is doing *nothing,*" she wailed. McClellan had just begun a second month of inactivity after his inconclusive Peninsula Campaign, despite desperate orders from Lincoln and Halleck either to attack Richmond or to march his army back north to defend Washington. The real situation was not recognizable in her words of comfort to McClellan. "I can readily understand how hard it *is* for you to be sitting still when you feel so anxious to advance. . . ." Sometimes her reassurances, when read closely, seem ambivalent, perhaps even a bit silly, as when she wrote to him near the end of that month. "I don't think it is at all surprising darling that the men still have confidence in you & still are glad to see you," her letter on August 23 said. "They *ought* to *adore* you & I believe they do almost. You certainly have done enough for them."[18]

Nearly a year earlier, McClellan had invidiously maneuvered Winfield Scott out of command of the Union Army. After he attended the old general's farewell ceremony in November 1861, when Scott boarded a train to leave Washington for the last time, McClellan sent Nelly a detailed account of it with a plea: "Should I ever become vainglorious & ambitious remind me of that spectacle." There was, of course, not the slightest chance that she ever would. From an examination of his many letters and the five of hers that survive, it is clear that what he wanted from her was approval, validation, praise. When she did not praise him enough, he demanded more. Apparently Nelly's appreciation for McClellan's role in the victory at Williamsburg was not fulsome enough because on May 8, he wrote: "Your two letters of Sunday & Monday reached me last night. I do not think you overmuch rejoiced at the results I gained." He continued unhappily: "I really thought that you would appreciate a great result gained by pure skill & at little cost more highly than you seem to." In that instance, her applause might have been fainter than usual because of McClellan's boast that he had "whipped" A. P. Hill, along with other Confederate commanders.[19]

It is possible, of course, that Nelly's consistent echoes of her husband's warped view of the world and of himself may have reflected her own considered perspective on the times and the man. She certainly convinced McClellan that she shared his views. "You do not feel one bit more bitterly towards those people than I do," McClellan reassured Nelly in one letter. "I do not say much about it—but I fear they have done all that cowardice, folly & rascality can do to ruin our poor country. . . . I have no respect for any member of [this administration] & *our* opinions do not differ in the slightest."[20]

Nelly expressed negative views of his superiors in derogatory language that matched, and sometimes surpassed, his. In one of her letters, she called Lincoln "an old reprobate," and in a lost letter, we can judge from McClellan's reply that Nelly used more colorful language. "I agree with you," McClellan wrote, "that a certain eminent individual is 'an old stick'—& of pretty poor timber at that." At times, those in Washington were "crazy," "scoundrels," and even "miserable traitors." Nelly joined McClellan in his dislike of Stanton, whom she had detested even before McClellan changed his opinion, as is clear from one of his letters: "I remember what you thought of Stanton when you first saw him. I thought you were wrong. I now know you were right. Enough of the creature!"[21]

Such talk was music to her husband's ears, and it would have made her life easier, too. Sharing, even anticipating, McClellan's perception that enemies within and without the Union vastly outnumbered him would have been a great convenience for Nelly. In a relationship largely defined by daily long-distance correspondence, reinforcing her husband's delusions would have been much easier and much more conducive to marital harmony than attempting to inject reality into McClellan's worldview from afar. Nelly was twenty-six; she was a new wife and a new mother. She matured in the midst of the most turbulent time in American history. She had been taught by society's traditions and by her training to support her husband. Her parents had pushed her to marry McClellan, whom they adored and to whom her father reported. Her country regarded him as a military genius and national savior. So it was only natural that Nelly should encourage McClellan in everything he thought and everything he did. Or was it?

Boosting a husband's morale and self-esteem in letters from the home front to the front lines has always been de rigueur. It has never been unusual, though, for wives to express differences of opinion or offer advice, even when the husbands' daily world is vastly different from their own. American women from Abigail Adams to Eleanor Roosevelt disagreed with their husbands in private correspondence during wartime, and they often provided excellent advice to their spouses. Though Jessie Frémont and Nelly McClellan never criticized their husbands (at least insofar as we have any evidence), the nineteenth century was by no means devoid of women who forthrightly tackled their husbands' judgments. Ellen Sherman and Julia Grant, for example, did not hesitate to let their husbands know when they disagreed with them. Nor was it unusual to find Southern wives frankly expressing contrary thoughts to their husbands in the field. The Confederacy's "steel magnolias" wielded a powerful combination of feminine charm and inflexible will.

Lydia Johnston was a case in point. Her husband, Joseph E. Johnston, was McClellan's Confederate counterpart in the winter of 1861-62, as commander of the Confederate Army of the Potomac. Johnston was also McClellan's faint echo in many of his self-destructive personality traits. Like Little Mac, Johnston was extraordinarily sensitive to real and imagined slights by his superiors, though in Johnston's case there were, in fact, plenty of the former. Like McClellan, Johnston could not set aside personal vanity and ambition for the greater good. Most damaging to his career and his cause, however, Johnston was secretive to the point of being incommunicative with his superiors.[22]

Perhaps no amount of prodding or cajoling by well-meaning friends or family could have altered the worldviews or actions of either Johnston or McClellan. Notably in the latter case, Nelly never appears to have attempted such an intervention. Johnston's wife, though, was cut from different cloth than was McClellan's. Lydia Johnston saw the folly of her husband's ways and at least on one occasion tried to change them. In a letter to Johnston, she encouraged her husband to "keep the government better informed about his situation." Johnston replied that her advice was "judicious" and then defended himself by telling her that he was reporting "in a general way . . . but the people of Richmond take no interest in any partial affairs [engagements] that may occur in this quarter." To Lydia Johnston's credit, at least she tried.[23]

Even if she was not prepared to contradict her husband's perverted worldview or offer him unsolicited career advice, Nelly had another option available to persuade him toward a more rational outlook on his superiors. Behind a shield of unbridled self-confidence, McClellan occasionally harbored self-doubts, and like all other thoughts of his, he communicated them to her. There is no evidence from either her letters or his, though, that she ever picked up on those openings or encouraged him to give weight to those thoughts.

In May 1862, as the Army of the Potomac approached Richmond, McClellan interrupted a letter to Nelly, complaining, "I have this moment received a dispatch from the Prsdt who is terribly scared about Washington—& talks about the necessity of my returning in order to save it!" An hour and a half later, he resumed the letter to her: "5 pm. Have just finished my reply to his Excellency! It is perfectly sickening to deal with such people & you may rest assured that I will lose as little time as possible in breaking off all connection with them . . . every day brings with it only additional proofs of their hypocrisy, knavery & folly—well, well, I ought not to write in this way, for they may be right & I entirely wrong, so I will drop the matter."[24]

As he camped south of Richmond on Harrison's Landing later in July, he wrote Nelly that the Administration's "cowardice and folly" had set the country on the road to ruin. He worried that his "day of usefulness to the country is past—at least under this administration," and then, he continued, "Perhaps I have really brought it on myself; for while striving conscientiously to do my best, it may well be that I have made great mistakes that my vanity does not permit me to perceive." Three days after that letter, he picked up the same thread when he wrote to her: "I have tried to do my best, honestly & faithfully, for my country— that I have to a certain extent failed I do not believe to be my fault—tho' my self conceit probably blinds me to my errors that others see." In the letter to her on November 7, 1862, the one interrupted by Burnside and Buckingham, relieving him of command for the last time, he again admitted he might have committed some errors. "Do not be at all worried—I am not . . . to the last I have done my duty as I understand it," he wrote. "That I must have made many mistakes I cannot deny—I do not see any great blunders—but no one can judge of himself."[25]

No indications exist that she ever sought to use his episodic expressions of self-doubt to encourage him to act differently, although she readily reinforced his messianic self-delusions and condemnations of Lincoln and his advisers. Based on everything we know about him, McClellan was almost certainly incapable of revising his opinions of events and people, especially of himself. Even if McClellan had possessed a more resilient mind, however, Nelly never gave him any mental space in which to change it.

CHAPTER 11

"I almost wish . . . they would displace you"

McClellan's relations with Lincoln were almost constantly fraught with difficulties. In that respect, too, McClellan's wartime experience mirrored Frémont's. But Nelly did not take it upon herself, as did Jessie, to intercede personally with the president on her husband's behalf. Although it became clear twice in 1862 that the general was in jeopardy of losing his command, Nelly never made a trip to the Executive Mansion to plead her husband's case. She had several good reasons not to do so. Perhaps the most important, or at least, the one most obvious in their correspondence, was that McClellan himself almost always expressed a strange ambivalence about his fate. Relying upon God to plot his course in this world and the next, McClellan perceived earthly decision makers, like Lincoln and Stanton, to be playing little more than bit parts in the larger drama of his life.

The first blow to his authority and ego fell on March 11, 1862. On that day, McClellan was relieved of command of all U.S. armies except the Army of the Potomac, which he was still readying for the Peninsula Campaign. That should have alerted him regarding Lincoln's expectations, but McClellan spent little time bewailing his loss of the supreme command. He still harbored hope that he would be restored to general-in-chief at the end of his successful Peninsula Campaign, and he told Nelly not to talk about it with anyone.

McClellan's next career crossroads came near the end of the Peninsula Campaign, when rumors began to circulate that Lincoln and Stanton might appoint a new general-in-chief, simultaneously eliminating McClellan's chance to regain the title and installing a superior officer over him. On July 17, he told Nelly that he would "not be at all surprised to have some other Genl made Cmder of the whole army, or even to be superseded here—& to tell you the truth I don't care how soon they do it. I have lost confidence in the Govt. & would be glad to be out of the scrape—keep this to yourself." The next day he elaborated on his plan for the future in a letter to her: "If they supersede me in command of the Army of the Potomac I will resign my commission at once; if they appoint Halleck Comg Genl I will remain in command of this army as long as they will allow me to. . . . I cannot remain as a subordinate in the army I once commanded any longer than the interests of my own Army of the Potomac require."[1]

Two days later, his suspicions were confirmed, and he wrote to her: "I see it reported in this evening's papers that Halleck is to be Genl. In Chief. Now let them take the next step & relieve me & I shall once more be a free man."[2]

By early August, as Pope began to direct some Army of the Potomac troops in defense of Washington, McClellan correctly anticipated a further denigration in his status. Rather than fearing it, he told Nelly he was prepared with a strategy of his own: "I see more clearly every day their [Halleck, Stanton, and Lincoln] settled purpose to force me to resign." According to McClellan, however, such a move would play right into his hands. "I am trying to keep my temper & force *them* to relieve me or dismiss me from the service," he explained to her. Faced with her husband's determined ambivalence, there is little wonder that Nelly never approached Lincoln to save his career.[3]

The McClellans' correspondence reveals, moreover, that on more than one occasion Nelly actively encouraged him to resign his position and she welcomed the prospect that he might be relieved. "You *have* reason to *love* that Army George, for they *do adore* you," she wrote on August 4. "*every* one says that & I wouldn't have you *desert* them—but I *almost* wish—as I have said before—they would displace you—& *then* you could not help yourself." When rumors of Pope's ascension reached her, she was apoplectic: "I have the most violent contempt for him [Pope] & that feeling seems to be pretty general. . . . Don't you think if Pope was put over you—you would consider it your duty to *quit? I* do. & should use all my influence to make you leave those circumstances. I *must* not *endure* the idea of you being *under that puppy. . . .*"[4]

Although McClellan's detractors did not know it, the best ally they had in their desire to remove McClellan from command was the general's own wife. The second best, as it happened, was the wife of the commander in chief. Less than a week before the president removed McClellan from command, Mary Lincoln urged her husband to do so. During a visit to New York on November 2, 1862, Mary wrote from her hotel:

Dear husband,

. . . Your name is on every lip and many prayers and good wishes are hourly sent up for your welfare. And McClellan & his slowness are as vehemently discussed. Allowing this beautiful weather to pass away is disheartening the North. . . . Many say they would almost worship you if you would put a fighting general in the place of McClellan. This would be splendid weather for an engagement. . . . [5]

McClellan had initially charmed Mary, whom he referred to as "the Lady President" in a letter to Nelly, but Mary's disenchantment with him grew as his martial reputation failed and his political support among Democrats increased. After the Battle of Antietam, her savvy political eye clearly perceived that he was a liability to her husband and a threat to her hold on the Executive Mansion. Mary Lincoln believed McClellan had to go.

McClellan's most ardent supporters were businessmen who saw a bright future for him in the Democratic Party, like Joseph W. Alsop, William W. Aspinwall, and John Jacob Astor. On more than one occasion, McClellan consulted them in confidential letters about whether he should leave the army in the middle of the war and seek civilian employment (some of which were published in the general's posthumous memoirs, *McClellan's Own Story*). The first request was occasioned by Halleck's ascension to general-in-chief; the second by Lincoln's Preliminary Emancipation Proclamation, issued just after the Battle of Antietam. McClellan was greatly disturbed by both developments, but his friends argued strongly against his voluntary departure from his command. "Dont think of resigning," Alsop wrote to him on July 24 in response to his letter asking help in finding a job in the civilian world. Aspinwall was even more emphatic: "Your sphere whilst the war lasts, is the army—you have no right to entertain any idea of a return to civil life just now." On July 24, Aspinwall wrote to Nelly, urging her to convince her husband not to resign, but she was then in full agreement with her husband. On that same day, McClellan responded to her letter: "You ask me whether my self-respect will permit me to remain longer in the service after Halleck's appointment? It will permit me to remain only so long as the welfare of the Army of the Potomac demands—no longer. Don't mind these things, I bide my time. Whatever God sends me, be it defeat and loss of rank, or be it success and honor, I will cheerfully submit. . . ."[6]

Aspinwall was so concerned about the general's opposition to Lincoln's Preliminary Emancipation Proclamation that he decided to visit McClellan. McClellan wrote to Nelly on October 5 that Aspinwall arrived in camp just as the president was leaving and was "decidedly of the opinion that it is my duty to submit to the Prsdt's proclamation & quietly continue doing my duty as a soldier." He continued, "I presume he is right . . . I shall surely give his views full consideration." Whether those men sought to deter McClellan from making a political misstep that would bar him from the presidency or whether they were reacting to his petty tantrums with admirable common sense, it appears that McClellan gave more weight to career advice from his business friends than from Nelly. He was right to do so. Nelly consistently encouraged his worst instincts regarding Lincoln and his military future; his friends saw more clearly the duty he owed his president and his nation.[7]

Of all of the mistakes McClellan made in the war, one of the most damaging to him and to the country was his failure to trust Lincoln. If Lincoln had erred in elevating the young warrior to supreme commander too swiftly, McClellan's refusal—or inability—to trust Lincoln sealed his fate. Nearly every historian's analysis of the Lincoln-McClellan relationship, from T. Harry Williams's to Stephen Sears's to Joseph Glatthaar's to John Waugh's, reaches the same conclusion. "[P]erhaps McClellan's greatest mistake of all was not bonding with Abraham Lincoln . . . ," wrote Waugh. "Lincoln had held out his hand to McClellan, but McClellan refused to grasp it. . . . Above everything else, that failure had been his Achilles' heel."[8]

Lincoln intuitively recognized McClellan's need for moral as well as military support, and he invested much of his energy during the first two years of the war in reassuring the general of his friendship. After one of many such expressions from Lincoln, McClellan wrote to the president: "I am well aware of the firm friendship & confidence you have evinced for me, & instead of again thanking you for it will endeavor to assure you that it is not misplaced." If he believed it when he put pen to paper, his suspicious mind altered its perspective almost immediately. Ten days after writing that letter, McClellan wrote to Nelly: "I feel that the fate of the nation depends on me, & I feel I have not one single friend at the seat of Govt." Nelly never encouraged him to think otherwise.[9]

She did, though, ask him questions at times, and McClellan did tell her some of the very things that Lincoln, Stanton, and Halleck desired to know: When will you move? When will you attack? No doubt her interest reflected her own personal concern about his safety and a natural desire to know what her husband was doing, but she must also have wanted answers to the mounting criticism of her husband that she encountered in newspapers, in Congress, and in her daily rounds in society. As McClellan entered the second month of his siege of Yorktown, which stalled his offensive up the peninsula to Richmond, Nelly was anxious to get his reaction to critical reports she was reading and hearing. On April 19, he wrote to her, obviously in response to her concerns: "Don't be at all discouraged—all is going well. . . . I can't tell you when Yorktown is to be

Portrait of George and Nelly McClellan, taken in 1861 or 1862, when she was twenty-six and he was thirty-five years old. (*Courtesy of the Library of Congress*)

attacked, for it depends on circumstances that I cannot control. . . . Never mind what such people as Wade say—they are beneath contempt." Sen. Benjamin Wade of Ohio may have been beneath McClellan's contempt, but he was not beneath notice; as chairman of the Joint Committee on the Conduct of the War, he held the most powerful seat in the wartime Congress. Despite her husband's reassurance, one keen Washington observer, Elizabeth Blair Lee, wrote to her husband in April "that abolitionists sent & said so many painful things to Mrs. McClelland that her Mother has taken her off to New York among her friends—fearing the effects of her distress here upon her health—this I had from a next door neighbor." Nelly's relative detachment from her husband's world did not shield her from public criticism of him.[10]

Three months later, McClellan was stalled again outside "the gates of Richmond," under heavy pressure from Lincoln and Stanton to disclose his plans and resume forward progress. On July 17, he responded to similar inquiries from Nelly. "You ask me when I expect to reach Richmond & whether I shall act on the offensive this summer. I am at the mercy of the Govt—after the first 9000 or 10,000 men sent to me they have withheld all further reinforcements. . . ." Then he advised her, "Don't think much about the war."[11]

At about the same time, General Marcy, who was ill and in Washington, expressed the same concern. The man of substantial military experience expressed himself in very diplomatic, almost tentative language in a telegram to his son-in-law: "It is very generally thought that an advance on Richmond at an early period would be received with more enthusiasm now than at any time since the war commenced," Marcy wrote. "The people seem to demand it. . . ." McClellan's response to him was more brusque than had been his letter to Nelly. "Your proposition is easily enunciated but not so readily carried out," retorted McClellan in a telegram. "You may rest assured that it is not necessary to urge me from a distance—I on the spot am quite as anxious to finish this agreeable game as any of my disinterested friends away from here."[12]

In fact, Nelly's father may have been another reason Nelly did not approach Lincoln, even had she been concerned about her husband's career. As McClellan's chief of staff, Marcy dealt with Lincoln on a regular basis, and if requests were to be made regarding military matters, he was surely the one to do it. On more than one occasion, Marcy manfully met the wrath of Lincoln, Stanton, and Halleck that should have rained upon his son-in-law. In the best known of such incidents, McClellan instructed Marcy to report to the president the failure of the vital effort to clear the upper Potomac River of Confederates in

February 1862, and the reason for it. Marcy reported that the operation had been frustrated in large part because the canal boats, which McClellan had ordered to Harpers Ferry, were six inches too wide for the lock. Upon hearing that, Lincoln's generally placid demeanor utterly failed him. According to John Nicolay, the president, who genuinely liked Marcy, had a "long and sharp talk" with McClellan's chief of staff. "Why in the Nation, General Marcy, couldn't the General have known whether a boat would go through that lock before spending a million dollars getting them there?" roared Lincoln. "I am no engineer, but it seems to me that if I wished to know whether a boat would go through a hole or a lock, common sense would teach me to go and measure it." Marcy had no answer to the president's complaint; McClellan was, after all, first and foremost an engineer.[13]

Marcy was a proud man who always comported himself in accord with strict military guidelines. In his role as McClellan's father-in-law, however, he was sometimes tempted to shade accounts of his son-in-law's actions and words. After McClellan's ignominious retreat from Malvern Hill to Harrison's Landing in July 1862, for example, Marcy once again traveled to Washington to report to the president on behalf of McClellan. According to Sears, Marcy "was closely questioned," particularly after he admitted that if McClellan was attacked again by overwhelming numbers and his communications cut, he might be forced to capitulate. That word was not to be used in connection with the army, Lincoln told him sharply. Marcy stammered that he spoke only of a hypothetical situation, which he later wrote, "seemed to afford great relief to the President." Hypothetical though the situation might have been, Marcy was likely telling Lincoln what he thought McClellan would do in such a situation.[14]

Marcy's embarrassment at candidly predicting McClellan's future action on the battlefield, was, perhaps, only possibly less painful than seeing at firsthand his son-in-law's often appalling personal behavior toward the commander in chief. Being part of McClellan's immediate family placed Marcy on such an intimate footing that he suffered more than any other man in his official capacity might have. Even though Nelly was in residence in Washington on one Sunday morning early in 1862, her father greeted a caller at the front door. Unexpectedly facing the president, who had traveled from the White House to McClellan's home to confer with his commander, Marcy was forced to inform the commander in chief that McClellan was not yet awake and could not see him. Marcy did so "with flushed face and confused manner." It could only have further embarrassed Marcy that the president himself covered for the disrespectful general, saying, "Of course, he's very busy now, and no doubt was laboring far into the night." McClellan's fortunate choice (for McClellan if not for Marcy) of his father-in-law as his chief of staff obviated any need for Nelly to interact with Lincoln in other than a social setting. Her father had urged her to marry McClellan and was in the position of the general's chief adviser. Surely, Nelly could trust her father to act in support of her husband's career.[15]

CHAPTER 12

"how the mighty are fallen"

What is apparent in hindsight, however, is that Nelly could not be trusted to burnish her husband's legacy. Shortly after McClellan's death in 1885, the couple's private correspondence during the Civil War, guarded by Nelly for more than twenty years, was published in a book in which the author credited Nelly with giving him access to the letters. If McClellan had chosen his chief of staff brilliantly, he was far less astute in his selection of a literary executor, although his choice of William Cowper Prime surely seemed a wise one at the time. Prime was a friend, a lawyer, an art historian, and a collector of ancient coins, pottery, and porcelain, who later became a trustee and vice president of the Metropolitan Museum of Art. Before the Civil War, he turned a journey to the Holy Land into several best-selling books—combination memoirs/travel guides—frequently carried by pilgrims to Palestine, Jerusalem, and Egypt. So purple was Prime's prose in his most famous volume, *Tent Life in the Holy Land* (1857), that Mark Twain could not resist satirizing it. Twain's irreverent take on Victorian society and religious pilgrimages, *Innocents Abroad, or the New Pilgrims' Progress* (1869), featured repeated jibes at a fictionalized book Twain called "Nomadic Life in Palestine," by a "Mr. Grimes."[1]

Prime's next foray was journalism. In 1861, he became a co-owner and editor of the *New York Journal of Commerce*. In the middle of the presidential election year, on Wednesday, May 18, 1864, the *Journal* and the *New York World* mistakenly published a bogus presidential proclamation that indicated the war was not going well. The forgery of the proclamation—an elaborate ruse by someone attempting to manipulate the gold market—quickly came to light, along with the fact that, while the bogus proclamation had been distributed to a number of newspapers, only the two most anti-Republican newspapers had printed it. That evening, the Lincoln Administration sent soldiers to close down the *Journal* and arrest Prime and Manton Marble, the editor of the

World. "McClellan, noble old fellow, was the first man here on Wednesday," Prime wrote three days later, when he had been freed from jail and regained his newspaper, "and he was the first man here today, literally the first." Mc-Clellan had good reasons, both professional and personal, to hasten to extract Prime from his sticky situation; by 1864, Prime was one of McClellan's most active political boosters and a tireless campaign manager. Prime admired Mc-Clellan from the first and defended him to the last. He always blamed the general's failures on Washington politicians, principally Lincoln and Stanton. To all appearances, Prime was McClellan's perfect choice for literary executor.[2]

McClellan began writing his memoirs shortly after his failed presidential bid, when he and Nelly were in Europe. He did so "not with any intention of publishing them at present," he vowed, "but only availing myself of the opportunity to place my side of the story on record." In addition to soliciting reminiscences from those who served with him, he used as reference material some of the information from his letters to his wife, which she had carefully retained per his instructions. McClellan's biographer Stephen W. Sears, who pieced together the intricate construction of McClellan's memoirs, maintains that in his own early manuscript, McClellan used excerpts from his letters to Nelly sparingly and did not include the incendiary descriptions of his superiors that were later to amaze and astound readers.[3]

After laboring for years on a final draft of his memoirs, McClellan stored the only copy in a warehouse in New York along with other valuable household goods when the couple sailed for Europe again in 1881. On the family's return several months later, Nelly and McClellan learned to their horror that a fire had destroyed the warehouse, and with all of their possessions, the manuscript was lost. Greatly disheartened, the general took up his pen again after urging by his friends. He struggled to reconstitute his earlier lengthy manuscript, but from evidence of surviving notes, according to Sears, "his new effort was more limited and entirely military, framed by the contents of his wartime *Report.*" The *Report* was a 763-page, wholly self-serving version of his actions that McClellan and his staff had prepared in 1863 to defend his conduct against accusations raised by the Committee on the Conduct of the War. Even with the massive *Report* as the basis for his second effort, however, McClellan made slow progress on his memoirs. Of course, he was a very busy man at that time: McClellan's postwar career included lucrative senior engineering responsibilities for major railroad, bridge, and dock projects, as well as an exemplary term as governor of the state of New Jersey (1878–81), punctuated by several lengthy trips to Europe with Nelly and their two children.[4]

And then, without warning, fifty-eight-year-old McClellan was struck dead by a heart attack in his home in Orange, New Jersey, on October 29, 1885. His forty-nine-year-old widow and their two children leaned on Prime for assistance in the wake of McClellan's death. Prime was one of two men "consulted by the family concerning arrangements for the funeral," and when McClellan's body was moved from Orange to New York City for the funeral, it was taken to Prime's house, where Nelly and the children stayed until the service on November 2.[5]

McClellan had made his will in 1873. In it, "the testator's beloved wife" was bequeathed his estate and made his executrix. Prime was named "literary Executor, with authority to make such disposition of Gen. McClellan's papers as he may think best." In giving Prime that responsibility, the general put his trust in a man whom he knew fully shared his views about himself, about the conduct of the war, and about the men in Washington who sabotaged his march to greatness. McClellan trusted his friend Prime to do his best for him. What McClellan could not have known was how bad Prime's best would be.[6]

At the time of McClellan's death, the best-selling book in the United States was actually two books: the two-volume *Personal Memoirs of Ulysses S. Grant.* Grant had died of cancer in July 1885, just days after he wrote the final word of his memoirs. He had pressed to finish the memoirs, desperate to provide for his wife Julia after his death. Mark Twain made him a generous offer to have Twain's company, Charles L. Webster & Co., publish the memoirs and sell them by subscription. When McClellan died—four months after Grant— nearly 300,000 subscriptions to Grant's memoirs had been sold. Julia Grant would receive nearly $500,000 from the sale of her husband's book (the equivalent of nearly $10 million today). Ten years earlier, Sherman had published his memoirs, which were a literary and financial success; they, like Grant's, have never gone out of print. Every day, it seemed, brought news of more military memoirs in the works. The men who had fought on battlefields twenty years earlier were refighting the Civil War on paper, and people all over the world were paying to read their stories.

After serving as an honorary pallbearer at McClellan's funeral, William Cowper Prime turned to his duties as literary executor. He rushed to get McClellan's story into print for that lucrative market. Prime soon let a friend know that Twain's company would be publishing the general's memoirs. Considering one of Twain's biting observations about the writing style of "Mr. Grimes" in *Innocents Abroad,* Twain may have been the only person on the planet who instinctively grasped just how little of *McClellan's Own Story* was, in fact, Mc-Clellan's own story—and how much was Prime's: "I love to quote from Grimes, because he is so dramatic. And because he is so romantic. And because he seems to care but little whether he tells the truth or not, so he scares the reader or excites his envy or his admiration."[7]

At the time of his death, McClellan had made little headway in his second attempt at his memoirs; he left only sketchy drafts of his wartime experiences, ending in early 1862, and he included only one extract from his letters to Nelly. Prime quickly seized upon McClellan's unfinished writings and within a year produced his version of the general's memoirs, which he called *McClellan's Own Story*. The reader of *McClellan's Own Story* can be forgiven if he doesn't immediately grasp the extent of Prime's responsibility for the content of the book, including the most sensational material: extensive excerpts from the intimate letters McClellan had sent to Nelly during the war. Not until after the title page (which lists only McClellan as the author), the table of contents, the list of illustrations, and the first two closely typeset pages of Prime's "Biographical Sketch" of McClellan do readers learn from Prime that they are about to encounter "letters which I have suffered to appear in this volume." That is the first hint that it was not McClellan who bared his tortured soul to the world.[8]

Today's penchant for sharing the most intimate details of daily life through social media is far removed from the standards of the nineteenth century. Privacy was highly valued in Victorian society. In 1887, Prime's publication of McClellan's personal correspondence was considered bad form, even though the letters were eagerly read. Quoting from one of McClellan's letters in their biography of Abraham Lincoln, Nicolay and Hay felt compelled to excuse their breach of generally accepted polite behavior. "We should hesitate to print these pathetic evidences of McClellan's weakness of character, contained as they are in private letters to his family," they explained in a footnote, "if they had not been published by Mr. W. C. Prime, with the singular misconception of their true bearing, as a basis for attacking the administration of Mr. Lincoln."[9]

Prime's many transgressions in the production of that book, in addition to his mind-boggling decision to publish the McClellans' personal correspondence, were long invisible to even the most dedicated historians. It has been only recently that Stephen Sears, who edited McClellan's papers, discovered and revealed Prime's premeditated literary crime of presenting his bastardized manuscript as McClellan's "own story." Of Prime's work, Sears wrote:

The general had left not even half a manuscript, with much of that only in early draft form and undergoing revision at the time of his sudden death. Prime took this as it was, undid some of revisions, and patched together the balance of the book from McClellan writings that went back twenty years and more. . . . [H]e then added excerpts from some 250 of McClellan's wartime letters to his wife. In these letters to Ellen it had been the general's habit to pour out his innermost feelings and opinions in unbridled fashion; at their publication McClellan surely turned over in his grave.[10]

Sears's flatly concludes that "McClellan was betrayed by his literary executor." In fact, however, a compelling case can be made for Nelly's complicity in the publication of her husband's personal correspondence. In his introduction to *McClellan's Own Story,* Prime described Nelly's contribution to his product:

The perfection of their love, the absolute confidence which [McClellan] re-posed, and wisely reposed, in her, made his letters not only graphic accounts of daily events, great and small, but also an exposure of his inmost feelings. I found among his papers some extracts from these letters, which he had made to aid him in writing his memoir; but the letters were supposed to have van-ished in the fire. When they were discovered, carefully sealed for the only per-son to whom they belonged, I asked for fuller extracts. I confess that I hesitated very much about giving any part of these letters, written in the most sacred confidence of life to the public eye.[11]

Though the McClellans had entrusted much of their household posses-sions and the general's only draft of his memoirs to the presumed security of a warehouse, Nelly—"the only person to whom they belonged"—must have been much more protective of her husband's letters.

Her action is routinely taken for granted by legions of historians and Civil War buffs, who have profited from quoting the correspondence without offer-ing Nelly praise commensurate with the remarkable act of preservation that it was. The vital historical contribution of Civil War wives through their careful protection of their husbands' correspondence has, by and large, escaped the specific notice and thanks of historians. So much of history would be lost with-out those letters, but the McClellans' correspondence is of particular note. It is nearly impossible to make any sweeping generalization about the thousands of books about Abraham Lincoln, except one: it is hard to find a narrative of Lincoln's war years that does not quote from the letters McClellan wrote to

Nelly. Despite their inestimable value to our understanding of the times, of the war, of McClellan, and of Lincoln, the letters that Nelly saved from the fire have become so embedded in the historical record that their existence is as readily taken for granted as their publication in *McClellan's Own Story*.

The letters' publication was not, however, the inevitable consequence of Nelly's success in preserving them from the fire. Indeed, had McClellan lived to finish his memoirs, Sears contends, the letters would not have been published. Sears found only two sentences quoted verbatim in any of McClellan's drafts of his memoirs. It is apparent that McClellan had no intention of including anything but minor excerpts from his letters, though he used them as an aid to recall his thoughts at the time. Prime's publication of extensive excerpts from the letters required McClellan's sudden death, Prime's inept handling of the general's memoirs, and Nelly's acquiescence—or her complete disengagement from the project. It appears that McClellan not only misjudged his literary executor, he was unwise to trust his wife to perform the conventional widow's duty of protecting her husband's legacy.

"First, shoot the widow" is the informal motto of biographers, according to one who has written about writing biographies. Widows are generally the bane of a biographer's existence because they so often interfere to safeguard or enlarge upon the legacy of their late husbands, as did, for example, LaSalle Corbett Pickett, Elizabeth Bacon Custer, and Jessie Benton Frémont. In this case, however, recourse to violence was not necessary, or even desirable. Unlike Martha Washington, who destroyed all of her husband's personal correspondence immediately upon his death, Nelly did not take steps to withhold her husband's letters in order to protect his reputation or her own. Whether she directly acceded to Prime's request for "fuller extracts" as Prime appears to claim, or whether Nelly explicitly disengaged herself from the publishing process, it is almost impossible to imagine that she was not aware that extensive passages from her personal trove of letters were being copied for Prime's use.[12]

Although it is not clear whom Prime "asked for fuller extracts," it was Nelly's daughter, May, who made those copies for Prime. May was twenty-four and single at the time, so it is possible that she was living with her mother while doing Prime's bidding. We know that May went to Europe with Nelly and her brother Max in the spring of 1886. Even had mother and daughter not lived under the same roof, it is unlikely that May could have—or would have—copied parts of more than two hundred private letters and given them to Prime without her mother's awareness and approval or, at least, without her mother's clear refusal to be involved.[13]

Nelly, her husband's executrix, might have felt obliged to allow Prime, her husband's literary executor, to review the correspondence for research in preparing his manuscript. That much would have been understandable. What is incomprehensible is her complete disengagement from the monumental effort that her husband had originally undertaken for his family's legacy and which would become his authorized historical record. Forty-nine-year-old Nelly was surely shocked and grieved by the unexpected early death of her husband. Even so, it is difficult to understand why she would have completely abandoned control over what should have been her most personal and treasured reminders of her husband.[14]

Nelly's relinquishment of her husband's letters to Prime is all the more puzzling considering that McClellan had often warned her against telling others their opinions of important men. In June 1862, McClellan had obviously heard rumors that she had been free with her opinions because he cautioned: "[D]o be very careful what you say. . . . The fact is that you & I cannot be too careful how we talk. . . ." That July, he returned to the same theme, writing to Nelly at a time when she was in Connecticut and her father was in Washington. "While I think of it be very careful what you telegraph & tell your father the same thing. I have the proof that the Secy reads all my private telegrams. If he has read my private letter to you also his ears must have tingled somewhat." A month later, McClellan felt the necessity to remind her again to be discreet. "Be careful not to say one word about Stanton, McDowell or any of my enemies," he wrote to her at midnight on April 27, 1862. "[L]et us present a contrast with those people & show by no word or act that we care what they say or do." Perhaps the most poignant of McClellan's words to Nelly in this regard were written when he became certain that Halleck would be named general-in-chief of the Union Army: "it will not do to parade the tattered remnants of my departed honors to the gaze of the world."[15]

Prime maintained that he was discreet in excerpting from the letters for publication: "[b]y far the larger portion of the letters, and of every letter, belongs to that confidence which not even death affects." In fact, it does appear that his elisions mask most of the truly personal exchanges between George and Nelly. The few extracts along those lines that escaped his editor's pen show a human and humorous side of McClellan that is largely missing from most accounts of the man. In early September 1861, for example, when Nelly heard a report that he had been killed, he reassured her swiftly and playfully: "What a shame that any one should spread such a wicked rumor in regard to my being killed! I beg to assure you that I have not been killed a single time since I reached Washington." Nearly a year later, McClellan described his dismay when a letter of hers had been delayed. "When the mail came, & my package of letters was handed to me, my heart sank way down to the toes of my slippers, was rapidly wearing a hole through one of them, for there was no letter from you," he wrote. "In about twenty minutes, Seth [his aide] gladdened my heart, saved my slippers & put me generally in a good humour with the whole world by handing me your glorious & splendid five pager."[16]

Two days later, he painted a comical portrait of his circumstances. "What do you think I have been doing for the last half-hour? Guess, guess!!!" he teased. "I have been sewing on buttons and patching my woollen shirts. . . . So you see 'how the mighty are fallen'—the general of a hundred thousand men sewing on buttons and mending his own clothes. It carried me back to the unhappy days of my miserable bachelorhood. . . ."[17]

McClellan was, in fact, quite a clever and funny man at times, but we have relatively few examples of that side of his personality because of the editing of his letters.

Prime's purpose in omitting those bits, he claimed, was to protect the McClellans' privacy. Prime followed a three-step process. First, he found some excerpts from the letters, which McClellan had copied as reference material for his memoirs. Prime reviewed them carefully but wished to see the passages that McClellan had omitted because, in Sears's words, the redacted letters "did not reflect enough of the general's personal qualities that Prime so much admired." It was at this point, that Prime must have asked for the original letters (almost certainly from Nelly, but perhaps through May), and then secured May's assistance in filling in the gaps, which she did by copying even more extensive passages from the original letters. The third (and fatal to the McClellans' reputations) step in the process was Prime's final selection of portions of copied letters to be included in *McClellan's Own Story*.[18]

According to Sears, the original letters were lost after that. As a result, the most complete extant versions of his letters are combinations of the general's "extracts of his letters" and May's copies of her mother's originals, now in the Library of Congress. Because his focus in *McClellan's Own Story* was on the general's military career, Prime determined to include numerous, extensive extracts of the letters relevant to that subject. He grouped his chosen selections into eleven separate chapters of the book and aptly, if ironically, titled them "Private Letters." If he had wished to paint a favorable portrait of the man he admired, and most assuredly he did, Prime would have done much better to have excluded much of what he included.

Certainly, Prime wanted to honor the man whom he admired so extravagantly. Assuredly, too, he sought to maximize income from the sale of the memoirs for Nelly and May and young Max. To be able to tout the inclusion of new and exclusive material could only help boost sales. And Prime was in a mad rush to cobble together the memoirs from the many articles (including the *Report*) that McClellan had written over the previous twenty years. Prime was wise enough not to include McClellan's worst insults of the martyred Abraham Lincoln in the manuscript, but Prime may have had his own reasons for including McClellan's slurs against Stanton, Halleck, and others. Prime had suffered his own humiliation at their hands in 1864—his newspaper closed, three days in jail—and he may have believed that McClellan's memoirs presented him with the perfect tool to put his tormentors in their place. Prime could use the words of General McClellan, which he likely thought would carry a great deal more weight, to settle scores for him and his hero.

Whatever the reason for Prime's inclusion of the letters, for well more than a century, historians have been grateful that Prime did what he did and that Nelly enabled him to do it. Even when Prime attempted to edit for discretion and good taste, the results were often more coy than diplomatic, and the reputations of neither McClellan nor Nelly benefited from Prime's alterations. As quoted earlier, one of McClellan's letters to his wife was published thusly (the elision was Prime's "tactful" edit): "So you want to know how I feel about Stanton, and what I think of him now? I will tell you with the most perfect frankness. I think . . . I may do the man injustice. God grant that I may be wrong!"[19]

Sears's scholarship revealed what Prime's teaser concealed and gives a much more complete picture of the McClellans' shared delusions. The elided portion, which remained in May's copy of the original, reads:

> . . . that he [Stanton] is the most unmitigated scoundrel I ever knew, heard or read of; I think that (& I do not wish to be irreverent) had he lived in the time of the Saviour, Judas Iscariot would have remained a respected member of the fraternity of the Apostles, & that the magnificent treachery & rascality would have caused Judas to have raised his arms in holy horror & unaffected wonder—he would certainly have claimed & exercised the right to have been the Betrayer of his Lord & Master, by virtue of the same merit that raised Satan to his "bad eminence."[20]

Through their memoirs, widows Jessie Benton Frémont, Julia Dent Grant, Elizabeth Bacon Custer, and Varina Davis, among others, all labored mightily to burnish their husbands' reputations. In contrast, Nelly McClellan is almost conspicuous by her absence on the literary scene of that era.

She was absent from the country itself for most of the post–Civil War years. General and Mrs. McClellan had literally fled to Europe after he lost the presidential election in 1864 to Abraham Lincoln. "The Young Napoleon has gone into exile," observed more than one wag of their three years in Europe. The Library of Congress holds three slim volumes of Nelly's diaries for the years after the war. Closely written in beautiful penmanship (and for one month, completely in French), she detailed travels, walks, dinners, visits from friends, and shopping, though she rarely expresses any of her thoughts. After Max Mc-Clellan's birth in late 1865, when Nelly was thirty, her diary entries almost always include vague references to pain, illness, and doctors. For example, she wrote on October 13, 1867, "a wretched day—dull and cloudy outside & duller and cloud(ier) inside." Although there are relatively few diary references to her husband, one entry contains McClellan's recounting of events during the war, which provides some insight into the version of history that he intended his memoir to contain:

> November 22 [1867]
> Evening—the Genl. & I have been having a chat on his experiences during the war & I am going to write it down—for it certainly is interesting & may be of interest to his children some time. I was questioning him about something from the time he was forced to withdraw his troops from Harrison Landing in Aug. 62. . . . If he had been listened to the battles of the 2nd Bull Run—Antietam, Fredericksburg,—Gettysburg, the Wilderness would have been saved & the war easily finished 2 years before it was—as 2 years after Grant brought up at the same place—the Genl was forced by the Authorities in Washington to leave.[21]

After her husband's death, forty-nine-year-old Nelly almost immediately took her son and daughter to Europe. No doubt she was attempting to escape painful memories, but on the other side of the Atlantic she could also escape even more painful contemporary commentaries on her husband. Certainly, criticism of McClellan did not end at the general's grave. For example, the *New York Times* obituary of October 30, 1885, portrayed a version of his wartime leadership completely opposed to the one Nelly recorded:

[T]he dash and vigor that had characterized him in his campaign in West Virginia seems to have left him altogether when placed in a position where it could be used to tremendous advantage. He exhibited an excessive caution which cramped all his better energies and practically disabled him for aggressive warfare. The record of his command of the army was one of indecision, procrastination, and inaction. . . . There is little doubt in the minds of those who have studied the history of the war of the rebellion that, but for his procrastination and excess of caution when Commander-in-Chief of the Federal Army, Richmond would have fallen in 1862. . . . [22]

There was nothing in those remarks that had not been said before and by many others, but Nelly did not need to hear it over and over again. Like Mary Lincoln, Nelly found respite in France after her husband's death. There, May met and married a French diplomat in 1893. The couple named their home in Nice for her father's greatest victory—in his eyes, at least. Nelly lived out her last days in Villa Antietam.[23]

Perhaps Nelly's failure to protect her husband's letters from publication was part of her estrangement from the United States and its painful memories of her husband's failures and rejection. Perhaps it was a continuation of her relative disengagement from her husband and his work during his life. In any event, her detachment from Prime's bastardized version of her husband's memoirs may, in fact, be most evident in the fact that Prime did not correctly print Nelly's name in either of the two places it appears in *McClellan's Own Story*. Nelly was in Europe when it was published, and one can only conclude that she did not see the manuscript to make corrections. After the title page is: "Copyright, 1886, by Ellen M. McClellan As Executrix of the last will and testament of Geo. B. McClellan, deceased." That version of her name might be excused as shorthand for "Ellen M(arcy) McClellan," an inscription Nelly herself used on the flyleaf of one of her diaries. That was not Prime's intent, however, as is evident from his second reference to her. In the introductory "Biographical Sketch of George B. McClellan by W. C. Prime, LL.D.," Prime wrote: "On the 22d May, 1860, he married Ellen Mary Marcy. . . ."[24]

Nelly died in France in 1915. Her body was later returned to the United States and buried alongside her husband, in the Riverview Cemetery in Trenton, New Jersey, where her parents are also buried. Her correct name is engraved on the headstone provided by her family: Mary Ellen McClellan. Among his many literary errors, Prime did not even get his benefactor's name right.[25]

During the war, Nelly's flawed appraisals of people and events, or, at least, her strident echoes of those of her husband, nurtured McClellan's messianic delusions and supported his mistaken judgments of his superiors. McClellan's lack of trust in Lincoln was the general's fatal mistake, and Nelly encouraged that mistrust, to her husband's detriment.

Without a doubt, though, McClellan was the architect of his own failure, just as Frémont was of his. As was the case with the Frémonts, McClellan's wife wasn't primarily responsible for her husband's bad decisions, or indecision, or delusions. But Nelly unquestionably played a role in the downward trajectory of McClellan's career and in his tarnished legacy. Nelly parroted and amplified his distorted visions of his world. She not only enabled his self-destructive thoughts and actions, she enabled the publication of his letters, damning McClellan for an eternity with his own words. While Jessie's aggressive efforts to help her husband backfired spectacularly, Nelly's contribution to her husband's downfall was the quiet, steady drip of acid on warped steel. Did she realize how badly those letters would reflect upon him? Did she realize how much more favorably they would reflect upon Lincoln, Stanton, Seward, and others that she and her husband disdained? Did she care? After all, according to McClellan, she *was* his alter ego.

PART THREE

True Faith and Allegiance

Eleanor Ewing Sherman

ELLEN SHERMAN'S CIVIL WAR

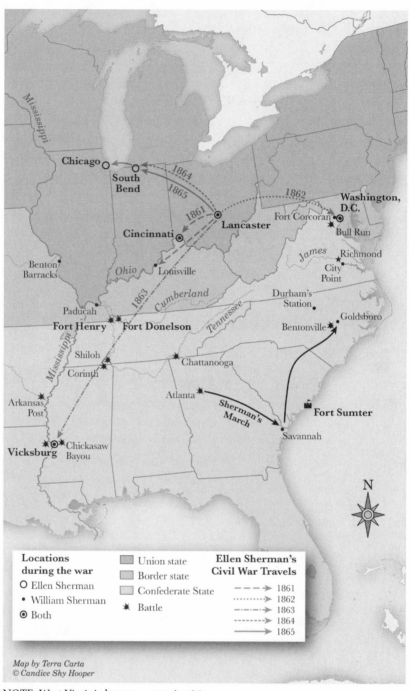

Map by Terra Carta
© Candice Shy Hooper

NOTE: West Virginia became a state in 1863.

CHAPTER 13

"It is high or low tide with us ever"

In March 1849, Abraham Lincoln completed his single two-year term as a U.S. representative, to all appearances ending the dream of a national political career that both he and his wife cherished. He returned to Springfield, Illinois, to ponder his future. Six months later, the forty-year-old father of two was a lawyer again, but his heart was not in it. Even as he sought an appointment as commissioner of the General Land Office, Lincoln was asking the secretary of the interior to find jobs for friends. His efforts on behalf of one of his acquaintances, a man named Simeon Francis, spawned a mind-boggling series of political machinations that in the end took a strange twist. Instead of accommodating Francis, the secretary offered Lincoln a job he had not sought, the position of territorial governor of Oregon. Friends urged Lincoln to take the post, which carried a generous annual salary of $3,000 and fed his keen interest in the far West. Although Lincoln felt awkward about obtaining a job for himself and not for his friend, he told an acquaintance that he had "made up his mind that he would accept the place if Mary would consent to go."[1]

Mary would not. She told her husband that she "had had enough of frontier life." She would not countenance a move to "that distant land," according to a newspaper article that appeared soon thereafter. In an effort to entice Mary to change her mind, Lincoln tried to persuade his best friend, Joshua Speed, and his wife to go west with them, but that also failed. Acceding to Mary's demands (as he so often did throughout their marriage), Lincoln reluctantly sent a telegram to the secretary:

September 27, 1849
To: Hon. Thomas Ewing
I respectfully decline Governorship of Oregon; I am still anxious that, Simeon Frances shall be secretary of that Territory.
A. Lincoln

For the rest of her life, Mary Lincoln never forgot that her firm refusal in this instance played a pivotal role in her husband's rise to the presidency. Nor did she allow her husband to forget it. According to Noah Brooks, the journalist and friend of the Lincolns during their tenure in the White House, Mary "did not fail to remind him that her advice, when he was wavering, had restrained him from 'throwing himself away' on a distant territorial governorship."[2]

Although Mary spoke often of her perspicacity, there is no record that Thomas Ewing ever reflected upon how nearly he had derailed Lincoln's career—and quite possibly the course of the Union. More probably, Lincoln's telegram was quickly forgotten in light of the many other things the secretary had on his mind at that time. In addition to his many regular duties, the secretary bent to the task of persuading the U.S. Army to grant a furlough to twenty-nine-year-old Lt. William Tecumseh Sherman, and "with other friends made every exertion" on Sherman's behalf. The ambitious young lieutenant had spent three frustrating years in California, serving in a succession of posts that utterly failed to engage his intellect or his energy. He had entirely missed combat in the Mexican War, which was the ticket to military advancement for so many of his fellow West Pointers. He was discouraged and lonely and wanted to see his family again. Despite Ewing's efforts and his influence, however, the secretary was no more successful with army brass than he had been with Lincoln. Sherman languished in San Francisco until December 1849, when some military dispatches arrived from Oregon Territory, and a sympathetic superior officer ordered Sherman to carry them to New York City.[3]

Elated at the assignment, Sherman traveled by ship, boat, and mules from San Francisco through Nicaragua to New York, and personally delivered the packet to legendary commanding general Winfield Scott. Mission accomplished, Sherman then impatiently headed to Washington. His destination was the four-story brick townhouse directly across Pennsylvania Avenue from the White House, owned by Francis Preston Blair. Secretary Ewing was renting Blair's house, and Sherman was going home.

There is no more complex or consequential web of family relationships in all of the Civil War than that surrounding William Tecumseh Sherman. At the age of nine, he became the foster son of Thomas Ewing, who had served two terms in the Senate by the first half of the nineteenth century. Ewing had also served as secretary of the treasury under presidents William Henry Harrison and John Tyler before becoming the nation's first secretary of the interior during the brief Administration of President Zachary Taylor. Sherman was also related by blood to another man who became U.S. senator from Ohio—his brother, John Sherman. At the outbreak of the Civil War, Lincoln appointed yet another of Sherman's brothers, Iowa banker Hoyt Sherman, to the post of paymaster of the U.S. Army with the grade of major. In addition, Sherman had four foster brothers, three of whom became generals in the Union Army (Thomas Jr., Hugh Boyle, and Charley Ewing). One of them (Thomas Ewing Jr.) also served as the first chief justice of the Kansas Supreme Court and later defended Dr. Samuel Mudd in the Lincoln assassination trial. Like the Blairs of Maryland, the Shermans and Ewings of Ohio combined fierce family loyalty with shrewd and powerful political influence, all of which proved invaluable to Sherman during the Civil War.

No male member of the family, though, was of more help to Sherman in the worst moments of his star-crossed life than was Eleanor Boyle Ewing. Ellen, as she was always known, was Thomas Ewing's eldest daughter, and from the age of four, she was Sherman's foster sister. Less than six months after Sherman appeared on the doorstep of Blair's house in 1850, Ellen became his wife, too.

With rare exception, Ellen Sherman has come down through history in the same sort of Manichean cast as Jessie Frémont. Ellen is portrayed as either a perfectly saintly woman of pious Catholic charity or a selfish, extravagant, nagging daddy's girl. The truth is that she was both. Both aspects of her character were sources of frustration, anger, and depression for her husband throughout their marriage. The more important truth, however, is that when Sherman experienced his worst setbacks during the Civil War, Ellen was at her very best. Even as she suffered along with him, Ellen found the strength to overcome her own despair and focused on reviving him, on reassuring him of her love and respect, on urging him to moderate his sudden swings of mood from overconfidence to self-loathing. She rebounded from the blows of fate or foe to help orchestrate their powerful family connections on his behalf. Perhaps most valuable of all, she placed each personal crisis into a spiritual framework that enabled her and her children to cope when disaster struck, relieving Sherman of some portion of his own mental distress. Ellen once observed of their lives together, "It is high or low tide with us ever." Throughout his life, Sherman chafed against his wife's tenacious attachment to her father and her fervent devotion to her religion, but when tragedy struck they proved invaluable to him. They were Ellen's staunchest allies in maintaining her family's equilibrium, and she was Lincoln's staunchest ally in sustaining one of the key architects of the Union victory.[4]

Sherman's thicket of powerful family ties was the consequence of his father's sudden, early death. Supreme Court Justice Charles Sherman died in June 1829, at the age of forty, probably of typhoid acquired in a boardinghouse where he lodged while on travel for the court. When typhoid claimed Charles Sherman, he left behind a widow and eleven children, but virtually no money. "His death left the family very poor," Sherman remembered vividly, "but friends rose up with proffers of generous care and assistance; for all the neighbors knew that mother could not maintain so large a family without help." Mary Hoyt Sherman made the emotionally difficult but financially necessary decision to find homes for most of her children with relatives and family friends. Thomas Ewing was a neighbor, a prominent lawyer, and a longtime friend. The many Sherman children had often played with the large Ewing brood. In all seasons of the year, the children of both families literally flowed through the two houses, which had been built less than a block apart because of their parents' friendship.[5]

When he learned of his close friend's death, Thomas Ewing, who was then also raising a niece and nephew in addition to his own children, did not hesitate. He walked down the hill to Mrs. Sherman's home and offered to take in one of her children. According to family legend, her third son was selected for Ewing's generosity because he was "the brightest." Shortly thereafter, Ewing walked the redheaded youngster up the hill to his new home. Fifty-six years later, that boy would recall, "I fell to the charge of the Hon. Thomas Ewing, who took me to his family, and ever after treated me as his own son."[6]

Thomas Ewing and Charles Sherman had much in common. They both loved literature. Tales of the two men's attachment to their wives and children are strikingly similar and bespeak a common love of family. Ewing was a giant of a man, large and muscular, who had earned money as a very young man for the education he craved by working at one of the most grueling trades of that era—making salt. The Kanawha River Valley of Ohio was noted for the presence of naturally occurring salt deposits; the area was often referred to as the "Kanawha salines." Rendering salt—the essential element to preserve meat and fish—from the brine of salt springs was demanding, distasteful, and dangerous. Ewing threw himself into the work that often broke his health solely because it provided the money he needed for schooling. All his life Ewing stayed in the salt business—buying and managing several saltworks—in order to feed his mind and maintain a cultivated lifestyle for his family. More than once in William Tecumseh Sherman's life, Thomas Ewing and his daughter would encourage Sherman to follow the same arduous but dependably lucrative profession. Sherman never would.

Like Thomas Ewing, Charles Sherman was a man of towering intellect, but in his case, it was touched with whimsy and creativity. The tall, spare man wrote poetry and at least one play, and he caused a stir in Lancaster, Ohio, with his admiration for an Indian warrior. Charles Sherman's most conspicuous legacy to his third son was, in fact, the name Tecumseh. Sherman wrote that his father, who served as a commissary in the War of 1812, "caught a fancy for the great chief of the Shawnee, 'Tecumseh,'" and wanted to name a son after the legendary Indian war chief and man of peace, who died a hero to his people during the War of 1812. Even though William Tecumseh Sherman always signed his letters "W. T. Sherman," his family and his closest friends always called him "Cump" or "Cumpy." It was as Cump that his new Ewing family welcomed Sherman, including pretty, intelligent four-year-old Ellen. It was as "Dearest Cump" that she addressed him in her letters, which began when he left for West Point in 1836, and continued for five decades.[7]

As remarkable as it is that Nelly McClellan, Julia Grant, and other Civil War military wives saved their husbands' letters through years of chaotic travel and living arrangements, it is even more remarkable that Sherman saved so many of his wife's letters. This was a man who was always on the march, even before the March. This was also a man who declared to Ellen at the beginning of the Civil War that he would be so busy chasing and fighting the enemy he could not possibly save her letters. Five days before Sherman led troops into combat at what became known as the First Battle of Bull Run, he warned her, "As I read [your letters] I will tear them up, for every ounce on a march tells." He lied. By the end of the war, he had carefully guarded hundreds of her letters. When hers are read together with the similar number of his that Ellen saved, their correspondence comprises perhaps the largest and most intimate view of the Civil War.[8]

While he was a cadet at West Point, Sherman's letters to Ellen show fondness that would ripen into affection between two young people who shared a family but were often apart. In 1837, seventeen-year-old Sherman wrote from West Point to nearly fourteen-year-old Ellen at St. Mary's Academy in Somerset, Ohio (the second Catholic boarding school she had attended by that age). He had "received your very welcome letter a few days since, indeed I thought you had forgotten me and the assurance that it was not the case gave me the greatest pleasure. . . . Ellen I shall expect an immediate answer to this. I am yours most affectionately, W. T. Sherman."[9]

Six years later, his affection had grown to ardor. On June 14, 1844, the young lieutenant, then stationed at Fort Moultrie in Charleston Harbor, South Carolina, indulged in a daydream about the next year. "[H]ope whispers that I might at the end of that eventful year throw off the selfish and hypocritical garb of old-Bachelorism and share my future life with one whom I have so long loved as a sister, yea more than any that now live. Is the picture either absurd or delusive?"[10]

Two weeks after that letter, Ellen wrote a long reply, in which she dreamed about them taking a trip to Europe in ten years, when as "her protector," Sherman would defend her against the slanderers of Catholics in England and help her "defy my Protestant friends." They had spent relatively little time together during the previous years. Through their letters their relationship advanced beyond that of foster siblings. They were in love.[11]

Although one modern biographer of Sherman refers to their relationship as "near-incest," the marriage of non-blood-related siblings brought together under one roof as the result of parents' remarriage or tragedy was accepted in that era, as it is now (though it was and still is often a point of gossip). Indeed, in the nineteenth century, when death rates were high, families large, and there was no public assistance, neighbors routinely reached out to help when disaster struck. Couples took nieces, nephews, neighbors, and grandchildren into their homes with little fanfare. As a result of this widespread pattern of private assistance in that era, the marriage of foster or stepsiblings was not a rare occurrence. If it was remarked upon at all, it was noted in passing, but there was no criticism attached to it. For example, the guests who accompanied the Lincolns to Ford's Theatre on the night of the president's assassination, Clara Harrison and Maj. Henry Rathbone, were stepsiblings who had recently become engaged. Its primary impact was on the principals, whose relationship to each other became more intimately complex. Ellen and Sherman could remember when they had been neighborhood playmates, before they lived under the same roof as brother and sister. They were always conscious of their own blood relatives even as they embraced their larger foster families. Throughout their lives, they treated each other as both sibling and spouse.[12]

By the end of 1844, the year of Sherman's daydream, Ellen had accepted his proposal of marriage, after he had formally asked Thomas Ewing for her hand. Marriage was years off for the couple, though, due to the poor state of his finances and her health. The meagerness of a lieutenant's salary in the antebellum U.S. Army, no matter where he was posted, was widely acknowledged. The purchasing power of Sherman's inadequate military pay declined precipitously during his posting to California. It was Sherman, relying on his West Point education, who officially verified that the metal dredged from Sutter's Mill in 1849 was, in fact, gold. Once that was established, the cost of living in California soared, and Sherman could barely live on his earnings, let alone support a wife.[13]

At the same time, Ellen was plagued with a series of illnesses. Her generally fragile health was further ravaged by persistent painful boils that afflicted her neck and by chronic shortness of breath that raised fears for her lungs. In 1845, the Catholic priest in Lancaster, Father Josue Young, reported to Bishop John Baptist Purcell in Cincinnati that "Ellen Ewing seems to be sinking into the grave." Although Father Young gave no specific description of Ellen's illness at that time, two years later, Young wrote to Bishop Purcell that Thomas Ewing's "daughter continues to suffer from scrofula."[14]

Scrofula is a form of external tuberculosis that appears as ugly, oozing, agonizing eruptions of the glands of the neck. We know now that it is a bacterial infection that can be ingested in milk from a tubercular cow, or it can be transmitted through the breath as a result of close, sustained physical contact, or through the breast milk of an infected mother. In the nineteenth century, before antibiotics, doctors prescribed a wide variety of highly toxic powders, oils, and tonics to attempt to deal with scrofula. In addition to medications administered topically and orally, doctors regularly lanced or excised the worst boils, which often drained for months and left ugly red scars.[15]

In May 1849, Ellen wrote Cump that she had just visited a doctor in Baltimore about her condition. "For my neck, which is now the seat of three ugly ulcers he gave me a nice dressing. His powder and ointment, with the frequent washings and dressings have already improved the old sore, which was gathering when you left and broke the following October. The other two sores I cannot hope to see improving for some time yet. My ear and cheek are involved in

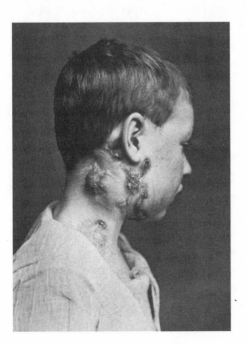

Medical photograph from 1893 of an anonymous victim of scrofula, the disease that cursed Ellen Sherman all of her life. (*Courtesy of the U.S. National Library of Medicine*)

the old and largest sore." Six years later she was "taking burdock and find it a very fine tonic. It is about the only remedy for scrofula that Dr. Powers gave me." Ellen suffered from this disfiguring disease for many years. She may have unknowingly passed it along to her own children, one of whom, she later reported to her husband, suffered from "scrofulous affection of the nostrils such as I used to have," and another whose "neck is full of glanular Swellings." Ellen suffered dreadfully from scrofula throughout her life, and in those years when she was a pretty young woman who loved to play cards and the pianoforte and who was contemplating marriage, the painful and hideous disease must have seemed an almost biblical curse. That Sherman saw past her affliction speaks volumes about his affection for her.[16]

Ellen's lungs were also a constant source of worry to her. In that era, when pulmonary tuberculosis killed countless men, women, and children, Ellen had good reason for concern. Her letters over four decades are filled with fearful references to weak lungs, bleeding lungs, tired lungs, cold on the lungs, and lung fever. To improve her health, she took cold baths and rode horses for exercise. She was never diagnosed with consumption, as pulmonary tuberculosis was called then, but her poor health made her fear it always.

So debilitating were her ailments during the years of her engagement to Sherman that she worried openly about whether she should marry at all. In January 1849, as Thomas Ewing sought the furlough that Sherman needed to escape California, Ellen filled a letter to her fiancé with her fears: "Time instead of releiving me has only proved the stern nature of the disease which afflicts me. It has also fully proved to me the folly of marriage in my case and induces me to resolve finally and *earnestly* to avoid the station for which I am rendered incapable and thus to avoid the transmission of the worst of all the ills which we inherit—disease—Am I not sensible? Am I not reasonable?"[17]

Sherman, who never believed she was as ill as she thought she was, dismissed her doubts. Fifteen months later, they were married.[18]

Because Ellen had not convinced Sherman to become a Catholic, they could not be married in the Church, to her deep chagrin. To her delight, however, the president of Georgetown University traveled four miles downtown from the Jesuit college on the northeastern bank of the Potomac River to Blair's house across from the Executive Mansion to perform the ceremony. Sherman was then thirty years old, Ellen twenty-six, and her wedding day was one of the highlights of the city's social season. Dressed in a beautiful silk-and-lace gown, the petite, slender, dark-haired Ellen carried her bouquet in a silver nosegay holder given to her by Henry Clay. Sherman later recalled, "The marriage ceremony was attended by a large and distinguished company, embracing Daniel Webster, Henry Clay, T[homas] H[art] Benton, President Zachary Taylor, and all his cabinet." With her brother Philemon (Sherman's lifelong best friend), they headed off on a honeymoon that encompassed Baltimore and Philadelphia, the beginning of a nearly forty-year union. Nine months later, their first child, Maria Ewing Sherman (Minnie) was born.[19]

Theirs was not a fairy-tale marriage of deathless passion that one reads in the letters of Jessie Frémont or George McClellan. Rather, the Shermans' letters speak of a steady development of deep devotion, solid commitment, and abiding concern for the welfare of each other and of their children. It was a relationship that withstood strong differences of opinion. Ellen Sherman did not hesitate to disagree with her husband on family matters, financial transactions, and sometimes even on his military decisions. She also nagged him regularly and stridently about his refusal to join the Catholic Church. In fact, although the Shermans' antebellum correspondence is filled with affection and detailed news of their lives and their children, it is also freighted with dissension. The recurring themes are religion, money, housing, and Sherman's choice of jobs.

Religion was a sticking point early in their relationship. Thomas Ewing's wife was a leading force in establishing a Catholic church in Lancaster (with significant help from her Presbyterian husband's money), and she inspired and nurtured Ellen's devotion to Catholicism. Once the church was established, mother and daughter rarely missed a morning's walk to the church to decorate the altar; Ellen forever cherished those memories. By the time she was old enough to know she was in love with Sherman, Ellen was a devout Catholic, her religion inseparable from the rest of her life. In the letter to Sherman, when she daydreamed about traveling together to Europe to learn how to defy Protestants, Ellen felt under siege. Long-standing religious tensions between Protestants and Catholics were exacerbated by the economic impact of the flood of poor Irish Catholic immigrants seeking jobs and housing in the teeming industrial cities of the Northeast. In 1844, emotions flared into violence, and a riot in Philadelphia resulted in thirteen deaths. In another letter, Ellen complained about the Protestants: "taunt me they do now with everything, in every manner. Not an hour can be passed in their company (since the riots produced an excitement) during which you hear not some slur cast upon the Papists."[20]

Ellen was well versed in Catholic doctrine and firmly believed in it, something that Sherman simply could not embrace. In 1842, he wrote Ellen from

Mobile, Alabama: "I cannot with due reflection attribute to minor points of doctrine or form the importance usually attached to them. I believe in good works rather than faith, and believe them to constitute the basis of true religion both as revealed in Scripture and taught by the experience of all ages, and common sense." That was the line he hewed to his entire life, but Ellen never stopped trying to convert him.[21]

Sherman may have felt justified in refusing his wife's entreaties because his beliefs would not allow otherwise, and also because he had always before him the example of his foster father. Until the very last days of his life, Thomas Ewing remained stolidly Protestant in the face of his wife's and her clergy's concerted efforts. As one example of their collaboration, in 1848, Father Young wrote to Bishop Purcell: "Mr. Thomas Ewing's conversion is a matter of proper solicitude on the part of his lady and family. They believe that Purcell can further it." Ewing's persistent refusals to convert must have been known to his whole family, including Sherman. Sherman may have had another reason as well. In his memoirs, when he wrote about his own father's death, he said it "was universally deplored; more especially by his neighbors in Lancaster, and by the Society of Freemasons, of which he was the High-Priest of Arch Chapter No. 11." The historical enmity between Catholics and Masons may have led Sherman to honor his father's memory by remaining outside the Catholic Church.[22]

Whatever his reason, Sherman consistently rebuffed every attempt his wife made to convert him. In the main, though, Ellen's religious pleadings carried more warmth and less bite during Sherman's most stressful war years. "You must not give me credit for loving & respecting you as I do," she wrote Sherman in March 1862. "You only want Christianity to make you perfect & that you will have for my unceasing prayers for faith to you will be answered."[23]

Money, too, was a problem for the Shermans before the Civil War. Their financial conflicts were often inextricably bound to their conflicts over where to live and what profession Sherman would follow. Ellen's dream job for Sherman was manager of her father's saltworks, so the family could live in Lancaster. Not surprisingly, Sherman had entirely different plans for himself: "I have adopted the Army as my profession," he told her in 1839, while he was at West Point. Three years later, when she asked again if he would leave the army, he wrote to her from Fort Moultrie, South Carolina: "[N]ot a day passes without my meeting some old fellow who once was an officer but [resigned] and all with very few exceptions say it was the most foolish act of their life." He concluded,

"Believing myself similarly constituted, I intend of course to wait a more auspicious moment than the present to abandon my present life." When Sherman did decide to "abandon" the army, it was because his military pay could not support his growing family and Ellen's high standards for their home, their clothing, their education. Rather than go to the saltworks, though, he went into banking in San Francisco—not at all what Ellen had in mind. During the eleven years of their marriage before the Civil War, Ellen unsuccessfully tried twice more to urge him into the saltworks. It was a recurring source of tension in their marriage.[24]

Their discussions about money, too, had a sharper tone at times before and after the war than during it. "You want to know what I have done with the $500 balance on the California money," wrote Ellen to Sherman in early 1861. "You say you are entitled to that much confidence. My bank book my receipted bills my notes and every thing else that is mine is at all times ready for your inspection & if I withold any confidence ever it is that you may not be worried or that I may not seem to thwart your inclinations." That was just the warm-up. "You say if I have 'made up my mind to remain in L[ancaster] no matter what fate attends you, you ought to know it.' To one who has within the last ten years gone with you to St. Louis, New Orleans, San Francisco & Leavenworth & during that time has had to endure the sickness & pain of bearing & giving birth to five children this is rather unkind. I will not give the insinuation the weight of a serious accusation by denying it." She then proceeded to give him a two-year accounting of her expenses for the family—to the penny. It could not have helped Sherman's humor to note that one of her largest expenses by far was "The Church $250."[25]

Ellen was fiercely independent when it came to what she considered "her" money, much of which came from the sale of various pieces of property that her father had bought as investments for her, as he did for all of his children. In early 1860, Ellen wrote to her father protesting that her brother "Tom writes me that he has made Cump an offer for my property [in Leavenworth, Kansas], but he must be aware that Cump cannot sell what is mine, and moreover, that I would not trust to Cump's judgement implicitly, where the sale of property is concerned."[26]

All of her life, Ellen held independent opinions on a broad range of issues, and she held her ground, even when Sherman disagreed with her. In August 1862, she asked her husband to sit for a photograph and send copies to her. Ellen knew he hated that sort of thing, but she instructed him "to submit with the best grace you can—Remember there never was a hero that was not under cow of his wife. Father says Napoleon would have died successful & prosperous had he not exempt[ed] himself from this great natural law."[27]

Her spirited independence was not limited to private words or acts. Upon hearing news from Italy in 1870 of the imprisonment of Pope Pius IX in the Vatican by the Italian government, Ellen hung the flag of the papal state, draped in black crepe, from the front of their Washington, D.C., home in a defiant and very public protest. The Italian minister in Washington quickly contacted Sherman, then lieutenant general of the United States Army, and protested, but to no avail. Sherman acknowledged that he did live at that address, but that he was powerless to alter the situation. Historian John F. Marszalek termed the Sherman marriage "a contentious union," and while full of love, it was that, too, indeed.[28]

CHAPTER 14

"You will never be happy in this world unless you go into the Army again"

It is a tired cliché that Sherman failed at everything until he joined with Grant to win the Civil War, but even tired clichés hold an element of truth. As Sherman pursued careers in the army, banking, land surveying, law, and the streetcar business, Ellen and their children often followed him. She made enormous but unenthusiastic efforts to set up housekeeping in San Francisco, California; St. Louis, Missouri; and Leavenworth, Kansas. Nevertheless, whenever she could, which was often, she returned to Lancaster, the spot in the universe she loved most. Living in her childhood home, she could save money, enjoy ample help with the children, and be near her beloved parents. Throughout her life, she basked in the warmth of "Ewingville," as Lancaster was referred to within the family. A favorite family story was Sherman's claim that no matter where in the country they were, he could blindfold his wife, spin her around three times, and when she stopped, "*still blindfolded,*" she would always be facing in the direction of Lancaster.[1]

For Sherman, though, Lancaster held no charms. It was the place of his birth, but in that town he saw himself as a cast-off—a vagabond, an urchin—the son of a failed, dead man, living on the charity of a vital and successful man. He admired Thomas Ewing and sought his respect his whole life, but he strove to succeed outside the shadow cast by the giant.

Near the end of 1859, after a series of civilian business failures alternately spectacular (on the heels of two bank failures not of his making, he refused a third banking job because he was, he said, "the Jonah of banking") and banal (he utterly fizzled in his first court appearance as a lawyer), Sherman tried to reenter the U.S. Army as a quartermaster. Instead, he wound up as the leader of an institution of higher learning. As superintendent of the newly founded, but not yet formed, Louisiana State Seminary of Learning and Military Academy (predecessor of Louisiana State University), Sherman believed he had finally found his true calling. He threw himself into the work of completing the un-finished campus (including barracks and school buildings), hiring teachers, organizing curricula, securing books and supplies, and recruiting cadets for the school, which was located in a remote and relatively unpopulated area of central Louisiana, called Pineville, near the state capital of Alexandria.[2]

Sherman also designed a house to be built for his family on the grounds of the academy, and it was still under construction in the spring of 1860. The Sher-mans had been apart much of the time since thirty-six-year-old Ellen had given birth to Eleanor Mary "Ellie" Sherman in September 1859. When she wrote to her husband on May 1, 1860, Ellen revealed the passion they shared for each other. That day was their tenth anniversary, and after she told him she loved him more than ever, she wrote: "[Were] it not for one fear I would leave the children here, in good hands, and go down before the very hot weather comes on, to make you a visit. You can guess what that fear is I suppose when I tell you it is concerning myself & not a fear of yellow fever. If you think it will do to risk having another baby so soon I wish you would approve of my going down."[3]

But soon after that, the children fell ill with scarlet fever, so she could not make the trip.

Ellen had two strong reservations about moving the family to Louisiana. Yellow fever was a deadly and ever-present risk in the Deep South. In addi-tion, Sherman had warned her that she could not expect to find white servants to hire. Although she would move to a slave state, Ellen made it clear that she would not countenance owning any slaves. "I never could consent to buy or sell a slave," she wrote her husband on June 5, 1860, "so if I am to be consulted we never can own property of that sort but must depend upon labor of some other kind." Her concerns were short-lived, however: Louisiana was squarely in the anti-Lincoln/pro-slavery column, and its secession was imminent.

Appalled at Louisiana's impending disunion, Sherman formally tendered his letter of resignation to the Academy, to become effective whenever the state left the Union. That happened on January 26, 1861, but an intervening act by the Louisiana governor prompted Sherman to accelerate his own timetable. Six days before Louisiana officially seceded, Sherman wrote to U.S. Army Gen. George Mason Graham, one of the founders of the Academy, to explain his decision:

> I was waiting as patiently as a red-headed person could, for the official acts of the convention charged with the destiny of Louisiana, when tidings reached me that Governor Moore had caused the seizure of the forts and ar-

senals. . . . For this I see no justification and feel compelled to announce my determination [to resign]. . . . My own opinion is that Lincoln will be installed in office—that Congress will not repeal the Union. . . . The consequence is inevitable—war, and ugly war too.[4]

Although he could write with ironic detachment about himself in the midst of the unfolding political and personal crisis, the ugliness of the coming war struck hard at his emotional personality. When he did finally leave the military academy nearly a month later, Sherman addressed the corps of cadets with feeling. He firmly shook hands with the young men, so many of them secessionist firebrands whom he feared he might later encounter on the battlefield (and did). He could not, however, summon the words to say farewell to them or to the professors he had hired, including David French Boyd, who remained a close, lifelong friend. "You are all here!" he uttered in a choked voice, pointing to his heart.[5]

The relief Ellen felt at avoiding life in Louisiana was only barely repressed in the face of her husband's despair at leaving the first civilian job he truly loved. On January 16, 1861, she wrote to him from Lancaster that her father would welcome him into the salt business but then discussed another career possibility, based on his brother's likely future. "It is thought now that [Ohio's U.S. Sen. Salmon P.] Chase will go into the Cabinet and John Sherman into the Senate," she wrote. "John can easily procure you a high position in the Army if you desire it." Sherman's letter to Ellen four days later dismissed thoughts of returning to the military. "I feel no desire to follow an army necessarily engaged in Civil War," he wrote. With war on the near horizon, Ellen recognized her husband's innate attachment to military life. "Now I have for some time past been convinced that you will never be happy in this world unless you go into the Army again," she wrote on January 29. "I will own that I am less reluctant to have you go into the Army again because I believe that if war should rage you will be impatient of any other employment & join some volunteer regiment." She proceeded to apply some balm to the wounds that he had suffered in his Louisiana venture. "I am proud and happy in the knowledge that you have so promptly declared your disapproval of their rebellion," she declared, "& that you have so distinctly announced your opinion & position in the terrible state of affairs."[6]

Sherman's reentry into the army was anything but smooth. In February 1861, as Ellen predicted, the Ohio Legislature elected John Sherman to the U.S. Senate to fill the seat vacated by Treasury Secretary Chase. Sherman was then still in Louisiana, waiting for the much-needed $500 he was owed by the Seminary.

When John urged Sherman to accompany him to his swearing-in ceremony in Washington, D.C., he agreed to go. John planned to take Sherman to meet Lincoln, hoping the newly inaugurated president would be impressed enough by his brother's knowledge and insight into the situation in the South to offer him a senior military post. The two Sherman brothers visited the president in mid-March.

Whether Lincoln found William Tecumseh Sherman impressive is not recorded, but Sherman was certainly unimpressed by Lincoln, whom he concluded was dangerously naive. The president made a typically wry response to Sherman's heated warning about the South's readiness for war. "I guess we'll manage to keep house," said Lincoln, and Sherman's frustration boiled. Walking away from the Executive Mansion, Sherman blazed at his brother, "d—ning politicians generally" and warning that "the country was sleeping on a volcano that might burst forth at any moment." He recalled that "John begged me to be patient," but Sherman was exasperated and humiliated that his military skills and his sacrifice in leaving his job in Louisiana for the Union were not appreciated. In a letter to his dear friend David French Boyd, still teaching at the Louisiana military academy, he said, "I acted with great energy, went to Washington, satisfied my self that Lincoln was organizing his administration on pure party principles, concluded that it was no place for me who profess to love and venerate my whole country and not a mere Fraction—and forthwith to Lancaster. . . ."[7]

There, Sherman found a letter from his friend Henry Turner, the man who had previously invited him into the banking business. This time, Sherman avoided the Ewing saltworks by accepting Turner's offer to be president of the Fifth Street Railroad in St. Louis. It was a far less grand enterprise than its name, the term "railroad" then encompassing passenger wagon cars pulled by horses, and the salary was less than what Ellen would spend, he knew. But the job had one principal advantage: it was not in Lancaster. Conspicuously washing his hands of the developing national crisis for the time being, he moved Ellen, who was pregnant again, and their five children from Ohio to Missouri.

Over the following weeks, Ellen skillfully, though somewhat reluctantly, settled into a new home in St. Louis with the children, while Sherman brought financial and administrative order to the railroad company. The turmoil in the country—amplified in half-slave/half-free Missouri, as the Frémonts were to learn when they arrived in late July—continued to mount. With Ellen's encouragement, John Sherman continued his behind-the-scenes efforts in Washington to engage his brother in defense of the nation. In early April, Postmaster General Montgomery Blair, acting on behalf of the president, approached Sherman about a clerkship in the War Department that he promised would quickly lead to Sherman's appointment as assistant secretary of war. Sherman staunchly refused, unwilling to pull up his family's roots again so soon. Then, shortly after the attack on Fort Sumter in mid-April, Rep. and Gen. Frank Blair (who, Sherman told John, was regarded as "Lincolns Vice Roy" in Missouri) met with Sherman in St. Louis, offering the post of brigadier general and promising to put him in charge of the state's volunteer militia. He refused that, too.[8]

Outwardly unmoved, Sherman was torn inside. He was a soldier, even as he stood passively at a street corner in St. Louis, clocking his streetcars to check on their timeliness. There was a war going on, and he wanted to be in the fight—but only on his own terms. Sherman disdained the 75,000-man three-month volunteer army, which Lincoln's initial call had hastily assembled in the immediate aftermath of the firing on Fort Sumter. To Sherman's way of thinking, their numbers were too small, their time too short, and their lack of discipline, training, and commitment foretold trouble in camp and worse under fire. In addition, he believed that he personally deserved better from an administration that was handing out commands as political rewards to men who neither had the training nor had made the kind of sacrifice for their country that he already had. In his own mind, his reasoning for refusing the Blair brothers' offers was sound.[9]

Apparently, though, his refusals raised questions in other minds about whether the time he had spent in the South had weakened his allegiance to the Union. It had not; if anything, he was more fiercely loyal to the Union, even as he was "d—ning" those Northern politicians whom he believed were allowing it to be destroyed. By early May, however, "even my best friends were uneasy as to my political status." In an effort to make his feelings clear, he wrote on May 8 to Secretary of War Simon Cameron to explain his situation in light of Lincoln's recent call for volunteers to serve three years. The emphasis in the letter is his:

Dear Sir:

I hold myself now, as always prepared to serve my country in the capacity for which I was trained. I did not and will not volunteer for *three months*, because I cannot throw my family on the cold charity of the world. But for the *three-years* call, made by the President, an officer can prepare his command and do good service.... Should my services be needed, the records of the War Department will enable you to designate the station in which I can render most service.[10]

The day after he mailed that letter, Sherman's grave concerns about volunteer militia were played out before his own eyes, and nearly fatally for his family. Violence flared when Brig. Gen. Nathaniel Lyon of the Missouri Home Guards (the man who took the job that Sherman had refused) seized weapons and munitions from the hands of the St. Louis arsenal's chief, a Southern sympathizer. Sherman, his six-year-old son Willy, and two of Ellen's brothers were caught in the cross fire. Ellen vividly described the deadly chain of events in a May 11 letter to her father:

> They were in front of a line of Government troops and between the two parties when unexpectedly to them the firing commenced. Charley knocked Willy down instantly & then fell on the ground himself, covering Willy from the fire. Cump's first impulse was to run with Willy but when he found Charley had him down he too fell on the ground & the two completely sheltered Willy. Shots whistled past them and, as you will learn from the papers, quite a number were killed among them several little children.

In that letter, Ellen also told her father, "The papers say that Cump is to be offered a good position in the regular service," she wrote. "If offered a suitable position, he will instantly accept it, in which case we will all be back in Lancaster again."[11]

A week after the bloody St. Louis arsenal incident, which, coincidentally, Ulysses S. Grant also witnessed, Sherman received the formal offer of command in the regular army, with the grade of colonel. As Ellen had happily predicted, he accepted, and she and the children headed back to Lancaster. Sherman was ordered to report to Washington, and by the end of June, he had an active command—the 3rd Brigade of the 1st Division of the U.S. Army, camped at Fort Corcoran, just across the Potomac River from Georgetown. Sherman diligently applied himself to his duties.

For good reason, though, Sherman despaired of drilling his volunteer troops into competent soldiers in time for it to matter: battle was imminent. Confederate Gen. Pierre Gustave Toutant Beauregard and his army were camped thirty miles to the west of Washington at Manassas Junction near a creek named Bull Run. Union General-in-Chief Scott and commander of the Department of Northeastern Virginia, Gen. Irvin McDowell, had grave reservations about sending masses of raw troops into combat. Lincoln understood their fears but reckoned the rebel troops were equally untrained. He could not withstand the political imperatives of the moment or ignore the fact that the three-month enlistments were about to expire. He ordered McDowell to attack.

Marching west from Fort Corcoran on July 19 toward certain battle, Sherman found himself in precisely the situation he had strenuously attempted to avoid. He was in command of forces overwhelmingly made up of brand-new volunteers, many of them "*three months*" men near the end of their service. After initial Federal success on the field, the tide of battle reversed into a stunning Confederate victory. Sherman's men first retreated to Centreville, where they were ordered to stop and rest. Then everything came undone, and "they fell into disorder." Blindly, his men fled eastward, racing away from an enemy who was not in pursuit. Into Fort Corcoran and onto the city of Washington, the army bled a blue river of scared, dazed, wounded, hungry, angry men whose youthful dreams of glory had been cruelly smashed. Sherman was appalled. "I had read of retreats before, have seen the noise and confusion of crowds of men at fires and shipwrecks, but nothing like this," he wrote to Ellen in one of several lengthy letters describing the battle. "The proud army characterized as the most extraordinary on earth has turned out the most ordinary," he wrote her on July 28. "So it seems to be true that the North is after all pure bluster."[12]

There was no bluster in Sherman, however. Five days before he wrote that letter, one of his ninety-day wonders claimed the right to leave Sherman's camp at Fort Corcoran because his three-month enlistment had expired. Sherman declared to the man that his departure without signed orders "will be mutiny, and I will shoot you like a dog!" Later that afternoon, the president arrived at his camp with Secretary Seward as part of Lincoln's larger effort to boost morale within the army after the disaster. In the course of Lincoln's visit, the same soldier pressed forward from the crowd and presented his complaint. "I have a cause of grievance," he told the president. "This morning I went to speak to Colonel Sherman, and he threatened to shoot me." Lincoln knew no specifics of the soldier's charge, but in the short time they had been together that day, Sherman had impressed him with his seriousness of purpose. Pretending to be mortified, the president advised the soldier, in a clearly audible whisper, "Well, if I were you, and he threatened to shoot, I would not trust him, for I believe he would do it." The crush of troops roared in laughter, which Lincoln and Sherman shared. As they rode off together, Sherman hastened to justify his actions to the president, but the commander in chief shrugged off the colonel's explanation. As Sherman recalled, Lincoln assured him, "Of course I didn't know any thing about it, but I thought you knew your own business best."[13]

Carte de visite of Gen. William
Tecumseh Sherman, c. 1862,
when he was forty-two years
old. (*Author's collection*)

During that short visit, Sherman's earlier harsh opinion of the president
was altered by the brief remarks Lincoln made to his troops. Sherman later
described Lincoln's impact on the soldiers' morale that day: "That speech
reached every heart, nerved every arm, and made stern patriots out of timid
and wavering men." Although Sherman mentioned the president's visit only
in passing to Ellen in his July 24 letter ("Yesterday the President and Mr.
Seward visited me, and I slipped over for a few minutes last night to see your
father."), it is likely that Sherman elaborated on the visit with Ellen when they
were next together, since she specifically referenced that encounter in her later
conversation with Lincoln.[14]

In their brief time together that day, Lincoln would have absorbed much
about Colonel Sherman: his dedication to the task of forging an army from
civilians and his sense of duty. Soon after that visit, Sherman received surprising but welcome word that he had been made a brigadier general of volunteers,
along with a number of other colonels who, in his words, "had shared in the
common stampede" from Bull Run. Lincoln later claimed personal credit for

putting his name on the list. Though Sherman and his fellow officers had been "trembling lest we should be held personally accountable for the disastrous result of the battle," the figurative ax fell only on McDowell. He was out, and McClellan was in, "summoned from the West," wrote Sherman, but "[i]nstead of coming over the river, as we expected, he took a house in Washington, and only came over from time to time to have a review or inspection." Although Sherman disapproved of McClellan's remote management style, he believed the choice of the new commander of the Department of Northeastern Virginia (soon to become the Army of the Potomac) "at the time was fully justified by his high reputation in the army and country." From Sherman's memoirs, it is clear that he and McClellan established an easy relationship at the outset and could have enjoyed a good working relationship—for a time, at least. Inevitably, though, Sherman would have begun to chafe under the polished McClellan's pomp and immobility, and Little Mac would have begun to resent the tall, energetic Westerner's penchant for movement and his powerful political ties. A near-certain clash with McClellan could only have ended badly for Sherman.[15]

Fortunately, the new brigadier general was soon removed from ongoing duty directly under McClellan's watchful eye in the East. Of course, at that time, no one knew what the future held for Sherman. The fact that he was preserved to go on to success and glory in the western theater was due to Brig. Gen. Robert Anderson, although certainly no one could have predicted it. Anderson, the North's hero of Fort Sumter, selected Sherman, who had served under him in South Carolina nearly twenty years earlier, to accompany him west on a new assignment. In hindsight, Anderson's choice led to his subordinate's lasting fame. In the near term, however, it wrought disaster on Sherman. For Ellen, it proved her finest hour in the Civil War.

CHAPTER 15

"releive my husband from the suspicions now resting on him"

Sherman's date with disaster began not long after his Fort Corcoran encounter with Lincoln. Despite Gen. Robert Anderson's reluctance to assume another major command after Fort Sumter due to his fragile health, he agreed to take responsibility for the vast and hostile swath of the western region, which included the crucial border states of Kentucky and Tennessee. As a means of easing his burden of command, the Administration offered Anderson his choice of brigadier generals. Apparently Anderson favorably recalled Sherman's service under him at Fort Moultrie in the 1840s; when Sherman met with him at the Willard Hotel in mid-August 1861, Anderson "explained that he wanted me as his right hand."[1]

Sherman recalled Anderson's description of his mission as a two-step, defensive-offensive affair: first, to secure Kentucky firmly within the Union and then to move with force into eastern Tennessee to support Union sympathizers there. Sherman knew he and Anderson faced a daunting task, and as Anderson's "right hand," he worried that that task would fall to him. Unlike McClellan, who greeted every promotion as proof of divinely ordained superiority, Sherman feared rather than relished a promotion to command of any army. As was his manner, he quickly sought to insure it would not happen. As was also his manner, he did so bluntly and to the commander in chief himself, which produced one of the most oft-repeated Lincoln quips of the war. Sherman recalled in his memoirs: "In this interview with Mr. Lincoln I also explained to him my extreme desire to serve in a subordinate capacity, and in no event to be left in a superior command. He promised me this with promptness, making the jocular remark that his chief trouble was to find places for the too many generals who wanted to be at the head of affairs, to command armies, etc."[2]

While Sherman prepared to leave Washington, Ellen, unaware of his change in orders, sought to visit him there. She had given birth to their third daughter,

Rachel, soon after he had left for Washington in June. Now she proposed to travel from Lancaster "with baby & nurse" and set up temporary housekeeping for them in Washington. "I feel I must have the satisfaction of seeing you once more before our troops make any advance movement," she pleaded. In response to an earlier request, he had told her, "I have as much as I can do to keep my officers and men from living in Washington, and shall not set a bad example." He would not do as McClellan did.[3]

But a subsequent telegram from Sherman to a delighted Ellen asked her to meet him in Cincinnati at the end of the month. There, she spent a week with her husband in the Burnet House hotel, while he and Generals Anderson and George Thomas discussed the situation facing the Department of the Cumberland. After her visit, she returned to Lancaster and settled back into life with her active brood in her parents' comfortable home, not knowing when she would see him again. In a letter to her husband on September 21, she expressed her pleasure that he was assigned to "Kentucky & Tennessee [rather] than into Missouri." She foresaw good things for her husband and his "band of patriots," as she called his men.[4]

All too soon, however, Sherman's worst fears were realized. Anderson's health swiftly and completely failed. On October 8, Anderson's "right hand" was forced to take the Department's tiller against his will, notwithstanding Lincoln's earlier assurances. Sherman telegraphed to the War Department his desire "to remain in a subordinate position" and shortly "received reassurance that Brigadier-General Buell would soon arrive from California and would be sent to relieve me."[5]

As Sherman settled reluctantly into command, his concerns about his small, poorly trained, and poorly armed Union force escalated into overwhelming fears of destruction by what he incorrectly believed were more numerous enemy troops. Defending Kentucky, the first phase of Sherman's mission, seemed far beyond the ability of his few troops, and he requested more. Then he was even more overwhelmed when Adj. Gen. Lorenzo Thomas inquired about the timing of the second phase of his mission, the invasion of Tennessee. Sherman's stream of letters and telegrams to Washington became a flood. His demands for more men, more arms, more everything began to alarm his superiors. One telegram, addressed directly to Lincoln, ended with the sharp command: "Answer." In mid-October, Secretary of War Simon Cameron and Adj. Gen. Lorenzo Thomas decided to hear Sherman's concerns firsthand as they returned to Washington from Missouri after investigating charges of corruption and incompetence swirling around Frémont.[6]

On October 16, 1861, Sherman met Cameron and Thomas at the train station and accompanied them to the Galt House hotel in Louisville, where he had established his headquarters. Sherman looked askance at the clutch of civilians in the secretary's entourage, but Cameron assured Sherman that all of them could be trusted because they were "all friends, all members of my family." After discussing other matters, he turned his attention to Sherman and insisted that he "speak . . . freely and without restraint" about the military situation in Kentucky. Despite his unease, Sherman had no choice but to comply. He first locked the door of the room and then spread a map of the United States on a table. Pointing out the relatively shorter military fronts that Frémont and McClellan each had to protect and stating the numbers of troops under their commands, Sherman then calculated that on an equivalent basis of men-per-mile of front, he would need 60,000 troops for a sufficient defense and 200,000 to launch an offensive into Tennessee that would cripple the Confederacy. He also railed against the appalling shortage of arms for his men and the poor quality of those they had been issued.[7]

Even had Sherman spoken in the most calm and deliberate manner, his numbers would have shocked anyone in authority at that time. Normally excitable by nature and fueled by a string of sleepless nights and nonstop caffeine and cigars, Sherman was anything but calm and deliberate. Sherman's outward appearance mirrored his inner turmoil. Over the preceding month, he had become increasingly anxious. In the immediate wake of Cameron's visit, however, Sherman seemed confident that his demands would be addressed. On October 26, he wrote his brother in Washington that he was "glad that the secretary remembered my remark that to accomplish the only purposes for which Kentucky can be used there should be a force here of 200,000 men."[8]

Sherman could have expected that his description of the dangers and the manpower needs in Kentucky would be reported to President Lincoln, but he could not have imagined that it would be reported in the newspapers as well. Two weeks after the Louisville meeting, General Thomas's report on Frémont's Department and his interview with Sherman appeared in the New York Tribune, and other newspapers around the country quickly reprinted it. The report was highly critical of Frémont's management and of the general personally. By contrast, Thomas did not personally disparage Sherman, though he cast a shadow over Sherman's perception of possibilities in that region. He wrote that Sherman "gave a gloomy picture of affairs in Kentucky," citing Sherman's claim that he could not recruit sufficient troops from either the young, who were Confederate firebrands, or from the old, who were Unionists wary of declaring their allegiance. Thomas recounted that "On being asked the question, what force he deemed necessary, [Sherman] promptly replied 200,000 men," but he made no mention that Sherman had calculated that big round number with an offensive move into Tennessee in mind. Although the report raised questions about Sherman, it did not indict the brigadier general's leadership. The adjutant general's account was far harder on Frémont than it was on Sherman. Yet, Sherman suffered terribly in the immediate aftermath of the report's wide publication.[9]

Despite Cameron's reassurances to Sherman at the Galt House, one of the secretary's "family" in the room that day was a newspaper reporter. When *New York Tribune* correspondent Samuel Wilkeson returned east and wrote his story, he eagerly embellished Thomas's report with his own withering eyewitness account of Sherman's nervous state of mind. The reporter also included tales of the general's month-long feverish demands for more arms and more troops, including, according to Wilkeson, three anxious telegrams sent to Washington in one day. Sherman had never been popular with the press; it seemed he went out of his way from the first to irritate correspondents and editors. He denounced what he called their treachery and treason in printing information on troop movements, and he banned reporters from his camps. Though Sherman was rough with them, newspaper correspondents were somewhat circumspect in criticizing Sherman early in the war. Indeed, only five days before Sherman's meeting with Cameron, a *New York Times* correspondent's regret at Anderson's departure was tempered by his confidence that "the Department will not suffer by the change" because Sherman "performs his business with a Napoleonic dispatch." Once the *Tribune* printed Thomas's report with Wilkeson's criticism of Sherman, however, offended reporters jettisoned their journalistic inhibitions, and Sherman became their favorite punching bag.[10]

Angry, frustrated, depressed, and humiliated, Sherman shrank from the storm bursting over his head. As the days passed, he continued to withdraw into himself. "God Knows that I think of you and our dear Children all the time," Sherman wrote to Ellen on November 1, "and that I would that we might hide ourselves in some quiet corner of the world."[11]

Ellen did not want to hide. She wanted to fight. Her keenest weapons were her intelligence, her determination, and her family, especially her father. While Jessie Benton, Nelly Marcy, and Julia Dent were all especially close to their fathers, the bond between Ellen and Thomas Ewing was as close as a father-daughter relationship could be. True, Ellen adopted her mother's Catholic faith with a fervor that increased steadily through her life. Nevertheless, her

Presbyterian father was her lodestone, pulling her back to Lancaster time after time. Father and daughter corresponded regularly and lengthily all their lives; their love for each other was manifest. When her father died, Ellen wrote to his sister, her aunt Jane: "My best friend has gone from earth."[12]

At the age of fifteen in 1839, Ellen had journeyed with Thomas Ewing to Washington, where he had legal business and where he enrolled her in a Catholic boarding school. Decades later, Ellen recalled that her father took her to a dentist just across the street from the White House, who immediately determined that four of Ellen's molars "must come out." Her father then told her "he would go & get me some books to take with me to the Academy to read during recreation hours." Ellen wrote: "I did not realize then that Father's sudden desire to get me books was a ruse and he went because he could not bear to see me undergo such pain. . . ."[13]

If that episode illustrated that Thomas Ewing could not bear to see his daughter in agony, neither could Ellen bear to see her father in pain, no matter the cost to her or her husband. When she and Sherman moved to California in 1853 to pursue his banking career, Thomas Ewing convinced her to leave their firstborn, Minnie, with him and his wife in Lancaster, to ease their separation from Ellen. Ellen agreed, prevailing over her husband's opposition to the plan. Ellen, Sherman, and their second child, Lizzie, who was barely a year old, made the same dangerous journey to California that Jessie had made. Ellen bore another child in San Francisco, William "Willy" Tecumseh Sherman Jr., but even with two young children to occupy her, she missed her oldest daughter and her parents. In 1855, Ellen left three-year-old Lizzie and one-year-old Willy in the care of Sherman and a nurse in their brand-new home in the city and undertook the arduous journey back to Lancaster alone, ostensibly to bring Minnie back to live with them. Ellen's trip from the West to the East Coast was certainly worse in one major respect than Jessie's arduous trip six years earlier. On the first leg of Ellen's travel, from San Francisco to Panama aboard the steamer *Golden Age,* she was jolted awake at two o'clock in the morning of April 29 "by the grating, the crashing of the vessel's bottom upon a coral reef," Ellen wrote to Sherman later that day. By all accounts, she conducted herself with calm dignity as passengers and crew awaited rescue by a passing ship. Ellen continued her trip by a newly built railroad across the isthmus, boarded another vessel, and sailed around Florida to New York City.[14]

Her brother Charley greeted her at the pier with news that Ellen conveyed in a letter to Sherman from that city, even before she went to Lancaster. "Charley says that Father could not live without Minnie, so we must give her up during his lifetime," she wrote in an oddly detached vein. "The probability is we will have a large family and it would seem the more selfish to refuse one to Father. Do not ask me to take her away from him—I know you are too kind to insist upon it." Unlike Jessie, who sided with her husband against her father, Ellen often chose to disappoint her husband when forced to choose between him and Thomas Ewing. From 1861 to 1865, however, Ellen's closeness to her father proved an advantage to Sherman when he most needed help in dealing with military difficulties and mental demons, especially when the newspapers attacked him in that first winter of the war.[15]

In the fall of 1861, Ellen had become aware of her husband's military concerns, even before publication of the Thomas report, through his progressively fearful letters home. On September 21, she wrote that she still had "hope that no harm will befall you and that our cause will conquer in spite of the numbers against us." Her husband's spirits had not improved by late September, when she wrote from Lancaster that she was "sorry to find you so desponding. I have more hope than you and I cannot but believe that you will lead your army, be it great or small not to death but to victory." In a further effort to lift his spirits, she told him, "Two regiments came down on Saturday. Whilst they were in Camp a vote was taken to know where the majority wished to be sent & they were unanimous in their desire to be sent to you. . . ."[16]

Sherman remained depressed, though, and by October 4, her tone became more worried: "Yesterday Father received your letter of the 30th ultimo which has caused me the greatest anxiety & pain." Ellen sought to comfort him, telling him that Ewing had just left for the state capital to see the governor to beg for arms and troops for Sherman. On October 10, Ellen gave him more good news: "I received the kindest letter from John Sherman saying that he is, by [Ohio] Gov. [William] Dennison, Authorised to raise two Regiments which shall go to you. He says he is going with them himself." No Ohio troops materialized in Kentucky, however, and Sherman's fears of an impending enemy assault grew exponentially. Within a fortnight, his alarm over the Confederate threat approached pure panic as he took the reins of command with Anderson's departure.[17]

Less than a month later came the publication of Thomas's report and the first open criticism of Sherman in newspapers across the country: "Sherman was wild in his estimate," according to one account in the *Chicago Tribune*. Sherman's concern over the military situation became a fever in him. By day, he haunted the Louisville telegraph office, alternately brooding and voluble, smoking cigar after cigar and discarding the butts on the floor. They were humorously dubbed "Sherman's old soldiers" by newspaper correspondents, who also stuck close to the telegraph and thus had ample opportunity to scrutinize Sherman's increasingly nervous behavior. "He could not rid himself of the apprehension that he was due for defeat if the rebels attacked," recalled reporter Henry Villard in his memoirs. According to Villard, Sherman feverishly paced the hallway of his hotel by night, "smoking and obviously absorbed in oppressive thoughts. . . . His strange ways led to gossip, and it was soon whispered about that he was suffering from mental depression."[18]

His despair was obvious to his wife many miles away. Ellen tried to lighten his mood with her letters, one of which playfully begged him to "write me a cheerful letter that I may have it to refer to when the gloomy ones come." Sherman reacted irritably; he could not shake his sense of dread: "[Y]ou want me to write you a cheerful letter. How any body could be cheerful now I cant tell [-] even [Charles Dickens's eternal optimist] Mark Tapley could not be cheerful. Personally I am comfortable enough, but the forbodings of danger against which I have struggled keep me far from being easy. . . ."[19]

His only respite came from infrequent but far-ranging rides through the territory under his command. On horseback excursions, he sought to familiarize himself with the terrain—always a primary consideration of his military mind—but he also found solace in the exercise, the fresh air, and the natural beauty of the land. All of Sherman's life, personal exploration of America's vast and diverse geography served to exercise his active mind and body, and he could recall vividly the topography of places he had visited decades earlier. On the inside front flap of his small pocket diary for 1861 is a rough but strikingly accurate drawing of Charleston Harbor and its fortifications. No doubt Sherman drew it at the time of the firing on Fort Sumter in April of that year, based on his memories of having been stationed at Fort Moultrie under Anderson nearly twenty years before. In the words of one biographer, Sherman "loved the earth as the sailor loves the sea."[20]

Sherman's depression deepened in the fall of 1861. On November 1, two days after the Thomas report appeared in the *New York Tribune*, Sherman wrote despairingly to his wife: "I find myself riding a whirlwind unable to guide the Storm. . . . The idea of going down to History with a fame such as threatens me nearly makes me crazy, indeed I may be so now . . . in the quiet of your country you cannot feel as one surrounded by the importunities of contractors and the quiet observation of spies."[21]

In the midst of Sherman's troubles, major changes were taking place in the senior command of the U.S. Army. Winfield Scott stepped aside, and McClellan assumed overall command as general-in-chief. A week later, Sherman's immediate superior, Frémont, was relieved of his command in Missouri. Then, on November 8, McClellan telegraphed Sherman that Gen. Don Carlos Buell would be dispatched to take over command from Sherman, as Sherman had asked. Buell, who had been one of the original group of subordinate brigadiers chosen by Anderson (along with Sherman), had left California for Kentucky in late August; he would finally arrive in Louisville on November 13. At nearly the same time Sherman received McClellan's telegram, he also received orders to go to St. Louis and await further instructions from Maj. Gen. Henry Wager Halleck, who had just assumed Frémont's command of the Department of Missouri. Sherman and Halleck knew each other well. Sherman was one year behind Halleck at West Point, and they had shared the six-month-long voyage from New York around Cape Horn to San Francisco during the Mexican War. Their friendship had deteriorated in California when, in Halleck's opinion, 2d Lt. Sherman (then in charge of the state's military affairs) did not show due deference to 1st Lt. Halleck (then secretary of state, in charge of civil affairs) in positioning some batteries and building a blockhouse.[22]

Ellen first learned that her husband's superiors considered him unfit for duty on Friday, November 8, when she opened a note addressed to her father, who was not then at home, and read a dispatch from her husband's senior aide: "Send Mrs. Sherman & youngest boy down to relieve Gen. Sherman and myself from the pressure of business no occasion for alarm." She recorded in her diary that she "started in two hours for Louisville with Willy & Tommy." Shortly after her arrival, Ellen wrote to John: "Knowing insanity to be in the family & having seen Cump in the seize of it in California, I assure you I was tortured by fears, which have been *only in part* relieved since I got here." Family tales of Sherman's mentally unstable uncle and grandmother weighed on Ellen's mind, as did memories of Sherman's extreme nervous tension during the days in California when he unsuccessfully fought against vigilante rule and financial failure. She continued her letter to John: "Some time ago in writing to me he expressed a hope that Halleck would relieve him of command. Cump's mind has been wrought up to a morbid state of anxiety which caused him to request McClellan to make the change."[23]

At Ellen's scribbled request, John hastened from Washington to Louisville to join her in assessing his brother's health. They succeeded in getting her husband to see a doctor, but there is no record of his diagnosis or of any plan of treatment. Ellen remained with her husband until Friday, November 15, when John Sherman accompanied her back to Ohio. Even then, Ellen left Sherman reluctantly, hoping he would obtain leave to go home because, as she wrote on November 18, "Now that I know you to be in such low spirits I shall not have a comfortable or happy day away from you."[24]

By then, her husband had made his way to St. Louis, where Halleck believed that a relatively less stressful posting would enable the high-strung brigadier to recover his equanimity. Alas, this assignment also ended badly for Sherman. Sent by Halleck to assess the deployment of forces in the area, Sherman ordered several scattered posts consolidated, fearing that small, isolated camps could be easily overrun. Other generals in the area thought his fears unjustified, and Halleck concurred. He quickly overruled Sherman's deployments (though Halleck later ordered the same consolidation). Such confusion made it appear that Sherman was bringing to Missouri his Kentucky pattern of fearful and unrealistic projections of enemy strength.

Back in Lancaster, a worried Ellen continued to focus on her husband's deteriorating situation; his usually reliable letter writing had inexplicably fallen off. In the face of his silence, Ellen's anxiety soon drove her to St. Louis, where Halleck had just recently placed Sherman in charge of drilling troops at Benton Barracks. This was a substantial demotion, even for a man who had never sought a major command. Everyone who knew Sherman was conscious of his shame. On December 1, armed with Halleck's blessing (and a twenty-day leave), Ellen took Sherman back to Lancaster, Ohio, for rest and recuperation. Within a week it seemed that the worst of the storm in the press had passed, and with quiet days with his children, good food, and slightly fewer cigars, Sherman's mood began to improve. Storm clouds were on the horizon, though. On December 9, the *New York Times* remarked in passing that Gen. Franz Sigel was in temporary command "in place of Gen. SHERMAN, whose disorders have removed him, perhaps permanently, from his command."[25]

Then, on December 11, 1861, the *Cincinnati Commercial* informed the world that Gen. William T. Sherman was insane. Ellen, whose pocket diary entries were generally as brief as they were intermittent, simply noted for that Wednesday: "At Mrs. Daughherty's to tea. The slanderous article in the Commercial appeared this day."[26]

GENERAL WILLIAM T. SHERMAN INSANE

The painful intelligence reaches us, in such form that we are not at liberty to disclose it, that General William T. Sherman, late commander of the Department of the Cumberland, is insane. It appears that he was at the time while he was commanding Kentucky, stark mad. . . . He has of course been relieved altogether from command. The harsh criticisms that have been lavished on this gentleman, provoked by his strange conduct, will now give way to feelings of deepest sympathy for him in his great calamity. It seems providential that the country has not to mourn the loss of an army through the loss of mind of a general into whose hands was committed the vast responsibility of the command of Kentucky.[27]

The charge of insanity would pursue Sherman unfairly for the rest of his life. Both Shermans bowed under the force of this unexpected, vicious blow. Ellen's reaction was so profoundly wrenching that she apologized to her husband the following week. Her words paint a heartbreaking picture of the moment they both read the article: "I am sorry that I allowed myself to succumb to that

Portrait of Mrs. William Tecumseh Sherman by famed artist George Peter Alexander Healy, painted in 1865, when she was forty-one years old. (*Smithsonian American Art Museum, Gift of P. Tecumseh Sherman*)

horrible thing but I could not help it when I saw you so shaken by it." Their private shock reverberated through the community. She wrote John Sherman: "Nature will paint to your mind and heart what I felt when Tommy came in to us just now to say that a boy had told him that 'Papa was crazy.'" Perhaps the worst moment for Sherman came on December 12, when he sat down to write Thomas Ewing, who would have already heard of it in Washington. "Among the keenest feelings of my life," wrote Sherman to the man who had taken him in as a child, "is that arising from a consciousness that you will be mortified beyond measure at the disgrace which has befallen me by the announcement in the *Cincinnati Commercial* that I am insane."[28]

Upon the article's publication, the Sherman-Ewing family went into full assault mode. Ellen was involved in every aspect of the campaign, keeping note of every development—medical, military, political, journalistic. She corresponded with everyone involved in Sherman's situation—generals, newspaper editors, even the president. She relayed information to Sherman in a series of letters that combined detailed, serious attention to the unfolding drama with stout faith in his competence, earnest efforts to divert his morbid thoughts toward lighter subjects, and loving reassurance of his honor.

The day that the *Commercial*'s article appeared, Sherman and Philemon Ewing collaborated on a point-by-point refutation of the article, which Philemon personally carried to Cincinnati the next day. Thomas Ewing wrote letters to newspaper editors and began preparing a lawsuit against the *Cincinnati Commercial*. The elder Ewing also counseled Sherman to hold his emotions and opinions in check. In a letter on December 22, to "My Dear Son," Ewing wrote: "I would again impress upon you the necessity of avoiding all unfavorable expressions of opinions on any points connected with the contest or the service, *even to your most intimate friends.*"[29]

John Sherman also counseled restraint in dealing with the press but took up his brother's cause with vigor in Washington. Two days after the *Commercial* article appeared, John visited Lincoln and reported to Ellen: "It was manifest that the President felt kindly" toward her husband. "If I was in Cump's place," John wrote with feeling, "I would . . . quietly perform his duty wherever sent, and justify the President's remark that there was more *fighting* qualities in Gen. Sherman than in any Brigadier he had appointed." John also reviewed for Ellen the errors that Sherman had made since he arrived in Kentucky. According to John, his brother had written "letters & despatches . . . some of which were proven by subsequent events to be entirely erroneous and all were desponding, complaining, and almost insubordinate. He constantly exaggerated the number & resources of the enemy and looked upon all around him with distrust & suspicion. . . . [I]t is idle for him, for you or any of his friends to overlook the fact that his own fancies create enemies & difficulties where none exist."[30]

By this time, Sherman had returned to his post at the Benton Barracks, so Ellen reported by letter John's visit to the president and a similar one by her father. She told Sherman that "Father saw the President & John Sherman saw him after hearing from you & me & [the president] was most friendly toward you." She also reassured her husband that the Ewings would not air the Sherman family's mental history as part of their defense of him. "[Father] says the melancholy and depression to which your family is subject must not be brought up by us & it will be very hard for them to prove that because your Uncle & Grandmother suffered from extreme depression of spirits that therefore you were stark mad whilst commanding in Kentucky." Further, she urged Sherman to agree to sue the newspaper: "[Father] is anxious to hear from you as soon as possible, as he thinks no time should be lost in letting them know that suit will be commenced. . . . A simple denial by family or friends will not be the same—this is the only proof that can be given." She added, "P. S. Father wants to conduct the suit himself—just leave it to him."[31]

Ellen's own efforts to convince her husband's superiors of his sanity began with a letter to Halleck. She sought assurances that Halleck had not questioned Sherman's mental health in his official dispatches. He assured her that he had not used "insane" in any official report and told her he believed the strain of overwork simply required that Sherman have a temporary rest. Halleck's letter provided some reassurance to Ellen, and she sent an account of it to her husband, hoping it would also ease his mind.[32]

The letter Sherman wrote to her on the first day of 1862, though, was melancholy in the extreme. "Dearest Ellen," he wrote, "Again have I failed to write to you as I promised. Again have I neglected the almost only remaining chain of love & affection that should bind me to earth. . . . [T]he idea of having brought disgrace on all associated with me is so horrible to contemplate that I cannot rally under it." After two more gloomy letters from her husband in quick succession, Ellen altered her strategy. She was not satisfied that the attacks on her husband were being appropriately addressed by the proper authorities, and until they were, there was no hope of his rehabilitation—either in the army or in his own mind. First, she wrote her husband a loving letter of reassurance: "It is not in the power of your enemies to lower you in the estimation of those who know you." Then, like other military wives during those years, she took her case directly to the president.[33]

Ellen first sent the commander in chief a letter, and an exceptional letter it was. Unlike Jessie's arrogant appeal to Lincoln, Ellen's written petition to the president on January 9, 1862, was humble and quite diplomatic, if not shrewd. Her letter began: "Having always entertained a high regard for you and beleiving you to possess the kindest feelings as well as the truest honor I appeal with confidence to you for some intervention in my husband's favor & in vindication of his slandered name." Ellen's letter is remarkable in many respects, but perhaps most for its candid description of Sherman's generally agitated manner and his nervous breakdown in Kentucky. Although she did not reference any mental illness in Sherman's family, Ellen wrote of Sherman's "nervous temperament," and that his "mind is harassed by these cruel attacks." She enclosed copies of the newspaper articles, in case he had not seen them, and argued, "Newspaper slanders are generally insignaficant, but this you will perceive is of a peculiar nature, and one which *no* man can hear with stoicism—particularly one, who is nervous and sensitive." Even had Nelly or Jessie ever admitted to themselves that their husbands had flaws, it is inconceivable they would have ever committed such criticisms to paper for a third party (especially Lincoln) to read. Ellen recognized Sherman's failings and was willing to admit them when it might help her husband to do so. Ellen trusted in Lincoln's essential goodness and perhaps also in his ability to perceive the Ewing-Sherman political strength.[34]

Although her spelling was imperfect, Ellen's words were almost pitch perfect. Her letter is remarkable for the clear and concise manner in which she reviewed her husband's plight and for how she shrewdly contrasted Sherman's treatment at the hands of his superiors with that of his replacement. General Buell had barely advanced against the enemy, she noted to Lincoln, even though Buell's force was larger than Sherman's had been. In her words, Sherman's "request to be releived was *very cooly* complied with, and much *more readily* than any request for men and arms had been. His successor was immediately reinforced by three or four times the number of men he had when he was notified 'that he would be releived'; and with *this,* and *many other* advantages he has been there *longer* than Gen. Sherman and has moved but seven miles." Pointedly, she added, "Yet nothing from Adj. Gen. Thomas has been telegraphed over the Union holding him up to the ridicule of men or announcing that he is 'expected to push into Tennessee.'" Warming to her theme about Sherman's enemies in the army, she told the president: "Adjutant General Thomas has shewn himself, *more than once,* an enemy of my husband."

The press came in for its share of blame, too: "A week after he left St. Louis, and when the conspirators against him (with newspaper correspondents as tools) had time to arrange their plans, the statement that Gen W. T. Sherman *was a madman* was telegraphed from *Sedalia* to St. Louis, from St. Louis to Chicago, from *Frankfort* Kentucky to Cincinnati and from *Washington City* to New York, all about the same day."

She told Lincoln: "An article appeared in the Cincinnati Commercial the Louisville Journal and the St. Louis Democrat, on the same subject, about the same day, and all emanating from the same source." Sherman's family had attempted to set the record straight, but Ellen spelled out for the president the fruitlessness of the Ewings' tireless efforts: "Contradictions were immediately published, but who gives credence to them? Not more than half of those who read a slander, ever see a contradiction, and of the number of those who read this, the great part will consider it 'an effort of his friends to conceal his misfortune.'"

Ellen believed Lincoln held the power to restore Sherman's reputation. She petitioned the president in a manner that combined a sophisticated grasp of her husband's situation with insight into Lincoln's character and her own strong religiosity: "No *official* act contradiction has yet appeared, & no official act has yet reinstated him. As the minister of God, to dispense justice to us, and as one who has the heart to sympathise as well as the power to act, I beseech you, by some mark of confidence, to releive my husband from the suspicions now resting on him. He is now occupying a *subordinate* position in Gen. Halleck's department, which seems an endorsement of the slander."

Six days later, she had not received an answer from Lincoln (inexplicably, he never did reply to her letter), and she learned that her father was about to head to Washington. With Philemon Ewing, Thomas Ewing Jr., and John Sherman already in Washington, Ellen grasped the potential of the political firepower she could concentrate on her husband's behalf. Ellen decided to accompany her father. On January 15, she wrote to Sherman: "Father heard yesterday [that] he will be obliged to leave tomorrow for Washington. I will go with him & before I return we hope to have you ordered to a more agreeable post where you will be releived from the annoyance of feeling that you are out of place. A rumor reached us yesterday that Mr. Cameron had been sent to Russia & Mr. Stanton made Sec of War. If this be true we will have no difficulty in securing whatever may be desirable for you as Mr Stanton is an intimate friend of Father's."[35]

If she meant to comfort Sherman with news of her trip, she failed. Dismayed at the thought that his wife would petition his commander in chief, he telegraphed John to dissuade her. Too late. She had already left for Washington. On January 22, Ellen wrote Sherman: "I cannot yet say anything definite but we hope and believe that things will soon take a turn most agreeable and advantageous to you." Then she urged him: "Be patient my dearest husband & for the

Sake of your poor wife & little children keep as cheerful & calm as possible & in a very short time you will look back upon these dark days as a troubled dream—a night mare."[36]

The next day, John showed her the telegram Sherman had sent, which spurred Ellen to write to her husband that he should "not fear I will behave ridiculously here. I have not yet done anything myself or seen anyone but John Sherman. Father wished me to wait until he had seen the Sec. of War [Stanton]. He had seen him & McClellan but he has not even told me his plans or designs but bids me stay here awhile longer." On January 29, Sherman responded to her letter with immediate, heartfelt embarrassment. "Dearest Ellen," he wrote, "I received last night your letter from Washington and do feel ashamed that I should have telegraphed to John to prevent you being indiscreet—the idea is absurd—with such a load of indiscretion on my own shoulders that I should caution you against it."[37]

That same day, Ellen wrote Sherman: "Father & I go to the Presidents' to-day." Though she did not confess excitement or nervousness, her body betrayed her emotions: "I have not time to write you more now & my hand trembles I dont know why." Once the meeting was over, Ellen immediately reported to her husband. Dated "January 29, 1862 Wednesday evening," her letter is vastly different from Jessie's reports to Frémont after her encounter with Lincoln. Ellen's contains no secret code words. It does contain a precise, detailed, contemporary account of what was said by each of the parties. It also gives the full flavor of Ellen's determination and of Lincoln's early confidence in Sherman. It began:

> Dearest Cump, Father and I had a long & most satisfactory interview with the President today. He gave you the highest praise, said that he and Mr. Seward had been strongly impressed in your favor when you were in command at Fort Corcoran & that he had nominated you for Brig. Genl before the Ohio Delegation sent in your name or any names. He said he felt sorry to lose you when you went to Kentucky but he felt that the department was safer after you took command than before.[38]

Lincoln pulled no punches, however, and told Ewing and his daughter that Sherman's subsequent actions had shaken his faith in him. Echoing what John Sherman had earlier written, she wrote Cump:

> [The President] then intimated that after that, dispatches &c. had come from you had the effect of making him feel less comfortable &c. He seemed anxious

for us to know, and said that he wanted you to know that he had entertained the highest & most generous feelings towards you, and that he still entertained them; and he intimated that by testing, in your present position, that recent reports were unfounded your abilities would soon secure promotion.

Ellen was willing to accept Lincoln's wait-and-see prescription for Sherman's rehabilitation, but she was also determined to air her grievances to the president, as she wrote Sherman. She began with a direct assault on the insanity charge: "I asked Mr. Lincoln if he thought you insane when in command at Fort Corcoran. I told him you were no more so now. That I had known you since you were ten years old and you were the Same now that you had always been." Like Jessie, Ellen emphasized her suspicion of a conspiracy against her husband:

I told him you had enemies among your fellow Generals & that the newspaper correspondants were mere tools. . . . I told him that I did not come to ask for anything but to say a word against those who had conspired against you &c & in vindication of your name. He seemed very anxious that we should believe that he felt kindly towards you. He and Father are great friends just now. . . . Father was very much pleased with the entire interview.

Of course, Lincoln had good reason to respond positively to his guests that day. In stark contrast to Jessie's visit to the White House, all the elements of the Ewing-Sherman meeting were calculated to favor the supplicants, who— in this case—knew they were supplicants. To begin with, unlike Jessie's late-night meeting with Lincoln, Ellen's visit occurred at a reasonable hour of the day. Nor was it an unscheduled, last-minute meeting. Former Senator, former Treasury Secretary, former Interior Secretary Thomas Ewing knew the value of careful advance work, and he had taken pains to meet with Secretary of War Stanton ahead of the meeting. And, whether by extraordinarily good planning or extraordinary luck, the meeting with Ewing and his daughter took place on a relatively quiet day for the president during a very busy month of the war. It is the only event recorded on Lincoln's calendar on January 29, 1862.[39]

The tone of the meeting was vastly different, too. Unlike the Frémonts, Ellen and her father were not arrogant in their dealings with the president. They did not believe he was stupid, naive, or innately hostile to Sherman's interests. Although she could not vote, Ellen had been an early and outspoken advocate for Lincoln in his 1860 campaign. Through her father's connections, she had spent nearly as much time near the seat of presidential power as had Jessie, but she had not drawn from that experience a sense that she was entitled to treat the White House as her own or that the president was less than her equal. Thomas Ewing's dealings with Lincoln had begun more than two decades earlier. In addition to Ewing's 1849 offer of the Oregon Territory governorship, Lincoln had often petitioned Interior Secretary Ewing for patronage and routine favors during his congressional term. Throughout the Civil War, Lincoln continued to seek advice and insight from Ewing.[40]

Also, in contrast to Jessie's meeting with Lincoln, Ellen did not insist upon receiving immediate, favorable action from the president. Rather, Ellen accepted at face value Lincoln's expression of concern for Sherman, and she accepted Lincoln's plan for a patient rehabilitation of her husband's career. She did so not merely because she was being politic in not pressing the president, but also because her honesty prevented her from arguing with the president over Sherman's shortcomings.

Lincoln may also have reacted positively to Sherman's case in part because of his other generals' apparently insatiable demands for troops and weapons. Frémont, of course, had begun his tenure in Missouri with ceaseless requests (often in Jessie's hand) for more men, more arms, more munitions. McClellan, too, took up the cry for more, more, more as soon as he came to Washington. Lincoln may also have seen some justification in Sherman's calls for more men and arms in a wire from one of his most trusted friends and advisers, one who moreover was on the scene in Kentucky. On the day of Anderson's resignation, Joshua Speed wrote to Lincoln an assessment of the situation in that state, which combined a call for more troops with confidence in Sherman. He concluded, "If we wish to save Ky to the Union our force should be increased—to a point that will enable us to drive Buckner out of the State & carry the war into Tenessee. . . ." A week before Sherman had pleaded with Cameron in the hotel room in Louisville for more men with whom to mount an aggressive campaign into Tennessee, Lincoln was hearing from a trusted friend in the same city that more troops were indeed needed to accomplish that cherished military objective. Three months later, when he received Ellen and her father at the White House (soon after Speed and his wife celebrated Thanksgiving dinner with the Lincolns), the president could not have forgotten Speed's recommendation for more troops. Nor could he have forgotten the confidence in Sherman that Speed and other loyal Kentucky men had.[41]

Just as Jessie had done, though, Ellen could not restrain herself from warning Lincoln that her husband had been the victim of a conspiracy within his

Administration. As far as can be determined, Lincoln did not react with agitation to her charge as he had when Jessie had alleged a similar conspiracy. Lincoln was not at all happy that Thomas's report to Cameron had been published in newspapers. Despite the fact that the timing of its publication in late October had provided critical support for his removal of Frémont from command, Lincoln was mortified that the confidential government report had been published. On December 12, Lincoln penned a note to Brig. Gen. Samuel Curtis, apologizing for the publication of information the officer had imparted to Cameron and Thomas in what Curtis had considered a confidential interview: "You, and others, particularly, and the public service generally, were wronged, and injured by the publication of Gen. Thomas' report, on his return from the West. I have no apology only to say it never would have been done, if I had had the least suspicion it was to be done." Among the "others" who were "particularly . . . wronged" was, of course, Sherman.[42]

In Ellen's heartfelt accounts to Lincoln of Sherman's "nervous temperament," his public humiliation, and his being "in low spirits and in poor health," Lincoln may well have empathized, recalling his own bouts of melancholia earlier in his life and how friendship, patience, and passage of time had enabled him to recover. That was the same prescription he urged on his visitors for Sherman's recovery. Ellen and her father went away with—to be precise—nothing more than sympathy, good wishes, and expressions of confidence. Those were significant, of course, coming from the president of the United States. But Ellen's letter had asked for "some mark of confidence," and she surely had hoped for more definite, even public action on his part. Even so, father and daughter gladly accepted the words of encouragement they received, and Ellen urged Sherman to feel the same way. Her letter to Sherman following the visit with the president concluded with the very advice Lincoln had given her and with a firm and tender declaration of confidence in him: "If you will only keep a brave heart and not be desponding & not care how you may be judged your abilities will bring you out one of the first in the land."[43]

By the time Ellen returned to Lancaster in early February, Brigadier General Sherman was still in the rehabilitation stage of his Civil War career, training troops at the Benton Barracks near St. Louis under the critical eye of General Halleck. About 150 miles to the southeast, another of Halleck's brigadiers, Ulysses S. Grant, commanded at Cairo, Illinois. There, at the southern tip of Illinois on the Mississippi River, a warehouse of men, munitions, and supplies was assembled for action. Prompted by President Lincoln's Special War Order No. 1 on January 31, directing all Union forces under arms to advance against the enemy by February 22, Halleck approved Grant's plan to attack Fort Henry on the Tennessee River. On February 6, Grant's combined army-navy assault on the fort swiftly ended with the Confederate Army surrendering to Union gunboats in a nationally celebrated victory.[44]

While Grant sought to build on the momentum of victory, Halleck sought to leverage his subordinate's glory into greater authority for himself. At that time, Halleck was one of two equal commanders in the West; the other was General Buell. For militarily sound reasons, Halleck wanted the two armies consolidated under one leader. Unsuccessful in his preliminary desktop maneuvers to secure the combined command, Halleck watched as Grant moved toward his next military target—Fort Donelson, a more robust Confederate stronghold that protected the Cumberland River. Another victory by the quiet young officer under his command could provide more ammunition for Halleck's personal power play. As a result, Halleck resolved to hold nothing back in supplying Grant's every need. Surveying the resources he had at his disposal, he determined that Sherman's rehabilitation was at an end. On February 13, Sherman got what he had only recently fled in panic and depression, a command in Kentucky. This time, Sherman was ordered to Paducah, where he would command the District of Cairo and assist Grant's operations.

Although Sherman arrived near the very end of Grant's campaign against Fort Donelson, he threw himself into the job of sending men and supplies to the front. Sherman put his heart into the support role Halleck had assigned him, even though, technically, he was senior to Grant. On February 15, as the fighting blazed, Sherman also sent two messages to Grant that Grant never forgot. The first carried assurance that another regiment was on its way, with more to be sent if needed. Even more welcome, the message from Sherman carried a pledge of unqualified support: "[I]f I could be of service myself would gladly come, without making any question of rank." The second message to Grant, later in that day of heavy fighting, reiterated the earnest offer. "I feel anxious about you as I know the great facilities they have of concentration by means of the River & R[ail] Road, but have faith in you—Command me in anyway." For Sherman, Union victory was the goal. Adherence to the finer points of the military pecking order was a distraction from the goal. Grant appreciated Sherman's selflessness as much as he did the reinforcements. The day after he received those messages, Grant claimed a major victory for the Union.[45]

Grant's triumph at Fort Donelson was a signal event in the Civil War, denying Kentucky to the Confederates, capturing an entire army, boosting spirits in the North, and creating the persona of "Unconditional Surrender Grant." It inspired Sherman's confidence in the Union effort like nothing else had yet done. The victory lifted his own spirits, too, and made him feel useful. He was part of a winning team—and what a team it was, this pair of similarly unprepossessing but temperamentally disparate soldiers. "[T]here was something wanting in Grant, which Sherman could always supply, and *vice versa,* as regards Sherman," Adm. David Porter told Navy Secretary Gideon Welles in late 1864; "the two together made a very perfect general officer and they ought never to be separated."[46]

In February 1862, they moved together, gathering a massive force that Halleck planned to lead into battle himself. Halleck's target was a city, not an army, contrary to Lincoln's strategy, but it was without question an important city. Just as forts Henry and Donelson sat astride vital water transportation routes, so the city of Corinth, Mississippi, embraced one of the most valuable rail junctions in the South. The Confederate high command intended to hold Corinth, and in furtherance of that goal, Jefferson Davis's favorite general, Albert Sidney Johnston, was racing toward it, along with Generals Beauregard, Polk, Hardee, and Bragg. The race to Corinth was on as well among Union generals. As the Army of the Tennessee, under Grant's command, headed southwest with troops, boats, wagons, horses, guns, and supplies, Buell was pushing his Army of the Ohio to meet Grant's forces just north of Corinth, where their combined forces would rest and organize for the blow they would make against the city. Halleck was confident that the Confederates would await the consolidation of all the Union forces and would also await his own unhurried arrival from St. Louis. In the strictest military language, Halleck ordered Grant to avoid bringing on a fight with the enemy before Halleck—or at least Buell and his reinforcements—arrived.

In the end, Corinth proved not to be the site of the major battle. Gen. Albert Sidney Johnston determined to get the jump on Grant, to fight him before Buell could swell Union forces beyond the Confederates' ability to defeat them at Corinth. Johnston decided to attack Grant's forces where Sherman had placed them for the interim—in a large, well-ordered, tented camp on the Tennessee River at Pittsburg Landing, atop the high bluff that rose from the river, on the broad plain surrounding a tiny log church called Shiloh.[47]

By this time, Sherman was in what he called "high feather," cheerful and confident in the future. Ellen's satisfaction in her husband's improved circumstances can be seen in her letters, which returned to the antebellum themes she had pursued with Sherman: her need for funds ("I am ashamed to ask you for more money but I must get you to send me a part of your next pay as I am nearly out at the Bank & do not want to Spend my gold"); her desire that he help her brothers ("I am very anxious to know what Halleck says in response to your request about Charley. Please send me his letter, and please persevere until you get that Batallion"); and her fervent pleading that he accept the Catholic faith ("Why dearest Cump do you not prepare your soul, by the healing graces of the sacraments which bring forgiveness hope joy and consolation?"). She was no longer trying to distract Sherman from his demons. She was trying to get him to address her needs and wants.[48]

Ellen's demands were balanced with tender affection, as in one letter in which she recalled the days of their courtship when young Lieutenant Sherman was stationed near where forty-two-year-old Brigadier General Sherman was now at that very moment. After reminiscing about that time in their lives, thirty-eight-year-old Ellen turned to the present. "But here we are! old people almost now, & loving one another better than we could have done before. What a blessed compensation it is—the increased affection which length of attachment sorrow & exposure bring." The Shermans' momentary satisfaction with their world was not fated to last.[49]

Gen. Albert Sidney Johnston's forces struck the tented camps surrounding Shiloh on Sunday, April 6. Despite signs of major rebel activity nearby over the previous thirty-six hours, Sherman was comfortable in his preparations and even more so in the enemy's lack of will to attack the Union Army there. At dawn, Confederates charged through the woods, driving deer and rabbits ahead of them. Sherman's position was the most forward, and in the first few minutes of battle, a shot felled his orderly at his side, one of the first men killed in the Battle of Shiloh. Rebel troops fell upon the Union camp; some Confederate soldiers rummaged through Sherman's tent as others feasted on breakfasts that had been abandoned by their foe.[50]

Grant, who had made his headquarters nine miles downriver in the town of Savannah where telegraph service was available, heard the heavy thump of cannon just as he sat down to breakfast. He rushed by steamboat to Pittsburg Landing in time to see blue-coated soldiers streaming over the bluff from the battlefield into the river—even attempting to board his own boat. Soon, Grant was everywhere on the battlefield, as was Sherman. Grant later wrote: "I never deemed it important to stay long with Sherman. Although his troops were then under fire for the first time, their commander, by his constant presence with them, inspired a confidence in officers and men that enabled them to render services on that bloody battle-field worthy of the best of veterans." Grant used an exclamation point only twice in his memoirs to emphasize his own emotions, and one of those was when he wrote about Sherman's critical role at Shiloh: "A casualty to Sherman that would have taken him from the field that day would have been a sad one for the troops engaged at Shiloh. And how near we came to this! On the 6th Sherman was shot twice, once in the hand, once in the shoulder, the ball cutting his coat and making a slight wound, and a third ball passed through his hat. In addition to this he had several horses shot during the day."[51]

Everyone who saw Sherman that day and who wrote about him remarked upon his calm sense of control in the midst of the melee. The chaos of battle seemed to quiet his perpetually active mind. Sherman ever after demonstrated the same reaction to combat. On this day at Shiloh, though, despite the best efforts of Sherman and Grant and several other truly heroic Union generals, panic nearly made irrevocable what seemed by nightfall to be a certain Union defeat. Indeed, General Beauregard, who assumed command of the Confederate forces on Albert Sidney Johnston's death in the afternoon, called a halt to the action while there was still light in the western sky—to the disgust of some of his senior officers, who wanted to continue pushing Grant into the river. Beauregard believed there was little left to do but mop up in the morning, and after wiring Richmond news of a complete victory, he slept that night in Sherman's tent.

Between Beauregard and the river to his east lay a bloody, moaning, writhing carpet of wounded Union and Confederate soldiers. On the far side of that human carpet, Union soldiers huddled in a driving rain in makeshift camps at the edge of the river bluff. Surgeons and their desperately wounded patients invaded a small house atop the landing that had earlier served as Grant's headquarters. Soon, the terrible sights and sounds and smells drove Grant out into the dark and the rain, with only a tree and his hat brim for shelter. It was there that Sherman found him about midnight. Sherman, convinced by all he had witnessed that day that the wise course was to retreat and reorganize, intended to provide that counsel to his commanding general. Approaching Grant in the dark, though, Sherman was struck by something in the general's attitude that stopped that thought in his throat. Instead, he observed laconically, "Well, Grant, we've had the devil's own day." "Lick 'em tomorrow," replied Grant. And they did.[52]

Northern newspaper versions of the battle were at first confused and then highly critical of the officer corps at Shiloh, with one notable exception: Sherman. They praised Sherman for his fierce but calm leadership during the battle, while Grant and nearly everyone else in high command were reviled for their negligence in allowing the surprise Confederate attack. *Cincinnati Gazette* reporter Whitelaw Reid wrote a scathing article about the generals' failing, which included only praise for Sherman. Then Ohio Lt. Gov. Benjamin Stanton published his own version of the fight. He charged Grant and others—but not Sherman—with gross negligence in allowing the surprise attack. Sherman being Sherman could not bask in the glow of newspaper correspondents' praise while other honest, loyal officers were suffering at their hands. He was constitutionally unable to resist striking back on behalf of the army in general and his friend Grant in particular. If newspapers could blithely undermine soldiers' confidence in their officers through such reports (which he adamantly insisted were false and malicious), military cohesion and morale—and the Union cause itself—were in danger. With close tutoring from Thomas Ewing and from Ellen (who at one point bluntly advised that she would not forward a particular draft of his letter for publication), Sherman drafted and redrafted a response to Stanton's article, which was published. Then, of course, a battle between Benjamin Stanton and Sherman was joined. Unsurprisingly, it revived the insanity charge (what foe of Sherman could ever resist doing that?), but Sherman was beyond caring at that point. The experience at Shiloh pumped such confidence into him that, as his family and Lincoln had advised him in January, he did not look back. He could only look ahead to the next battle.[53]

Two signal events in the life of William Tecumseh Sherman would happen first. On Lincoln's order, he was made major general, the first positive act the commander in chief had made on Sherman's behalf since the visit by Ellen and her father in January. Ellen's brother Tom told her that the president had personally initiated, penned, and signed the nomination and asked Tom to "present his compliments to Mrs. Sherman 'to whom he had taken a great liking.'" Ellen wrote Sherman: "Tom assured him the liking was reciprocated & told him that I had run up the Republican flag on his nomination &c—He rubbed his hands & with much pleasure said 'that's first rate.'"[54]

The second significant occurrence was that Sherman emerged as the right person in the right place at the right time to convince Grant not to leave after Shiloh. Halleck, who had planned all along to take command of the troops before Corinth, took this opportunity to reorganize the army. In doing so, Halleck made Grant his second in command, "offering Grant a form of partnership intended to tide him over a crisis," according to one historian. But even though he had also just been promoted to major general, Grant viewed his new assignment gloomily; with Halleck at hand, he had no responsibility, nor could he bring Julia to live with him. When Grant threatened to leave the camp at Corinth, however, Sherman persuaded him to stay. The talkative redhead pressed on Grant his own phoenix-like rebirth from public humiliation to battlefield hero and promotion over the previous eight months. Sherman argued that if Grant would remain in a subordinate capacity in camp for a while longer, fortune might smile on him, too. Grant agreed to remain. Sure enough, within weeks, Halleck was summoned to Washington to become general-in-chief, and he turned over command of Union forces in the West to Grant.[55]

Sherman rejoiced in Grant's elevation and looked forward to continuing their successful partnership, but Sherman's martial seesaw was about to teeter again. His next major engagement—the battle of Chickasaw Bayou, fought north of Vicksburg, Mississippi, in the last four days of December 1862—proved to be a debacle for Sherman, but only in part because of his own actions. Ordered by Grant to make an assault on Vicksburg (the first of many of Grant's attempts to take that Confederate fortress), Sherman headed south from his headquarters, then in Memphis, Tennessee. He and his troops comprised one of the three forces that Grant hoped could work in concert to launch a coordinated attack against Confederates entrenched in Vicksburg. Gen. Nathaniel P. Banks and General Grant himself were to spearhead the other two forces. Unfortunately, neither Banks nor Grant arrived as promised. Without those troops or even confirmation that they were near (which they never were), Sherman nevertheless ordered three successive, brutal, deadly frontal assaults on the Confederate position before retiring in the face of relentless carnage and superior defenses.[56]

Unaware of Grant's design for a larger campaign, reporters made their own assault—against Sherman's "insane" desire to attack a much larger force than his own. The disastrous result of the frontal assaults was amplified by misinformed newspaper outcry over it. Further muddying the situation was the fact that at that point, Gen. John McClernand (also a prominent Illinois politician) appeared on the scene to take over Sherman's command. McClernand and Sherman together went on to a small but signal victory in the battle of Arkansas Post, a swift assault that Sherman had conceived before McClernand had arrived, but Sherman got no credit for it. Once again, newspapers had a field day speculating about Sherman's competence and his future. Their published slanders added to the accumulated stress of battles and swamped Sherman's earlier confidence.[57]

It was all enough to make Sherman contemplate resigning from the army, and he threatened to do that in a letter to Ellen in February 1863. Unlike Jessie and Nelly, who agreed with—even encouraged—their husbands when they vowed to resign, Ellen would have none of it. She was furious at Lincoln for placing McClernand in command over her husband and privately fumed that the president should be impeached, but she scolded Sherman as soon as she read his letter: "[I]f you abandon your country & her cause when so few are competent & willing to Serve, I shall then indeed be distressed. . . . Whatever happens Cump hold on to your commission. Do not desert the good ship whilst she is in danger of Sinking—you cannot do it—If you have sent in your resignation let me beg you to recall it."[58]

A week later, she wrote: "Nothing that you are capable of doing could cause me deep mortification except your resignation at this time." Then she played her trump card: his hatred of newspapers. "In addition to the fact that you would be abandoning your country in her hour of peril do you not see that you would thus be giving your enemies—the correspondents—the triumph they wish. They will then have written you down." The day after her second letter, she received a letter from her husband that eased her mind: he would remain where he was for the time being. In a second letter on the subject just days later, Sherman backtracked, assuring her that he "did not intend to resign unless the public opinion of the North made it prudent for the President to recall me nominally to some other command. . . ."[59]

In June 1862, six months after her visit with President Lincoln, Ellen Sherman had sat at the window of her home in Lancaster, writing a letter to her husband. Through the glass, she could see her children playing in the yard. As she paused to watch her seven-year-old son climb a tree, the sight brought to mind a vivid childhood memory. She took up her pen again and wrote: "Willy is on the top of the trees after cherries already. How well I remember seeing you climb the cherry trees when not much larger than he." This recollection led her to reflect upon how much had happened in their lives since then and particularly upon the difficulties they had faced in the previous six months. Ellen continued, "Little did I think when I looked at you then—timid shrinking & wondering at your boldness that in later years my courage would be called up to enable you to bear the bitter trials of life." Ellen concluded that part of her letter with warm words of respect and of love. "I thank God that in our day of trouble my heart did homage to your peerless virtues & more than ever before held you as the first best dearest one on earth to me." Ellen's courage had indeed served them well after the *Cincinnati Commercial's* insanity charge.[60]

Neither of them could then have imagined that her courage would soon be called upon again to help them weather an even harsher blow.

CHAPTER 16

"I have never dared to murmer at God's decree"

Beginning in March 1863, Ellen petitioned her husband to allow her to visit him in camp near Vicksburg. Grant was pursuing a host of strategies and tactics to topple the city known as the Gibraltar of the West, and Sherman was his right hand in those schemes. In addition to requests to her husband, Ellen even asked one of his aides about the feasibility of making the trip to Vicksburg via a well-known steamboat landing. On March 16, she asked Gen. Stephen Hurlbut, "Would you be shocked to see me come down soon? Could I get to Young's Point?" It was not until after the fall of Vicksburg on July 4, 1863, however, that Sherman allowed Ellen and their children to visit him in Mississippi. "I have a healthy camp," he wrote, urging her to come. A delighted Ellen replied, "The thought of going down to you has spread a sunshine over everything . . . all have gone to bed to dream happy dreams & my own heart is full of joy." Then she added her standard cautionary prayer: "God grant that nothing may occur to mar the happiness we anticipate."[1]

 With Minnie, Lizzie, Tommy, and Willy in tow (babies Ellie and Rachel stayed in Lancaster with her parents), Ellen arrived in Vicksburg as summer turned to fall. The family moved into a cluster of large tents that had been erected for them, except for nine-year-old Willy and seven-year-old Tommy, who bunked like soldiers with their uncle Charley Ewing in a tent a short distance away. The Shermans, who were apart for most of the war, spent one of their most enjoyable family interludes in years at the camp on the Big Black River, even though their visit pivoted upon the aftermath of a terrible siege. They toured the ravaged city, peering into elaborate cave homes dug by residents to avoid shells from the Union's naval guns; they helped with civilian and military relief efforts; and they visited with Grant and Julia and their children. Sherman even took time to indulge in drawing. The man who had graduated number one in his West Point drawing class sketched the camp

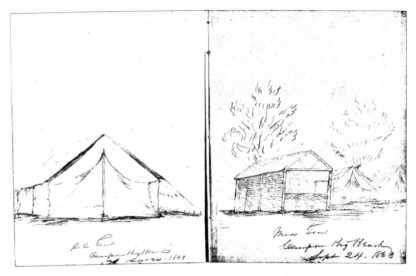

General Sherman sketched "Mess Tent, Camp on Big Black (River), Sept. 24, 1863," one of several sketches Sherman made for his daughter Minnie's scrapbook, called "Album of the Heart." (*Courtesy of the University of Notre Dame Archives*)

for Minnie, drawings that she later preserved in a small scrapbook she titled "Album of the Heart."[2]

All too soon, though, Grant ordered Sherman to Chattanooga, Tennessee, where Confederate forces under Gen. Braxton Bragg had entrapped the U.S. Army of the Cumberland after defeating it soundly in the Battle of Chickamauga. Sherman's mission was to relieve what "threatened to become a Union Vicksburg." At the end of September, Sherman gathered his headquarters staff and his family and boarded a riverboat to make the trip to Memphis. There, Sherman and his forces would move overland to Chattanooga, while Ellen and the children would head back to Lancaster.[3]

Soon after they embarked, though, it became clear that nine-year-old Willy was not well. What at first seemed like a mild case of diarrhea turned deadly. With the young boy's life at stake, the boat raced to Memphis. The moment it docked, Sherman scooped Willy in his arms and rushed to the Gayoso Hotel, where a doctor was waiting. Willy appeared to have contracted typhoid or cholera in camp, and the doctor had no cure to offer. Father Joseph Carrier, a Catholic priest whom the Shermans knew well, arrived shortly, and with Willy's grieving parents and most of his siblings at his side, the young man was administered the last rites. Ellen's recollection of her last conversation with her son sounded a theme of love and resignation. "I asked him if he was willing to die if it was God's will to take him," she later wrote to Sherman in one of the many letters in which the two relived Willy's last hours. "He said yes and that he would pray for us to follow him. I told him how we loved him, and asked him if he knew it, and he said he did."[4]

Sherman wrote in his memoirs: "Ellen, Minnie, Lizzie and Tom were with him at the time, and we all helpless and overwhelmed saw him die. . . . We procured a metallic casket and had a military funeral, the battalion of the 13th U.S. regulars acting as escort from the Gayoso Hotel to the steamboat *Grey Eagle,* which conveyed him and my family up to Cairo, when they proceeded to our home where he was buried."[5]

Sherman was utterly inconsolable. He blamed himself for his son's death. At midnight on October 4, the day after Willy's death, he wrote to Capt. C. C. Smith of the 13th Infantry, which had awarded Willy the grade and insignia of sergeant. "Consistent with a sense of duty to my profession and office, I could not leave my post," he lamented, "and sent for my family to come to me in that fatal climate, and in that sickly period of the year, and behold the result! The child who bore my name . . . floats a mere corpse, seeking a grave in a distant land, with a weeping mother, brother, and sisters clustered about him."[6]

Willy was his favorite child; there was no mistaking that. He loved them all, but Sherman adored Willy. He admitted it to John Sherman: "Somehow he was more to me than the other children. . . . I miss the child in my thoughts because I had in his future the best hopes. Tom the younger is more violent & headstrong, but not so patient & persistent." To Phil Ewing, he wrote: "this boy seemed to me more a part of myself than any other human being . . . he seemed to inherit an instinct I have of going across the country direct to the object regardless of beaten roads or paths." Willy was the repository of all of Sherman's hopes and dreams. Now that son and those dreams were dead.[7]

Sherman had no time to stop and mourn. In the letter to Captain Smith he wrote: "But, for myself I can ask no sympathy. On, on, I must go til I meet a soldier's fate, or see my country rise superior to all factions." His comrades in the Army of the Cumberland were besieged in Chattanooga, so on to Chattanooga he must go. As he did, he poured out his heart in letters to an array of comrades, friends, and family. He wrote about Willy to Halleck, to Grant, to Adm. David Porter, to the doctors who had attended Willy on the boat and in Memphis. To Ellen, he revealed his heartache and self-accusations. "Sleeping—waking—everywhere I see Poor Little Willy. . . . I will always deplore my want of judgment in taking my family to so fatal a climate at so critical period of the year. . . ." He wrote his children to comfort them. Fumbling to express his feelings to Tommy, he penned words that must have been equally welcoming and unfeeling: "You are now our only Boy, and must take Poor Willy's place, to take care of your Sisters, and to fill my Place when I too am gone. I have promised that whenever you meet a Soldier who knew Willy that you will give him half you have. . . . Your loving father, W. T. Sherman." To Sherman's benefit, he had serious, complicated work to do, and that work could help keep the demons from his mind—for a portion of each hour, at the very least.[8]

Ellen's grief matched Sherman's, and she wept along with her parents as Willy was buried in the Catholic cemetery in Lancaster. Unlike her husband, she had no new overarching project right then to take her mind off her loss (although she would soon learn that she was pregnant for the seventh time), but she had plenty to distract her. "I am lonely at heart but my time is fully occupied," she wrote. Her five children demanded her attention. Though her letters were filled with recollections and regrets about her care for Willy during their encampment, there is no indication that she faltered at all in caring for her living children in the aftermath of Willy's death. Nor did she withdraw from society generally. She suffered Willy's loss terribly—of that there can be no doubt—but when her reaction to the death of her Willy is placed alongside that of Mary Lincoln upon Willie Lincoln's death in February 1862, the contrast is striking.[9]

Observers almost universally described Mary Lincoln as "prostrated" at her Willie's death. She was alternately hysterical and mute. Her seamstress and confidante, Elizabeth Keckley, was her constant and often sole companion in those days. Mary closeted herself in her room in the White House, refusing to see even her young son Tad, who had just lost his brother and constant playmate. She hardly saw her oldest son Robert, who came home from Harvard for Willie's funeral. Mary did not attend Willie's funeral—she sent word that she could not, and there is no doubt she was correct. Just as Mary provided no support for her grieving children, she provided no consolation for her grieving husband (for whom Willie was his favorite son as well). Of course, Mary was isolated within a White House where her every move was scrutinized, while Ellen was at her childhood home surrounded by her family.[10]

While Lincoln "increasingly turned to religion for solace" during this time, according to historian David Herbert Donald, Mary sought to communicate with Willie in séances and with spiritual mediums, which became widely known and made her an object of ridicule among many. For the remainder of her days in the White House, Mary never went into the room where Willie died or into the Green Room, where his body lay before burial. One day, Elizabeth Keckley watched as Abraham Lincoln, himself awash in sorrow, took Mary to the win-

Willy Sherman, who died at the age of nine of typhoid, contracted at the family's camp in Vicksburg. On the back of the photograph is written, "This picture is blessed." (*Courtesy of the University of Notre Dame Archives*)

dow of her bedroom and pointed to a distant but recognizable landmark: the Government Hospital for the Insane (now known as St. Elizabeth's). "Mother," he said gently, using the name he'd called her since the birth of their first child, "do you see that large white building on the hill yonder? Try and control your grief, or it will drive you mad, and we may have to send you there."[11]

In contrast to Mary Lincoln, though not in criticism of her, Ellen Sherman proved a tower of strength within her family, despite the fact that her grief-stricken letters were full of recriminations, guilt, and regret, all of which she aimed at herself. "I would give every thing I have on earth if I had only paid more attention to him that Monday he was taken," she lamented. "Do write me Cump if you can remember doing anything for him. There were so many persons on the boat &c. I was so engrossed with Minnie (who was sick at the time) & in so much pain myself that I did not give him the attention he ought to have had."[12]

In some letters, she (like Sherman) wished that God had taken her instead of Willy. "Life seems sometimes insupportable & were it not that I must live as long as God wills for the other children I would pray that he might suffer me to die now," she wrote two weeks after Willy's death. Her letters are tragic, to be sure, but they are not hysterical. She was a woman in deep mourning, but above all she was a bereaved mother looking to God for strength to endure the death of her child. Although in one letter she expressed concern about her mental health, it is clear she believed God supplied her with spiritual strength enough to match her sorrow. Her fervent faith provided a framework within which she could place Willy's death as part of a larger mosaic of her life and her church. She knew with the certainty of a devout Catholic—and she taught her children—that he had gone to a better place, and that in the teachings of the church, he was there to intercede for her and every other member of his family to help them attain the same Kingdom of Heaven he had already entered. "What a joyful meeting it will be in heaven should we be blest in getting there to find our darling waiting to receive us."[13]

Her faith enabled Ellen to move through each day with some consolation even in the midst of profound sadness because, she believed, the tragedy was God's will: "I have never dared to murmer at God's decree." Catholicism was a bulwark for Ellen, providing a stable worldview for her from this world to the next. Even the child growing inside her was connected to Willy and her faith. The first mention of her pregnancy in her letters to Cump is in early February 1864. "The anniversary of dear Willy's birth month we will have another added to our little flock," she wrote. When her beloved mother died later that month, Willy was a part of that, too, and the thought comforted her. Ellen wrote Sherman: "She has joined our darling Willy now, and together, I trust they watch over us."[14]

The only person in the Sherman family to whom the Catholic religion did not afford direct comfort was Sherman. Nonetheless, he benefited from the Catholic doctrine he had consistently refused to embrace through the strength and peace it brought to his brokenhearted wife. Her letters made it clear that she was coping with Willy's death, albeit with great difficulty. Unlike Lincoln, Sherman did not fear his wife would suffer complete emotional collapse. He could find proof of Ellen's mental health in the many details she provided about her days, the children's activities, financial and household affairs, gossip about family and friends, and her occasional sharp political insights. Relieving him of that worry was critical to his own mental health as he continued in his military assignments, which took him farther and farther from his family.

That he could and did worry about her is evident from a letter he wrote in July 1864, when there was an unexplained hiatus in letters from Ellen. He gently scolded her: "You should write occasionally or make Lizzie write or Minnie who must now be at home, or get some one for I should not be kept uneasy about you, when my mind is kept on such a stretch by the circumstances that surround me." After Willy's death, Sherman neither asked for leave to be with his wife and children, nor did his superiors offer it. Lincoln said of Grant after Shiloh, "I can't spare this man, he fights." After Vicksburg, Grant might have said the same of Sherman. The red-haired general had become his indispensable right arm. Grant could not spare Sherman, so Sherman did not spare himself.[15]

Ellen's correspondence with her husband rarely flagged, though, and if the news in her letters was not always cheering, at least it came regularly. Even when they disagreed, Sherman did not mind. Occasionally, though, she stepped over the line, in his opinion, and he let her know it. "I don't object to your having strong likes and dislikes & expressing them to me," he told her on January 11. In reference to a critical letter she wrote to her husband's quartermaster, he continued, "but I do object to your stooping to writing any man with whom you may be as a stranger or putting anyone between me and you. Leave me to play my game of life and I honestly believe you will be satisfied." He concluded his scolding on a light note, echoing Ellen's earlier efforts to raise his spirits. "I am now past forty & according to Natural Law can't change and you must take me 'for worse.'" Because of their close relationship, he could scold and tease his wife even as he shared her overwhelming sorrow. Ellen was coping as well as could be expected after the sudden, shocking death of her son. With her husband far away, she had buried her boy, managed her children, nursed her parents, and buried her mother, too.[16]

ఆ CHAPTER 17 ဲ

"for the privilege of whipping negro wenches"

Sustained by her religion, Ellen's grief did not paralyze her, nor did it soften at all her fierce desire to crush the Rebellion. Her hatred for the Confederacy had been apparent to her family and friends from the very beginning of the conflict. One year before Willy's death, as she sat reading a newspaper in Lancaster, Ellen learned the first intimations of a terrible battle four hundred miles to the east, the portent of a second disastrous Union defeat near Manassas Junction in Virginia. Rumors that Gen. Robert E. Lee and his Army of Northern Virginia were crushing Gen. John Pope and the Army of Virginia had flown by telegraph to Cincinnati in late August 1862. Ellen's brother, Hugh Boyle Ewing, was on that battlefield in what would become known as the Second Battle of Bull Run, and she worried for his safety. Perhaps as a means of allaying her fears by expressing them, she took up her pen to write to her husband. Sherman was then more than six hundred miles from her in the opposite direction, in Memphis, Tennessee, building fortifications and managing a hostile population of Southern sympathizers.

Ellen was a great letter writer (according to her father, she was a better letter writer than the famous seventeenth-century French woman of letters, Madame de Sévigné). Like her husband, Ellen wrote easily and often, and nearly every letter she wrote sizzled with blistering opinions of people on both sides of the war—military and civilian leaders, newspaper reporters and editors, abolitionists, slaveholders, Catholics, and secessionists. Most of her letters were quite long, spilling over page after page. Her letter on August 30, 1862, though, was uncharacteristically short, only three brief paragraphs. After expressing concern for her brother and his comrades engaged in combat at that moment, the mother of two young sons and four young daughters vowed to her husband, "My boys shall go when strong enough to carry a musket—Would they were all boys to offer their lives in exterminating & punishing foul treason." In the midst of her writing, she paused to frame her thinking about the future. What Ellen then wrote was a grim hope, but it proved to be a prophecy, a prophecy of her husband's pivotal role in the terrible civil war: "I hope this may be not only a war of emancipation but of extermination & that all under the influence of the foul fiend may be driven like the Swine into the Sea. May we carry fire & sword into their states till not one habitation is left standing."[1]

Two years later, in the fall of 1864, as Sherman's army marched from Atlanta to the sea and beyond, he would "carry fire and sword" into Georgia, South Carolina, and North Carolina. Ellen was a wind at his back. He would have done it without her blessing because Sherman believed his march was militarily justified as the best and quickest path to ending the war. In the ferocity of his devout Catholic wife's hatred for secessionists, though, he would have found reassurance that his "hard war" path to the sea was also a morally acceptable path. Ellen Sherman was not perfect, but she was good—a good wife, a good daughter, a good sister, a good mother, a good Catholic, and a good patriot. She was also a very good hater. She was a complex mix of parts, and in that she closely resembled her husband. Popular history has painted Sherman as a fiend, bent on destruction and punishment of the South, unyielding in his attacks on defenseless widows and orphans. Most recent historians have been more nuanced in their treatment of Sherman, though, providing substantial evidence of his feelings of friendship toward Southerners, his regret at having to make war upon them, his belief that the hardest war was the most merciful as the quickest path to ending the conflict, and his desire to quickly resume good relations with the enemy once the fighting was over.

By comparison, contemporary historians generally acknowledge Ellen as the devout though often nagging little woman behind the man but give virtually no insight into her own perceptions of the war. In that regard, her letters are astonishing. They reveal a fierce, unrelenting hatred of secessionists. Ellen's language is fiery, often poetic, even breathtaking in its vitriol. She reserved her most bitter loathing for Catholic Confederates, whom she denounced as having broken the laws of man and God in supporting disunion and slavery. Whenever possible, she shunned any contact with Confederate sympathizers and urged her husband to do likewise; she made no exceptions for prewar friendships. Like her husband, she believed the enemy encompassed the entire Confederate population, including women. Her vision of postwar Reconstruction policy was far different from his, however. Hers was not quite apocalyptic, but it focused far more on punishment of the traitorous society than on an early and easy reunion of North and South. To the extent that Sherman is the name associated with desire for merciless total war in the middle of the nineteenth century, Ellen Ewing was more Sherman than Sherman himself.

Ellen's political views were evident early: she was for Lincoln from the start. In the fall of 1860, she wrote Sherman about how she expressed her political preference in public: "At a Lincoln demonstration the other evening Sis & I went out to the gate and waved—so I suppose we are on that Side—I am for the North against the South as soon as they take sides." A week after that, she wrote that she was sending Willy and Tommy to a Republican rally, where John Sherman was planning to speak, instructing the boys "to hurrah for Lincoln." After Lincoln's election but before his inauguration, Ellen raged against President Buchanan's vacillation in the face of Southern threats and seizures of Federal arsenals. "Buchanan is a superannuated woman or a traitor. I hope when Lincoln holds the reigns of Goverment he will protect United States property."[2]

Ellen also attacked one of the Shermans' closest friends. Henry Turner, a West Point classmate of Sherman, had hired him three times before the war—as a banker in San Francisco, as a banker in New York, and as the president of the St. Louis streetcar company. The Shermans had been close to the Turners; Ellen's letters to her husband from 1853 until 1860 were filled with friendly references to the major and his wife Julia, who were devout Catholics with whom they had frequent social contact. Nevertheless, those substantial personal and professional ties counted for nothing when it became clear to Ellen at the end of 1860 that Turner sympathized with the Southern cause. "Cump I ask it as a particular favor that you will not go to see the Turners," she wrote her husband. "[T]o refuse it will be to show me a personal slight which you would not be unkind enough to inflict at this time." A month later, Ellen wrote her husband about Turner again. "Were I a man in firm health he & I would fight together—not side by side but face to face." Less than a week after that, Ellen returned to the subject of Major Turner, and her fury was heightened by reflection upon his religion: "A catholic should be governed somewhat by the fact that the Church has always treated Slavery as an evil which should be abolished by wise & moderate means. It is hard to think that freemen . . . could sacrifice country & honor for the privilege of whipping negro wenches. . . ."[3]

In August, she found an opportunity to send a letter to Sherman via "a Dominican Priest," who was heading toward Sherman's camp. In her next letter to her husband, she told him that she later learned that the priest "was on his way to see his Uncle who is under sentence of death. If so I sincerely hope he may be hung or shot when the time comes after having had grace to repent his treachery to his Government & to receive absolution from his nephew who has gone probably in hopes of giving him the sacraments." Her ferocity against Catholic secessionists was not limited to laymen, though. Ellen feared that such men and women would taint all of that faith with a badge of disloyalty, under which loyal Catholics like her and her family would suffer. "I am disgusted with the Catholic Clergy generally—I have turned my heart against them. Their disloy-alty will be long remembered & laid up against Catholics generally & may even cause difficulties to arise which will make martyrs of our children."[4]

This was not an unusual concern among Catholics loyal to the Union. While the pope had issued a statement against the slave trade in 1843, the Catholic Church was mainly silent on the practice of slavery in the United States even as the Civil War was fought. Only two Catholic archbishops in the United States openly preached against the institution; one of them was Ellen's, the Very Rev-erend John Baptist Purcell, archbishop of Cincinnati. Even before the war, as evidenced by young Ellen's letter to Cump dreaming of a trip to Italy, Catholics were under siege by Protestants for religious and economic reasons. Catholic secessionists provided an additional point of conflict, a political one that could only make life worse for all Catholics, even those fiercely loyal to the Stars and Stripes. In the fall of 1864, Ellen estimated that in Lancaster, "nine tenths of the catholics are disloyal & would rather vote for Jeff Davis or McClellan than for you or Father or any honest patriot." Throughout the war, Ellen made her feelings about the duty that all Catholics owed the Union perfectly clear. In late 1864, she wrote Sherman: "I understand that two of the Dominican Priests at St. Joseph's have been drafted. I hope they will not be able to get substitutes."[5]

Though she feared that Catholic rebel sympathizers would taint others of the faith with the stain of disloyalty, her hatred of secessionists was firmly rooted in secular love for her country. In January 1861, she praised her husband's brother, who was a more radical Republican than Lincoln. "John Sherman has made another speech which is called by some ultra—I go with it heart & soul," she wrote Sherman. "If we have a government it should be sustained and if we have not power to punish traitors we have no government." Later in the war, she praised her husband in words that drew upon her devotion to Union and liberty. She was proud that he was "fighting for justice and legitimate author-ity against the foulest usurpation that ever ambitions sought to impose upon a free people." Ellen was clear in her hierarchy of hates: "I used to dislike the Abolitionists but their folly sinks into insignificance when compared with the treason of the South."[6]

Her descriptions of the enemy were withering—"inhuman blood thirsty wretches who have brought all this suffering upon us—their women as well as their men," she wrote in April 1862. When the Confederate Army evacuated Corinth a couple of months later, her father "was pleased," but she was not. The Confederate Army had escaped untouched. "I want the serpent's head crushed," Ellen declared to her husband. Two years later, her patriotic passion had not cooled and her confidence in her husband was firm. On July 16, 1864, she wrote: "I expect to hear soon of your being in possession of Atlanta." Sounding much like Lincoln, she continued, "I wish you could defeat & scatter Johns[t]on's Army."[7]

By the time Sherman was at the gates of Atlanta, it was no longer Johnston's army he faced; it was Hood's. Johnston had nimbly sidestepped several attempts by Sherman to engage him in battle around Atlanta, and Davis's dislike of Johnston prompted him to act on his fears that the general would abandon the city. On July 17, 1864, Davis replaced Johnston with Gen. John Bell Hood, whom he judged a better fighter than Johnston. Fight Hood did, but escape he and his army did, too. When Sherman telegraphed to Washington on September 4, 1864, "Atlanta is ours and fairly won," Lincoln rejoiced in the news as a harbinger of his electoral success in November. It was a truly significant military victory in an election year so thin on Union success that the president had believed in late August that he would be defeated at the polls.[8]

The capture of one of the Confederacy's prime manufacturing and transportation centers was cause for widespread celebration in the North, but Sherman knew that much harder work remained before the rebels would stop fighting. As a first step, he intended to destroy Atlanta's industrial and railroad capacity before moving on. As a corollary of that, he issued an order expelling the residents, so he would not have to weaken his army by leaving behind troops to garrison the city. When city officials protested the order, Sherman replied in one of the most famous public statements of the Civil War: "You might as well appeal against the thunder-storm as against these terrible hardships of war. . . . But, my dear sirs, when peace does come, you may call on me for any thing. Then will I share with you the last cracker, and watch with you to shield your homes and families against danger from every quarter. . . ."[9]

Of course, Sherman's eloquence did not stop Confederate city officials, women, and generals from continuing to moan in the most passionately aggrieved tones of his "barbarity" and "cruelty." Even some in the North thought he had violated the norms of civilized warfare. Ellen, though, cheered him on: "I am charmed with your order expelling the inhabitants of Atlanta as it has always seemed preposterous to have our Government feeding so many of their people—their insolent women particularly." No doubt she recalled Sherman's tales of how

Southern women had cursed him when she wrote: "[T]hey are responsible for the war and should be made to feel that it exists in sternest reality." She did not agree completely with him, however. If her husband was ready to share his last cracker with former rebels as soon as peace was declared, Ellen was not. "I, for one, shall be sorry to see the south received into the union again until her slaves are free & she is humbled in that which has led to her pride & wickedness."[10]

Sherman's initial desire had not been to humble the South, but to convince its men to acknowledge that their cause was wrong—or at least lost—and to resume their devotion to the Union. He had said as much in a letter to his brother John in May 1861, even before he rejoined the army. "The greatest difficulty in the problem now before the country is not to conquer," he wrote, "but so conquer as to impress upon the real men of the south a respect for their conquerors." By the fall of 1864, however, Sherman had altered his opinion of what was required from the rebels. What was needed was not the respect of the men of the South. What was needed was the psychological defeat of the rebellious population.[11]

What was needed, he believed, was a march.

CHAPTER 18

"the Government requires sacrifices from wives"

The Civil War was full of marches, but there was only one March: Sherman's March to the Sea—and beyond. The calculation of what might be achieved by such a march percolated in Sherman's mind long before he sought Grant's approval for it. As he moved from battlefield to battlefield from 1861 to 1864, Sherman's active mind took note of the eager young secessionists in Kentucky, the epithets of Southern women who begged rations while cursing his name, and the frustration of chasing nimble enemy armies through a vast territory that supplied and hid them. He knew that Lincoln was right to want to defeat armies instead of capturing cities (though Atlanta was a prize that even Lincoln found irresistible), but what if the will of the Southern citizenry to support its army could be defeated? Sherman determined it was time for the U.S. Army to bring war to the people of the South, just as his wife had prophesied.

In a late-September letter to Grant outlining his plan, Sherman lightheartedly concluded, "If you can whip Lee and I can march to the Atlantic I think Uncle Abe will give us a twenty days' leave of absence to see the young folks."[1] Grant was not enthusiastic about the idea at first, and he suspected that Lincoln would not like it either. Like Lincoln (and Ellen Sherman), Grant wanted Hood's army whipped, broken, defeated, and he had given that assignment to Sherman with full confidence in his subordinate. Now Sherman wanted to make Hood's army the responsibility of his subordinate, Gen. George H. Thomas. Instead, Sherman wanted to lead 65,000 men south from Atlanta— precise route unknown—to the sea—precise point unknown. Why? In his memoirs, Sherman said, "my aim then was, to whip the rebels, to humble their pride, to follow them to their inmost recesses, and make them fear and dread us." To Grant he reasoned, "Instead of being on the defensive I would be on the offensive, instead of guessing at what he means to do he would have to guess at my plans. The difference in war is full twenty five percent."[2]

Not quite convinced, Grant unenthusiastically pushed the plan further up the chain of command and found Halleck, Stanton, and Lincoln equally lukewarm about it. In the back of all four men's minds was fear that Thomas would be unable to defeat Hood, and Hood's army (soon to become Joseph Johnston's again) would slip away east and join with Lee against Grant. Sherman was confident Thomas could handle Hood, but he had even greater confidence in the value of his march to demoralize the Confederacy. Though Grant still had reservations, he ultimately decided to trust Sherman and his plan. On November 2, Grant telegraphed Sherman final approval: "I say then go as you propose." Sherman's preparations were thorough, his men and wagon trains superbly organized, his orders explicit—except those regarding the ultimate destination.[3]

On November 8, the North signaled its readiness to continue the war: Abraham Lincoln was reelected president. Less than a week later, Sherman acknowledged a telegram from Gen. George Thomas and telegraphed a last, brief message to Ellen.

Nov. 12, 1864

Headquarters, Military Division of the Mississippi, In the Field, Kingston Geo.,

Mrs. W. T. Sherman

Lancaster, Ohio

We start today . . . I have all your letters to include Nov. 3.

Write no more until you hear of me. Good bye.

W. T. Sherman

Soon after the messages were sent, some of Sherman's soldiers "burnt a bridge, which severed the telegraph-wire, and all communication with the rear ceased thenceforth."[4]

Sherman next wrote Ellen on December 16, from the outskirts of Savannah, Georgia. In those four weeks, Sherman and his 65,000 men had cut a swath more or less sixty miles wide through nearly three hundred miles of Georgia heartland. Remarkably few men fell victim to disease during the march, and a few died in brief, bloody fighting along the way. Sherman's later calculations placed total Union casualties for the March to the Sea at 764. He would have been apprised of those casualties along the way, but it was not until December 30 that he learned of another death that occurred during that time. Baby Charles Sherman died on December 4.[5]

The birth of her seventh child in July had been difficult for thirty-nine-year-old Ellen. Immediately after the boy was born, "I was so ill & had such raging fever that my life was in great danger," she had written Sherman on July 9, while he faced off against Johnston outside Atlanta. Worse, "the second day's fever dried my milk entirely & I have the trial of seeing my poor little baby fret & cry . . . & am deprived of the pleasure of gratifying him." Within a week, however, he was "strong & healthy," and on August 22, Ellen described Charley as "healthy & fat & happy as possible." She was still pleased with his health on August 30, when she traveled to South Bend, Indiana, to put the oldest children into school at Notre Dame. She was soon back in Lancaster, though, because "the baby has a very bad cold settled on his lungs and his cough is so troublesome that the dear little fellow keeps me disturbed very much in the night." Two weeks later she wrote again of Charley's "severe cold on his lungs and a cough." By the end of October, the baby was "quite sick . . . I have the most serious apprehensions that he will never recover altho' I do not think him in very immediate danger. . . ."[6]

Willy was still so much on the couple's minds that he was a regular feature of discussions about baby Charley. In late October, Ellen's religious bent informed her reflection on the baby's declining health. "It may be that Willy has prayed for him to come to him," she told her husband. On Election Day, she wrote that she feared the baby's lung problems would end in consumption. Almost certainly, the last letter Sherman received before he set out on the march told him the child was ill.[7]

Sherman's first letter to Ellen after the march, on December 16, does not mention the baby at all. In the full flush of excitement at his spectacular military achievement, he briefly reviewed for her the course of the march and his "safe arrival on the Coast." He wrote: "I Should like to hear how you all are, but suppose of course you are at South Bend." Even so, he addressed that letter to Ellen in Lancaster, as he did one on Christmas Day. Sherman had presented the city of Savannah and its guns and cotton to Abraham Lincoln as a Christmas present, but Sherman's family's own Christmas was a sad one, though Sherman himself did not know it. On Christmas, he also wrote to Minnie at Notre Dame: "Tell Mama if she is at South Bend that I have written to her twice at Lancaster, as I have not yet heard whether She has actually moved up to Notre Dame." He was still unaware of the tragedy he and Ellen had suffered in his absence, but he wanted news of his new son. "I have not even heard if the baby got well of the Cold with which he was suffering at the time I left Atlanta."[8]

On December 30, he got the sad news. "The Steamer *Fulton* arrived at Hilton Head yesterday, bring[ing] N.Y. Mails," he wrote Ellen on the very last day of the year. The mail included newspapers that carried a "full obituary and reports of the funeral services at Notre Dame." In addition, he told her, "I got a letter from yr. father at Washington, Hugh in Kentucky and John Sherman all alluding to the death of our baby, but I got nothing from you or the girls at school." He then turned philosophical: "I had hoped that the little fellow would weather the ailment, but it seems he too, is lost to us, and gone to join Willy . . . amid the Scenes of death and desolation through which I daily pass I cannot but become callous to death. . . . You on the Contrary surrounded alone by life & youth cannot take things so philosophically but are stayed by the Religious faith of a better and higher life elsewhere."[9]

Even though Sherman had not heard from Ellen since the baby's death, he knew that her faith would help her cope with the second loss of a son. He was correct. The day before Sherman read the newspapers and letters about Charley's death, Ellen finally received his letter of December 16, which he had sent to Lancaster. She replied to it within hours. Ellen spared Cump the sad details of the baby's prolonged suffering, but not her hopes for her husband's salvation through his two dead sons: "His long agony & my woe in witnessing & recalling it I will not dwell upon at present. The loss, aside from the present lonliness it involves I do not deplore on my own account for it is so much better to have him safe with his heavenly Father than to feel that we ever might leave him here without our care. . . . God grant that his prayers and Willy's may ensure my perseverance and obtain for you the gift of faith." Even though he had not the gift of faith, Ellen was enormously proud of her husband, and told him so. "You are so crowned with earthly fame and honor and glory now it is not necessary for me to Say anything on the subject of your acheivements." She told him, too, of her supreme confidence in him. "What astonishes and charms the world at large does not surprise me for I knew when you were denounced that you were more capable of accomplishing great things for the country than any man they had."[10]

Ellen did voice a complaint that she and the other women Sherman and his men left behind must have shared—lack of communication. She had dealt philosophically with Sherman's failure to write her in the month before the march, when she acknowledged to him, "the Government requires sacrifices from wives as well as from husbands." The strain of the baby's death, however, pushed her to express her disappointment more sharply after she finally heard from him. Even though Sherman had one of the best excuses of any soldier in the war for not writing, Ellen scolded him: "Considering your orders to me not to write until I heard from you I think you have been a long time in getting a letter to me. . . . I think you ought to have telegraphed me earlier and more than once, for I have been too long alone here without hearing from you or the means of writing to you."[11]

Ellen was not the only one in the dark during the march. Even President Lincoln could not provide any information on Sherman's whereabouts to his brother John, who approached the commander in chief on the subject in December. "We know what hole he went into," Lincoln told the senator, "but we don't know where he will emerge." On another occasion, as he stood in a receiving line at the White House, Lincoln appeared lost in thought. He was quite unconsciously ignoring his guests until he suddenly snapped back to reality, explaining simply, in words they immediately understood, "How do you do? Excuse me for not noting you. I was thinking of a man down South."[12]

Once Ellen and Sherman were back in touch during his stay in Savannah, she wrote: "I hope it will be different hereafter." It would not. Before Sherman even received her scolding, Cump had written to warn her: "It will not be long before I sally forth again on another dangerous & important Quixotic venture." By the time she read that, Ellen had regained her equilibrium and cheered him on. "We are beginning to have reports of you through Southern papers & all parties north and south think you must make Charleston or Augusta your objective point," she wrote in early February. "On the other hand peace rumors gain ground every day and since Mr. Lincoln and Mr. Seward went to meet peace Commissioners the hope of peace is almost general." Ellen's thinking on peace and on the Copperheads had not changed, nor had her confidence in her husband. "I do not hope for or desire any peace that will leave it possible for Jeff Davis or any of his partners in guilt ever to have a seat in Congress. If they will let you alone you will soon conquer a peace & they will be glad to escape to Mexico where so many of their northern sympathisers are going."[13]

"Sherman's march to the sea was one of the major events of the Civil War," wrote historian John Marszalek, noting that through it, "[Sherman] more than any Union general, demonstrated the hopelessness of the Confederate cause." The March to the Sea had indeed accomplished much for the Union cause and for Sherman's confidence and reputation. It frightened and demoralized the South. It cheered the North. It spurred desertions from the Confederate ranks. It brought popular fame to Sherman and his men. It won Sherman respect from prominent military men in America and Europe (even McClellan wrote him a letter of congratulations). It was a highly complex logistical challenge, one that demanded fierce focus by a leader unencumbered with excessive regard for Victorian notions of chivalry. And yet, in execution, "really it was easy," Sherman wrote Ellen in early January. "[L]ike one who has walked a narrow plank I look back and wonder if I really did it." Easy—that was his opinion of the march from Atlanta to Savannah.[14]

The march north from Savannah would be more arduous. Originally, Halleck and Grant contemplated that Sherman's army would move by ship up the Atlantic coast from Savannah to meet Grant's on the outskirts of Richmond. But when Sherman focused on the logistics required to move his men by water that distance, he immediately grasped the disadvantages of such a maneuver. The two months required to secure and move enough transports up the coast were far too long for a war that was entering a desperate endgame. Sherman also feared that the superb physical and psychological health of his men—toughened by marching on average ten miles per day, well fed by foraging, and proud of their achievements—would be imperiled by unhealthy conditions in camps awaiting the transports' arrival and aboard the ships.

In fact, Sherman's confidence in his men and in himself led him to consider what no other military leader—Union or Confederate—believed feasible. He proposed to march his men through rabidly hostile South Carolina and through the notoriously impassable swamps of North Carolina to link up with Grant outside Richmond. Once again, despite much second-guessing in Washington, Sherman's plan prevailed. And again, his logistically talented mind left nothing to chance. Though the first march had its fair share of bogs and creeks, this time he laid in even more axes for the backbreaking work of corduroying roads and more precious portable pontoon bridges for traversing deeper and wider bogs and water. During their march through Georgia, Sherman's men had been highly efficient in destroying railroads, but their almost superhuman ability to restore rail lines damaged by the Confederates inspired the legend that Sherman carried "extra tunnels." As they traversed the armpit-deep marshes and meandering rivers of the South, Sherman's army also, in effect, carried its own dry land.

Delayed by weather until February 1 (in his pocket diary, he scrawled "rain" day after day after day), Sherman and his men finally departed Savannah. All of Sherman's previous orders prohibiting wanton destruction and theft of purely personal property remained in effect. Designated foragers spread out ahead each morning and returned each evening with wagons full of food and forage, often trailing contraband horses, cattle, goats, and purloined rebel possessions. Though the terrain was far more difficult, the pace dictated by Sherman was the same ten miles per day he had specified through Georgia.[15]

Since Sherman did not tell his wife not to write him on this march, she did, and since this march tracked nearer the Atlantic coast, naval vessels could deliver mail. On February 15, Ellen sent him a letter full of family tales, expressions of sorrow over Willy, thanks for money he had sent her, and surprising news that she was planning to travel to Chicago within a week. She included in that letter a request for a particular favor: would he please send her "anything that will be either a curiosity or of value"? For the first and only time, Ellen was asking for a trophy of the war. It was for a good cause: "Indeed, to tell the whole truth, I am going as the guest of the Lady Managers of the Great North Western Sanitary Fair. It is to take place the last of May and is to be the greatest thing of the kind ever held in the west. I have been invited by the ladies first and then by Bishop Duggan (a most enthusiastic Republican) to preside at the Catholic Table. . . . Do not write to me to keep out of it for before this reaches you I will be fully committed."[16]

Sherman received her letter when he arrived in Goldsboro, North Carolina, on March 23, and replied immediately. He was unenthused about her proposed role in the Sanitary Fair. In the first place, he said, with perfect Victorian-era pitch, "I don't much approve of ladies selling things at a table." In the second place, "I could collect plenty of trophies," he told her " . . . but I prefer not to do it." In fact, it was against military rules to take trophies in the field, and it was against his specific orders to take items of personal rather than military value at any point in the march. Certainly he saw the hand of the Catholic Church in her willingness to participate in such a public event; she generally shunned gatherings of any kind not limited to family. "Still, do as you please," he told his wife, whom he knew would do as she pleased.[17]

For her part, Ellen surely rejoiced in her ability to leverage Cump's fame into good works for the soldiers who would benefit from the money raised at the fair. Even better, though, "each congregation [was] to be represented" at tables like her Catholic table, in what several clergymen called "friendly rivalry for the palm of well-doing." In effect, the fair was staging a contest among religions to raise money for soldier relief, and Ellen would have the supreme pleasure of using Sherman's swelling popularity to support her Catholic faith.[18]

Neither she nor her husband could have imagined that before the fair took place, Sherman would once again suffer a dreadful national blow to his reputation, this one far worse than even the insanity charge four years earlier.

CHAPTER 19

"my opinion of you is unaltered"

The wings of Sherman's army folded together in Goldsboro on March 22 and 23, as he had planned. Resupplied by a fleet of vessels carrying clean clothing and mail, the men set about readying themselves to continue north—to join Grant and, rumor had it, to fight Bobby Lee. Sherman was yet unclear on Grant's precise plans for his army, perhaps because Grant was not quite clear himself. Headquartered 150 miles north of Goldsboro at City Point (now Hopewell), Virginia, Grant had sent Sherman two letters "giving a general description of the state of facts," Sherman recalled in his memoirs. Grant wrote him that "Lee's army is much demoralized, and great numbers are deserting," but at the same time Grant admitted, "It is most difficult to understand what the rebels intend to do." Lee was still guarding Richmond and nearby Petersburg, the political/military/social heart of the Confederacy, and Grant was besieging Petersburg, in preparation for assaulting Richmond. Sherman and his army were to continue north, Grant wrote. Then he concluded with a statement that echoed their first communication in the war, Sherman's message to him during the Battle of Fort Donelson. "Let me know if you want more troops, or anything else," Grant wrote on March 22. Sherman understood the need to remain flexible in the face of such a nimble foe, but he later wrote: "Nevertheless, I deemed it of great importance that I should have a personal interview with the general, and determined to go in person to City Point."[1]

Sherman's decision to travel north to see Grant in person set the stage for one of the most consequential encounters during the Civil War, one that neither general had planned. Abraham Lincoln had arrived at City Point on March 24, in response to an invitation from Grant that his wife Julia had urged her husband to send. So, by serendipity, Sherman and Grant met together with Lincoln twice at the close of the war. The second of those meetings was truly momentous, both for who was there and for what was said—or, more precisely, for what Sherman believed was said.

On Sherman's arrival at Grant's headquarters at City Point on the afternoon of March 27, Brig. Gen. Horace Porter (one of Grant's aides) later recalled that he, Grant, and several other officers walked toward the pier when they learned Sherman's boat had arrived. "Before we reached the foot of the steps, Sherman had jumped ashore and was hurrying forward with long strides to meet his chief. ... Their encounter was more like that of two school-boys coming together after a vacation than the meeting of the chief actors in a great war tragedy." Grant and General Porter were soon hearing firsthand Sherman's equally riotous and sorrowful tales of his March to the Sea and to the north. More than an hour passed before Grant recalled the president's presence nearby and suggested they go to Lincoln's quarters on the *River Queen* paddlewheel steamer for further talk. An hour later, General Porter and Julia were in the headquarters cabin having tea when the generals returned. According to General Porter, Julia immediately asked the men if they had seen Mrs. Lincoln. Grant replied that they had gone "on a business errand" and did not think to ask for the First Lady; Sherman said he did not know she was there at all. "Well, you are a pretty pair!" exclaimed Mrs. Grant. "I do not see how you could have been so neglectful." Abashed, the generals promised to do better when they saw Lincoln again the next day.[2]

The next morning, March 28, Grant, Sherman, and Adm. David Dixon Porter went aboard the *River Queen* to meet with Lincoln. First, though, as Julia had instructed, Grant "was particular to inquire after Mrs. Lincoln, and to say that we desired to pay our respects to her," but when Lincoln went to find Mary, he returned with the news that she was not well enough to join them. Then the men settled into their chairs, and Grant laid out before the president the situation facing his armies: Lee occupied Petersburg, and Grant planned to continue his maneuvering to Lee's right, hoping to outflank him. "Lee might move out before and evacuate Petersburg and Richmond, but ... if he did there would be a hot pursuit." Sherman, moving his troops north, could hold Lee and Johnston in that case until Grant arrived, and "then the enemy would be caught in a vise and have his life promptly crushed out." Lincoln expressed the hope that the war could be ended without another major battle: "Must more blood be shed? Cannot this last bloody battle be avoided?" Sherman took the point on that question. Whether there was to be more bloodshed was not in the hands of the president's generals, he counseled, but was rather a decision that "must rest necessarily with the enemy."[3]

Admiral Porter wrote the account written closest in time to the meeting, based on notes he made soon after it concluded. He sent this information to Sherman in 1866. Three themes emerge from Admiral Porter's description of the meeting. First, since all four of the men believed that the end was very near, Lincoln wanted to stop the bloodshed and avoid further battle if at all possible. Second, according to Admiral Porter, "Lincoln came down to City Point with the most liberal views toward the rebels. He felt confident that we would be successful and was willing that the enemy should capitulate on the most favorable terms. . . . He wanted peace on almost any terms." Further discussion about "*the terms*," according to Admiral Porter, took place between Sherman and the president, and Lincoln "insisted that the surrender of Johnston's army must be obtained on any terms." Finally, Admiral Porter insisted that had Lincoln lived, he would have approved of the surrender terms that Sherman proposed to Johnston less than a month after the *River Queen* meeting.[4]

Although Grant did not include a description of the meeting in his memoirs, he did debrief Julia and General Porter after it. According to General Porter's recollection, Grant first reassured Julia they had asked for Mary Lincoln, but she was indisposed. Then Grant proceeded to describe the meeting in general terms that agreed with Admiral Porter's later version. "Lincoln spoke about the course which he thought had better be pursued after the war, and expressed an inclination to lean toward a generous policy," General Porter recalled Grant saying after the hour-and-a-half-long meeting. "In speaking about the Confederate political leaders, [Lincoln] intimated, though he did not say so in express terms, that it would relieve the situation if they should escape to some foreign country."[5]

Because Sherman relied on his understanding of Lincoln's intent in framing his surrender terms to Johnston, it is Sherman's recollection of Lincoln's wishes that are most important. Sherman did not make a contemporaneous account of the meeting, so ten years after the event, Sherman relied on his memory and on the account that Admiral Porter sent him in 1866, when he wrote of both meetings at City Point that

> Mr. Lincoln was full and frank in his conversation, assuring me that in his mind he was all ready for the civil reorganization of the affairs at the South as soon as the war was over; and he distinctly authorized me to assure Governor Vance and the people of North Carolina that, as soon as the rebel armies laid down their arms, and resumed their civil pursuits, they would at once be

guaranteed all their rights as citizens of a common country; and that to avoid anarchy the State governments then in existence, with their civil function-aries, would be recognized by him as the government *de facto* till Congress could provide others.

Sherman recalled that at the second meeting on the *River Queen,* he initiated the questions about "What was to be done with the rebel armies when de-feated? And what should be done with the political leaders, such as Jeff. Davis, etc.? Should we allow them to escape, etc.?" According to Sherman, Lincoln said, "all he wanted of us was to defeat the opposing armies, and to get the men composing the Confederate armies back to their homes, at work on their farms and in their shops. As to Jeff Davis, he was hardly at liberty to speak his mind fully, but intimated that he ought to clear out, 'escape the country,' only it would not do for him to say openly. . . . I inferred that Mr. Lincoln wanted Davis to escape, 'unbeknownst' to him."[6]

By the conclusion of the meeting with Lincoln, Sherman wrote that he was "more than ever impressed by his kindly nature, his deep and earnest sympathy . . . and that his earnest desire seemed to be to end the war speedily without more bloodshed or devastation, and to restore all of the men of both sections to their homes." What Sherman heard from Lincoln at that meeting was in tune with his own philosophy of hard war, soft peace. Unlike their first meeting al-most exactly four years earlier, this one was harmonious. They had not agreed at all in 1861 on how to begin fighting the war, but in Sherman's mind, the two men agreed on how it should be ended. "Of all the men I ever met," Sherman reflected in his memoirs, Lincoln "seemed to possess more of the elements of greatness, combined with goodness, than any other."[7]

Sherman left immediately after the meeting. Returning to Goldsboro, he prepared his army to move north to Petersburg, intent on preventing Johnston from linking up with Lee before his forces could arrive. He also took time to write Ellen. "I made a hasty visit to City Point to see Genl. Grant, to confer with him on points of importance and am back before Joseph Johnston or the newspapers found out the fact." He did not mention meeting Lincoln. He knew she was in Chicago about the Sanitary Fair, and he feared reporters would learn about the visit from her. "Don't go near those Tribune men. They are as mean sneaks as possible," he told her later in her visit there. "They would report your conversations, and pick your pockets of my letters and publish them if it would contribute to their temporary advantage."[8]

On April 5, he wrote Thomas Ewing: "I am preparing to go butt end, at Joe Johnston towards Raleigh." He also told Ewing that he was sending a messenger to Ellen with "the Rebel flag that was over the State House of Columbia S.C. as a contribution to the Fair of which it seems she is a patroness." Sherman remained concerned about the propriety of sending the flag. "The Col. of this Regt. Sends the flag to Ellen for the Fair, and I cannot well say nay, but if you think there is any impropriety in Ellens touching it as a trophy, telegraph her. . . ." To Ellen he wrote teasingly the same day: "I have no late letters from you, none since you wrote in Chicago, but you too are becoming a public character and the busy newspapers follow you. I see that the public authorities & citizens of Chicago paid you a public visit with speeches & music & that Bishop Duggan responded for you. If these give you pleasure I am glad of it for I would rather that you and the children should be benefitted by any fame I may achieve than that it Should Enure to me personally."[9]

Sherman and Grant had agreed that Sherman's troops would begin their march north to Petersburg on April 10. "But the whole problem became suddenly changed by the news of the fall of Richmond and Petersburg, which reached Goldsboro on the 6th of April," Sherman recalled. With Grant in hot pursuit of Lee, who was fleeing southwest toward Danville, Virginia, Sherman aimed his army northwest on April 10 to prevent Johnston's army, then "known to be at Smithfield," North Carolina, from joining Lee's. Within a day, Sherman reached Smithfield, but Johnston had fled toward Raleigh.

On that evening, April 11, Sherman received word from Grant that he had accepted Lee's surrender two days earlier at Appomattox. "Of course, this created a perfect *furore* of rejoicing, and we all regarded the war as over, for I knew that General Johnston had no army with which to oppose mine," wrote Sherman in his memoirs. "So that the only questions that remained were, would he surrender at Raleigh? Or would he allow his army to disperse into guerrilla-bands, to 'die in the last ditch,' and entail on his country an indefinite and prolonged military occupation, and of consequent desolation?" The latter prospect was as antithetical to Sherman as he knew it was to the president. "I then remembered Mr. Lincoln's repeated expression that he wanted the rebel soldiers not only defeated, but 'back at their homes, engaged in their civil pursuits.'"[10]

On April 14, he directed his troops that "the inhabitants will be dealt with kindly, looking to an early reconciliation." By that time, he had cornered Johnston near Raleigh at Durham's Station. The same day Johnston sent Sherman a request for a temporary suspension of hostilities and for Sherman to "communicate to Lieutenant-General Grant, commanding the armies of the United States, the request that he will take like action in regard to other armies" in order that the "civil authorities" meet to determine the terms "to terminate the existing war." Sherman replied stiffly, "I am fully empowered to arrange with you any terms for the suspension of further hostilities between the armies commanded by you and those commanded by myself." If Sherman had confined his actions to those armies, he would not have brought the wrath of Stanton—and indeed much of the entire country for a time—down upon him. With Lincoln's desire to end the war and the president's words of generosity toward the enemy still in his ears, Sherman prepared to travel to Durham's Station to negotiate with the man he had earlier fought to the gates of Atlanta but whom he had never met.[11]

As Sherman boarded a private train on the morning of April 17 to meet Johnston, a telegraph officer raced to stop him. A ciphered message had just arrived from Morehead City, North Carolina, which demanded Sherman's attention. Waiting impatiently for more than thirty minutes for it to be decoded, Sherman was finally handed a telegram from Secretary of War Stanton. It contained the chilling news that Lincoln had been assassinated, Seward had been attacked, and there were indications of plots against Grant and other high-ranking officials. Indeed, Stanton warned that an assassin was on Sherman's trail. Sherman, Grant, and Lincoln had feared that civil war might degenerate into chaotic murder, but no one could have imagined anything this terrible.[12]

"Dreading the effect of such a message at that critical instant of time," Sherman swore the telegraph officer to secrecy, placed the telegram in his pocket, and boarded the train to Durham's Station for his appointment with Johnston. "As soon as we were alone together I showed him the dispatch announcing Mr. Lincoln's assassination, and watched him closely. The perspiration came out in large drops on his forehead, and he did not attempt to conceal his distress." Sherman told Johnston he had not yet informed his men about the assassination, that "Mr. Lincoln was particularly endeared to the soldiers," and he "feared that some foolish woman or man in Raleigh might say something or do something that would madden our men, and that a fate worse than that of Columbia would befall the place." It was then that the two men began discussing the desirability of preparing "terms that would embrace all the Confederate armies." Johnston pressed for such a sweeping agreement, but said he would have to obtain Jefferson Davis's permission to surrender all of the remaining armies in the field. He vowed to do so, and the two men agreed to meet again the next morning. Sherman returned to Raleigh, where he issued

Special Field Orders No. 56 on the afternoon of April 17: "The general commanding announces, with pain and sorrow, that on the evening of the 14th instant, at the theatre in Washington city, his Excellency the President of the United States, Mr. Lincoln, was assassinated by one who uttered the State motto of Virginia. . . . Thus it seems that our enemy, despairing of meeting us in open, manly warfare, begins to resort to the assassin's tools. . . ."[13]

Johnston and Confederate Secretary of War (and former vice president of the United States) John Breckinridge met Sherman the next morning with the confirmation that Johnston "had authority over all the Confederate armies." Sherman, "recalling the conversation of Mr. Lincoln, at City Point . . . sat down at the table, and wrote off the terms, which I thought concisely expressed his views and wishes, and explained that I was willing to submit these terms to the new President, Mr. (Andrew) Johnson." He then took the opportunity, as Lincoln had slyly suggested, to urge Breckinridge "that he had better get away . . . and [he] intimated that he would speedily leave the country forever. I may have also advised him that Mr. Davis too should get abroad as soon as possible."[14]

Whether or not Sherman's generous terms reflected Lincoln's wishes, there is little doubt that Sherman sincerely believed they did. More importantly, he acknowledged that his terms were not final until the new president approved them. Sherman fully believed his proposal would be approved in Washington, even though it dealt in depth with issues that went well beyond military terms. In addition to disbanding the Confederate armies, all "arms and public property" were to be returned to state arsenals; state governments were to be recognized by the U.S. president when state officers and legislators took loyalty oaths; federal courts were to be reestablished in the states; and all of the rights and guarantees of the Constitution were to once again be returned to all citizens.[15]

Sherman's relief and pride in his achievement were evident in the letters he sent to Grant, Halleck, and Ellen. To Grant, he enclosed the surrender terms, which, he wrote, "if approved by the President of the United States will produce Peace from the Potomac to the Rio Grande." To Halleck, Sherman laughingly brushed off the general's earlier warning that had elaborated on Stanton's, "describing the man Clark detailed to assassinate me. He had better be in a hurry or he will be too late." Then he turned serious in discussing Lincoln's assassination, and how his terms would avoid further disasters. "I cannot believe that even Mr. Davis was privy to the diabolical plot, but think it the emanation of a set of young men of the South who are the very devils. . . . Had I pushed Johnstons army to an extremity these would have dispersed and would have done important mischief."[16]

Before Sherman wrote to Ellen on April 18, he may have received her letter of April 10. She was not at all happy with the far less generous terms that Grant had offered to Lee. "I think the rebels ought not to have been allowed their side arms or horses, but I suppose Genl Grant knew best," she wrote her husband, and then said confidently, "The next news will be from you & then the whole affair will be closed." Whether or not he had read that letter when he wrote to her, his letter was full of confidence, too. He announced that he had "arranged terms for the disbandment of *all* the Confederate Armies from this to the Rio Grande. . . . I can hardly realize it, but I can see no slip. The terms are all on our side." On April 22, he wrote to her again: "We await a reply from Washington which finishes all the war by one process or forces us to push the fragments of the Confederate Army to the wall."[17]

Sherman believed that he had obtained the best possible surrender terms. If they were accepted in Washington, he would emerge from the war fully vindicated. His original estimate to Lincoln of the seriousness with which the North needed to wage war would be shown to be accurate; the charge of "insanity" would be erased from public consciousness in light of his manifest success. He could return to his family—his formidable foster father, his distinguished siblings and foster siblings, his long-absent wife, and his children—in triumph. Such confidence marked a shift in Sherman's outlook. Though he knew his marches were of lasting significance, Sherman had repeatedly expressed fears during the preceding six months that his rising reputation might be undone before the fighting stopped. In October 1864, he had written Ellen: "In Revolutions men fall & rise. Long before this war is over much as you hear me praised now you may hear me cursed & insulted. Read History, Read Coriolanus and you will see the true measure of popular applause." Sherman knew his history (and his Shakespeare) well; Roman general Coriolanus led the city's army to a magnificent victory, but its citizens did not appreciate his sacrifice, drove him from Rome, and branded him a traitor.[18]

While Sherman awaited a reply from Washington regarding his surrender terms, a national outcry over his actions erupted. According to one historian, no event of the Civil War other than Lincoln's assassination sparked as much newspaper coverage as did the controversy over Sherman's surrender terms to Johnston. The country had ridden an emotional roller coaster from triumph and joy after Lee's surrender, to grief and panic after the night of April 14. Fears of conspiracy and endless guerrilla warfare swept the city of Washington, and few in positions of power were in a mood to follow Lincoln's advice regarding lenient surrender terms, much less Sherman's proposal for sweeping reconciliation.[19]

When Sherman's courier delivered the proposed surrender terms to Grant in Washington on April 21, Grant recognized at once that Sherman had gone beyond acceptable limits of scope and leniency, and later that evening, Lincoln's Cabinet secretaries, meeting as President Johnson's Cabinet, unanimously rejected Sherman's proposed surrender terms. They could have stopped at that, but they did not. Fueled by panic and fear, the men who had benefited politically from Sherman's victories over the preceding three years now engaged in rank speculation about his motives. Navy Secretary Gideon Welles was one of the few voices of reason. He acknowledged that Sherman had committed an error, "but this error, if it be one, had its origin, I apprehend, with President Lincoln who was for prompt and easy terms with the Rebels." Welles defended Sherman, protesting, "we must not forget what good he has done," but Stanton could not say enough terrible things about Sherman. According to Stanton, Sherman had deliberately stepped beyond the military sphere in order to secure recognition of the Confederate government; Sherman had given guarantees of property rights that could embrace the continuation of slavery; Sherman had ordered that his troops step aside from the path of Jefferson Davis's flight from Richmond; and Sherman had facilitated Davis's removal of millions in Confederate gold, some of which, no doubt, would end up in Sherman's pockets. Stanton's accusations in that closed-door Cabinet session were awful, but they were not the worst that he did.[20]

Grant said little during the Cabinet session and left immediately after it to go in person to tell Sherman his terms had been rejected. Because of heightened security concerns, Grant's travel was kept secret, so Grant's unannounced appearance at his camp surprised Sherman. In a brief conversation, Grant described the terror that had washed over the city and led the Cabinet to reject Sherman's terms, circumstances that Sherman's isolation in rural North Carolina had kept from him. Sherman then dutifully contacted Johnston, and in short order, they agreed to the same terms that Grant had given Lee. Grant never revealed that Stanton had also ordered Grant to take command of Sherman's army.

It was not until Grant returned to Washington that Sherman became aware of the full extent of Stanton's treachery. The day after the Cabinet meeting, the secretary of war had released to a host of New York reporters his account of the meeting and his accusations against the general. Newspapers all across the country snatched up the first reports and were soon eagerly feasting on Sherman's honor and reputation. Some could not resist chalking up Sherman's latest disaster to his "insanity." Others charged that Sherman had deliberately chosen not to impose upon Johnston the same terms Grant had given Lee. For example, the *New York Times* of April 24 reported and editorialized:

GEN. SHERMAN'S EXTRAORDINARY NEGOTIATION FOR PEACE.
The loyal public will read with profound surprise the terms which Gen. SHER-
MAN tendered to the rebel government . . . [O]ne is at a loss to know which
side agreed to surrender. . . . The act, viewed in its purely military bearings,
must be regarded as one of most dangerous insubordination.[21]

The accusation of insubordination—a grave charge against a military officer—focused on Stanton's claim that Sherman had knowingly stepped beyond
his military authority to settle civil issues and in doing so, had violated the express wishes of the late President Lincoln. More than a month earlier, Lincoln
had issued orders to Grant, in a telegram from Stanton, forbidding the lieutenant general from discussing any civil issues with Lee, and Stanton wanted
the world to believe that Sherman had previously seen that telegram. Helpfully,
Stanton provided a copy of the telegram for the newspapers to include in their
stories. Stanton also, helpfully, gave a copy of the telegram to Grant for him to
give to Sherman. Grant carried it with him when he traveled to North Carolina
to negate Sherman's surrender terms on April 24. As a result, Sherman saw the
telegram for the first time on the same day it was published in the newspapers.[22]

Not only was the existence of the telegram news to Sherman, but Lincoln's
alleged express order to Grant not to discuss civil issues with enemy military commanders had not been raised during the conversations at City Point.
Stanton's worst was perfected when the newspapers included Stanton's wholly
fabricated charge that Sherman was allowing Davis to escape with millions of
dollars in gold. In addition, Stanton had sent word of his suspicions to Henry
Halleck, then commanding the forces of occupation in Richmond. As a result,
Halleck issued an order to Sherman's subordinate officers that they were not
to obey his commands. In short order, Sherman was proclaimed to the world
as a traitor, Coriolanus redux.[23]

That world included Lancaster, Ohio, where Ellen had been waiting confidently for the glorious news that her husband had concluded the final peace of
the war. When, on April 24, she saw the newspapers, she was no doubt stunned
by the news and by the savage press outcry. Adding to her deep humiliation,
Sherman was hanged in effigy on the lawn in front of the Ewing house, and
Minnie's classmates harassed her at school. When later newspaper editions

verified the generous terms that Sherman had offered Joseph Johnston, she sat down on April 26 and wrote one of the most remarkable letters of the war.[24]

Dearest Cump,

News electrified us on Monday of your mild terms to Joe Johnson. You will see the strictness & the abuse of the newspapers. You know me well enough to know that I never would agree in any such policy as that towards perjured traitors as many of them are being deserters from the Regular Army of the United States.

But my opinion of you is unaltered and my heart not having been set on the popular favor I care nothing for the clamor they have raised. I know your motive was pure. . . . [H]owever much I differ from you I honor and respect you— for the heart that could prompt such terms to men who have cost us individually one keen great pang which death will alone assuage—the loss of Willy. . . .

I think you have made a great mistake but it is well enough for you do not wish to be a politician & you have done no harm to even yourself except in a political view. Your record no man can tarnish and to the latest posterity it will shine pure and bright & none the less so for this last act which is so thoroughly unpopular. . . .

Mr. Stanton in his summing up against you proves that he has been nursing wrath against you & you have now given him occasion to pour it out at a time and in a way to most deeply embitter the "many=headed=monster thing"— the people. So be it.

God is over all and He will bring good out of evil to those who trust in Him. My only prayer for us all is that we may have eternal life. What is earth's fame & glory now to Mr. Lincoln or Genl McPherson and what does Willy pray for now?

As to this world's view—your record is made it is grand—it is high—it is unalterable & imperishable as long as time lasts.

As to yourself, you are incapable of a mean selfish sordid motive & to me you are far dearer when people blame than when they praise you. . . .

Ever dearest Cump Your truly affectionate,

Ellen

Ellen knew her husband, heart and head, and she knew he had no sinister motive for the terms he proposed. Despite their many differences, or perhaps because they dealt with them so directly and honestly, Ellen knew that Sherman would be as mortified as she at the slander of the newspapers and the calumny of Stanton. Under similar circumstances, it is not difficult to imagine that another general's wife (Jessie? Nelly?) would have avoided mentioning her own negative opinion of his actions and instead would have focused only on soothing her husband's wounded honor. Ellen, though, did something that was far more valuable and far more constructive: she told her husband the whole truth. She told him she believed his judgment flawed but his motives pure. Ellen had always recognized Sherman's weaknesses and his mistakes, and she never shrank from admitting them, even to him. It was precisely because she was so honest about what she thought were his failings that Sherman could have complete confidence in her praise, absolute assurance that her admiration was genuine and well deserved. Through Ellen's combination of remonstrance and respect, he could understand why so many disagreed with him, and he could believe that those who disagreed with him could nevertheless esteem him.

At that moment, though, he was furious at Stanton and Halleck, and he did not care who knew it. He also wanted revenge, and he was not reticent about letting people know that either. Among his generals, he poured out his rage, "pac[ing] up and down the room like a caged lion," calling Stanton a "mean, vindictive, scheming politician." Ten years later, the charges still stung: "I was outraged beyond measure, and was resolved to resent the insult, cost what it might," Sherman wrote in his memoirs. As Sherman's army continued its march north from Raleigh, his officers and his men were as outraged by the slanders as he was. Notwithstanding Halleck's directives, they obeyed Sherman's orders. They also joined in snubbing Halleck when they marched through Richmond on their way to Washington. As Halleck stood facing the lines of soldiers who marched by, he could not help but notice that, to a man, they directed their gaze stiffly away from him. Halleck attempted to make up to Sherman, assuring him, "If . . . I used language which has given you offense, it was unintentional, and I deeply regret it," but Sherman rejected both his lame apology and his invitation to meet: "When you advised me of the Assassin Clark being on my track, I little dreamed he would turn up in the direction and guise he did."[25]

After recovering from their shock at Sherman's surrender terms and the savage newspaper attacks, the Sherman-Ewing family team once again swung into action. Their tactics were different this time. The family made no effort to publish statements in support of Sherman's agreement with Johnston, since the terms were odious to the Ewings; nor did Sherman's family try to refute, point by point, all the falsehoods that Stanton had broadcast. But they did publicly defend his honor. Soon thereafter, reason prevailed when it became clear that Sherman had never been told of Lincoln's telegram to Grant, and that Sherman's military orders in no way assisted Jefferson Davis's escape.[26]

"Let some one newspaper know that the Vandal Sherman is encamped near . . . Alexandria," he informed Grant's chief of staff on May 14. He had just arrived outside the capital city in preparation for a final review of the Union armies and the subsequent mustering out of most of his army. Controversy over his surrender terms still raged, and Sherman still vowed vengeance against Stanton. So outspoken was he on the latter score that his brothers John and Charles Sherman and his foster brothers Hugh and Thomas Ewing Jr. sought each other out, dragging Tom Jr. from a barber's chair at the Willard Hotel to strategize on how best to tamp down Sherman's ferocious temper. They sent John to talk some sense to Sherman, but in fact, time was again their greatest ally.[27]

In mid-May, Ellen wrote her husband a letter of joy and praise. "I assure you we are truly charmed to find that you have had so good an opportunity of returning the insult of that base man Halleck." Desirous of moderating further efforts at revenge on Sherman's part, she also offered good counsel. "Father is very anxious to See you. He thinks Stanton & the President will lose no means to destroy you if you lay your self liable to or compromi[se] yourself in any way towards Stanton as he is a 'Superior Officer &c' . . . I hope you will not give them the truimph of a court martial over you for breach of military etiquette." Ellen devised a clever means of chastising Stanton: "Two days after Stanton fulminated that astounding falsehood," she told Sherman in the same letter, "I telegraphed you through him. Stating that 'Father & I highly approved your [reply to Stanton]' &c. &c. Stanton replied that he would forward the dispatch without delay & signed himself very truly my friend. I think you never got it."[28]

Though some newspapers and some officials worked hard to keep the controversy alive, the nation soon regained its perspective on the man who had done so much to defeat the Confederacy. By the time Sherman marched at the head of his Western armies down Pennsylvania Avenue in the Grand Review on May 24, his reputation had largely been restored. In fact, it was Sherman himself who pointedly revived the controversy that day. He dismounted at the reviewing stand in front of the White House to join Ellen, eight-year-old Tommy, and Thomas Ewing, and, according to his memoirs, "Passing them, I shook hands with the president, General Grant, and each member of the cabinet. As I approached Mr. Stanton, he offered me his hand, but I declined it publicly, and the fact was universally noticed. I then took my post on the left of the President, and for six hours and a half stood, while the army passed. . . . It was, in my judgment, the most magnificent army in existence. . . ."[29]

Satisfied that he had bested both Halleck and Stanton with his very public snubs, Sherman then characteristically turned to his duties, executing all the orders and paperwork necessary to disband his historic army and bidding his men farewell. Ellen was still worried, though, that Stanton had the means and the desire to humble her husband. Without her husband's knowledge, since Sherman certainly would never have agreed, Ellen paid a courtesy call on Stanton. There is no record of the substance of the meeting, but always conscious of the possibility of a wife's influence on her husband, Ellen also arranged for flowers to be sent to Mrs. Stanton.[30]

CHAPTER 20

"No greater glory than to fill a patriot's grave"

The rest of the Shermans' life together was relatively quiet, but relative only to their Civil War years. It was in a letter to her father in 1869, when the family was in St. Louis during an outbreak of erysipelas, a painful and often fatal disease, that Ellen wrote: "It is high or low tide with us ever." Their postwar years were indeed filled with highs and lows. Immediately after the Grand Review, Ellen had the great joy of being escorted to the Sanitary Fair in Chicago by her husband, who was named its president, and the pleasure of seeing the Catholic table triumph over the Protestants' in raising funds. Sherman then settled into his post as commanding general of the Military Division of the Mississippi. In that capacity, he was responsible for the heartland of the country, where his own heart had always been. The region held many challenges, including nearly 200,000 Indians, at least half of whom still contested the presence of the white man on their land. They also contested the building of the transcontinental railroad that Lincoln had begun, so Sherman organized the western army to protect the working parties. He always considered his early advocacy for the railroad and his role in assisting its completion in 1869 among his most valuable contributions to the nation and made a point of being in the telegraph office in Washington to learn that the golden spike was driven at Promontory, Utah, connecting the two tracks.[1]

During that time, the Shermans' personal relationship was recharged by their opportunity to live together in a home of their own in St. Louis, where the general placed his military headquarters. In 1867, at the age of forty-three, Ellen gave birth to their eighth and last child, Philemon Tecumseh Sherman, who was always called Cumpy. Upon Grant's inauguration as president in 1869, the new chief executive made Sherman lieutenant general of the U.S. Army. But the two men's friendship soon suffered when Grant supported Secretary of War John Rawlins rather than Sherman in a dispute about the lieutenant general's authority.[2]

Ellen suffered her own great blow in 1871, when her eighty-two-year-old father died. But her loss was mixed with a great joy. In his final hours, surrounded by his family, Ewing accepted conversion to the Catholic faith. Ellen's persistence had accomplished what her mother had begun. The Catholic conversion of such a prominent Protestant did not go uncontested, however, and Ewing's soul was fought over even as his mortal remains were committed to earth. A Methodist newspaper characterized Purcell's funeral mass as an attempt "to eulogize the Romish Church, to the shameful neglect, if not positive insult, of the memory of the distinguished citizen, over whose senseless body mummeries were performed and statements made that in any rational hour of his former life he would have spurned with contempt."[3]

To counter such charges and deal with the loss she felt, Ellen compiled a book of tributes to her father. She worked on the project for more than a year, asking distinguished men in politics, law, and business to write about Thomas Ewing, with special emphasis on his conversion to Catholicism. One of those requests went to Sherman, but he refused to take the bait. Instead, he wrote an elegant encomium to his foster father's brilliance and erudition and charitable nature, while pointedly avoiding discussion of the conversion to Catholicism that he knew was still the object of Ellen's fondest hopes for him. "It struck me as something out of my line entirely," he wrote of the request to "allude to the fact that your father died in the Catholic Church . . . it would sit awkwardly on my pen." While Ellen undertook her memorial tribute to her father, Sherman set out on a long-planned tour of Europe. There, royalty and the Continent's most famous military men feted him. He also traveled to Italy and met Pope Pius IX. Though Ellen did not accompany her "protector" on that visit as she had hoped more than twenty years earlier (perhaps because of her health or the Victorian-era custom of a year's mourning for the loss of a parent), it was one of the great thrills of Ellen's Catholic life that her husband met the pope.[4]

Minnie's wedding in 1874 was one of the grandest events of the Washington social season—rivaling even Nellie Grant's wedding in the White House that year. Prominent Washingtonians and friends from across the country were treated to the pomp, ritual, and mystery of a Catholic ceremony (though Ellen instructed the bishop that she had "decided on a low mass since there will be so many impatient and unappreciative persons" attending). It was a personal, social, political, and religious triumph for Ellen, who finally had the Catholic wedding she had dreamed of for herself so many years earlier. The next year saw publication of Sherman's memoirs, which proved successful in generating income and controversy.[5]

The year 1877 marked the fiftieth anniversary of the elevation of Pope Pius IX, and at the earnest request of her archbishop, Ellen took on the massive task of collecting the United States' tribute to the pope's Diamond Jubilee celebration. In gratitude for her work, Pius IX sent her a letter and a rosary he had blessed. It seemed then that her bond to her church could not be made stronger, but the very next year her son Tom announced that he had decided to become a priest. Ellen's profound joy at the realization of her greatest hope for Tom was muted in the face of her husband's bitter rage and grief over what he perceived to be the loss of a third son. For a time, their conflicting passions wrenched the family apart, and Ellen moved to Baltimore briefly to live near where Rachel and Cumpy attended Catholic school. Though reconciliation with Tom was years away for Sherman, soon Ellen and Cump reunited and once again took pleasure in each other and in their expanding family of grandchildren.[6]

All too soon, though, tragedy struck in the midst of their joy. Within the space of two weeks in 1882, two of Minnie Sherman Fitch's young daughters died of a typhoid-like illness. Their deaths were a terrible blow to the Shermans, who knew that pain all too well. For a time after that, Minnie and her husband lived in the Shermans' home. In 1884, when another of Minnie's daughters crawled into bed with her grandmother, little Eleanor Sherman Fitch felt under the pillow and found some folded clothing. Grandmother Ellen explained that it belonged to an uncle that young Eleanor had never met. Ellen had kept Willy's "sergeant's uniform" under her pillow for more than twenty years.[7]

Sherman's friendship with Grant had revived by the time Grant lay dying of cancer in 1884. Sherman visited Grant at his home in New York City in December of that year as the impoverished hero of the Union raced against death to complete his memoirs. Cump reported to Ellen, "General Grant says my visits to him have done him more good than all of the doctors." While Grant lay dying, Sherman lobbied Congress to secure a Federal pension for Grant and his soon-to-be-widow Julia. At Grant's funeral, fellow mourners saw Sherman standing at attention, his frame shaking while tears streamed down his face.[8]

The sad times were leavened, for Cump at least, by the sheer magnitude of his celebrity. Historian Lee Kennett called his postwar life his "banquet years." Sherman faithfully attended reunions of his beloved Army of the Tennessee; he never forgot his "boys." He also loved the theater and opera and dining with friends; it was a rare evening when he was not engaged. Sherman enjoyed the company of women and made a point of kissing as many of them as he could. Historian Michael Fellman provided excerpts of intimate correspondence with

Ellen Sherman (*center*), with her children (*left to right*) Lizzie Sherman, Father Tom Sherman, Ellie Sherman Thackara, Rachel Sherman, Cumpy Sherman, Minnie Sherman Fitch, and four grandchildren (William, Eleanor, and Thomas Fitch, and Elizabeth Thackara). This photograph was taken at the house in Oakland, Maryland, 1882, after the death of Minnie's two daughters. (*Courtesy of the University of Notre Dame Archives*)

two women in his later years. Kennett said that Sherman engaged in "discreet liaisons" that "only came to light long after his death." Historian John Marszalek wrote that he "constantly placed himself in situations where he had the opportunity to philander" and concluded, "there must have been some flings."[9]

But Sherman always returned to Ellen. Even when Sherman entertained at home, though, Ellen encouraged her daughters to play the role of hostess. "I am glad [Minnie] will so soon be able to relieve me of a duty that is irksome and too much in addition to my other cares, for my present age," Ellen wrote her father in 1867, when she was forty-three. As time went on, Ellen withdrew further and further from Sherman's social life. When Minnie married, Lizzie and then Rachel took her place as hostess. Ellen spent her energies on numerous church-related projects. She had no stamina for entertainments after a day of soliciting funds for the young women's shelter she established in Washington or for Indian missionary work that her brother Charley was advancing.[10]

No doubt, she was also reluctant to appear often in public next to her perpetually youthful-looking husband. Cump had earned his wrinkles early from a life outdoors, riding and camping, so his face changed little over the years, though his red hair and beard turned grey. He always moved with energy and barely put on weight. By contrast, Ellen had aged appreciably by the end of the war, eight pregnancies taking their toll. Though the George P. A. Healey portrait of her, painted in 1865, depicts a beautiful, slender, mature woman, petite Ellen steadily gained weight throughout her life, and it bothered her. In 1887, apparently piqued by some remark by Cump about her health, she shot back at him: "I was weighed in a Drug Store last week & I weigh exactly the same as when I left St. Louis 165 lbs. When we went to Washington in 1869, Mrs. Grant weighed 175 & I weighed 150—so I am not a monstrosity even yet nor in danger of dying of mere fat. I know about Mrs. Grant's weight & mine because we were weighed at the White House one afternoon when I was spending the afternoon with her."[11]

Ellen's health, never good, deteriorated as she aged. Her scrofula recurred, the hideous boils a source of pain and embarrassment. She began to exhibit signs of what was then called dropsy, or congenital heart failure—difficulty in breathing and swelling of her legs and ankles. The Shermans had been living in a series of hotels and rented homes, but finally in the summer of 1888, Sherman bought a house of their own in New York City. A thoroughly delighted Ellen had only months to enjoy it.[12]

Though Sherman had long believed that Ellen's frequent complaints about her ill health were exaggerated, it was clear that her heart was weak and her health failing. Once she moved into her bedroom on the top floor of the house that autumn, she never left her suite. Sherman paid every attention to her as she rapidly faded; he spent most of each day at her side. At the very end, on November 28, 1888, he had just returned to his basement-floor office when Ellen's nurse called to him that his wife was dying. Racing up two sets of stairs, he was heard to shout, "Ellen, wait for me! No one has ever loved you as I loved you!" His sixty-four-year-old wife was dead when he entered the room. "[H]ers was the easiest [death] of all," he wrote to a longtime friend. "In the last hour she seemed twenty years younger exactly like the Healy portrait . . . and as such I shall ever remember her. To her the world was a day—Heaven Eternity—and could I, I would not bring her back."[13]

Ellen's death sparked an international outpouring of sympathy for Sherman. Letters and telegrams flooded the New York City brownstone at 75 West Seventy-First Street. They spoke of Ellen's good works and of the Shermans' lifelong companionship. Many were from prominent people, including Julia Grant, John Hay, and a host of politicians and military acquaintances. The bulk of the letters, though, were from "his boys," old men who had once served under Sherman and who remembered those days as the high point of their lives. They grieved at his loss, but it was clear they also welcomed the chance to reconnect with the man who had made them immortal.

> Toledo Ohio, Nov 30th
> Gen W T Sherman
> Accept our loving sympathy with you in your affliction. I could not rest untill I sent this messenger.
> Yours truly
> James T Baldwin
> I followed you through to the sea[14]

According to those around him, Sherman was genuinely shocked by Ellen's death; he truly had not believed she was as ill as she was. She had been an integral part of his life for nearly all of his sixty-eight years. Her absence plunged Sherman into profound depression. A week after her funeral, he was unable to respond personally to messages of sympathy. Although he was an active and healthy man at the time of her death and gradually regained his interest in the world, Sherman lived barely two more years. In early 1891, he again contracted erysipelas, a streptococcal infection that manifests itself in large, angry, painful red patches on the face and throat and legs. He had suffered from it before, but this time, he soon contracted something worse, perhaps pneumonia or sepsis, since erysipelas can migrate into the bloodstream. His breathing became labored; his family began gathering. Contacted in London, Father Tom Sherman boarded the first ship to New York.[15]

As he took to his bed, Sherman began reading *Great Expectations*. The choice of author was not surprising; Dickens had always been a favorite of Cump and Ellen, who had each read all of Dickens's novels and reread many of them several times. The choice of novels was, perhaps, not surprising either. Sherman's seven decades had taken many turns, was marked by many highs and lows, and hinged upon many contingencies. Perhaps Sherman thought even at that late date he might find a clue to the "why" of his own life by parsing that novel again. Two days before his seventy-first birthday, Cump opened the book and began reading: "My father's family name being Pirrip, and my Christian name Philip, my infant tongue could make of both names nothing longer or more explicit than Pip. So, I called myself Pip, and came to be called Pip." First published in 1864, it is the tale of a young, orphaned urchin with an unusual name, who was raised by a man who inspired independence, whose life had as many lows as highs, and whose rise from obscurity to success was equally motivated and frustrated by a most difficult woman.[16]

The ailing Sherman soon set the book aside. Gathered in his bedroom were his daughters Minnie, Lizzie, Rachel, and Ellie, his son Cumpy, and his older brother John. Tom was still at sea, but a Catholic priest was there, summoned by his Catholic children, though Sherman, like Thomas Ewing, had not embraced the faith during his active life. Nor would Sherman do so on his deathbed, not even to be reunited with Ellen and his beloved Willy. He had written shortly after Ellen's death that she "would have given anything if I would have simply said Amen; but it was impossible." Sherman would leave the world as much his own man as he had faced it.[17]

As he slipped from consciousness, however, his children sought to redeem his soul, as their mother had tried all her life. On February 13, as Sherman lay comatose, they had the priest administer the last rites. Sherman rallied enough at the last to mumble a few words, without really communicating with those around him. In particular, he gasped a phrase that recalled his West Point oath of "true faith and allegiance" to the United States. Before he died on the afternoon of February 14, 1891, more than once Sherman whispered the words he had previously instructed to be engraved on his monument: "Faithful & honorable; faithful & honorable."[18]

Newspapers had been publishing daily bulletins about the general's health, the same sort of national deathwatch they had instigated during Grant's last illness six years earlier. When they learned about the last rites, they could not resist raising a storm about it, as they had about so many other events in his life. Sherman's brother John, they claimed, had stepped out of the room for a brief time, and the general's children took that opportunity to direct the priest to perform a ceremony that both Cump and John would have prohibited. John was genuinely outraged and slammed the story shut: his brother was "too good a Christian and too human a man to deny to his children the consolations of their religion." For good measure, John avowed that he would have allowed the ceremony if he had been present. Public fascination with Sherman's deathbed drama echoed that over Thomas Ewing's.[19]

The nineteenth century reverberated with ugly anti-Catholic prejudice, with charges that Catholics served only their pope and not their country. But if there were any question whether a Catholic could be a loyal American, Ellen Ewing Sherman was the definitive answer. In her words and deeds, in private and in public, Ellen displayed a passion for the United States of America that the most avid Protestant might hope to match but could never excel. Ellen had instructed Tommy and Willy to "wave the flag" for Lincoln's election in 1860. Even before the Civil War began, she urged Cump to rejoin the army to defend the Union. When he wanted to hide in the wake of the charge of insanity, she rallied his spirits and battled to keep him in the war. When Sherman threatened to resign, she sharply rejected that course as desertion, urged him to remain on duty, and prophesied great victories for him. She wished she were a man so she could fight. She wished her sons were old enough to fight. She wished her daughters were sons so they could fight. Of her beloved brother's possible death at Second Bull Run she declared, "No greater glory than to fill a patriot's grave." The thought of Catholic secessionists drove her to pray fervently that "vengeance will fall upon them yet for being false to their country." Fortified by her faith, Ellen weathered the tragic deaths of two young sons even as she urged her husband to stay in the field and wage unrelenting war against the Rebellion.[20]

The religion that sustained Ellen's soul never competed with her loyalty to the Union or to her family. Looking out over her sixty-four years, they were all seamlessly woven into the tapestry of her life. For many of those years, Cump resented her devotion to Catholicism and her attachment to her father, but her loyalty to her husband was enduring. Each time a crisis struck during the Civil War, Ellen rose to the occasion. Ellen's fierce passions were ever for her husband, her faith, and her country.

PART FOUR

Center of Gravity

Julia Dent Grant

JULIA GRANT'S CIVIL WAR

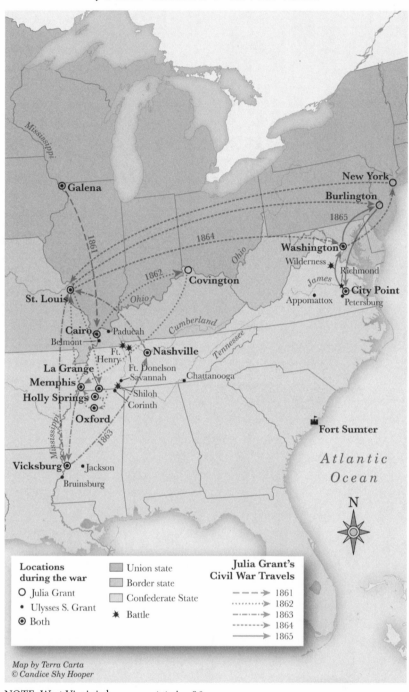

Map by Terra Carta
© Candice Shy Hooper

NOTE: West Virginia became a state in 1863.

Chapter 21

"sunshine"

As dusk settled on the Ohio River on a chilly February day in 1862, the United States steamer *New Uncle Sam* pulled away from the dock at Cairo, Illinois, heading toward Fort Henry in rebel-held Tennessee. Onboard, thirty-nine-year-old Brig. Gen. Ulysses S. Grant "seemed anxious, and more than usually silent." A week earlier, his commanding officer, Maj. Gen. Henry Wager Halleck had brusquely vetoed Grant's plan to assault the strategically positioned Confederate fort, then reversed his decision on January 30. Fearful that Halleck might have another change of mind, Grant "carefully observed the river behind them with his field glass," and when the boat carried him past the final Union telegraph station on the riverbank, "the anxiety imprinted upon his face, changed into an expression of satisfaction." To his chief of staff, Assistant Adj. Gen. John Rawlins, Grant exclaimed, with uncharacteristic enthusiasm, "Now we seem to be safe, beyond recall by either electricity or steam. . . . We *will* succeed, Rawlins; we *must* succeed."[1]

Delighted as he was to be safely underway, Grant's thoughts soon turned from anticipation of the battle ahead to thoughts of the woman he was leaving behind. His wife Julia and their children had lived with Grant in camp over the past three months. Through those same field glasses, he could have seen them on the riverbank watching his departure, and no doubt he wondered when they would all be together again. For Grant, that question was not a matter of mere sentiment but one more akin to survival.[2]

Ulysses Grant needed Julia in a way that none of the other generals needed their wives. He craved constant reassurance of her love, her steadfast confidence in him, and the cheer she always brought to his days. She could sustain him through his greatest troubles. Three times in his military career and more than half a dozen times as a civilian, he found himself in a condition of near occupational immobility. Despite the fact that in every one of the military instances he had just been awarded higher grade, there was no corresponding increase in responsibility or meaningful work to occupy his mind, and there was little hope for future advancement. Each of those instances occurred during a significant period of time without either Julia's presence or satisfactory correspondence from her. Each of those times, Grant slid into despair and depression. Each of those times, he contemplated leaving the army. One time, he did. By contrast, in his civilian life, although he repeatedly suffered frustration, boredom, crushing financial failure, scorn from his father and father-in-law, pity from his former army colleagues, and bleak prospects for improvement in his situation, he maintained his emotional equilibrium. Grant moved relentlessly from one setback to another with determination and often with a sense of optimism, without falling prey to paralyzing melancholia. The most significant difference between the military and the civilian episodes was that during the latter, Julia and his children were with him. Her presence nourished his soul. But she could not accompany Grant on his mission to capture Fort Henry, and as he lost sight of her on the dock, he feared losing touch with her as well. Aboard the *New Uncle Sam*, Grant's personal concerns blossomed into empathy for all of the men under his command who longed for their families and treasured the letters they received sporadically via the war's early, chaotic mail service. Grant's thought soon became father to the deed.

With him aboard the steamer was Absalom H. Markland, a special agent of the U.S. Post Office Department. Markland, Grant's childhood schoolmate, had recently been detailed to Cairo to investigate problems with the U.S. mail service in that important military hub. On the eve of the steamer's departure, Markland remembered that Grant "asked me if I did not want to see a fight, and invited me to go to Fort Henry with him." Markland eagerly accepted. Though their paths had crossed earlier during Markland's stay in Cairo, it was not until Grant began the trip away from Julia that the general "inquired if it were not possible, to keep the mail up to the army and to take the soldier's letter home," wrote Markland in an account penned more than twenty years later. "On my answering that I thought that this could be done," recalled Markland, "he gave me that branch of the service, and from that beginning sprang the great army mail service of the war, and to Gen. Grant the credit of originating that service belongs."[3]

Mail service was one of Grant's highest priorities throughout the war; its importance to him was apparent from the beginning. Grant's Special Field Orders No. 1, issued February 6, 1862, placed Markland in "charge of all mail matter from and to the troops." Five days after Union forces occupied Fort

Henry, on the eve of the Battle of Fort Donelson, Grant issued General Field Orders No. 10, specifying that "Here after there will be a daily line of steamers between this place and Cairo . . . taking on the mails. Two good boats will be put on the line for this purpose."[4]

The battles of Fort Henry and especially Fort Donelson, where Grant entered history as "Unconditional Surrender Grant," served as the general's springboard to the nation's highest military grade and worldwide fame. Lincoln had taken note of the man from Galena, Illinois, earlier in the war because of Grant's decisive actions at Paducah, Kentucky, and Belmont, Missouri. Grant's success at Forts Henry and Donelson, which shut the Confederacy out of western Tennessee and western Kentucky and opened vital waterways, riveted the president's attention on the young brigadier. As he signed the commission promoting Grant to major general of volunteers in the wake of the Fort Donelson victory, Lincoln's quiet but proud observation to Secretary of War Stanton revealed that the general's victories were of special interest to him. "If the Southerners think that man for man they are better than our Illinois men, or Western men generally," observed the president, with evident pride in his fellow Illinoisan, "they will discover themselves in a grievous mistake."[5]

Those victories also marked the beginning of another war-long partnership that aided the Union war effort immeasurably. Cloaked in Grant's authority and carried along with his army, Markland labored tirelessly to provide reliable mail service that helped soldiers and families bridge the anxious and lonely gap between the front line and the home front. No action Grant took as military commander during the Civil War more clearly reflected his personal priority—love of family—than Grant's devotion to organizing efficient mail service for the men in the field. Doubtless, Markland's efficiency improved the morale of the general's troops, who received letters from their loved ones more reliably, but ironically, it may have increased Grant's loneliness at times. The more frequent the arrival of mail shipments, the more vulnerable Grant was to disappointment when they contained nothing from his beloved Julia.

Julia was a faithful lover, but she was a faithless correspondent. Grant's letters to her from 1844 to 1862 brim with painful pleas for her to write to him. They are often truly heartbreaking to read. Despite Grant's reliable output of letters to her, Julia neglected her correspondence with him, often for months at a time. When she did write, her letters were usually short and oddly aloof from his. She rarely responded to Grant's specific requests for information about her and the children, though he asked her over and over about them. She almost never provided him reassurance that funds and other items he sent to her arrived safely, even when he repeated requests that she do so. Almost assuredly, Julia fibbed to him from time to time to hide her failings—claiming alternatively that some of her letters to him or some of his to her had been lost in the mail system. In her memoirs, she wrote time and again of the many lovely letters she received from "Ulys" from battle zones and remote military outposts. She never mentioned her own meager output or how it drove Grant to anguish and depression.

One cannot read Grant's letters to Julia without a rising sense of compassion for him and indignation at her; Julia's behavior appears thoughtless, at times even callous. The vast evidence of her expansive, loving personality and her undying affection for Grant, however, belies those adjectives. There is no complete answer to why she neglected to write to him, although a physical defect in one of her eyes played an important role. There is no doubt that she felt real guilt about her failure to write, but neither love nor guilt could move her to act. Debilitating depression gripped Grant in the dark, lonely months without letters from Julia. By the time the Civil War began, it seemed apparent to both of them that she would not—or could not—change.

Because reliable mutual correspondence was simply not an option for the couple, Grant resolved to keep Julia near him as much as possible. Julia lived with her husband in the field more often and for longer periods of time than any of the wives of Lincoln's other generals. Julia was with Grant at every opportunity. The amount of time she spent with her husband during the war is extraordinary.

Her reassuring companionship preserved Grant's equilibrium, that quiet calm that struck every person he encountered and that particularly marked his demeanor as a military leader. Julia provided equal parts of love, confidence, and cheer, and Grant made certain that she understood just how important the last quality—"sunshine," he called it—was to him. The consequences of Julia's presence in camp with Grant were, however, not confined to their effects on her husband, as important as those were. Of course, it is never possible to know how history might have unfolded if circumstances were changed, but the course of events would have changed, even if only slightly, with any difference in people, actions, or timing. Because of Grant's insistence that Julia live with him for what proved to be the final four months of the war, at least three important events in the last week of Abraham Lincoln's life unfolded as they did. One of those was Lincoln's last night, at Ford's Theatre on April 14, 1865.

CHAPTER 22

"this, to me, most delicate subject"

Hiram Ulysses Grant was born in a small, comfortable house on the banks of the Ohio River at Point Pleasant, Ohio, on April 27, 1822. He was the first son of Hannah Simpson Grant and Jesse Root Grant. Not long after his own mother's early death, Jesse had been apprenticed to his older half-brother, who was a tanner, and Jesse followed him into the trade. Jesse's fear of debt and his relentless focus on money helped to make him a sharp businessman but also made him stingy and mean. Young "Lyss" was put to work early in his father's business, but he so hated everything associated with the sight and smell of butchering animals that he sought refuge as a delivery boy, where his love of horses found a productive outlet in his father's eyes.[1]

Jesse Grant had worked for a time at a tannery owned by a brother of the abolitionist John Brown and was an outspoken opponent of slavery. In fact, he was outspoken about many things. His fierce interest in politics found an outlet in a steady stream of letters to politicians and newspapers. He was extravagant in his praise for his son when Grant succeeded but equally harsh in expressing disappointment on the many occasions when Grant failed to meet his high expectations. Hannah, too, loved her son, though her contemporaries could never recall that she displayed affection toward him—or anyone else, for that matter. Although Grant wept when he learned of her death, nothing known about her life suggests a nurturing nature. Grant never indicated that his childhood was an unhappy one; indeed, he said it was quite the opposite. Dominated by Jesse's stern parsimony and Hannah's severe demeanor, though, he grew into a quiet, shy youth.

In the spring of 1840, according to the records of the U.S. Military Academy, seventeen-year-old Grant stood five-feet one-inch tall and weighed 117 pounds. Four years later, when the army measured him again before his graduation, the young man had shot up six inches, but because of a worrisome respiratory illness, he still weighed only 117 pounds. The skinny lieutenant had smooth, wavy auburn hair, a high forehead, and brilliant blue eyes, which were usually calm, but could twinkle on occasion. Grant's son and his granddaughter recalled that he smiled at them often, though he didn't smile with his mouth, he smiled with his eyes. Without a beard, his face was smooth, his features refined, almost feminine, in the opinion of more than one observer. Like Lincoln, when he did grow a beard, it aged him agreeably. Grant revealed a dry sense of humor among intimates, but he most often displayed quieter qualities of composure and reticence. Grant never learned to dance, disliked music all his life, and, according to at least one close acquaintance, never initiated a conversation with a woman. He was not at ease in noisy, crowded, social events. He sought to avoid the limelight, even as ambition to be worthy of it burned inside him.[2]

Julia's childhood was as warm as Grant's was cold. Julia Boggs Dent was born near St. Louis in January 1826. She always insisted, particularly during the Civil War, that her family was from the West and not the South, but her upbringing was Southern to its core. Her father, "Colonel" Frederick Dent, was one of those "juleps-on-the-veranda farmers," bred in the South with the barest hint of a military pedigree. On his plantation, called White Haven, with the aid of more than a dozen slaves, he lived a life of splendid ease more commonly associated with the Deep South. Probably relating family lore, Julia's biographer wrote that Dent gave a "ginger colored" slave girl as a gift to his beloved first daughter when Julia was born, but no records have been found. The slave's name was also Julia, but she was often called Jule or Black Julia.[3]

Dent's beautiful wife, Ellen, originally from Pennsylvania, hated the isolation of the plantation, so the colonel built a small townhouse for her in St. Louis, where she and the children enjoyed parties, music, and theater. Within the Dents' social circle were Thomas Hart Benton and his family. "Julia knew his daughter, the fascinating Jessie," according to Julia's biographer, Ishbel Ross, "although neither she nor Ulysses would ever learn to like her husband." It was, however, White Haven, the white-pillared plantation mansion surrounded by nearly five hundred acres on the Gravois Creek, that Julia remembered most fondly. In her memoirs, written when she was in her seventies, the White Haven of her youth took on mythic proportions. It was the most picturesque and productive land, with the most beautiful house, with the most lovely furnishings, with the most delicious food, presided over by the best mother and father, who denied nothing to her or her handsome brothers and lovely sisters. Julia wrote that White Haven's slaves were well cared for, too, and they were content, "though the young ones became somewhat demoralized about the beginning of the Rebellion, when all the comforts of slavery passed away forever."[4]

According to Julia's memoirs, her childhood was blissful, but that is not the whole truth. Julia's memoirs provide a wealth of information about her life, and most of it is accurate. What she omitted, though, is often at least as important as what she included. In writing of her childhood, Julia neglected to mention one very important fact: she was born with eyes that crossed.

As a young girl, Julia was small, barely five feet tall, and looked deceptively fragile, though she was always physically strong and agile. She had tiny hands, which were almost always remarked upon by her contemporaries, and beautiful long chestnut hair she wore up in a chignon or a cascade of curls. Among family and friends, she was known for her exuberant, lively personality, always ready for adventure and drawn to romance, although she recalled that she was the "shyest of little girls." She was not beautiful, but she might have been called handsome, perhaps, except for the physical defect that was, unfortunately, apparent at first glance. One of her large brown eyes was not aligned with the other, spoiling the symmetry of her face.[5]

When Julia recounted her early years in her memoirs, they are full of parties and soldiers and courting. Though she said she was bashful, she never mentioned that her eyes made her dreadfully self-conscious, but there is not the slightest doubt they did. The clearest evidence of that can be found in photographs of Julia. In most of them, she presents a profile or a bare three-quarters view, so one of her eyes is obscured, and the contrast between the two eyes is not as apparent. Full-face photographs of Julia are rare; her lifelong preference for profile is absolutely pronounced, almost militant. In more than one photograph with her family, she has turned so stiffly to one side that she appears to be snubbing her beloved husband.

Julia's reluctance to confront a camera head-on was probably a mannerism she adopted when she was in society. It is more than likely that she had a habit of averting her eyes when meeting someone for the first time and continued to minimize eye contact until she was comfortable with the person. Julia's shyness on first meeting made her less boisterous than her memoirs or her contemporaries' accounts of her would have the reader believe. In keeping with the "life was perfect" theme of her memoirs, however, Julia's self-consciousness surfaces only briefly in the Grants' own words—just once in her memoirs and once in a letter from her husband. In February 1848, before they were married, Grant responded to news from Julia about one of her friends. "I should like to see Fanny Higgins very much," he wrote, "to see the alteration it makes in her

Top: Julia (fourth from left), shows her decided preference for being photographed in profile, standing next to her husband at the Big Bonanza Silver Mine in Nevada, 1879. (*Courtesy of the Library of Congress*)

Above right: Photograph of Julia after the war. (*Courtesy of the Library of Congress*)

Above left and detail at left: A somewhat rare full-face photograph of Julia with Nellie, Jesse, and her father, "Colonel" Dent. (*Courtesy of the Library of Congress*) having her eyes straitened." Perhaps Julia had written to her beau about Fanny's experience in the hope of getting some encouragement from Grant to undergo the same operation. There is no record of his reaction if he ever saw Fanny Higgins's eyes, but Julia never stopped thinking about the possibility.[6]

Indeed, when the subject arose between them again many years later, he positively forbade it, but in the most loving way. When Julia traveled to St. Louis to care for her son Fred in late 1863, she visited the head of the St. Louis Medical College.

> I had often been urged in my girlhood by Dr. [Charles A.] Pope, the most distinguished surgeon in the country at that time, to permit him to make a very simple operation upon my eyes. I had never had the courage to consent, but now that my husband had become so famous I really thought it behooved me to try to look as well as possible. So I consulted the Doctor on this, to me, most delicate subject, but alas! He told me it was too late, too late. I told the General and expressed my regret. . . . He drew me to him and said: "Did I not see you and fall in love with you with these same eyes? I like them just as they are, and now, remember, you are not to interfere with them. They are mine, and let me tell you, Mrs. Grant, you had better not make any experiments, as I might not like you half so well with any other eyes."[7]

Despite Grant's expressions of satisfaction with her eyes as they were, Julia's embarrassment persisted, as is apparent from most of her photographs, until the end of her life.

Beyond her self-consciousness about her looks, however, Julia's vision troubled her throughout her life. Most biographers of Julia and of her husband note that she had a condition called strabismus and comment on her weak eyes, but they often leave it at that. In her book, *Civil War Wives*, historian Carol Berkin provided insight into Julia's struggle with her vision as an adult. To understand fully how strabismus affected Julia and her relationship with Grant, though, it is important to consider the host of consequences from strabismus that begin in early childhood.

Strabismus, "a misalignment of the visual axes of the two eyes," can manifest as either crossed eyes (one or both eyes turning inward) or walleye (the outward turning of an eye). It appears from photographs of Julia that most often her right eye looked inward and downward, although some accounts say that each eye alternated such movements. In either case, her eyes would have crossed when she tried to focus on an object. Her misaligned right eye would have impaired her vision in significant ways. Based on decades of study, we also now know that even if she had undergone surgery to have her eyes "straitened," it is highly unlikely that her vision would have improved.[8]

Julia would have been unable to focus properly on objects, and from time to time she probably saw two of everything before her brain suppressed one of the images. (Some strabismics do see both images persistently and train themselves to ignore one.) It is more than likely that her regular, or binocular, vision was less than perfect. Strabismus is usually accompanied by poor binocular vision. Julia was always referred to as having "weak" eyes, though she refused to wear glasses her whole life. She probably also lacked depth perception. It is also likely that she could not see in stereovision. That is, Julia probably never viewed the world in three dimensions. Almost certainly, she never even knew that she was stereoblind.[9]

Julia's condition would have affected her early life in many subtle ways. Like most strabismics, she was probably slow to walk as a baby. She was almost surely clumsy, too, constantly bumping into things or dropping them when her misaligned eyes and her untrained brain failed to gauge distances properly. Such mishaps, combined with the confusing sensation of objects floating unfocused in space before her, probably frustrated her and made for a fussy baby Julia. She surely claimed much of her parents' attention and affection as a consequence. And of course, since eyes are such a prominent feature of babies, her big and beautiful but crossed brown eyes probably inspired an especially protective attitude in her mother and father. Among her young peers, though, she was almost certainly an object of innocent but nonetheless painful mocking.

Julia's own account of her earliest years in her memoirs mentions no unpleasantness, but it contains important clues to how she adapted to her handicap, or rather, how those around Julia adapted their behavior to accommodate her. Her memoirs are full of tales of being the "pet" of her family, which may attest to the coddling and concern of her four older brothers and her parents. Her father, in particular, doted upon his oldest daughter and could rarely refuse any request she made of him. Julia recalled that as a child she was always followed into her fields of play by a "dusky train of eight to ten little colored girls of all hues" who waited on her. She did not have to walk, and therefore stumble, to school as a young child; her brothers carried her across the fields to the country school. There, where other children sat on benches or stools, "Mamma sent a nice armchair for my use," she recalled. Her whole world conspired to pamper Julia. "I cannot remember ever having been coerced into doing anything." When she quailed at the schoolroom challenge of learning Roman numerals (imagine all those lines swimming before her eyes), the teacher who had just punished her sister for not reciting the lesson properly simply told Julia, "Never mind, don't trouble your little head about it any more now. You will learn it in good time." Later, she confessed, "I never did."[10]

Indeed, it appears that Julia was never disciplined, nor that she ever learned the value of self-discipline. At Miss Mauro's boarding school in St. Louis, she recalled, "I remained for about seven years, studying about what I liked." Mostly what she liked were novels and romantic stories, which she read at her leisure. Despite her claimed proficiency in the liberal arts, "In every other branch I was below the standard," she confessed, "and worse still, my indifference was very exasperating."[11]

Reading was a lifelong challenge for Julia. While she wrote of reading books, she wrote more often of being read to—by her mother, by her brother, and all through their lives together by Grant, who shared her love of novels. Small print especially vexed her. On returning home one day to find calling cards left by visitors, "I handed them to the General to read," she recalled, "as even then I was unable to read a card except in very strong light." When in the White House, Julia had the newspapers read to her by a maid as she dressed. Handwriting would have been even more difficult for her to decipher.[12]

If reading was a challenge for Julia, writing was an ordeal. Certainly, when it came to numbers, Julia had difficulty manipulating figures on paper. She ascribed her problems with calculations to her lifelong difficulty with mathematics, but flawed vision may have contributed to her frustration. Julia laughingly described her earliest efforts to track her household expenses in an account book. Her husband, she wrote, characterized the result "mathematical conundrums." Grant, who once considered a future as a teacher of mathematics, refused to tutor Julia or help her balance her accounts, however, simply promising to make up whatever deficit mysteriously materialized (no small offer, considering their persistently strained finances).[13]

Indeed, as Ross related, "All through their married life the General tried to save her eyes when he could, reading to her, writing letters that normally would fall to her, and helping her in sundry small ways." Researching her biography of Julia in the late 1950s, Ross had access to three of Julia's grandchildren, Gen. Ulysses S. Grant III and Princess Julia Cantacuzéne (children of Frederick Dent Grant), and Mrs. William Pigott Cronan (daughter of Jesse Root Grant). They plied Ross with firsthand recollections and secondhand family tales of their grandparents. Foremost in their memories was their grandfather's devotion to Julia. His thoughtful accommodation to the problems caused by her strabismus,

Ross observed, "was a quiet and sympathetic acceptance of a handicap to which they did not often refer. . . ." After Grant's death, Julia had others transcribe personal letters for her, and she dictated much of her memoirs to her son Fred. Most biographers attribute her delegation of writing to the weakening of her eyes in old age. But even as a young woman, according to Ross's sources, although she certainly could write, "[s]he did not like to write when she could avoid it," and avoiding things she did not like to do was a skill Julia mastered as a child.[14]

In one of Grant's references to her self-indulgence, Julia recorded his wry response to an observation she made in a house in LaGrange, Tennessee, in the summer of 1862. Grant had chosen the house, from which its secessionist owner had fled, as his headquarters, and Julia joined him there. As she sat on the floor of the bedroom near the fireplace, Julia noted the washstand anchored to the floor that had been left by the owners. She remarked offhandedly to her husband that she disliked stationary washstands but did not know precisely why. Grant immediately grasped her unconscious reasoning, she recalled. "He said: 'I'll tell you why. You have to go to the stand. It cannot be brought to you.'" From her earliest days, Julia's life assumed a pattern of pampered self-indulgence remarkable even for upper-class Southern belles of the time, attributable in part to her flawed vision and the accommodations made in acknowledgment of it by her family and friends. Although she claimed that she was "not spoiled," Julia grew up believing that the world revolved around her, and in fact, her world did. Such cosseting surely pleased the young debutante, but when she and Grant fell in love, it served them poorly. Her lack of discipline wrought havoc on him time and again.[15]

They met when he was twenty-two, a year after his 1843 graduation from West Point. The choice of schooling had been his father's. It was in the paperwork for entrance to the military academy that the congressman who appointed him mistakenly changed his name from Hiram Ulysses Grant to Ulysses Simpson Grant. At West Point, U. S. Grant became "Sam," as in "Uncle Sam," to his classmates.[16]

After graduation, 2d Lt. Grant was stationed with the 4th Infantry Regiment at Jefferson Barracks, near St. Louis, close to the home of his roommate from his senior year, Frederick Dent. Though Dent was stationed elsewhere, he encouraged Grant to visit his family. So, along with Dent's cousin, James "Pete" Longstreet, a bear of a man who had also befriended the shy cadet at West Point, Grant rode to White Haven for dinner now and then. Colonel and Mrs. Dent lavished the young men with food and engaged them in merry conversation. The atmosphere was gracious and affectionate; Grant must have basked in its warmth. With the Dents' encouragement, he returned weekly, sometimes on his own. Grant became a particular favorite of the Dents' younger daughters, Ellen, or "Nellie," and Emma, but he did not meet their seventeen-year-old daughter, Julia, until she returned from boarding school in St. Louis. When they met, he felt something he had never felt before. "In February she returned to her country home," Grant wrote in his memoirs. "After that I do not know but that my visits became more frequent; they certainly did become more enjoyable." "We would often take walks, or go on horseback to visit the neighbors. . . . If the 4th infantry had remained at Jefferson Barracks it is possible, even probable, that this life might have continued for some years without my finding out that there was anything serious the matter with me. . . ." What was "the matter" with him, of course, was that he was in love.[17]

Ulysses and Julia Grant lived one of the great love stories in American history. There is not the barest question of their mutual devotion, as has been raised in the case of the McClellans, certainly none of the accusations of infidelity that hounded Frémont all his life, nor even the hints of flirtations that followed Sherman's later years. They fell in love, and they stayed there for nearly forty years. Their love for each other was obvious to all. Years after Grant's death, one of his sisters-in-law, who had earlier fallen out with Julia and Ulysses over a financial matter, vented her spleen to a newspaper reporter. The bitter woman pulled no punches, and one of her most heated criticisms was reserved for their demonstrations of affection. "To see them together when there were no other pairs of eyes about was a sight," she sputtered, somewhat oxymoronically. Seeing them in her mind's eye more than twenty years before, she fumed, "He was much past 40 and she was nearing that, but no two people of that age ever deported themselves quite like that pair. . . . They still carried on as young lovers which did not flatter a couple that advanced in years." And they carried on that way for twenty years more.[18]

Few biographers express any difficulty in understanding why Julia fell for Grant. Years before they met, while she was at school in St. Louis, a romance novel titled *The Dashing Lieutenant* captured her fancy. One day, when she and the other young ladies in her school were fantasizing about the kind of men they wanted to marry, Julia declared that she would prefer to marry an officer above all other men. Grant was a handsome young officer when they met, the man of her dreams.

Why, though, did Grant find Julia so appealing? On this question, Grant's biographers seem puzzled. Although contemporaneous descriptions of Julia are generally oblique, they are almost always favorable, stressing her small hands and beautiful hair. Critical eyes have scrutinized her photographs, however, and cannot imagine that the attraction was physical. "Julia was no beauty," wrote one. "[E]ven at seventeen her figure was stumpy, she had more neck than chin, and . . . [a] malfunctioning muscle caused her right eye to move up and down involuntarily." There is light speculation that her father's wealth was a not inconsequential part of her charms, but such an attraction could never have inspired the passion that seized Grant and possessed him for a lifetime. Julia was not beautiful, to be sure, but she was not ugly. Perhaps it was her very "homeliness," as one historian called it, owing in large part to Julia's eye defect, which engaged Grant's sensitive nature and inspired his loving, protective instincts. Julia would certainly have been less intimidating to the socially awkward young Grant than any of society's beauties he encountered in outings with his fellow officers. No doubt when the two met, it was the introduction of the bashful to the reserved, but Julia was never a wallflower. Even with her deformity, Julia could not sustain her initial shyness among those she knew. Her cheerfulness and her pleasure in people and entertainments were infectious. Grant would not have been immune. Julia's warm personality, her gracious family life, her enjoyment of the outdoors, and her love of riding horses were assets that counted much in Grant's simple, austere world.[19]

Horses figured especially prominently in that world. Grant was a superb rider, always known for his ability to bond with horses. First as a child and later at West Point, he exhibited astonishing feats of horsemanship. He was so comfortable on a horse that courting on one would have put the shy young suitor much more at ease than wooing a young lady in a drawing room. Fortunately for them both, Julia was an excellent horsewoman, and she, too, had reasons to prefer courting in a saddle. Though it seems somewhat counterintuitive, her lack of depth perception and difficulty in focusing her eyes did not impair either her ability or her enjoyment of riding. In fact, strabismics often speak about how much pleasure they derive from having their bodies in motion; moving through space seems positively thrilling to them.[20]

In addition to the pleasure of movement, Julia would have found riding alongside Grant a perfectly natural way to hide one of her eyes. Her self-consciousness, heightened when conversing face to face in a parlor, would have been minimized on horseback, enabling an easy, shared enjoyment of their time together. Moreover, the scenery, the adventures of the trail, the horses would have provided plentiful subjects for conversation by even the most reticent suitor or the most bashful ingénue. Julia's description of the first time she met Grant dissolved immediately into joyous memories of their rides together: "About three days after my return [from school in St. Louis], Lieutenant Grant called to pay his usual weekly visit to our house. After that first visit he became a daily visitor to our house. Such delightful rides we all used to take! . . . Well I cannot tell of those two winged months. He was always by my side, walking or riding."[21]

Julia and her world worked magic on Grant, and she captured the young lieutenant's heart. He had claimed a bit of her heart, too. She began to feel something for Grant, but Julia was young for her age, and she could not easily make the leap from friendship to love. Before leaving Jefferson Barracks with his regiment in 1844, for Camp Salubrity in Natchitoches, Louisiana, Grant asked her to accept his class ring, a prelude to a real engagement. Julia refused: "Oh, no, mamma would not approve of my accepting a gift from a gentleman," she told him, at which "he seemed rather put out . . . and soon after took his leave, lingering near me and asking me if I would think of him in his absence." Almost immediately, she began to regret her decision; she began to feel something more than mere friendship. Indeed, if one applies a Freudian analysis to her tale of naming one of her tall bedposts for Grant ("according to custom"), she was unconsciously feeling much, much more. After several anxious days without him, he appeared again on a short leave of absence. When he renewed his proposal, she agreed to accept his ring, but only on the condition that their desire to be engaged be kept secret from her parents, whom she knew would not approve.[22]

The Dents had grown fond of Grant, especially Mrs. Dent, who believed the young man wise beyond his years. When later she finally became sure that Julia was not merely infatuated with Grant but loved him, Mrs. Dent supported their engagement. Even then, however, she did not do so openly; her husband did not want his cherished Julia to marry a military man. Sounding remarkably like Thomas Hart Benton and Randolph Marcy, "Colonel" Dent made clear his preference in a son-in-law, and army officers need not apply. Dent wanted a better life than that of a military wife for his favorite daughter, he said, preferably a young man of fortune at least commensurate with his own, who could give Julia the same cosseted existence she enjoyed at White Haven. It was a tall order, one that Lieutenant Grant could never hope to fill. Grant did not back down. He would leave the army if that were required, he told Julia; he was confident he could obtain a position as a mathematics teacher at an Ohio college. He loved Julia, and, knowing Dent's affection for his daughter, Grant was confident that the two young lovers could overcome her father's resistance.

Meanwhile, the army claimed the young officer, and Grant was off to Louisiana with his regiment. His happiness at Julia's acceptance of his class ring gradually deflated as time passed without word from her. His loving patience in the face of her failure to write was a monument to his self-control, but his confidence began to erode. Did she still love him?

Fear of losing Julia's love gripped Grant time and again during the succeeding two decades when his military service separated them for months and sometimes years at a time. When he and Julia were together, the fear vanished, but when they were apart, it sank sharp claws into his psyche. Grant's letters to Julia during the next twenty years expose his intense need for her. They are almost always long and full of descriptions of his surroundings and his activities. They feature intimate gossip, absorbing narrative, expressions of love, and anguished cries for her to write. He rarely touched directly on military actions (except for a few mesmerizing instances during the Mexican War), and whenever he recounted his own part in battle, his modesty was astonishing. Even in private letters to the woman he loves, he never struts; at most, he expresses quiet confidence in the value of his service.

Grant's Civil War superiors and subordinates were the first to appreciate his simple, lucid style of writing. The many orders, dispatches, and telegrams he wrote were always clear and coherent, even when written under fire. His reputation as a truly great writer was cemented in perpetuity in his monumental *Personal Memoirs,* written at the end of his life under even greater duress. In his earliest surviving letters, though, especially those to Julia during the Mexican War, Grant's remarkable facility for observation and description are most readily apparent. To read Grant's *Memoirs* is to get a solid sense of the engaged, observant military officer he was. To read his letters to Julia is to get to know the man.

Only by stripping those letters bare of all but his pleas to hear from her, however, can one get a true sense of Julia's hold on him. Those excerpts reveal Grant's desire for Julia, his mounting sense of despair in the absence of communication from her, his anxiety about her commitment to him, and above all, his unwavering, total devotion to her. When this aspect of Grant's letters is highlighted, it becomes clear that each letter from him is singularly focused on eliciting one from Julia in return. The reader can almost feel him willing her from a distance to write to him. Nearly every extant letter to her during his time in Louisiana, Mexico, on the West Coast, and through the Battle of Shiloh contains such a plea, even those that acknowledge a letter received from her. Her procrastination compelled him to urge her at every opportunity to write more faithfully.

If the discussion of Julia's failings as a correspondent seems one-sided, it is necessarily so. Julia saved more than 250 letters from Grant to her, and for that, once again, history is grateful beyond measure. Although there is evidence that Grant often carefully preserved Julia's letters for a time and reread them again and again to tide him over during the long months without word from her, only two short notes from her to him have been found. Unlike McClellan, Grant traveled light, even as lieutenant general, and moreover, he was often in the thick of battle. It is easy to imagine that her precious letters might have been lost or, possibly, protectively destroyed.

Without Julia's letters, it is difficult to get an accurate sense of the disproportion in the number and length of time between his letters and hers. We have only Grant's calculations: eleven in twenty months at one point; one for every five of his at another; just one during a cold and isolated four-month period. Nor do we have the explanations that she might have given about why she wrote so infrequently, though in one letter to Julia, Grant notes pointedly that she "offered no excuse at all" for an especially lengthy hiatus in her correspondence. Finally, some letters by each of them likely were, in fact, lost in the chaotic mails. In the absence of Julia's letters, however, there is commentary on their correspondence from Julia herself, written many years later, in her memoirs. The best that can be done is to contrast Julia's narrative about his letters with extracts from some of Grant's for each substantial period of time they were apart. What emerges from this "he said/she said" exercise is dismaying. In their first six months apart, his letters included many pleas:

> Julia! I cannot express the regrets that I feel at having to leave Jeff. Bks. at the time I did. . . . You must not forget to write soon. . . . It has been but few days since I wrote to you but I must write again. Be as punctual in writing to me Julia and then I will be compensated in a slight degree,—nothing could fully compensate—for your absence. . . . Your two letters of July and August have just been recieved and read you can scarcely imagine with how much pleasure. . . . Take example in punctuality by me, Julia, I have rec'd your letters only to day and now I am answering them . . . wont you be as punctual in answering mine in the future? You don't know Julia with how much anxiety and suspense I await there arrival. . . . It has now been nearly two months since I heard from you. . . . Julia you must answer this quick wont you? I know you can.[23]

In her memoirs, Julia wrote succinctly of that time without him: "Lieutenant Grant went direct to Camp Salubrity, La., where he remained until the next spring. I was still at White Haven, occasionally going to Jefferson Barracks and to St. Louis to attend parties and weddings. I was constantly receiving letters and books from Mr. Grant."[24]

Julia had many pleasant distractions at White Haven and in St. Louis to entice her away from the writing desk, and it is unlikely that those around her, particularly her parents (who at that time did not favor the match), would have encouraged her to respond promptly. Neither did she have anyone to assist her in reading Grant's letters, and that may have played a large role in her failure to write regularly. Julia was accustomed to having things read to her, but surely she would not have turned to her disapproving parents to read her beau's letters, or to her teasing siblings. Nor could she have obtained this intimate service from those in the household who existed to tend to her every need—slaves were rarely able to read; most slave states outlawed the teaching of reading to them as a security measure. At this early stage in the relationship between Julia and Grant, with no formal engagement between the two, a six-month separation punctuated by three letters from Julia (according to Grant's count) was bearable, but did not portend well.

In the spring of 1844, Grant was finally able to obtain a brief leave of absence, and he rode toward White Haven with one thought in mind. On a Sunday afternoon, just as her father was about to leave on a long trip, Julia recalled, "who should dash up to the front gate, mounted on a superb dapple gray, but Lieutenant Grant!" The dashing lieutenant had come to ask her father for permission to marry her. Grant later told Julia of the interview between the two men, which she recounted in her *Memoirs*. When Grant asked for Colonel Dent's permission to correspond with his daughter with the object of asking for her hand, Julia's father told the young suitor "he did not think the roving life [Julia] would have to lead as a soldier's wife would suit [her] at all." When Grant offered to resign his commission and take a job as a mathematics professor, Dent urged against that course of action and then proceeded to make a most amazing statement, as Julia related Grant's version of the conversation: "My father thought it best for him to stick to his profession, and to convince him that he had no objection to him personally, said: 'Now if it were Nellie, I would make no objection, but my Julia is so entirely unfitted for such a life.'"[25]

At that moment, surely, the scales fell from Grant's eyes. "Colonel" Dent, who affected an unearned military title in order to sustain his inflated ego, was not opposed to Grant's army service after all. Although Dent would have preferred a son-in-law with more money and status, if the "Colonel" were willing to allow his younger daughter to endure the perils and penury of military life, then his concerns lay not with Grant, but with his precious, disfigured Julia.

"The Lieutenant was not eager to avail himself of this Laban-like suggestion," Julia wrote laconically of Grant's response (Grant forever teased Nellie that she had been offered to him but he turned her down), "and, I am sure, convinced papa that if the life did not suit me, he would make me happy. At all events, permission was obtained for us to correspond." Dent did not totally capitulate to the request for her hand, however, recalled Julia: "If we who were so young should not change our minds in a year or two, he would then make no objection. This was satisfactory to both of us, and we considered the matter settled." Grant and Julia spent nearly two weeks together at White Haven in the spring of 1844, in full enjoyment of the present and in anticipation of their future wedded bliss. When Grant departed for Louisiana in early May, they believed they would be married in a year or so. They were, sadly, wrong. They did not see each other again for four years.[26]

During the first two years of their separation, as tensions between the United States and Mexico grew, Grant's regiment moved closer to the border, from Camp Salubrity to New Orleans Barracks, and then to Corpus Christi, Texas, and he wrote many letters to her:

My Dear Julia—It has been but few days since I wrote to you but I must write again . . . nothing could fully compensate—for your absence. . . . It is now seven weeks since I wrote to you and about three weeks since I began anxiously to expect an answer, but as none has come yet. . . . Mr. Hazlitt wishes to be remembered. He says that he was not two months in answering your letter. . . . Mrs Higgins and husband have arrived. . . . She says that I have a dangerous rival in Missouri, and that you do not intend to write to me any more &c. &c. . . . You will write to me soon wont you and contridict the above statement. . . . Two or three Mails have arrived at Corpus Christi in the last few days and by each I confidently expected a letter from you, but each time was disappointed. As a consolation then I come to my tent and got out all the letters yo[u have] ever written me—How many do you think they amounted? only 11 Julia, and it is now twenty months that we have been engaged. . . . [27]

For two years, Grant faithfully, regularly, lovingly wrote letters to Julia. She rarely answered him. When her long-sought replies came, according to Grant, they were mostly brief, and she often neglected to respond to specific questions he had posed. When her letters were long, or when she sent more than one in quick succession, Grant's gratitude poured forth as self-reassuring promises that she would discipline herself to write more often in the future. He was always disappointed.

On April 25, 1846, two days before Grant's twenty-fourth birthday, Mexican Army troops ambushed American forces north of the Rio Grande, and less than two weeks later, Congress approved President Polk's call for a declaration of war. By that time, though, U.S. forces under Gen. (and future president) Zachary Taylor had defeated the Mexican Army twice. Grant wrote to Julia on May 11, 1846: "After two hard fought battles against a force far superior to our own in numbers, Gen. Taylor has got possession of the Enemy's camp and now I am writing on the head of one of the captured drums."[28]

Grant had tried but failed to secure a leave of absence before his regiment was ordered into Mexico. Forced to endure what proved to be an additional two years away from Julia, he was comforted episodically with her infrequent letters, but at least he had much to occupy his mind and body. At the beginning of his combat tour, Julia apparently did post more letters than ever before, but they were never enough to satisfy Grant. Unreliable mail service added to the young lieutenant's woes. He was wild to be with Julia. By the end of those four years, Grant seriously contemplated leaving the army without any assurance of gainful employment in order to be near her. At one point, he told her he was toying with the notion of pretending to be sick enough to be shipped home for medical treatment. His sense of honor overcame his passion; he was no shirker and discarded that gambit. Grant finally determined on the more honorable course of resignation, but by then, even that exit route from Mexico was closed to him. "Gen. Scott will let no officer leave who is able for duty not even if he tenders his resignation," he told Julia, adding dryly, "So you see it is not so easy to get out of the wars as it is to get into them."[29]

In many respects, Grant emerged from the war a different man. When he returned, he was a lean, hardened combat veteran, skilled in logistics, cool under fire, with a superb ability to appraise topography critically, spot tactical opportunities, and evaluate the men around him—superiors and subordinates. He had learned lessons in strategy, tactics, and logistics from Taylor and Scott, lessons that he later acknowledged proved valuable during the Civil War.

In his memoirs, Grant also recalled the value of serving with many men in the Mexican War whom he would later oppose on the battlefield, including Robert E. Lee. When Grant came east in 1864 as lieutenant general of the U.S.

Army to face Lee, he heard endlessly of the Confederate general's "almost super-human abilities." Grant confidently demurred. "I had known him personally," he wrote, "and knew that he was mortal; and it was just as well that I felt this."[30]

Grant was a genuine hero in the Mexican War, even if his own letters never made the case for it. Though he was quartermaster (a staff position against which he appealed in vain) and thus not expected to expose himself to fire, he did so more than once. On one occasion, during the fiercest fighting in the streets of Monterrey in September 1846, Grant volunteered to ride back to headquarters to summon needed ammunition. "Like a trick rider in a rodeo," wrote Jean Smith of the daring mission, "he hooked one foot around the cantle of his saddle, one arm around the neck of his horse, Nelly, and with his body clinging to the sheltered side, galloped away at full speed." Grant avoided a hail of Mexican bullets, safely delivered the message, and when he told the story to his family, gave more credit to Nelly than to himself. A year later, in the battle for Mexico City, Grant convinced an artillery officer to help him muscle a how-itzer up the steeple of a church and into the bell tower, where it rained down a killing fire on a vulnerable Mexican position he had spotted. His action was nothing less than brilliant, and several officers noted it in their reports.[31]

However, in a war studded with such luminaries as Winfield Scott, Zach-ary Taylor, Robert E. Lee, A. P. Hill, and George Brinton McClellan, Ulysses Grant's tactical triumphs were crowded out of the headlines. Grant had not approved of the war—from the beginning, as he wrote in his *Memoirs,* he thought it "one of the most unjust ever waged by a stronger against a weaker nation"—but he never questioned his soldier's duty to fight for a policy deter-mined by civilian politicians. Grant was brevetted Capt. Ulysses S. Grant, or Captain Sam to his comrades, though he did not get official notice of it until months later. He had been a full participant in the fiercest fighting of the age.[32]

During the forty-eight months he had been separated from Julia, Grant had grown physically and mentally beyond his years. In one respect, though, he was the same. His love for Julia, his need for Julia, was as strong as ever.

CHAPTER 23

"how forsaken I feel here!"

Grant hastened back to White Haven and insisted they be married as soon as possible. The wedding was set for late August 1848. "I had had four years in which to prepare for this event, and therefore required only a week or so to make the few last arrangements," Julia recalled with some pride. While she made those last-minute arrangements, Grant traveled on to Ohio to visit his parents and tell them of his impending marriage.

Glad as his parents were to see their brave son again, they did not attend his wedding. Perhaps Jesse did not want to leave his business for long, but his fierce opposition to slavery may have also figured into their absence. Ulysses Grant's attachment to Julia enabled him to live in plantation society and even accept Julia's ownership of slaves, although he was always uncomfortable with the institution. His parents, though, were implacably opposed to slavery and patently displeased that Ulysses was marrying into a slave-owning family. Jesse and Hannah did not want to be guests in the home of slave owners, "did not wish to subject themselves to plantation airs," even if it meant missing their son's wedding.[1]

Grant and Julia married August 22, 1848, in the Dents' St. Louis townhouse. Their wedding was "necessarily a simple one," she recalled. "The season was unfavorable for a large gathering, and our temporary home in St. Louis was small." Her dress was "magnificent, rich, soft, white watered silk," a gift from her beautiful, wealthy cousin, Caroline O'Fallon, and another friend brought, "in a moss-lined basket, a lovely corsage bouquet of white cape jessamines, also a number to fasten my veil with." The bridesmaids were Julia's sister Nellie and two cousins; her husband's attendants included Lt. Cadmus Wilcox and Bernard Pratte, who "surrendered to General Grant at Appomattox," and probably James Longstreet, too. It was all perfection in her memory: the wedding cake, the music, the house lit with candles. She mentioned nothing of the groom, but, no doubt, he thought it all perfect, too.[2]

The first day of their marriage began the first of the many travel adventures the Grants shared. It was Julia's first trip away from St. Louis and her first time on a boat; she marveled at its power and speed. Julia most enjoyed "sitting alone with Ulys" on deck. They visited wealthy Grant cousins in Louisville, Kentucky, then arrived in Bethel, Ohio, where Julia's mounting anxiety at meeting her in-laws melted with their "cordial welcome." Her descriptions of Grant's grandmother, parents, and siblings at that time were wholly favorable. At that moment, in her own words, she was "well satisfied with my dear husband's family."[3]

Brevet Captain Grant's three-month leave of absence from the army was nearly up, and he received orders to Detroit. They returned to White Haven, where preparations to leave her childhood home drove Julia to tears. As she later recalled, her father happened upon them at that point, and said:

> "Grant, I can arrange it all for you. You join your regiment and leave Julia with us. You can get a leave of absence once or twice a year and run on here and spend a week or two with us. I always knew she could not live in the army." Ulys's arm was around me, and he bent his head and whispered: "Would you like this, Julia? Would you like to remain with your father and let me go alone?" "No, no, no, Ulys. I could not, would not, think of that for a moment." "Then," he said, "dry your tears and do not weep again. It makes me unhappy." There was never again a word said about my staying at home. . . . [4]

Their trip to Detroit proved a frustrating introduction to the vagaries of military life. On arrival, Grant was immediately redirected to Madison Barracks at Sacket's Harbor, New York, near Niagara, due to preference in assignment given another officer. Though it was a posting that Grant initially indignantly protested as violating regular army order, Madison Barracks provided some of the happiest times of their lives. There, they enjoyed winter sports and social entertainments with men and women who became lifelong friends. There, too, Julia first practiced the womanly arts of housekeeping.[5]

One of Julia's most endearing charms is the utterly unconscious irony in so many of her descriptions of events and people, especially of herself. Her reference to the loss of the "comforts of slavery" is only the first of many in her memoirs, but by far the most naively touching recollections surround her early married life. As she recalled, she had "four years to plan her wedding," but apparently, that was the only day of her future life she had contemplated in any detail. Her romantic sense of marriage and perhaps her mother's re-laxed attitude toward housekeeping may have made the need for preparation unthinkable to her. "We had such fine servants at home that I was under the impression that the house kept itself," Julia later confessed, adding, "And I do not think mamma was very thorough either." Even if her mother had at-tempted to pass along domestic skills, Julia's chronic lack of discipline would probably have defeated the effort. In any event, as she and Grant settled into the small house in Sacket's Harbor in the winter of 1848, it became apparent that Julia was utterly unprepared to manage their household.[6]

"Manage" is the key word because throughout her life she had help. From the beginning, Grant knew she would require household assistance, and even in the worst financial times, he made sure she had it. He had pledged to Dent that he would do everything he could to enable Julia to cope with military life. Grant recognized that her pampered upbringing, her eyesight, and her tem-perament required assistance in keeping house. Julia's slaves traveled with her where slavery was legal. "Black Julia" even lived with the Grants in military camps during the Civil War. When the Grants "went North," her slaves were left behind at White Haven to avoid being freed by operation of law or by es-cape. At those times, Grant hired a cook and, later, a nurse, to help Julia. Along with help for Julia, on the trip to Detroit and then to New York, they also had with them a young manservant, a Mexican orphan named Gregorio, or Greg-ory. The young boy had attached himself to Grant in Mexico during the war and stuck to him afterward. In addition to helping with horses and polishing Grant's shoes and buckles, Gregory aided Julia in tending to the heating and cooking fires at home.[7]

Julia worried most about meals; Grant was a picky eater, and she missed the Southern style of cooking, which neither she nor any Northern cook could replicate. She suffered many failures in this department. Ten years later, when they had moved to Galena, Illinois, she tried to teach her sister-in-law how to make "Maryland biscuit":

> . . . to my sorrow, I found I did not know exactly myself. The biscuits were utter failures. Each one had a soggy, black spot in the middle. They were not at all like home biscuits. I told the Captain it was because the flour was not good . . . [When the cook returned], for tea and breakfast we had delicious bread.

The Captain, turning to me, said facetiously: "I see, Julia, you have come to a good stratum in the flour."[8]

In response to Grant's protest against the New York assignment, he was almost immediately reassigned to Detroit, but winter made the move impossible. When travel resumed after the spring thaw on the lakes and rivers, the Grants set up housekeeping in Detroit, a posting they came to love. Julia was pregnant by then, and in May, she traveled to White Haven to be with her mother and a full complement of staff to have her baby. Their first son, Frederick Dent Grant, was born May 30, 1850. A year later, wanting to show off their son to his grandparents, Julia traveled with Fred, "the little dog" as Grant called him, to Grant's parents in Bethel, Ohio, and then to White Haven in Missouri. Once again, her correspondence was sparse. Although the trip had Grant's blessing, he very quickly became impatient for her return. By June, he was urging her to come back; by August he was positively frantic: "I am getting quite uneasy about you and Fred. I have not had the scratch of a pen from you since a bout week after you left. . . . After a lapse of more than one month I at length received a letter from you yesterday. I do not see that you had any excuse whatever for not writing before. . . . Do you think [Fred] recollects me? Has he any more teeth? You don't tell me anything about him. . . ."[9]

Julia recalled the separation with more than equanimity; she enjoyed her stay at White Haven greatly. Of this period, Julia wrote coyly: "I had a very happy summer at dear old White Haven. In September, Ulys wrote that I must come; that he was anxious to see his little son and I *think* he said, me also."[10]

Their correspondence during this time had resumed on the same terms it ended after the Mexican War: Grant wrote often and pleadingly; Julia wrote rarely and briefly. Grant's exasperation at Julia's lack of communication during the summer of 1851 was only a faint foreshadowing of what he was to endure beginning the next June. In the spring of 1852, Grant received orders to report to the West Coast for duty as quartermaster at Fort Vancouver, Oregon Territory (now Washington State). The Grants initially planned that Julia and Fred would travel with him, but by then she was pregnant again. Grant feared for her safety during the dangerous trip, which required the same perilous sea and land crossings that Jessie and Ellen had made. Reluctantly, he decided Julia should not accompany him. Hopeful that either his stay would be short or she would join him in short order, he arranged for her to stay with his parents in Ohio. Leaving her in late June, he traveled to New York and there embarked on a steamer to Panama with his 4th Infantry Regiment and a relatively large contingent of civilians, including women and children.

Cholera and yellow fever attacked Grant's party of soldiers and civilians as they crossed the isthmus in the steamy, deadly month of July. Assuming ad hoc leadership of the stricken band, Grant exceeded army regulations to secure mules and medicine, personally ministering to the sick when frightened nurses refused. Nearly one hundred died before they left the west coast of the isthmus. Those who survived the nightmare never forgot Grant's care for them and forever credited him with saving their lives. One of his charges remembered him as "a ministering angel to us all." In his frequent letters home during the harrowing trip, Grant expressed relief to Julia that she had not made the lethal journey, particularly since she was about to give birth.[11]

Grant disembarked the steamer *Golden Gate* in San Francisco and had the chance to visit two of Julia's brothers, who had set up business in town. He marveled at the vast amount of money that was being made and gambled away, as the gold rush persisted in warping the region's economy. From San Francisco, Grant traveled up the coast to Fort Vancouver, where the chaos of the rough-and-tumble territorial settlement overwhelmed him. There, too, the search for gold was paramount, and it pushed prices for everything beyond the reach of a single man on a lieutenant's pay, much less one with a wife and two children. Grant quickly grasped that his goal of bringing his family to live with him could not possibly be realized unless he could supplement his military pay.

At first, that seemed to be an easy prospect. So many men were abandoning their regular occupations to hunt for treasure that Grant concluded he could make good money in his spare time by supplying commodities such as potatoes, lumber, pigs, and chickens. Disaster struck all of Grant's efforts. His potato crops were drowned in two freak deluges, chickens shipped for lucrative sale in San Francisco died en route, and speculation in a social club failed when the manager fled with money that Grant and several partners had entrusted to him. Although Grant lived with other army officers in an effort to save money and enjoy companionship, his spirits suffered. In addition to disappointments from his time-consuming, backbreaking, and invariably unprofitable attempts to enable his family to join him, he lost touch with Julia—again: "My Dear Dear Wife—Another mail has arrived and not one word do I get from you directly or indirectly. . . . Just think, our youngest is at this moment probably over three months of age, and yet I have never heard a word from it, or you, in that time."[12]

Amazingly, Julia had not moved heaven and earth—or even pen and paper—

to make certain that Grant learned about the birth of the son named after him (but quickly nicknamed Buck, for the Buckeye State in which he was born). It would be almost exactly six months from Ulysses Junior's birth on July 4, 1852, before the anxious father got the news, and then it came in six letters, all at once.

> My Dear Dear Wife—You can scaresly conceive how hapy this Mails arrival has made me. . . . Your letter, and Clara's too, said so much about dear little Fred. & Ulys. You have no idea how hapy it made me feel. . . . Write to me often dearest. . . . I would prefer sacrificing my commission and try something to continuing this separation. When you write to me again dear Julia say a goo-deal about Fred. and Ulys. . . . By this Mail I received no letter from you, nor from any one at your house. Where Mails come but twice per month it does seem as though I might expect news from you and our dear little boys. . . . [13]

Worse was to come. In January 1854, Grant was transferred from Fort Vancouver to an even more isolated posting on Humboldt Bay, California. "The greatest trial of their marriage," author John Y. Simon wrote, "came with Ulysses's assignment to the Pacific Coast in 1852." The brain- and heart-numbing isolation on remote Humboldt Bay plunged Grant into debilitating depression. Reflecting on that grim and sorrowful period of Grant's life, biographer William McFeely wondered: "The hardest thing to understand in the story of Grant's intense unhappiness while on the Pacific Coast, which culminated in his resignation from the army is Julia's seeming unconcern." The real reason for her bewildering silence is necessarily shrouded in uncertainty, since we lack her version of events. By piecing together clues from his letters and from her memoirs, though, there is ground for reasonable conjecture. McFeely wondered why Julia did not "get on the next boat for California," but surely, Grant's accounts of the deadly crossing of the isthmus, his earnest relief that his family had not made the trip, and his poor financial situation were solid deterrent to Julia—and to her father, who would have had to finance her trip and the subsequent living expenses. Julia's frustration at her own situation during this time, marked by her increasingly fractious relationship with Grant's parents, might have led her to write as little as possible to Grant to avoid adding to his unhappiness. McFeely also described Julia as "inarticulate," a possible excuse for her failure to write lovingly and often. Yet, the young woman whose rare letter to her fiancé in 1846, when he was under fire in Mexico, vowed that she would "willingly share my tent, or my prison if I should be taken prisoner," cannot be faulted for lack of passionate imagination or ability to express it.[14]

Another explanation is possible, though, one that is both simple and grounded in the couple's shared history before his posting to California. Despite her failure to write and his many complaints, their separations had always ended well in the past. Though Grant was greatly frustrated, and she experienced guilt, his love had never faltered, and he had always survived their separations. Julia had no reason to believe this separation would end otherwise, and so she would have had little incentive to behave differently.

Julia's earlier attitude toward writing to Grant had been slow, tardy, remiss, lazy, even negligent. During this separation, though, it approached cruelty. Half a year went by before he received his first letter from her, months regularly passed without a word from home. Mail service was slow and unreliable, for sure, but other men at the post received mail from home, and Grant got letters from other members of his family—and from Julia's, too. Grant knew that Julia could write; her infrequent letters proved that. But her lack of self-discipline, which prevented her from keeping up her side of their correspondence, appeared to him to be laziness at best, indifference at worst. Her rare letters affected him powerfully. In one, "She had traced [Buck's] infant hand in pencil on the last sheet and Grant was touched to the quick," according to Ross. "He showed the sketch to an artillery sergeant named Eckerson, who noted that he 'folded the letter quickly and left without speaking a word; but his form shook, and his eyes were wet.'" Others also saw his hunger for his family, including a sergeant's wife, who recalled, "Oftentimes, while reading letters from his wife, his eyes would fill with tears, he would look up with a start and say, 'Mrs. Sheffield, I have the dearest little wife in the world, and I want to resign from the army and live with my family.'"[15]

Though the landscape was beautiful, the human environment at Fort Humboldt was bleak. There was no society, just gold miners and the Indians whose lands they were invading. Beyond drills and distributing wages, Grant had nothing to occupy his time, literally nothing. He tried again and again to secure leave to visit his family, but permission was always denied. It was during this time of his life that Grant's reputation for drinking too much and getting drunk was born, one that dogged him throughout the war and unfairly continues to the present day. As a corollary of his legendary affinity for the bottle arose the myth surrounding Julia: that she was dispatched to live with her husband during the war—by his chief of staff, John Rawlins, by Stanton, even by Lincoln—to keep Grant from drinking.

We know little for certain about Grant's drinking during his Pacific Coast tour of duty. There are accounts from fellow officers at Vancouver and Humboldt about Grant's occasional slurred speech and stumbling gait. One story has George McClellan arriving at Fort Vancouver to head an exploratory expedition, disgusted to find an inebriated quartermaster charged with outfitting the expedition. Nor do we know for certain if or how Grant's drinking contributed to his resignation. The most persistent story, although it is by no means solidly verified, is that Grant appeared intoxicated one payday as he sat at the paymaster's table before a line of soldiers. His superior officer called Grant out and, according to the most common version of events, gave him a choice: resign or face a court-martial.[16]

The one incontrovertible part of the story is that Grant's letter of resignation is dated April 11, the same day he wrote a letter to the same man accepting promotion to the grade of captain.

April 11 1854—Fort Humboldt, Humboldt Bay, California
To Col. S. Cooper, Adj. Gen. U.S.A., Washington DC
Col. I have the honor to acknowledge the reciept of my Commission as Captain in the 4th Infantry and my acceptance of the same.
I am Col. Very Respectfully Your Obt. Svt. U.S. Grant, Capt. 4th Inf.y

April 11 1854—Fort Humboldt, Humboldt Bay, California
To Col. S. Cooper, Adj. Gen. U.S.A., Washington DC
Col. I very respectfully tender my resignation of my commission as an officer of the Army, and request that it may take effect from the 31st July next.
I am Col. Very Respectfully Your Obt. Svt. U.S. Grant Capt.4th Inf.y[17]

In his memoirs, Grant placed his desire to have his family near him at the heart of his decision to resign: "My family, all this while, was at the East. It consisted now of a wife and two children. I saw no chance of supporting them on the Pacific coast out of my pay as an army officer. I concluded, therefore, to resign. . . ." A decade before he wrote his memoirs, though, he told an old and trusted friend visiting him at the White House that the "vice of intemperance . . . had not a little to do with his decision to resign."[18]

The real question about Grant and liquor, though, is not whether or how much. It is, rather, why? A reading of his letters makes the answer obvious. "Grant did not leave the army because he was a drunk," biographer McFeely observed. "He drank and left the army because he was profoundly depressed."

Although Grant had enormous resilience and great reserves of mental strength upon which to draw, those resources were not inexhaustible. Loneliness and boredom were destructive to a man with Grant's energy and drive. The boredom of those two years was profound, but it might have been bearable if he had heard from Julia, if she had sent stories of the children and of their days and of their extended families. In the communication vacuum that Julia created with her long stretches of silence, he lost confidence in her love and in himself until it crushed him.[19]

Without money and without plans, he left the army and headed east. He worried that Julia would not welcome him back. Grant was so mentally estranged from her at that point that he told her only that he was returning on leave, not that he had resigned from the army. His last letter from California was the coldest letter he ever wrote Julia, though it ended with his usual tender farewell:

May 2d 1854, Fort Humboldt California

Dear Wife—I do not propose writing you but a few lines. I have not yet recieved a letter from you and as I have a "leave of absence" and will be away from here in a few days do not expect to. After recieving this you may discontinue writing because before I could get a reply I shall be on my way home. You might write directing to the City of New York. . . . My love to all at home. Kiss our little boys for their pa. love to you dear Julia. Your affectionate husbd. Ulys.[20]

Grant's journey east from California was nearly as difficult as the deadly one west to California. Sorely lacking money, he attempted to recover investments he had made in San Francisco, but he failed. With few coins in his pocket, he nonetheless pressed several on a veteran and on two gold miners he perceived to be in worse straits. His situation continued to deteriorate when he arrived on the East Coast. Grant's visit to the New York City post office proved as fruitless as had his trips to meet mail steamers three thousand miles to the west; it held no letter from Julia. Grant sought to make use of his time in New York by collecting on a debt owed to him by another erstwhile business partner at Sacket's Harbor. Encountering an old friend from West Point and the Mexican War on the streets of New York City, Grant borrowed funds from Simon Bolivar Buckner Jr. to enable him to journey north to claim the money due him. Naively, Grant had written to the debtor of his impending visit, and of course, the deadbeat fled town just ahead of Grant's arrival. When Grant returned to the city empty-handed, Buckner was hesitant to lend the dusty, disheveled, impoverished man any more cash, but he did agree to guarantee his bill at a boardinghouse.

Tellingly, Grant did not rush to Julia's side; the first member of his family he went to see was his sorely displeased father. Although Grant had not told Julia he had resigned, he sent the news to his father from California. Jesse immediately wrote Secretary of War Jefferson Davis, urging him not to accept the resignation, saying his son really only wanted a much-deserved leave of absence to be with his family. Davis rightly refused the father's request on behalf of the son, and Jesse was embarrassed and disappointed when Grant appeared on his doorstep. "West Point has spoiled one of my boys for business," was Jesse's welcome. "I guess that's about so," Grant conceded. His visit home was not long, however; he soon traveled to White Haven to see his family.[21]

Ten years earlier, the unexpected arrival of a dashing young lieutenant astride a spirited gray horse had dazzled the crowd on Colonel Dent's white-pillared piazza. But on the day that a dusty figure, "with the look of a man who had suffered," drove an old buggy up to the entrance, there were only two young boys playing outside. Halting the horse, the man jumped down and pulled the startled boys to his chest. From inside the house, one of the slaves recognized Grant, informed the boys he was their father, and shouted for Julia, who came running. If Fred and young Ulysses had not expected his arrival, Julia had. Though she did not know for sure the day on which he would arrive, according to her biographer, "she had been preparing herself for his return." Julia was Julia, though, and her preparations for her husband's return were as singularly focused as they had been on her wedding day: "she had dressed each day most becomingly, her summer muslins crisped and flounced around her short, trim figure."[22]

Julia later recalled her activities from Grant's departure in 1852 to his return in 1854 in word pictures that convey a stark contrast to her husband's Pacific Coast nightmare. Her account of those years is full of weddings and parties and details about her boys that Grant had sought so voraciously: "[While he was gone m]y dear husband made every provision for my comfort and independence (this he always thought of), sending me more than I needed always. . . . A number of parties and receptions were given and attended. . . . After an absence of over two years, Captain Grant, to my great delight, resigned his commission in the U.S. Army and returned to me, his loving little wife. How very happy this reunion was! . . ."[23]

At their "very happy" reunion, Grant's joy in hugging his boys must have been as evident as his frustration at the agony that Julia had wrought on him for two long years. Julia made an oblique reference to it in her memoirs when, after he told about his fruitless trip to collect the debt, Julia chided him for being such a bad businessman. "Ulys turned to me," Julia recalled at that point, "and said: 'You know I had to wait in New York until I heard from you.'" Her embarrassment at that memory of his disappointment is most apparent in her abrupt change of subject immediately after that sentence.[24]

CHAPTER 24

"Is this my destiny?"

After Generals Frémont and McClellan left the army after the Mexican War—one under the cloud of court-martial, the other bearing laurels from the peacetime antebellum army—they went on to successful civilian occupations. Even Sherman could claim that he had found both income and contentment as a civilian at one point after the war in his capacity as superintendent of the Louisiana Military Academy. Grant's civilian life, though, proved to be a series of severe trials in occupations that were often repugnant and never provided the independence and security he needed: farmer, tanner, leather goods salesman, farmer again, surveyor, customs house inspector, unsuccessful candidate for county engineer, real estate agent, leather goods salesman again. He could not later point to a single stretch of remunerative and enjoyable employment between his resignation in 1854 and the firing on Fort Sumter in 1861. Notably, though, seven years of nearly unrelieved disappointment at job after job never disheartened Grant as had his absence from Julia and the children; Grant was with his family again, at last, and that is what mattered most to him.

It mattered so much that he refused the first job offered to him. Leaving White Haven after making broad but unacknowledged hints of his willingness to help Dent manage the plantation, Grant and Julia traveled to Covington, Kentucky, because Jesse had written in a more encouraging vein of work to be had. In fact, Grant's father offered him a job at his store in Galena, Illinois, but only on the condition that Julia and the children stay with the senior Grants, where Jesse could more easily control what Julia spent on their upkeep. By this time, the relationship between Julia and her in-laws had degenerated into one of civil hostility. Julia later characterized the cause of the break candidly but ruefully: "They considered me unpardonably extravagant, and I considered them inexcusably the other way and may, unintentionally, have shown my feelings." Nearly out of options, Grant determined to farm the sixty acres of land next to

White Haven that Julia's father had given her as a wedding present. He had said more than once that he liked farming; this was his first full-time devotion to it.[1]

Grant faced the many challenges of farming with determination and stamina. He worked the fields alongside two free black men he hired, paying them more than the going wage, to the severe disapproval of Dent and his slave-owning neighbors. The Grants were then living close by in a beautiful home, called Wish-ton-Wish (an Indian name for the whip-poor-will), owned by Julia's brother, Lewis. It was there, on July 4, 1855, that Julia gave birth to a daughter Ellen, called Nellie (or Missy, by her father). As pleased as Julia was to live at Wish-ton-Wish, Grant determined to build his own house; his dignity demanded independence. So, when he was not working in the fields, he was felling logs, trimming them, and assembling them into a log house. It was a work of backbreaking physical effort and of great pride to Grant, but of embarrassment and dismay to Julia, who looked longingly down the road to her brother's house. "I cannot imagine why the Captain ever built it, as we were then occupying Wish-ton-Wish, a beautiful English villa," Julia recalled wonderingly. "This house suited me in every way, but I supposed the Captain was tired of going so far to his farm and decided to build. . . . It was so crude and homely that I did not like it at all, but I did not say so." In fact, Julia's description of every aspect of their farming days is unrelievedly cheerful, except for that of the log house. "Ulysses was really very successful at farming," she wrote. "His crops yielded well . . . but not as much as he anticipated from his calculations on paper—and I was a splendid farmer's wife."[2]

Grant named his house "Hardscrabble" with the same note of irony that Jessie had christened her "White House" in the remote gold-mining territory of California. Although Julia got the joke ("we facetiously decided to call it Hardscrabble"), she did not appreciate it. In fact, her dissatisfaction with Hardscrabble provides more insight into her actual experience of those days than do her sunny tales of raising chickens and potatoes and churning butter. Reflecting upon the log house in her memoirs, Julia described the only time in her life that she felt the kind of despair that Grant had already experienced more than once:

[S]oon after we had moved up to the new log house on the Captain's farm, I was feeling quite blue (which was rare with me), when a feeling of the deepest despondency like a black cloud fell around me, and I exclaimed (aloud, I think): "Is this my destiny? Is this my destiny? These crude, not to say rough, surroundings; to eat; to sleep, to wake again and again to the same—oh, sad is me!" All at once the dark shadow passed away and a silvery light came hovering over, and something seemed to say, "No, no *this* is not your destiny."[3]

The spartan, homemade surroundings of Hardscrabble momentarily shook Julia's supreme confidence in Grant's glorious future as nothing else ever did or ever would, and for once, she feared her dreams for him and their family would not come true. Ironically, Julia's deepest despair came at a time when she was with her husband; Grant's descended upon him only when he was without her. Julia's fears were short-lived. Her belief in Grant's future rebounded, as Mary Robinson, one of the Dents' slaves, later recalled:

> One day—I will never forget the circumstances—Mrs. Grant was sitting in a larger rocking-chair talking to some of her relatives about family matters. She referred to the financial embarrassment of her husband and then added: But we will not always be in this condition. Wait until Dudy (meaning Grant) becomes President. I dreamed last night he had been elected President. The rest all laughed and looked upon it as a capital joke. The idea that her husband, who was then a very poor farmer, would ever become president of the United States. Mrs. Grant always had great confidence in her husband, and she never relinquished the belief that he was destined to become one of the greatest men of the nation.[4]

Others who saw Grant during that time were far less willing to believe in a great future for him. As he felled trees for the log house, he chopped firewood, which he loaded onto a wagon with a team of horses and headed into St. Louis to sell. Against the winter chill, he wore his old army overcoat, stripped of its insignia, but recognizable to former colleagues he came across on those trips. He never shrank from greeting them; he sought them out and reveled in their conversations. If his more successful friends were uncomfortable to see how close to the economic margin he was, Grant did not let embarrassment at his situation deprive him of companionship. When one friend stumbled upon him in his wagon and threadbare coat and asked in amazement what Grant was doing, he replied philosophically, "I am solving the problem of poverty," and they both laughed. Grant enjoyed reminiscing about old times with old friends and telling Julia about his encounters when he returned home to Hardscrabble. On one of his trips to St. Louis, he ran into Sherman, also down on his luck again and unhappily relying on the generosity of the Ewings for maintenance of his family. Each man quickly sized up the other. "West Point and the Regular Army were not good schools for farmers, bankers, merchants and mechanics," Sherman ruefully observed to Grant. Grant readily agreed.[5]

November 1856 found Grant voting in a presidential election for the first time in his life. Testifying to the heightened sectional tension and to Grant's close reading of it, he recalled, "It was evident to my mind that the election of a Republican President in 1856 meant the secession of all of the Slave States, and rebellion. Under these circumstances I preferred the success of a candidate whose election would prevent or postpone secession, to seeing the country plunged into a war the end of which no man could foretell." He voted for Democrat James Buchanan over the standard-bearer of the brand-new Republican Party, John Charles Frémont.[6]

A month later, Grant wrote to his father for a loan to buy seed, but Jesse did not respond. Julia's revered mother died in January 1857, plunging her into depression. Grant appealed again to Jesse, stressing how economical he and Julia had been, in the hope of forestalling his father's criticism of his wife. "My expenses for my family have been nothing scarcely for the last two years," Grant wrote. "Fifty dollars, I believe would pay all that I have laid out for their clothing." There is no record that Jesse replied. Somehow, Grant secured money to plant potatoes, melons, cabbages, but the Panic of 1857 wiped out all his hard work. Prices of farm goods tumbled; bankruptcies swept the nation. By December 1857, Grant had no income and another mouth to feed on the way; Julia was pregnant again. To buy Christmas gifts for his family, Grant pawned his hunting watch and its gold chain for $22.[7]

Jesse Root Grant, their last child, was born in February 1858, at White Haven, where the whole family had moved, to Julia's great relief. After his wife's death, Dent had asked Grant to manage the plantation, and Dent moved to St. Louis with his youngest daughter, Emma. Though Julia and the children were more comfortable in the spacious surroundings with well-trained household help on hand, 1858 proved no better than had 1857 for the Grants. In some respects, it was worse. Nine-year-old Fred was ill for months with typhoid fever. The whole family suffered from unspecified chills and fever. Julia could barely tend to the children, and Grant "was attacked by fever and ague," he remembered, using the nineteenth-century term for malaria. "I had suffered very severely and for a long time from this disease while a boy in Ohio. It now lasted a year . . . [and it did] interfere greatly with the amount of work I was able to perform."[8]

It was clear that Grant's health could not survive such exertions, and he and Julia began to discuss other occupations. He made several earnest attempts—

real estate, county engineer, customs house clerk—but none panned out. They sold his beloved Hardscrabble, which enabled them to send the boys to a good school in St. Louis and live modestly for a time while they sought other options. At this low point in his life, Grant achieved the impossible. He succeeded in getting his abolitionist Republican father to agree with his slave-holding Democratic father-in-law on one thing: in the eyes of both, Grant was worthless. According to a neighbor of Jesse Grant, the disappointed father predicted that "he would have to take U.S. [Ulysses] and his family home and make him over again, as he had no business qualifications whatever—had failed in everything." Julia's father, too, was "coldly unsympathetic at this time," recalled a member of the family, "and ridiculed Ulysses, to the deep grief of his daughter."[9]

The escalating estrangement within the Grant-Dent family was a faint, personal echo of the growing schism in the larger American society. By late 1859, the collision of slavery, states' rights, and abolitionism sparked a flame that rising political intolerance fanned. John Brown's October raid on the federal arsenal at Harpers Ferry, Virginia, launched spirited if not ferocious debates throughout the nation. They were nowhere as vigorous as they were in Missouri, where both slavery and its abolition were fiercely defended. Grant was never a vocal opponent of slavery, nor vocal at all in his political views. His close connections with the Dent family led many in St. Louis to assume he was a Democrat, and moreover, one with pro-slavery sentiments (such assumptions, in fact, cost him the elected post of county engineer). In point of fact, he was largely apolitical at the time, but he always turned away from any hint of support for secession. As the presidential election of 1860 loomed on the horizon, political options for avoiding a major, violent national conflict narrowed. So did Grant's economic options for supporting his family.[10]

By early 1860, Grant had only one option left, and as distasteful as it was to both of them, Julia encouraged Grant to pursue it. She urged him "to go to Kentucky to see his father . . . telling him that his father had always been not only willing but anxious to serve him (in his own way, to be sure)." Julia did not forget or forgive Jesse's fractious behavior toward her and toward Grant, but she recognized the same *"poverty, poverty"* that six years earlier Grant wrote her had stared him in the face in California. She determined they would beat it. He protested that with their strained finances, he could not afford the trip; she insisted they could not afford for him not to go. He went, and in response to one more—perhaps the most desperate—plea, Jesse allowed Grant to join his brothers in running his store in Galena, Illinois, the regional sales headquarters of Jesse's leather goods empire.[11]

Carte de visite of the "Grant Family." *Left to right:* Ellen (Nellie), Grant, Jesse, Fred, Julia, and Ulysses Jr. (Buck). (*Author's collection*)

In preparation for the move into a state where slavery was illegal, Grant freed a slave that he had acquired from Dent. He could surely have used the money that the sale of William Jones would bring, but that was not an option Grant would entertain. At her father's urging, Julia left her slaves Jule, Eliza, Dan, and John with him in St. Louis. In April 1860, the Grants arrived by steamer at Galena. Taking up residence in a modest brick house high on the banks of the river, which they rented for about $100 a year, Julia bravely began a new effort at housekeeping with another untested cook.[12]

Grant, unenthusiastic but determined to succeed, threw his energy into business with his brothers Orvil and Samuel Simpson (Simpson, or Simp as he was called, was ill with tuberculosis). Though his income was small, the Grants were content by all accounts. Grant especially rejoiced in being with his children. His daughter Nellie was his special pet, and his sons were unceasing delights. Most entertaining of all was young Jesse. Nearly every evening, after Grant climbed the steep hill home for dinner, Jesse greeted him at the door, spoiling for a fight. "I do not feel like fighting, Jess," Grant protested, while being pounded by the knee-high rascal, "but I can't stand being hectored in this manner by a man of your size," and the two would commence a wrestling match that ended only—and always—with Grant's surrender. The evenings would conclude with "the Captain reading aloud the papers which were teeming with interest just then," recalled Julia. "Oh! how intensely interesting the papers were that winter! My dear husband Ulys read aloud to me every speech for and against secession."[13]

Grant recovered his physical and financial health in Galena; the work was not physically demanding, and he could pay his bills. Though the job fed his family, it starved his soul. He had no aptitude as a clerk and even less interest in being one. He could be found most days sitting in the store, listening to political conversations and occasionally offering quiet, thoughtful commentary. But Grant never learned the inventory or the knack of customer service, and he was always poised to escape out the back door should a patron appear ready to ask him for assistance. The one aspect of the job Grant did like was traveling through the region on sales trips. He enjoyed the journey and the people and the scenery, but he found no satisfaction in selling leather goods. His mind was not engaged. He had not found his calling. Years later, Grant's great friend and former aide, Horace Porter, put his finger on the missing piece of the Galena puzzle when he said, "He was made for great things, not little."[14]

Six years before Grant landed in Galena, in one of history's many minor ironies, a man named John Livingston had sent Grant a letter. Dated July 5, 1854, and woefully misdirected to Fort Vancouver, the letter informed Grant: "Your name has been proposed as a suitable one to occupy a place in our 'Portraits & Memoirs of Eminent Americans now living.'" Livingston, publisher of the forthcoming volume, encouraged Grant to furnish a daguerreotype as well as some personal recollections of his Mexican War experiences. "This great work," Livingston wrote, "contains some of the highest names in the country including President Pierce & his cabinet with several prominent Army officers." As the letter began its long journey west, Grant had just resigned from the army and was beginning his long journey east. It is not apparent when, in the course of Grant's wholly undistinguished series of civilian jobs, it caught up with him. The letter is contained in Grant's papers, but there is no indication that he ever answered it. When the book was published, Grant was not among those "eminent Americans." His time had not yet come.[15]

In fact, the popular historical conception of Grant during that time is that he was a great man in waiting. More so than even Abraham Lincoln, Grant's first thirty-five years were arduous and anonymous, but that only made his journey great and his story irresistible. His is such a compelling tale that writers of fiction have been drawn to its creative force. F. Scott Fitzgerald reflected upon Grant's rise from obscurity when he created one of his own iconic characters. "The foregoing has the ring of biography," Scott wrote in *Tender Is the Night,* after describing Dick Diver's early years, "without the satisfaction of knowing that the hero, like Grant, lolling in his general store in Galena, is ready to be called to an intricate destiny."[16]

The novelist hit precisely on the pivot of the Grant story—Grant's presence in Galena in April 1861. While Grant's slough of despond made his rise to the heights of glory so amazing, it was the serendipity of his presence in Galena, Illinois, at that particular time that made so much of it possible. It was then, with boredom beginning to seep into the hours of his longest successful stretch of civilian employment, that Confederates fired on Fort Sumter, and Grant's life took its turn toward greatness. He had resigned from the army under the weight of debilitating depression, caused by Julia's failure to write and his own business failure after failure after failure. Because Julia urged him to go to his father for help, the outbreak of the Civil War found him "lolling" in the general store in Galena in the spring of 1861. Galena was one of the keys that unlocked Grant's intricate destiny, and because she urged Grant to ask his father for work, Julia had much to do with the couple's presence in Galena in the spring of 1861.

"secesh wives with their own little slaves"

News of the firing on Fort Sumter flashed to Galena by telegraph the same day. Four days later, on April 16, Grant joined a throng of townsmen in the courthouse. The local congressman, Elihu Washburne, whom he had not yet met, and attorney John Rawlins, whom he had, both eloquently stated the case for renunciation of partisanship and defense of the Union. Impressed by their words and moved by the spirit of the hour, Grant left the meeting with his brother Simpson, determined to offer his services to the United States.

When Grant returned home and told Julia of his decision to fight for the Union, his slave-owning wife gave him her full support, even though, for months, she had been feeling "much disturbed" in her "political sentiments," and understandably so. Julia was torn between her father's politics and her husband's. Before the firing on Fort Sumter, as Grant read aloud newspaper accounts of the arguments for and against secession, she tried to find a compromise to suit her conflicting emotions. At one point, she told Grant that she thought "the states had a right to go out of the Union if they wished to, and yet thought it the duty of the national government to prevent a dismemberment of the Union, even if coercion should be necessary." Grant gently pointed out her inconsistency with some amusement and urged her to hold to the latter view, which he said had more moral and legal weight behind it. But it was love, not reason, that swayed Julia. Though she did not record her feelings on that April evening, she later pointed to another aspect of the situation that informed her actions. "I did not think Captain Grant's occupation in Galena entirely congenial to him," she admitted, "and was willing, therefore, that he should go out on this expedition as he wished to, no matter how lonely I should be without him." Julia would not prevent her dashing lieutenant from returning to the profession they both knew suited him best.[1]

Further evidence of the discussion between them that night is found in a letter Grant wrote to Julia's father two days later. In it, Grant firmly explained his decision to fight for the Union, and then went on to discuss the implications of the war, predicting an end to the White Haven way of life. "[N]ow is the time, particularly in border slave states for men to prove their love of country," he declared to Dent. "No impartial man can conceal from himself the fact that in all these troubles the Southerners have been the aggressors. . . . In all this I can but see the doom of Slavery." Grant also needed to inform his father of his decision. His April 21 letter to Jesse brimmed with enthusiasm and loyalty: "There are but two parties now, Traitors and Patriots and I want hereafter to be ranked with the latter, and I trust, the stronger party." He recalled Jesse's decision to send him to West Point. "Having been educated for such an emergency, at the expense of the Government," Grant reminded his father, "I feel that it has upon me superior claims, such claims as no ordinary motives of self-interest can surmount. . . ." Perhaps Jesse asked his son where Julia's sympathies lay, for shortly thereafter, Grant wrote his father that "Julia takes a very sensible vue of our present difficulties. She would be sorry to have me go but thinks the circumstances may warrant it and will not through a single obsticle in the way. . . ."[2]

On April 18, when the Galena town fathers held a meeting to respond to Lincoln's call to the states for volunteer militias, they asked Grant to chair the session and sign up volunteers. According to Grant's memoirs, his West Point education and his service in the Mexican War were unique credentials in the town, and his perceived Democrat sympathies could help take the edge off the politics of the situation. "With much embarrassment and some prompting," Grant later recalled, "I made out to announce the object of the meeting." Grant did not volunteer then, but his efficiency and his demeanor impressed Washburne, who was introduced to him at the meeting. When Grant told the group he hoped that a boyhood friend, Ohio Gov. William Dennison, might give him a regiment to command, Washburne urged him to stick with Illinois and offered to intercede with that state's governor on his behalf. So Grant remained to manage the raising, drilling, and clothing of the Galena volunteers. When the troops headed to Springfield to be officially mustered into the ranks of the army, Grant went with them. Without commission, without uniform, and without cadence, he walked behind the new soldiers as they marched to the train station on April 25.[3]

Even with Washburne's help, though, nothing came easily to Grant. Weeks passed as Grant was given clerk's duties, sent on inspection missions, pressed to drill green troops, and authorized to muster some regiments into duty. More than a month later, when he visited his family in Covington, Kentucky, he learned that Maj. Gen. George McClellan was on the other side of the river at Cincinnati, and he decided to see if the general could use his help. When he was told to wait outside the general's office, Grant's stamina proved greater than Lincoln's was to be in McClellan's parlor in Washington later that year, but he was equally disappointed. After two full days of watching McClellan's aides "busy with quills," Grant abandoned the effort. McClellan, who may have recalled with distaste the inebriated quartermaster at Fort Humboldt, later claimed some credit for Grant's success, pointing to Grant's unsuccessful journey to see him. McClellan said he was out of town those days: "This was his good luck; for had I been there I would no doubt have given him a place on my staff, and he would probably have remained with me and shared my fate." Whether or not McClellan was telling the truth, Grant returned to Springfield, sincerely disappointed. Washburne continued to counsel patience. Grant finally got his command when a regiment from southern Illinois appealed to the governor to dismiss its erratic, alcoholic commander in favor of the quiet, no-nonsense man who had mustered it in weeks earlier. On June 15, thirty-nine-year-old Col. Ulysses S. Grant assumed command of the 21st Illinois Volunteer Infantry Regiment.[4]

Racing to Galena to secure funds for horse and uniform (which he borrowed from a former business partner of his father), Grant found Julia sorely tried by the burdens of home. Young Jesse had been unaccountably ill for several weeks, and the escalating political ferment roiled her emotions. The Dent family was splitting apart. On one side stood White Haven and all that made it the paradise Julia remembered. Her father claimed loyalty to the Union, "but is opposed to having an army to sustain it," Grant observed. "He would have a secession force march where they please uninterrupted and is really what I would call a secessionist." Dent's rebel sentiments were echoed by Julia's youngest sister, Emma, and by her brothers Lewis and John, the latter of whom was "thinking about a colonelcy in the secession army." The rest of the Dent family remained solidly in the Union camp. Sister Nellie followed the politics of her husband, Alexander Sharp, a strong Unionist, whom Grant later appointed brigade surgeon. Their brother Fred, then stationed on the West Coast, wrote a letter to Grant that "breathes fort[h] the most patriotic sentiments," Grant informed Dent. "He is for the old Flag" and would remain in the U.S. Army. Julia now faced one of the most dismal Civil War prospects—brother fighting brother.[5]

At the same time, "woman's work" assumed new challenges that Julia was particularly ill prepared to meet. Fabric for uniforms needed cutting and tailoring, flags for each military unit required sewing, and all manner of socks and sweaters begged to be knitted. Julia bravely threw herself into the fray of flying needles, but she was simply not cut out for such work. In her *Memoirs,* Julia recalled with great fondness making clothes for her children and was especially proud of her tiny gold thimble, which was the envy of her peers. By all accounts except hers, though, Julia found it very difficult to sew. Her eyes were surely part of the problem; some strabismics have pointed to sewing as their greatest challenge. Julia's probable lack of depth perception likely rendered her golden thimble less-than-perfect armor against the needles she wielded and wrought havoc on her attempts to produce quick, neat, consistent stitches. She did sew one item for the cause, but when she was handed yarn to make a pair of socks, she confessed to the sewing bee's organizer that she did not know how to knit and "feared that the war would be over" before she could complete them. After her initial foray, "I never attended the sewing meetings again," Julia remembered with some embarrassment.[6]

The notion of a very short war was a near consensus. In the North, Lincoln's initial call was for volunteers to commit to three months' service, and a South Carolina senator was so certain of Federal cowardice and quick Confederate victory that he offered to drink all the Yankee blood that would be spilled before the South achieved its independence.[7]

As Grant prepared to embark upon his second career in the army, Julia faced their separation with a surprising air of equanimity, despite her worries about her family in Galena and her family in White Haven. Julia's recollection of their parting has more than a touch of unreality, but thoughts like hers were not unusual in those early days when war was still chivalry and dash and romance: "Strange to say, I felt no regret at his going and even suggested that our eldest son, just then eleven years old, should accompany him. I think it was a tender thought for my beloved husband that prompted this suggestion, as well as a desire to gratify the importunings and pleadings of our boy Fred. You must not forget, though, that these regiments were only called out for three months, and I considered it a pleasant summer outing for both of them."[8]

That "tender thought" for her husband was one of the greatest proofs of Julia's love for him, and, at the same time, recognition of her limitations. She could not go with him; her young children, two under the age of six and one of them sick at the time, claimed all of her attention. They both knew that she would not write faithfully in his absence, no matter her promises, and they both knew, too, that Grant would suffer as a result. So Julia bravely offered to send their eleven-year-old son with him as companionship and as a tangible token of her love. It was another of Julia's efforts to find a compromise, and Grant agreed completely with this one.

With Fred happily at his side, Grant quietly and firmly embarked on his first command. He brought discipline to his unruly volunteer soldiers through his calm but unmistakably resolute manner. Unlike Sherman, he did not disdain the volunteer forces. He recognized that they had to be treated differently from regular army troops, not because they were less capable of discipline but because he believed, in the words of Bruce Catton, that "these raw soldiers were men who could be reasoned with, men with a sense of responsibility that would respond if anyone bothered to appeal to it." He gained such respect and loyalty from his men that—aided by timely patriotic speeches by Congressmen Washburne and John Logan—when their three-month term of enlistment was up, nearly all signed on for three more years. Grant's determination to do his job well was also evident in a request he sent home. "If you have an opportunity," he asked Julia, "I wish you would send me McClellands report of battles in the Crimea. You will find it about the house."[9]

Just then, his house in Galena was one of mourning. Tuberculosis had finally claimed Grant's brother Simpson, who died in St. Paul, Minnesota. His body was returned to Galena for burial. "This sad event brought Colonel Grant's father and sisters also to Galena," Julia recalled, "and I had the pleasure of entertaining them." Grant found no pleasure at all in a visit he made about the same time to St. Louis, though, where he sought to calm Dent's fury at him. Dent, whose relationship with Grant was always chilly, had turned icy. Convinced that his son-in-law was throwing away an easy opportunity for a more prestigious and lucrative senior command in the Confederate Army, Dent regarded Grant with disgust and anger. But Grant not only reaffirmed his loyalty to the United States, he also disdained the notion of gaining by favor what ought to be won by the sword. He told Dent that he would never seek personal or political influence to rise in the ranks. Dent again proposed that Julia and the children live with him in St. Louis, but Grant rebuffed that, too. Not too long thereafter, Dent, outraged and obstinate, told Julia that there would always be a plate at his table for her, but her husband was not welcome in his home.[10]

If Grant never sought political favor, he received it unbidden in July. A newspaper listed his name among those promoted to brigadier general of volunteer troops, and when Grant learned of it, he immediately told the chaplain who had brought the paper from St. Louis, "It never came from any request of mine. It must be some of Washburne's work." Indeed, on his own, Washburne had championed Grant's name when Lincoln offered the Illinois congressional delegation the opportunity to make four promotions. Grant did not rise without acknowledgment of his merits, though. He was a hard-working, firm disciplinarian, with excellent logistical skills and a rare lack of overweening ego. His direct superior, John Pope, had written to the recently arrived commander of the Department of Missouri, Maj. Gen. Frémont, on August 5, that Grant was "thoroughly a gentleman & an officer of intelligence & discretion."[11]

Grant was so pleased with his promotion that he wrote Julia a letter unlike any other—this one was surely penned with an eye to having Julia share it with friends in Galena: "I certainly feel very greatful to the people of Ill. for the interest they seem to have taken in me and unasked too . . . from what I have heard from there the people, who were perfect strangers to me up to the commencement of our present unhappy national difficulties, were very unanimous in recommending me for my present position. I shall do my very best not to disappoint them. . . . All my old Regt. expressed great regret at my leaving them and applied to be attached to my Brigade."[12]

His troops' regard for him must have been particularly gratifying, since he had yet to earn the respect of his father-in-law or of his father. When Jesse learned of his son's promotion in the volunteer force, he urged Grant to seek appointment in the regular army. Grant threw back in his father's face the greeting Jesse had given him seven years earlier, when Grant resigned from the regular army and left California. "You ask if I should not like to go in the regular army," he wrote. "I should not," he declared adamantly. "I want to bring my children up to useful employment, and in the army the chance is poor." He ended the letter with some family news. "Fred. has been with me until yesterday. I sent him home on a boat."[13]

Fred had the time of his life for a month, and Grant did, too. "Fred. enjoys it hugely," Grant wrote Julia delightedly in early July. "The Soldiers and officers call him Colonel and he seems to be quite a favorite." Soon, however, the 21st Illinois was ordered to Quincy, Illinois, and it appeared a battle loomed in Grant's immediate future. With concerns for Fred's safety and for Julia's fears, Grant reluctantly decided it was time for Fred to leave the army. As he sent Fred home, Grant wrote Julia that it was because "we may have some fighting to do," sure that she would appreciate his paternal caution. Instead, Julia was incensed—not because young Fred would have to travel back to Galena by himself, but because Grant was planning to send him back at all. Grant's action produced one of the few recorded instances in which Julia immediately responded to a letter from her husband. "I received a prompt letter in reply decidedly disapproving my proposition," recalled Grant. "Do not send him home," she insisted, calling upon her history lessons. "Alexander was not older when he accompanied Philip. Do keep him with you." It was too late; Fred was already making his way home alone, thoroughly unhappy. A month later, Grant felt the same. "I am sorry that I did not keep Fred with me," the letter to Julia said. "He would have enjoyed it very much." So would have his father.[14]

It appeared to Grant that Julia was once again faltering in her correspondence. "I should like to hear from you and the children oftener," he wrote on July 19. "I got but one letter from you since I left Springfield and no doubt you have writ[ten] others." Then, a thought—perhaps a hope—occurred to him: "But I am kept so on the wing tha[t] they do not reach me." For once, he was correct; Julia had made a prodigious effort to stay in contact with her husband after Fred's return to Galena. On August 26, Grant expressed joy at the "big batch of letters" from Julia that had arrived all at once. He was puzzled, though, because in one of those letters, Julia claimed she had not heard from him "in so long a time." She also failed to confirm arrival of some important items he sent to her. "There is one letter of mine which you have not acknowledged the receipt of which I think you would have noticed," Grant wrote from Cairo on September 29. "I enclosed you my commission as Brigadier General. Did you get it?" Grant assured her that he had usually written more than once a week, but both Grants were on notice that mail service was unreliable and would likely prove more so as the war progressed.[15]

Though he missed her letters, the newly minted brigadier general had plenty to occupy him. With his new grade came the privilege of choosing his own staff, and the first among those chosen was his Galena neighbor, John Rawlins. Grant fervently wanted the intelligent, lawyerly, yet profane, man as his aide. He wrote Julia to ask Orvil to entreat "Rollins" to join him. Rawlins was still in Galena; he had not yet volunteered because his wife was terminally ill with tuberculosis. He finally accepted Grant's offer, leaving the bedside of his dying wife in one of many doleful wartime parting scenes played out in homes across the United States. Rawlins was a self-made man, whose alcoholic father had left the family when he was a child. In Galena, he read the law and practiced with a local lawyer. In 1857, he was also elected city attorney. Grant had been impressed with him from the start, admired his political integrity, and came to rely upon him as a friend as well as an aide.[16]

Rawlins's fear of alcohol's devastating power made him hypersensitive to its presence anywhere near Grant. Rawlins's forceful removal of liquor from camp and his vocal reproach to those who drank in the general's presence may have fed the gossip about Grant's drinking even more than Grant's actual drinking did. Rawlins has been portrayed as "the man who saved the man who saved the Union," but it would be overstatement to say, as some have said, that his primary role was to keep Grant sober. Certainly there is no indication that Grant chose him because of his aggressive approach to temperance. In fact, Grant later told a colleague that Rawlins's greatest service was that he handled the swearing for both of them. But it is fair to say that in time, Rawlins believed Grant's sobriety was as much his responsibility as his military duties and claimed it as a core aspect of his own legacy of service to Grant and the Union. In addition to Rawlins, Grant brought onto his staff Clark B. Lagow and William S. Hillyer. Hillyer was a most fortunate addition to Grant's military family, since his wife traveled with Julia throughout the war and became one of Julia's closest lifelong friends.[17]

Kentucky declared its neutrality in mid-May; Federal and Confederate forces perched along the neutral state's borders, each side hoping the other would make a misstep fatal to its interests. Although it was clear that any overt attempt to seize the state by force risked tipping it the other way, it was at this juncture that Frémont decided upon a bold plan to advance against the Confederate forces under Gen. Leonidas Polk, whose ultimate aim was to seize control of the Mississippi River. To lead the field command, Frémont made another bold move: on August 28, he chose Brig. Gen. Ulysses S. Grant to command the Department of Southeast Missouri.

The two men had met before, and Frémont later recalled that Grant had impressed him as a "man of great activity and promptness in obeying orders without question or hesitation." The Pathfinder's staff, however, was less impressed and whispered against Grant "for reasons that were well known," Frémont later wrote, in one of the many code phrases for Grant's reputation as a drunk. When Grant reported to him in St. Louis for an interview (even with the summons, it took an effort to get through the guards to see the Pathfinder), Frémont looked past those whispers and past Grant's threadbare civilian clothes; the young brigadier carried himself with dignity and determination. Frémont could have selected another brigadier for the job, but he chose Grant, plucking him if not from obscurity, at least from the shadows. Frémont's orders to Grant on the day he gave him command of the forces in southeast Missouri were consistent with Frémont's strategy for securing the Mississippi River: "I told him that the purpose was to make Cairo (Illinois), and Paducah (Kentucky) opposite, the base of important operations against Memphis and Nashville."[18]

The tense face-off over Kentucky could not last long, nor did it. Confederate Gen. Gideon Pillow's September 4 movement on Columbus, Kentucky (which surprised Jefferson Davis as much as it did Abraham Lincoln), provided an excuse for Grant's rapid movement on Paducah, which he occupied without opposition on September 5. Frémont had issued his emancipation order a week earlier in St. Louis. In Paducah, the first Union Army outpost in fragile Kentucky, Grant issued his own proclamation to its citizens on September 6. He had no intention to "injure or annoy you," he declared, "but to respect the rights, and to defend and enforce the rights of all loyal citizens.... I have nothing to do with opinions. I shall deal only with armed rebellion and its aiders and abettors." During the same week that Frémont and Jessie parried fruitlessly and annoyingly with Lincoln about Frémont's emancipation order, the president found favor with Grant's handling of the Paducah situation. Absalom Markland, who met with Lincoln in Washington at that time, later recalled the president saying, "The modesty and brevity of that address to the citizens of Paducah show that the officer issuing it understands the situation, and is a proper man to command there at this time."[19]

The Kentucky General Assembly, dominated by Union sentiment, lost no time in punishing Polk and his superiors for breaking the neutrality. Legislators passed a resolution demanding that Confederate forces leave the state and promptly overrode a veto of that resolution by the state's governor, a Confederate sympathizer. The Assembly then ordered that the flag of the United States be hoisted above the capitol. By September 7, Kentucky was officially in the Union ranks.

Grant's new command was headquartered in Cairo, Illinois, the leading town in the southern portion of that state known as "Little Egypt." (Though named for the Egyptian capital, locals pronounce their city's name "kay-ro.") Cairo was a thriving commercial center, a bustling river port, and a major railroad hub. It had everything necessary for the transport, care, and maintenance of an army and—so important to Grant—of a family, too. "He wrote me many times," Julia recalled of her husband's move to Cairo, "urging me to visit him there, which I, at length, with much timidity, decided to do." Daunted by the logistics of such a move, she delayed her departure again and again, in large part because "[h]e desired the children to accompany me. This wish it was that deterred me in the first place, I thinking it such an undertaking to go with four children." Finally, though, she bravely gathered up her courage and her children, and headed south. She stopped for a visit with her father in St. Louis, where, it is likely, she convinced him she needed to take her slave Jule with her to Cairo.[20]

Ulysses Grant was a warrior, but Julia Grant was the Civil War's road warrior. Beginning with that first journey, she covered more than ten thousand miles in four years—nearly four thousand in just the first year—to be with her husband. Even those numbers understate the effort required to travel at the mercy of unreliable trains, ferries, and carriage, in bad weather, and over poor roads, sometimes in enemy country. With poor eyesight and four children, Julia could not have made it without her slave Jule to help her, especially in those early years. They arrived at Grant's headquarters soon after November 7, the day that Grant fought his first major engagement, near Belmont, Missouri.[21]

Grant and approximately three thousand untested troops had traveled by transport down the Mississippi River, across the river from Confederate-occupied Columbus, Kentucky, where a small Confederate force was garrisoned on a spit of land called Belmont. Grant had the advantage of surprise, and his green soldiers initially routed the Confederate troops. The gleeful bluecoats tarried to divide the abandoned campsite spoils, though, and were overwhelmed when General Polk rushed Confederate reinforcements across the river on steamboats. Viewing the chaos and panic in his ranks, Grant proved a cool but aggressive leader, urging the men to reload and fight their way through the enemy. "We cut our way in, we can cut our way out," he called to them, and they did, fleeing to transports waiting to return them to Cairo. The Confederates rightfully claimed a victory, since they had chased the Yankees from the field, but Grant found value in the engagement. His men and officers had had their first serious fight and had learned lessons from it, and he was pleased about that.

He was even happier when Julia arrived in Cairo soon after that battle. So eager was Grant to see his family, according to Julia, that "Ulys met me almost before the train stopped." Julia, who from this point in both her life and her memoirs referred to her husband as "the General" (or "Ulys," or "Mr. Grant," but never "the President"), began to ease into military life in Cairo, finding limitations as well as unexpected pleasures: "The General, the children, and I had rooms at headquarters, as did Colonel Hillyer's family. . . . The children and I managed to be comfortable in the great barracks our house resembled. . . ."[22]

Life in Cairo introduced Julia to a broad array of new experiences, including her new social status as the wife of the senior commander in the field. Grant's troops memorialized Julia's presence by naming a sixty-four-pounder cannon "Lady Grant."[23]

It was during this time that Julia wrote the only letter during the war to her husband that has survived. On December 9, they were both in Cairo—he at his headquarters and she at the pier waiting to board a boat for a trip to St. Louis to see her father—when Grant's aide Captain Lagow delivered a note from Grant, asking her to run an errand for him in St. Louis and to give "love to all at your fathers house." Grant signed it with her nickname for him, "Dode." On the back of that note, she wrote her own: "Dear Dode Come up & sit with me a while wont you? I am so lonesome bring up St. Louis Papers too & be sure & send or bring this back to your Juje." Carefully preserved at the Library of Congress, it is clear that the reason this note from her has survived is because she was committed to saving every letter from her husband.[24]

Her stay in Cairo also transformed Grant—literally. The face of the Ulysses Grant we know today is Julia's handiwork. Grant "had always worn his beard trimmed short until he was appointed colonel of the 21st Illinois," his son Fred later recalled, "but during the time he was serving in Missouri, he did not trim his beard, nor did he do so on being stationed in Cairo as brigadier-general." Of all of the exotic Civil War facial hairstyles, from Union Gen. Ambrose Burnside's flamboyant sideburns to Confederate Adm. Raphael Semmes's fantastically waxed and pointed mustache, Grant's beard of October 1861 was surely one of the very ugliest. Under a modest mustache, a waterfall of a beard fell in waves to his chest, where it was roughly trimmed straight across. That was not all; into the front of that beard, it appeared that a "U" was sculpted just below the chin. It was a beard on top of a beard, and when Julia saw it, she decided it was at least one beard too many. Frederick Grant, then eleven years old, remembered well his mother's reaction: "one of the first things that my mother said to him was, that she did not like the length of his beard." Julia, always conscious of appearances, insisted he trim it. Though Grant resisted for two months, Julia was determined her general would lose this battle.[25]

Rarely viewed today, the double beard was immortalized in a daguerreotype made in October 1861. The image is also rare because it captured Brig. Gen. Ulysses S. Grant in full military plumage: an ill-fitting sideswept hat perched back on his head, buttoned-up dress coat with epaulets at the shoulder, tasseled sash around his waist, and sword in his lap (he had not yet received his sword belt). When his brigadier general's uniform arrived in October, he had hastened to document his promotion. Grant pulled together his newly acquired and similarly attired headquarters staff, and they all headed to a daguerreotype studio in Cairo. Grant was proud of what seems in retrospect an almost comical photograph of himself; he sent a number of copies to his family, including aunts, uncles, and cousins. To his sister Mary he sent one each of himself and his staff, asking proudly, "A good looking set aint they?" As pleased as he was to have tangible proof of his advancement in the form of the uniform, Grant soon set aside all but the shoulder straps and returned to more comfortable clothes—a well-worn jacket over a private's blouse and trousers. That would be his working uniform for the rest of his army career. In Mexico he had witnessed firsthand the exceptional military skill shown by two very differently costumed generals: Old Fuss and Feathers (Winfield Scott) and Old Rough and Ready (Zachary Taylor). Grant knew the uniform did not make the man.[26]

What he did not know then but soon learned was that his reputation as a drunk would serve as a convenient weapon for his personal enemies to wield against him. The most persistent of the many men who sought to undermine Grant in this fashion was William Kountz, whom Grant reprimanded when Kountz failed miserably in his role as supplier of materiel transports for Grant's army at Cairo. Julia was in her husband's headquarters when Rawlins angrily ordered the man to leave Grant's tent after he had exhausted the general's patience. "Of course, Captain Kountz was very angry," according to Julia, "and at once proclaimed broadcast that General Grant and his staff were all drunk." Stomping out, the enraged Kountz (who was later arrested for disobeying orders) embarked on a fierce and methodical battle to destroy Grant's career. Kountz's charges ultimately came to naught, derailed by crucial gaps in his evidence and by Grant's much-heralded successes at Forts Henry and Donelson. But if Kountz accused Grant of being a drunkard with the most fury, he was not the only one. Others whose interests Grant foiled, including some powerful newspaper editors and friends of the president, used charges of drunkenness—and other personal failings—to attack the brigadier.[27]

Although Grant never had as rocky a relationship with the press as did Sherman, he created enemies in that quarter in a most peculiar fashion. Unlike Sherman, Grant caught grief for allowing too much freedom of the press. According to editors and correspondents with antislavery and abolitionist views, Grant exhibited "secesh" sympathies by allowing equal access to his camp by Democratic and Republican newspapers. When hard-line Republican newspapers urged Grant to deny access to—and even to stop circulation of—Democratic newspapers, he refused. Trying to place Grant in a bad light for that reason alone, however, was a nonstarter with Grant's civilian superiors, especially Lincoln. So, the general's critics most often wrapped their real motives within allegations of drunkenness and worse. It was in this manner that Julia Grant first came to Lincoln's notice. In early January 1862, the president read an unsigned letter with the startling words: "Until we can secure pure men in habits and men without secesh wives with their own little slaves to wait upon them, which is a fact here in this camp with Mrs. Grant, our country is lost." That anonymous letter was enclosed in another letter, addressed to Secretary of War Simon Cameron by William Bross, an editor of the *Chicago Tribune and Press.*[28]

Bross was a Republican political activist in Illinois with strong antislavery views, whom Lincoln knew well enough in 1861 to appoint postmaster of Chicago. By late December of that year, Bross was furious at Grant. He and the other *Tribune* editor, Joseph Medill, consistently protested Grant's refusal to halt distribution of their Democratic-owned rival, the *Chicago Times,* which, they declared, sought to undermine Union morale and publish confidential military information. Grant agreed with their assessment of the highly inflammatory *Times* and other similarly inspired newspapers, but with few exceptions through the long course of the war, he believed military attempts to silence the press would cause more harm than good.[29]

In addition, the *Tribune* had recently published charges of "fraud on the Quartermasters service" in Grant's department, which Grant had dispatched Hillyer to investigate, and that may have caused tension, too. Grant's refusal— probably brusque—to bend to the *Tribune*'s demands was likely the "treatment" referred to in Bross's letter to Cameron, which read in part:

> Evidence entirely satisfactory to myself and Associate Editors of the Tribune has become so convincing that Gen U.S. Grant commanding at Cairo is an inebriate, that I deem it my duty to call your attention to the matter. The inclosed anonymous letter would not deserve a moment's attention, were not facts abundant from other sources that what the writer says is true. His treatment to myself refered to in the first paragraph I care nothing about, but I was satisfied that he would not have acted as he did, had he been sober. . . . We think it best call your attention to this painful matter, rather than to attack Gen. Grant in the Tribune. As you may not know me personally I refer to Dr Chas V. Dyer & His Excellency President Lincoln.[30]

We know that Lincoln read this letter, including its anonymous enclosure, because it carries Lincoln's troubled endorsement of January 4, 1862: "Bross would not knowingly misrepresent. . . . Gen. Grant was appointed chiefly on the recommendation of Hon. E. B. Washburne—Perhaps we should consult him." Coincidentally, Washburne already had a document that he could have passed along, a firsthand report from Rawlins on the subject of Grant's drinking, prompted by yet another letter recently received by the congressman on that same matter from a citizen from Galena. In his lengthy letter, Rawlins had flatly, sincerely, and in great detail rejected the charges of Grant's drunkenness.

Insofar as can be determined, though, neither Rawlins nor Washburne commented on the issue of Julia's slave living with her and the general at U.S. Army
headquarters in Cairo.[31]

By late January 1862, Lincoln had met Frémont, McClellan, and Sherman
and their wives, some of them on more than one occasion. He formed his opinions of them based on his firsthand observation, as well as on reports from
sources trusted and spurious. More than two years would pass, though, before
Lincoln would meet either Grant or Julia. Until early 1864, he was forced to
evaluate them based on accounts—some flattering, but even more damning—
that arrived bidden and unbidden at the Executive Mansion. The anonymous
letter, passed along by a close political crony of his, was calculated to make
the president think ill of Julia Grant and worse of her husband. It is entirely
possible, though, that the missive instead sparked empathy in the president,
whose own wife's shortcomings—including Mary's rumored "secesh" tendencies—were routinely wielded as a weapon against Lincoln. In any event, this
particular effort to tarnish Grant's character produced no discernible results.

With battlefield command experience under his belt and his family at his
side in Cairo, Grant turned to the challenges and opportunities ahead. Like
Frémont and Sherman, he viewed the Mississippi River as the chief strategic
feature of the United States' heartland and its control as vital to Union success.
As winter settled in, he pored over maps and made reconnaissance trips. Grant
was eager to continue on the offensive, and he thought he knew just where to
begin. He went to St. Louis to talk to his new boss.

Just a week before the battle of Belmont, the U.S. Army had undergone
two major changes in its leadership. McClellan succeeded Scott to the post
of general-in-chief, and Lincoln relieved Frémont from command. In Frémont's place, after a brief interim, Lincoln appointed Maj. Gen. Henry Wager
Halleck. After the Mexican War, Halleck left the army and made a fortune as
a lawyer and land speculator in California. When the Civil War began, he
returned to his true love, military service. He had written a book—really, *the*
book—on military strategy and tactics, *Elements of Military Art and Science,*
in the 1840s. It was so well known and highly regarded that Lincoln borrowed it from the Library of Congress to further his own military education
when his frustration with McClellan was at its peak. Halleck had been one
of Lincoln's first major generals, initially ranking fourth in the army after
Scott, McClellan, and Frémont. Upon Frémont's removal as commander of
the Department of Missouri, Halleck was the logical candidate to succeed to
that post. During the war, Grant had high regard for Halleck's intelligence,

but he learned very early and at firsthand that Halleck's military instincts were vastly different from his own.[32]

Arriving in St. Louis on January 23, 1862, Grant soon conferred with his new chief about a plan he had devised to dislodge the Confederates from control of Fort Henry on the Tennessee River. Cautious, plodding, always by the book (by his book, in fact), Halleck barely deigned to listen to Grant's proposal for an aggressive, combined assault by gunboats and infantry to capture the strategically important but poorly constructed, badly sited, and weakly fortified enemy target. According to Grant, Halleck brusquely denied permission for the expedition in the most emphatic and condescending terms: "I was cut short as if my plan was preposterous." Grant left his commander's office sorely disappointed and prepared to return to his headquarters.[33]

It is not clear whether Grant engaged a barber before or after his meeting with Halleck, but according to Fred, "[d]uring that visit, he was shaved—the first time in my recollection that he was ever shaved; the second and only other instance was when he was President." Julia had won the battle of the beards, though she did not know it yet. In point of fact, she had little reason to rejoice right then. As Grant was about to leave for Cairo, he was handed a telegram from that very city, informing him that young Ulysses was gravely ill. "A medicine which could be procured only at a French chemist's in St. Louis," was the only possible remedy, according to the doctor at Buck's bedside. "When the General arrived at seven A.M. [with the medicine], Ulysses was delirious with pain and fever," Julia recalled. "The doctor began at once to administer the medicine and at the same hour the next day the little fellow was sitting up in his chair eating his breakfast."[34]

Soon, Grant was feeling as chipper as his son, and it was the commander in chief who delivered the general's tonic. On January 27, Lincoln issued his General War Order No. 1, demanding movement by February 22 against the Confederate Army and Navy everywhere along the Union line. While McClellan peevishly ignored the order as an insupportable imposition on his glacial preparations for the peninsula, Grant received the news as a gift. His renewed petition to Halleck for a combined operation to attack Fort Henry also carried the endorsement of celebrated U.S. Navy Capt. Andrew Hull Foote. This time, Halleck approved his proposal with alacrity. Operating in the capacity of a staff officer, as he later did so well when he became army chief of staff, Halleck quickly organized and forwarded to Grant troops, munitions, materiel, and soon thereafter, perhaps most important of all, William Tecumseh Sherman. Preparing for battle with intelligence, skill, and zeal, Grant coordinated the combined assault with Captain Foote, a decorated naval hero of enormous talent but modest demeanor. Within four days, Grant readied his forces, Foote prepared his gunboats, and they both set off. Foote's gunboats—more specifically, his naval guns—got there first, and the Confederate Army commander surrendered to a navy captain before Grant and his army arrived. Grant prepared to build on that success by immediately advancing against another nearby Confederate target, Fort Donelson, almost a dozen miles east on the Cumberland River.

Fort Donelson's strategic location made it a bigger prize than Fort Henry, but it was a much greater military challenge, too. In the first place, the physical structure was much stouter. In addition, it held more guns, more Confederate soldiers, and at that moment three high-ranking Confederate officers. Notwithstanding significant initial setbacks, Grant's determined assault prevailed. The two senior commanders, Generals John B. Floyd and Gideon J. Pillow, fled ahead of Grant's demand for surrender, leaving their colleague, Gen. Simon Bolivar Buckner Jr., the most humiliating of military duties. Huddled dejectedly inside the fort, Buckner found the message from his former friend, former West Point colleague, and one-time debtor "ungenerous and unchivalrous":

> Feby 16th 1862—Hd Qrs. Army in the Field, Camp near Donelson
> [To] Gen. S. B. Buckner, Confed. Army
> Sir: Yours of this date proposing Armistice and appointment of Commissioners to settle terms of Capitulation is just received. No terms except unconditional and immediate surrender can be accepted. I propose to move immediately upon your works. I am, sir, very respectfully Your obt. Svt. U. S. Grant Brig. Gen.[35]

When telegraphed to the War Department in Washington and splashed across Northern newspapers, Grant's words electrified the Union home front. Securing the two forts on two key rivers and capturing an entire Confederate Army were unqualified strategic victories for the Union. The Confederates lost their hold on Kentucky, and Tennessee seemed on the brink of slipping from their grip. Subsequently dubbed "Unconditional Surrender Grant," the newest Union hero gained more than popularity from his successes to that point. Battlefield experience strengthened his determination to advance and his preference for aggressive forward movement over cautious maneuver.

Grant received many telegrams, letters, and words of praise in the aftermath of the twin successes but nothing from Halleck, who was busy claiming the victories as his own. Immediately upon receiving word of Grant's victory, Halleck had wired McClellan: "Make Buell, Grant and Pope major-generals of volunteers and give me command in the west. I ask this for Forts Henry and Donelson." In pure McClellan fashion, however, the general-in-chief had already angled to steal the thunder Halleck tried to steal from Grant. In a note to Charles A. Dana, editor of the *New York Tribune,* Secretary of War Edwin Stanton wryly reviewed the ego at the top of the army: "Was it not a funny sight to see a certain military hero [McClellan] in the telegraph office at Washington last Sunday organizing victory and by sublime military combinations capturing Fort Donelson *six hours after* Grant and [Gen. C. F.] Smith had taken it sword in hand and had victorious possession!" Neither Stanton nor Lincoln was fooled about the identity of the man of the hour, however. Grant was promoted to major general of volunteers, and as he signed the commission, Lincoln made his satisfied pronouncement about the worth of Illinois men.[36]

As much as the senior civilian leaders lauded the new major general, Grant's military superiors, Halleck and McClellan, still retained serious doubts about the unpolished officer's abilities. Unknown to either man, for more than three weeks, Grant's regular reports to Halleck on his army's strength, location, and movements were deliberately interrupted (whether by a Confederate telegraph operator or a Union soldier whom Grant had cashiered for insubordination is unclear), as were Halleck's increasingly infuriated demands to Grant for information. Halleck reported Grant's apparent refusal to communicate to McClellan, and on March 3, McClellan authorized Halleck to arrest Grant. Then, with no basis in fact at all, Halleck revived the specter of Grant's drinking, wiring Washington: "A rumor has just reached me that since the taking of Fort Donelson General Grant has resumed his former bad habits." Halleck did not arrest Grant, but his doubts about Grant's competence led him to place Gen. C. F. Smith briefly in charge of Grant's advance column. Bewildered and outraged, Grant was unable to hide the tears in his eyes when he showed the order to a friend. Grant asked Halleck to relieve him from duty, but Halleck refused. Over the next ten days, the increasingly frustrated Grant twice renewed his request to be relieved, but Halleck did not respond.[37]

Ironically, at this precise juncture, "Unconditional Surrender" Grant's victory at Fort Donelson was becoming more widely known and his celebrity assured. For example, on March 8, three weeks after the battle and days after Halleck's allegation of Grant's drinking, *Harper's Weekly* magazine introduced to the world a bearded "Hero of Fort Donelson," with a full-length engraving of him on its cover. (Though Grant had shaved his beard two months earlier, the "hirsute appendage," as *Harper's* called it, persisted for months in images circulated by the press.) The nationwide heralding of Grant the Hero pushed

Harper's Weekly carried this engraving of Grant, "The Hero of Fort
Donelson," on its cover more than a month after he had bowed to
Julia's strong wishes and shaved the beard. (Harper's Weekly, *March
8, 1862*)

Lincoln to ask Stanton to prod Halleck for proof of his charges. Covering his
tracks, Halleck intimated to Grant that he had been Grant's champion in the
whole affair, and he restored Grant's command. Grant rejoined his army in
the field and headed south toward Corinth, Mississippi. Halleck intended to
assume personal command of all the armies at some convenient point along
the way and then lead them into battle for that strategic rail junction. Grant
particularly delighted in being reunited with Sherman, who scouted ahead

and selected a campsite on the bluffs above Pittsburg Landing, about twenty-five miles northeast of Corinth. Grant made his headquarters in the town of Savannah, Tennessee, some nine miles downriver (to the north), where there was telegraph service and where Buell's army was expected to arrive.[38]

Grant's departure from Cairo in early February had marked the beginning of a four-month-long absence from Julia. They had previously discussed the possibility that military necessity might keep him away from Cairo for some time, and in that case, he urged Julia to take the children to Kentucky and stay with his parents. "If I want you to visit me—and I am sure you will want to come, will you not?—you can leave the children with my people and can come to me without anxiety," Julia recalled Grant's reasoning. "We agreed to this arrangement," she wrote, and sure enough, "[s]hortly after this, the General wrote me, asking me to visit his family for a week or two and, if I found it agreeable to all, to make arrangements to remain there for the present." All seemed well for Julia and Grant during this separation, until early April. "One day, following soon after the most enthusiastic and thrilling encomiums that filled the Cincinnati newspapers over the surrender of Fort Donelson to Grant and his army," Julia recalled bitterly, "I sat shocked and almost stunned at an article (many of them) in ribald abuse of my husband just after the battle of Shiloh . . . the report went out that General Grant was not in the field, that he was at some dance house. The idea!"[39]

Dancing was not the focus of the many "ribald" reports that disturbed Julia, however. Drinking was the charge, more specifically that Grant had been drunk during the night of April 5. As a result, according to the newspapers, his army, camped on the bluffs above Pittsburg Landing, had been surprised at daybreak on the 6th by a massive Confederate attack, his troops initially routed, and many killed and wounded. Lincoln's recent elevation of Grant to major general gave critical newspapers the chance to strike both men with one blow. "The massacre at Shiloh, wherein 8,000 Union soldiers were lost through GRANT'S drunkenness, or incompetency, or both," wrote the Washington correspondent of the *New York Times*, "is a severe commentary on the thoughtless enthusiasm which nominates GRANT for a Major-General. . . ."[40]

Grant refused to comment to newspapers about the battle, and in particular ignored the charges of drunkenness, although in one letter to Julia, he carefully noted that he had been as "sober as a deacon." For the rest of his life, he protested that he had not been surprised at Shiloh, that even if he had had definite warning of the impending attack, he could not have done anything more to prepare for it than he already had. Whether or not that was true (and there are many historians who believe it was not), there is no doubt that Grant's grim determination to counterattack on the second day and his inspired leadership seized a Union victory from gaping jaws of defeat. That was not the story that sold newspapers in 1862, however. Accusations that men died because he was drunk hurt him terribly, though, and he worried that his family would suffer from articles that condemned the man for Shiloh whom they had previously honored for Fort Donelson.

Jesse Grant's distress at the national scourging of his son was palpable. He mounted a letter-writing campaign that at one point included publication of one of Grant's private letters to him, which other papers soon reprinted. Grant reprimanded his father sharply (and thereafter was even more circumspect in writing to Jesse), but he knew that the false reports of his cowardice and drunkenness had brought shame to his family. Congressman Washburne initiated his own defense of Grant in a speech on the floor of the House of Representatives on May 2. Two weeks later, Julia sent a letter to Washburne thanking him for his support of Grant. "It is indeed gratifying to know that he finds in you so true a friend," wrote Julia, who was staying with Grant's parents at the time, "and one who manifests such a ready willingness to exonerate him from the malicious and unfounded slanders of the press." Her letter was written on May 16, coincidentally (or not) the same day that Jesse Grant wrote a similar letter of thanks to Washburne.[41]

Within a week of Shiloh, Halleck arrived at Pittsburg Landing, where he established his headquarters and proceeded to take charge of the situation. Though Halleck thought Grant "brave & able on the field," he noted that Grant's army was "undisciplined and very much disorganized." Halleck's eyes and his orders quickly focused on minor infractions of army regulations in the midst of a major war. (One order, for example, sternly noted that regulations required that letters "*should relate to one matter only, and be properly folded.*") When he turned to the big picture, Halleck combined the several armies in the field into one army. According to Grant, he was made second in command and "was also supposed to be in command of the right wing and reserve."[42]

Being second in command to detail-oriented Halleck meant light administrative duties, and when it came to the armies in the field, Grant later wrote: "For myself, I was little more than an observer. Orders were sent direct to the right wing or reserve, ignoring me, and advances were made from one line of intrenchments to another without notifying me." Halleck's reorganization looked to Grant like a harsh rebuke. In reality, it was nothing personal, just Halleck's brusque manner of doing business, which may actually have been motivated by a desire to help Grant, as he had helped Sherman earlier. At this point, though, Grant could have echoed McClellan's plaint, "I am in command of *nothing*."[43]

As Grant's days dragged by with less authority and less action, his mind once again began to turn on itself. He had little to do. Disgrace stared him in the face. He feared he would not recover his command. He began to think of applying for transfer to the East or to the far West, of taking an extended leave, even of resigning, although his experience in command had convinced him that the army was his true calling. "My position was so embarrassing in fact that I made several applications during the siege to be relieved." More than anything, Grant needed the tangible reassurance of Julia's love and of her confidence in him that he could find in her presence. Having her in camp with him, though, was impossible in his rapidly eroding position of authority. Halleck had accompanied the order reorganizing the army with a note to Grant that his new duties "render it necessary that your Head Qrs should be near mine."[44]

With Halleck hovering so near, Grant could not bring Julia and the children to live with him in camp. On April 25, he wrote:

> Dear Julia , . . . Again I write you from this place where I verily believ it has rained almost continuously since the beginning of the year. . . . I however am no longer boss. Gen. Halleck is here and I am glad of it. . . . If the papers only knew how little ambition I have outside of putting down this rebellion and getting back once more to live quietly with my family I think they would say less and have fewer falsehoods to their account. . . . [45]

In desperation, Grant wrote Halleck a letter on May 11, oddly belligerent and beseeching: "[A]s I believe it is generally understood through this army that my position differs but little from that of one in arrest . . . ," Grant protested, "I respectfully ask either to be relieved from duty entirely or to have my position so defined that there can be no mistaking it." Halleck did not reply directly to his request: "If you believe me your friend you will not require explanations; if not, explanations on my part would be of little avail."[46] In his frustration, Grant's aggravation spilled over in a letter to Julia on May 13:

> Camp near Corinth, Miss
> Dear Julia—I have just received two letters from you one written on the 3rd and the other on the 4th of this month both complaining of not receiving letters from me. I write usually twice a week and why in the world you do not get

my letters I cant tell. . . . In my last letter I told you that it would probably be
my last this side of Corinth. But we move slow Gen. Halleck being determined
to make shure work. . . . If you do not get letters don't blame me with it for I
write every three or four days. . . . [47]

His first target was Julia. Even though, surprisingly, she had written two days
in a row, he was irritated with her complaints about his failure to write. His
second target was Halleck, whose ponderous, creeping pace toward Corinth
exasperated the man of action (though, unlike McClellan, Grant cloaked his
frustration in soldierly deference to his superior). The third source of his vexa-
tion was his own situation. A letter he wrote the next day makes clear that he
was near the breaking point. Grant had always abhorred even the slightest
appearance of courting political favor, but he poured out his anguish and frustration to Washburne, the politician who had become a friend:

May 14th 62 Camp near Corinth, Miss.
Dear Sir: . . . . To say that I have not been distressed at these attacks upon me
would be false, for I have a father mother, wife & children who read them and
are distressed by them and I necessarily share with them in it. . . .[48]

The march to Corinth from Pittsburg Landing, a journey of about twenty-
five miles, or two days' march, took more than a month under Halleck's direction, dissipating all of the momentum produced by Grant's victory at Shiloh. As Johnston had done to McClellan, General Beauregard and the bulk of
the Confederates at Corinth skedaddled ahead of the massive Federal force,
whose trail could be traced for miles across the countryside in the scars of its
time-consuming entrenchments.

May 31st 62 Corinth Miss
Dear Julia—Corinth is now in our hands without much fighting. . . . What the
next move, or the part I am to take I do not know. But I shall apply to go home
if there is not an early move and an important command assigned me. . . . Write
often to your long absent husband.[49]

But Julia did not write, nor did Halleck restore Grant's command, nor did he
approve Grant's renewed request for a leave of absence. In early June, Grant
again petitioned Halleck for leave. His optimism gone, Grant could not bear to
remain, useless, in the field. This time, Halleck granted him thirty days' leave.

Grant was preparing to depart camp, when fate intervened in the unlikely form of his rangy, redheaded colleague. To Sherman's eye, the substantial packing underway at Grant's tent indicated that the general had no plans to return, so he asked Grant if he were leaving and why. "Sherman, you know . . . I am in the way here," Grant told him. "I have stood it as long as I can, and can endure it no longer." He told Sherman he was going to St. Louis, and in response to Sherman's inquiry about whether he had business there, Grant admitted, "Not a bit." Sherman recalled the conversation vividly: "I then begged him to stay, illustrating his case by my own. Before the battle of Shiloh, I had been cast down by a mere newspaper assertion of 'crazy,' but that single battle had given me new life, and I was now in high feather; and I argued with him that, if he went away, events would go right along, and he would be left out; whereas, if he remained, some happy accident might restore him to favor and his true place."[50] Grant wrote to Sherman the next day that "he had reconsidered his intention and would remain," but he had, in fact, made up his mind shortly after Sherman left. Writing to Julia that evening, he confirmed that he had been contemplating more than a leave of absence.

> My Dearest Julia—I expected by this time to be at home, but fate is against it. . . . Privately I say to you that when I talked of going home and leaving my command here there was quite a feeling among the troops, at least so expressed by Gen. officers below me, against my going. I will have to stay. . . . Although Gen. Sherman has been made a Maj. Gen. by the battle of Shiloh I have never done half justice by him.[51]

For once, the toxic stew of loneliness, despair, and boredom had not worked its dark magic on Grant. In the absence of expressions of Julia's confidence in Grant, Sherman fell into line as her replacement. Sherman's verbal volley of arguments against resigning shook Grant from his self-absorbed funk, and his colleague's expressions of deep regard restored Grant's faith in himself. Grant picked himself up, brushed Halleck off, and resolved to stay in the fight.

On June 14, Halleck placed the Army of the Tennessee once again under Grant's command. Grant swiftly took action to improve his living situation—and his emotional equilibrium. He moved his headquarters to Memphis and sent for Julia and the children. Grant may have welcomed this resumption of his old command as Sherman's predicted "happy accident," the serendipitous consequence of remaining in camp at Sherman's recommendation. In fact, though, the action that wholly justified Grant's trust in Sherman's advice came several weeks later. On July 11, Halleck learned that Lincoln had appointed him general-in-chief. "Old Brains," as Halleck's troops dubbed him after the Corinth victory, then summoned Grant to Corinth and turned over his command to the forty-year-old general. Grant took the reins of the bulk of the armies in the West with as little fanfare and as much equanimity as he had assumed command of his first regiment.

Beneath his always-calm exterior, however, Grant had changed. The post-Shiloh, near-death-of-his-career experience proved cathartic. Reflecting on the depth of his despair, on the few options he had outside the army, on how nearly he missed receiving Halleck's transfer of command, or (most likely) on all three, Grant underwent a subtle but powerful transformation. He had always displayed tenacious determination and physical courage, but Grant's outward imperturbability barely concealed his emotional fragility. He had no problem ignoring most jeers and broadsides of the press and politicians, though he hated their impact on his family. Harsh words or neglect from his family and those he admired, however, could wound him deeply. More than one person had seen Grant reduced to tears by Halleck or Julia. No more. After Shiloh, Grant acquired a mental toughness he had not had before. He was not more severe toward other people; he became, rather, more inured to their slights.

The Grants' four-month separation, marked by the battles of Fort Henry, Fort Donelson, Shiloh, and Corinth, had been unavoidable, unfortunate, and almost fatal to Grant's career, but the danger posed by his forced inactivity and by Julia's failure to write was over. For the balance of the war, Grant's expanding military duties fully occupied his mind, and he rarely felt bored or lonely. As important, his increasing military authority enabled him to arrange more frequent family visits, since he could easily secure rail, river, or road transportation throughout Union-held territory. Fred often campaigned with his father, even when the action was hot, and Grant sent for Julia and young Jesse—and the other children, if they were not in school—between every major operation he undertook. Julia's celerity in joining him when he sent for her, her readiness to endure danger, fatigue, and stationary washstands, and her willingness to allow Fred to travel with his father during operations were solid, enduring, satisfying proofs of her commitment to him.

Evidence of the change in the Grants' circumstances and its impact on Grant's temperament is strikingly apparent in his letters to Julia for the duration of the war. His May 31, 1862, letter, asking her to "write often to your absent husband," was virtually his last appeal for her to correspond. Those pleas had been a feature of nearly every letter he had written to her over the preceding eighteen years. The fact that Grant had more opportunity to have his family with him, of course, reduced the need for correspondence. Even so, the change in his letters is significant. It is unlikely that Grant stopped asking Julia to write to him because he did not care about her, or because their separations were short (some were months in length), or because he simply forgot to include the request in his letters. It is more likely that he finally, fully accepted the fact that she would never change, and so, therefore, he had to change if he were to maintain his peace of mind. He could not make her write, but he could stop begging for letters from her. In doing so, he could spare himself the anguish of pleading and the aggravation of having his direct requests ignored.[52]

In addition to that sea change in his letters, he also began to comment more often on Julia's complaints and neglect with a wry detachment largely absent in his letters before Shiloh. For example, in November 1863, Grant wrote to her: "How long did you stay in Cincinnati? Who did you see? And who did you find to abuse me half as much as you do when you are mad[?]" The next April she received a letter from him dated the 27th, which read: "This is my forty second birthday. Getting old am I not? I received a very short letter from you this evening scratched off in a very great hurry as if you had something much more pleasing if not more important to do than to write to me." But this time, Grant did not despair at evidence of her carelessness; instead, he reassured her of his affection, adding, "I'll excuse you though. It is only gratifying a little desire to appear angry that I am indulging in it." In January 1865, he blithely concluded a letter with "I receive all your letters. Some of them are rather cross. Love and kisses for you and the children."[53]

A close reading of Grant's correspondence with Julia and with his father from mid-1862 forward reveals another significant change in Grant, an alteration in his role within his extended family. Reflecting his growing self-confidence, Grant's letters to Jesse and to Julia assume an increasingly authoritative tone, and his references to Julia's father contain more pity than resentment. Even while directing Western armies and, later, the entire U.S. Army, Grant found time to manage finances, arrange for employment of relatives, and mediate disputes within and among the families in tones that brooked no opposition. The two men who had only ever agreed on the assessment that Grant was worthless began to look to him for a host of tangible and intangible services. As Grant climbed the hierarchy of the U.S. military establishment, he also quietly but firmly assumed the role of patriarch of the Grant and Dent families.

Grant's ordeal of anguish caused by those he loved and those he served, from Fort Salubrity to Corinth, was an annealing process that ultimately strengthened him for the great work he would undertake. In the absence of Julia's nurturing presence, Sherman's faith in him fanned the spark of self-confidence that Halleck's treatment of him had almost extinguished. At times, Julia distressed him terribly, but he knew that she did not mean to hurt him. She loved him deeply. His obvious love for her never wavered from the day they met; his need for her never waned. She was his center of gravity.

Julia and Ulysses struggled to manage the impact of the war's inevitable, painful separations. Theirs was "a marriage tested by war," and Grant's military career barely survived the dangerous aftermath of Shiloh. From that time forward, however, Julia's more frequent visits, and, in her absence, Fred's companionship, promoted the inner calm and outward composure that marked Grant's command and enabled his rise to greatness. A heartier strain of self-confidence grew steadily within Grant. By the time of his victory at Vicksburg in July 1863, Grant had become the man, the general, to whom Lincoln could trust the execution of the war.[54]

CHAPTER 26

"Do stop digging at this old canal"

After her initial reluctance to travel with four children from St. Louis to Cairo, Julia never again hesitated when Grant sent word for her to join him. She knew he needed her, and she always had a bag packed, ready to respond instantly to a telegram from her husband, naming some faraway place to meet him, alone or with one or more of the children. As one historian put it, "Julia's only home was with Ulysses."[1]

The few times she stayed with her husband's family, she felt less than completely welcome. Julia was well aware of Jesse's criticisms of her, which did not stop when she left his house. In November 1862, while Julia was with her husband in LaGrange, Tennessee, Grant bluntly wrote Jesse: "I am only sorry your letter, and all that comes from you speaks so condescendingly of every thing Julia says, writes or thinks." Grant admonished: "You without probably being aware of it are so prejudiced against her that she could not please you. This is not pleasing to me." If her in-laws were not the solution to her housing problem, neither was Julia's own family. Staying with "Colonel" Dent in Missouri became more uncomfortable as the war continued. Her father was an outspoken pro-slavery rebel who had nothing good to say about her successful Union Army general husband. Nor did her neighbors, who "were all Southern in sentiment." Grant's desire to have Julia with him was matched by Julia's preference always to be with "Ulys," no matter what the hardships or danger.[2]

Grant's attachment to Julia was well known at the highest levels of the Union command. Stanton telegraphed Grant about Julia's movements to ease her husband's mind. The Confederate military hierarchy was equally interested in her whereabouts and circulated information on her arrival and departure from Grant's headquarters as actionable intelligence of Federal military plans. For example, when Julia traveled to Vicksburg just after it had fallen,

Gen. Joseph Johnston wired Gen. Samuel Cooper (the man to whom Grant tendered his resignation from the U.S. Army in 1854, and who had joined the Confederate Army) that her presence signified "General Grant would make that place his headquarters for some time."[3]

Halleck's promotion and transfer to Washington in the middle of 1862 were part of Lincoln's effort to organize all the Union armies into a coordinated effort against the Confederates. McClellan was still struggling on the peninsula, and rebels still blocked the Mississippi River from just north of the town of Vicksburg, Mississippi, for more than two hundred river miles south. Grant, ever focused on the strategic value of opening the mighty river to Union traffic and splitting the Confederacy in half, turned his attention to Vicksburg. Grant pressed southward from Memphis as he explored a variety of options for overcoming Vicksburg's defenses, which had been considerably strengthened over the previous six months.

Julia, young Jesse, and her slave Jule traveled with Grant in this earliest stage of the Vicksburg Campaign. "When I visited the General during the war, I nearly always had [Jule] with me as nurse," Julia recalled in her memoirs. Because they were traveling in areas where owning slaves was legal, Julia felt even more comfortable bringing the woman, whom Julia described as "a slave born and brought up at my old Missouri home." During their stay in LaGrange, Tennessee, Julia found "everything was so familiar—the old Negro quarters, the colored people warming themselves in the sun, the broken windows filled with old clothes—all seemed so familiar that, as I had never been there before, I must have seen them in my dreams" or in her memories of White Haven. Julia was traveling deeper into the South, seeing firsthand the war's impact on plantations so very much like her beloved childhood home. From LaGrange, Julia, Jesse, Jule, and Mrs. Hillyer traveled to Holly Springs, Mississippi, a major Federal supply depot. She had been told by Grant—who continued his push south—that "as soon as the [rail]road was finished through Oxford (Mississippi, about sixty miles south) he would have me come to him."[4]

Arrangements were made for Julia to stay in a home occupied by several women and children of the family of Mrs. Pugh Govan, whose husband, son, and brother-in-law served in the Confederate Army. There was good reason for Confederate sympathizers to open their homes to Union officials: "[N]o matter what their political stance, some local citizens realized that their best wartime insurance was the occupation of property by high-ranking Federal officers."[5]

Julia revealed her naiveté when she recalled her arrival there:

I did not realize for a moment that I was actually in the enemy's camp until [after breakfast], arising from the table with the family, we entered the hall, and I naturally, or thoughtlessly, turned towards the door of the drawing room where I had been received the night before; when suddenly the hostess stepped forward, and placing her fair hand on the doorknob, said: "Excuse me, Mrs. Grant, but I have set aside a drawing room for your use." Only imagine my chagrin and mortification. . . . [6]

One can also imagine the bewilderment of her hostess, contemplating the wife of the Federal general accompanied by her slave. She asked Julia, "You are Southern, aren't you?" Julia replied, "No, I am from the West. Missouri is my native state." The Mississippi matron persisted, "Yes, we know, but Missouri is a Southern state. Surely, you are Southern in feeling and principle." Indignantly, Julia declared, "No, indeed, I am the most loyal of the loyal." Political differences aside, Julia's stay with the Govans proved pleasurable; the family included a young boy just about Jesse's age.[7]

Grant, on the other hand, faced a myriad of problems, the least of which at this particular time might have been the Confederate Army. Lincoln's Preliminary Emancipation Proclamation, issued on September 22, first led to a trickle of runaway slaves entering Union lines. That trickle soon became a flood, as many plantation owners abandoned their field hands and fled with their personal slaves west or further south, ahead of Grant's troops. News of hundreds, then thousands of men, women, and children flocking to Union lines brought joy to Northern citizenry, but the unfed, homeless, and unemployed former slaves brought chaos to military camps. Grant sought the help of Chaplain John Eaton of the 27th Ohio to establish a means of putting the former slaves to work, for pay, for the military or on plantations. Grant knew that blacks would work without the lash; he had labored in fields side by side with them. As a result, he had come to recognize their humanity and inherent dignity, and he hoped that other whites would learn as much from his larger experiment. "Grant's plan embodied the important assumption that the only way to challenge racism was to repudiate stereotypes and ignorance," according to historian Brooks Simpson. Similar in some respects to Sherman's later Sea Islands program, "It was another example of applied common sense, something in short supply."[8]

On the morning of December 19, Grant sent word to Julia in Holly Springs that the railroad to Oxford was open and she should visit him. She wasted no time in responding to Grant's request. "I was delighted," recalled Julia, "and inviting Mrs. Hillyer to accompany me, we started in the afternoon of the same day I received the notice, taking Jesse and my maid with me. We had a long, fatiguing ride," before arriving in Oxford to find the headquarters in a tumult. Grant had not expected her so soon, but it was well that she had rushed to her husband's side. He had just received word that Confederate Gen. Earl Van Dorn and his cavalry were heading toward Holly Springs, and every effort was being made at Grant's headquarters in Oxford to alert the Federal officer in charge to prepare "a warm welcome" for the Confederate forces.

Nonetheless, when Van Dorn arrived early the next morning, he surprised the Union troops there as much as he did the town's inhabitants. One of the raiders who attacked at dawn on December 20 later described the "wild and exciting" scene: "torches flaming, guns popping, sabres clanking, negroes and abolitionists begging for mercy, women in *dreaming-robes* clapping their hands with joy." Col. Robert C. Murphy had received Grant's advance warning of Van Dorn's trajectory the evening before but had failed to act decisively upon it. After a brief fight, Murphy surrendered two thousand men at the Holly Springs depot and handed over sizable hospital and commissary supplies to the Confederates.[9]

That was a great haul for the rebels, but they sought an even greater prize. The marauders knew Mrs. Grant had been living in the town, according to Julia, and "some of Van Dorn's staff officers rode up to the house of which I had lately been an inmate and asked for me." Mrs. Govan "assured them I was not there, that I had gone the previous evening to visit General Grant," she recalled. "They demanded my baggage, and this also the kind and noble lady protected by her earnest and personal requests." Although the Confederate cavalrymen did not succeed in capturing Julia or her baggage, they did burn her carriage and steal her horses, which she had left in Colonel Murphy's safekeeping.[10]

"The most loyal of the most loyal" barely missed becoming one of the greatest prizes captured by the Confederates in the war. The military and political consequences of her capture, though substantial, would have paled in comparison to the emotional anguish it would have wrought on Ulysses Grant. That it was a near thing is evident from the many widely varied versions of the story that still circulate. In more than one, Van Dorn's surprise raid did in fact capture the general's lady. Depending on which narrative you choose, in a most chivalrous manner, Van Dorn either posted guards around the house where she, her son, and her slave were staying, or he immediately freed her to return to her husband at his headquarters. Those accounts are surely false. All her life, Julia relished tales of adventure and intrigue, so when she dictated her memoirs more than twenty years later, she would surely have portrayed herself as a captive redeemed by chivalry, if at all possible. She did not. It was a very close call, though. Only because she had impetuously, anxiously, lovingly rushed so quickly to be with her husband did she avoid capture.[11]

Van Dorn knew precisely where Julia was staying, and it is possible that he knew Jesse and Jule were with her, too. In fact, Jule might have been an even greater catch for the Confederates than Julia that morning. Capturing Julia Grant would have pained and embarrassed one Union general. Capturing her slave Jule at that particular time would have embarrassed the president of the United States. Twelve days from then, as the whole world knew, Abraham Lincoln would sign his Emancipation Proclamation.

Once Van Dorn fled, Grant moved his headquarters from Oxford to Holly Springs, where Col. William H. Coxe of that town (a man of Unionist sympathies) invited Grant to use his home, "a beautiful Italian villa," for his offices and his family. During that time, Julia played the mediator between Grant and his senior officers, which she often did during the war. Grant's "impatient generals," as Julia called them, sought her out at the Coxe house and asked her to intercede with her husband. Grant had given Sherman command of an expedition to Vicksburg, they protested, which Grant had the right to command and which, moreover, could bring glory to their commander—and to them, too, of course. "We want you to tell the General he is too unselfish, but if there is a chance, we young men would like to add a few leaves to our wreaths," they beseeched Julia, who went to Grant with their petition—"and what do you suppose he said, smiling at my anxiety for his fame?" Grant said, of course, he hoped Sherman would prevail and thus deserve the laurels. Though none of them knew it at the time, patient Grant and his impatient generals would have plenty of opportunities to crown themselves in glory. That particular mission, which resulted in Sherman's disaster at Chickasaw Bayou, was only one of Grant's many attempts to take Vicksburg over the following six months.[12]

The Grants were in Holly Springs on January 1, 1863, and Jule had reason to rejoice on that Day of Jubilee. According to Julia, Jule was no longer a slave. "Eliza, Dan, Julia, and John belonged to me up to the time of President Lincoln's Emancipation Proclamation," Julia Grant noted in her memoirs. Technically, because the proclamation did not free slaves in areas under Union control, Jule and the others might have remained in bondage, but a slave attached to Grant and his army of liberators would have been manifestly untenable after New Year's Day 1863. Even after that date, Jule continued her service to Julia, most likely as a paid servant. Shortly thereafter, Grant moved headquarters—and Julia—again, this time back to Memphis. "As General Sherman's expedition was not a success," Julia noted in her memoirs, "another was proposed, and General Grant went in person, taking Fred along, who was on a visit to us in Memphis." Her husband and son headed south toward Vicksburg, while Julia and Mrs. Hillyer remained in Memphis with their children.

On the morning of February 11, 1863, forty-year-old Grant confronted a challenge more urgent than capturing the Confederate stronghold. "This morning I met with a great loss," he wrote Julia from temporary quarters aboard the steamer *Magnolia*, anchored near Vicksburg. "Last night, contrary to my usual habit, I took out my teeth and put them in the wash [basin] and covered them with water. This morning the servant who attends to my stateroom, blacks my boots, &c., [came] in about daylight and finding water in the [basin] threw it out in to the river, teeth and all." Grant thought the dentist might be in Memphis, and since Julia was there, Grant urged her to try to find Dr. Hamline and "tell him of my misfortune." The dentist was located, but Julia's stay in Memphis was otherwise uneventful. "I remember nothing of interest now except there was great restlessness and anxiety and some murmuring at the army's seeming inactivity," wrote Julia. "General Grant was . . . waiting for the waters to subside that he might move on Vicksburg."[13]

Vicksburg, Mississippi, was "the nail head that holds the South's two halves together," according to Jefferson Davis. To Lincoln's eye, the city looked like a different implement. "Vicksburg is the key," he had said in November 1861. "The war can never be brought to a close until the key is in our pocket." Grant's campaign to put that key into Lincoln's pocket proved one of the most difficult and one of the most brilliant of the war.[14]

In late 1862, Vicksburg sat atop the highest ground along the twisting, two-hundred-plus-mile course of the Mississippi River that was still under rebel control. High ground it was—the cliffs rose dramatically, more than two hundred feet above the river, which was at record flood levels during most of Grant's efforts to take the city (Vicksburg lost its riverfront in 1876, when a flood altered the Mississippi's course). Vicksburg was "the Gibraltar of the Confederacy" in another favorite metaphor of the day, and Confederates had fortified those bluffs, which bristled with guns. It was Grant's next logical target in his southward thrust to reestablish Union control of the vital Mississippi River. The fortified city appeared impregnable from the river, and Grant's movements southwest from Corinth through LaGrange, Holly Springs, and

Oxford had all been part of his calculation that Vicksburg could most effectively be assaulted by an overland campaign from the north. Several failed attempts convinced him the assault should be launched from south of Vicksburg instead. Accordingly, he bent his mind to the task of moving an army down the western bank of the Mississippi well below Vicksburg and ferrying it across to the eastern bank of the river. From there, he would swing the army in an arc northeast, capturing Mississippi's capital city of Jackson, on the way to capturing Vicksburg and the Confederate Army charged with its defense. And it had to be done with enough stealth and diversions to catch Jefferson Davis and his generals unprepared for the final assault.

To organize the combined operation, Grant coordinated with Adm. David Dixon Porter, who commanded the "brown water navy" of river gunboats, in much the same "meeting of equals" approach Grant had used with Captain Foote at Fort Henry. Porter's transports, then safely in Union-controlled waters above Vicksburg, would have to "run the batteries" on the fortified Vicksburg bluff, continue south to meet Grant's soldiers (awaiting the transports some distance below on the west bank), and ferry them across to the east bank. Only then would Grant's troops be on the same side of the river as their target. Porter reacted with pleasure to Grant's modest demeanor and thoughtful plan. The Vicksburg batteries were formidable, but Porter recognized that the prize was worth the risk. Moreover, he believed his flotilla could do the job.

Julia's recollection of the "restlessness and anxiety" of the nation during the long Vicksburg Campaign was accurate. As Grant exhausted more than half a dozen separate efforts to defeat the Confederate stronghold's defenses, the press and congressional critics alternated lamentation with ridicule. A canal project, to carve a passage through one of the points closest to the city's batteries to enable boats to pass beyond the range of the guns, earned the lion's share of public derision. Julia, too, criticized it immediately when she arrived in camp in early April 1863. Even with her flawed vision, she could see at once its similarity to McClellan's interminable siege works. Instinctively, she feared it as a harbinger of doom for her husband's career, and she hesitated not at all to advise him on military tactics. "I had hardly said 'how do you do' before I began to make suggestions, asking the General, 'Why do you not move on Vicksburg at once? Do stop digging at this old canal.'" With no prompting from Grant, she offered her own plan. "Mass your troops in a solid phalanx at a point north of the fortress, rush upon it, and they will be obliged to surrender," she instructed. Amused, her husband gently chided her that such an attack was precisely what he wished to avoid because it "would involve great loss of life and not insure success." Then he confessed, "But it is true I will not use the canal. I never expected to, but started it to give the army occupation and to amuse the country until the waters should subside sufficiently to give me a foothold and then, Mrs. Grant, I will move upon Vicksburg and will take it, too."[15]

If Julia's military counsel proved unhelpful, her presence was welcome, providing Grant with the warmth and optimism so essential to his equanimity. At the same time, however, her arrival in camp at Vicksburg was interpreted by some of Grant's detractors as proof that he had continued drinking. Vicksburg was, allegedly, the site of Grant's most extensive drunken spree. Indeed, an officer in Grant's command who was angling unsuccessfully for higher rank claimed to have "telegraphed to [Grant's] wife & brought her on to take care of him. . . ." Years later, several men wrote about a three-day roaring, vomiting, drunken spell by Grant aboard a steamer on the Yazoo River. The most famous of those accounts was by Sylvanus Cadwallader, a newspaper reporter who claimed to be an eyewitness. Several key elements of his story stretch credibility to the breaking point. More recent analysis reveals fatal flaws in his narrative, but the most important conclusion to be derived from close study of the episode is the one aspect of the story upon which all accounts agree: even if Grant drank to excess at times, he did not do it when there was serious work to be done or where his men could observe his behavior.[16]

By mid-April, Grant was ready to test the key element in his plan to take Vicksburg from the south. The record floodwaters had receded, and the time had come to determine whether boats launched from a point on the west bank of the Mississippi north of Vicksburg could avoid destruction by Confederate guns on the city's bluffs and arrive safely at a point south of Vicksburg. Soon after Julia arrived in camp, her husband revealed that she was "just in time to watch the running of the batteries." On the moonless night of April 16, Julia and Grant sat next to each other onboard the steamer *Henry von Phul*, anchored safely away from the action, holding hands—and no doubt their breath, too—as Admiral Porter, on his flagship *Benton*, stealthily led a small flotilla of eleven vessels, steamers, transports, and gunboats around the bend at Vicksburg. The Grants made a memorable family picture; with them were their sons, Fred and young Ulysses.[17]

In Vicksburg, Confederate Gen. John C. Pemberton had anticipated that Grant would at some point try to run the batteries. He soon realized the game was afoot and lit the skyline with bonfires to silhouette the flotilla as targets for guns on the bluffs. Julia thrilled to the action: "All was going well when a red glare flashed up from the Vicksburg shore and the flotilla of gunboats and transports . . . was made plainly visible," she recalled. "Indeed, it was a grand sight. . . . How vividly that picture is photographed on my mind; the grand roar of the cannon rests in my memory. . . . The air was full of sulphurous smoke."[18]

By early morning, Grant had the answer to months of speculation. All but one of the vessels made the run successfully. Grant was ebullient; his plan was working. He immediately turned to implementing the combined land and riverine operation, though it would take two and a half months more for Vicksburg to fall. Nevertheless, the success of that April night brought cheer to the Northern public, which had grown weary of the string of unsuccessful assaults on the Gibraltar of the West. The *New York Times* heralded the good news on April 22 under the headline, "Gallant Work at Vicksburg": "The feeling of disappointment that has, for some time, existed over the supposed failure of our army and gunboats before Vicksburg, was suddenly removed yesterday by the news from the Southwest. It is announced that on the night of Thursday last, the gunboats Tuscumbia, Lafayette, Benton, Pittsburgh, Carondelet and Gen. Price, with three transports, ran the rebel batteries at Vicksburg, and all went out safely below except one transport, which was burned."[19]

Good news was in short supply in the Executive Mansion at that particular moment. Joseph Hooker—whom Lincoln had named commanding general of the Army of the Potomac in January 1863, to succeed Burnside (who had succeeded McClellan in the fall of 1862)—was bogged down in Virginia's legendary spring mud as he sought to crush Lee's army. Adm. Samuel Dupont's confident plan to avenge Fort Sumter and retake Charleston had ended in failure in less than two hours in Charleston Harbor. The preliminary success at Vicksburg was welcome news in the White House.

On April 17, the day after they watched the boats in the moonlight, Julia and young Ulysses returned to St. Louis, leaving Grant and Fred (who remained with him through the rest of the Vicksburg Campaign) to begin the marching and fighting required to execute Grant's planned counterclockwise swing toward the landward defenses of Vicksburg. Troops under his command fought some of the war's fiercest battles to get to the outskirts of the city, where Grant settled into a siege. By late June, as the siege entered its second month, desperate citizens inside the city turned to mule meat to assuage their hunger. Outside the beleaguered city, Confederate Gen. Joseph Johnston and President Jefferson Davis debated whether it was worth the risk to mount an attack for the relief of Vicksburg. (Mississippi plantation owner Davis was certain it was; Johnston was reluctant to commit.) It was July 3 by the time Confederate reinforcements began marching toward the ceaseless boom of Union cannon on the outskirts of the city. Independence Day dawned unsurprisingly hot but surprisingly quiet, and the reason soon became apparent. The day before, Pemberton had concluded to surrender. By noon on the Fourth of July, the Stars and Stripes had been hoisted above Vicksburg's courthouse.

Two months earlier, on Julia's return to St. Louis, she had told some of her "Southern" neighbors there that she would shortly again leave to join her husband—as soon as he captured Vicksburg. With unwavering confidence in Grant, Julia endured their sneers at the notion that the Gibraltar of the West would ever fall, so it was with enormous satisfaction that Julia told them in early July that she was leaving. Her happy departure was, in her words, their "first *authentic* information of the fall of Vicksburg."[20]

Lincoln's joy exceeded Julia's. Grant had secured the key that Lincoln had eyed from the beginning. Figuratively putting it in his pocket, the president declared, "The Father of Waters again goes unvexed to the sea." Nine years earlier, Capt. Sam Grant had resigned in despair if not disgrace from the regular army. Now, the president of the United States brought him back into it at its highest possible grade. On July 7, Lincoln commissioned Ulysses S. Grant major general in the U.S. Army, effective three days earlier, the day Vicksburg fell. (Grant also retained his grade as major general of volunteers.) Lincoln was effusive. "I do not remember that you and I ever met personally," read the first line of the president's letter to Grant. "I write this now as a grateful acknowledgement for the almost inestimable service you have done the country." After confessing to doubts about Grant's various Vicksburg strategems, he concluded, "I now wish to make the personal acknowledgement that you were right and I was wrong."[21]

No doubt Lincoln appreciated the victory in the West even more because events in the East continued to dishearten him. The president's delight in Grant's performance was in stark contrast to the grimly disappointed tone of the letter Lincoln wrote to Gen. George G. Meade, who had so recently succeeded Hooker in command of the Army of the Potomac. Meade won the Battle of Gettysburg the day before Vicksburg fell, but he failed to pursue Robert E. Lee from the field, enabling the Confederate Army to escape to Virginia. Lincoln was bitterly disappointed but decided not to send a searing letter he had written to Meade. Fortunately, Lincoln had Grant's news to satisfy his own and the country's desperate need for unqualified victories, and he did not hesitate to send his congratulatory letter to his general in the West.

Julia's return to Vicksburg in August meant that Grant would be in head-quarters there for some time, as General Johnston informed General Cooper. While the Union general met with subordinates and plotted his next move, Julia absorbed the grisly sights, sounds, and smells of the recently besieged city. Houses atop the ridge had been shelled for months, and even before the siege began, families (almost exclusively by then old men, women, and children) dug caves in the bluffs, where they endured the sound and fury of daily bombard-ments and scrambled for the town's dwindling rations. In the wreckage of the once beautiful city and the defeat of its proud slave-holding aristocracy, Julia would have recognized much that was familiar from her childhood, as she had earlier in Tennessee. She would have recognized, too, her husband's pivotal role in bringing more and more former slave territory under Union control.[22]

As Julia traveled with her husband and kept house with him and his army, she had a front-row seat at the drama of her old world turning upside down. She applauded Grant's performance; she was, as always, his biggest fan. Other intelligent, educated, slave-owning women with strong Unionist fervor, like Jessie's onetime friend Lizzie Blair, opposed Lincoln's Emancipation Procla-mation. They were willing to endure war to save the Union, but "clung to the chimerical idea of gradual emancipation and colonization."[23]

Except for Julia's sadness in her memoirs about losing the "comforts of slav-ery," though, she did not comment openly about the end of the institution, or about abolitionists, or about Lincoln's decision to make the end of slavery a major focus of the war effort. It is a remarkable display of self-discipline in a woman not known for that virtue. There is, in fact, no evidence that Julia har-bored ill thoughts toward Lincoln at all, or that she ever sought to color Grant's feelings for the president, as did Jessie Frémont and Nelly McClellan. As her president and her husband relentlessly battled to destroy the Confederacy, Julia calmly absorbed the destruction of the lifestyle she had loved so much. Her White Haven childhood became all the more precious in her memory—and doubtless all the more perfect therein, too—because it would soon disappear and could never be replicated.

In mid-September, Federal forces commanded by Maj. Gen. William S. Rosecrans lost the bloody Battle of Chickamauga, near the Georgia–Tennessee border, the greatest defeat the Union suffered in the West. Rosecrans was swiftly trapped inside Chattanooga, Tennessee, by a Confederate force under Gen. Braxton Bragg. About the same time, Maj. Gen. Ambrose Burnside and his Federals found themselves besieged in Knoxville, Tennessee. East Tennessee, toward which Lincoln had precipitately and unsuccessfully launched Frémont two years earlier, was again a top White House priority. In mid-October, Grant was summoned to Louisville, Kentucky. Still suffering from a severe injury to his leg, caused by a fall from a borrowed horse during a brief trip to New Orleans (a riding accident so rare for him that allegations instantly sprang up that he had been drunk at the time), he and Julia immediately left Vicksburg. "Arriving in Cairo, we found a special train to take to Indianapolis, where the General met Secretary Stanton," wrote Julia later. "After this, we went to Louisville, where we were detained an hour waiting for a ferryboat." Julia was disturbed the army had not wired ahead to arrange for quick passage, but she soon learned a lesson she would take to heart for the rest of the war. "[T]his seeming neglect was intentional, as it was not considered safe to telegraph in the portion of the country through which we passed in the presence of the Secretary and the General."[24]

Indeed, when the secretary revealed the purpose of their rendezvous, she learned that Grant's safety was about to become arguably as important as Stanton's. Halleck had combined the three western armies—the Tennessee, the Cumberland, and the Ohio, which had not always cooperated smoothly—into a newly created Military Division of the Mississippi. With Stanton's and Lincoln's blessing, Grant was assigned command of the whole. This practical but woefully belated military reorganization (which Halleck had sought during his tenure in the West) gave Grant command responsibility for the entire western theater of the war. His movements and deployments were still, of course, subject to approval in Washington, but they could no longer be directly frustrated or altered by officers in the field. Grant replaced Rosecrans with Gen. George Thomas in Chattanooga, while he laid plans to feed the troops that were said to be starving inside the city because of the Confederate siege.

Grant successfully organized the "cracker line," as he styled it, to Thomas's stranded men. He then turned his attention to Knoxville, Tennessee, which Julia's cousin, Confederate Gen. "Pete" Longstreet, was besieging. Grant's armies then claimed decisive victories in the Chattanooga Campaign, including those at Lookout Mountain and Missionary Ridge. Grant's unremitting pressure on Confederate military assets all along the line in the western theater was just what Lincoln had always wanted, but which none of his previous generals had delivered.

So great was Grant's acclaim and the Northern public's interest in him by the conclusion of the Chattanooga Campaign that the English-born artist John Antrobus was dispatched from Chicago to Tennessee to paint his portrait in the field. Grant might have resisted such flattery if that was all that was intended, but the work had been commissioned by a group of prominent Illinois citizens for a charitable cause. It was to be displayed to paying spectators to raise funds for the Chicago Soldiers' Home. With talk swirling through the press about raising Grant to the heralded but then nonexistent grade of lieutenant general, which George Washington had last held, Antrobus determined to paint him in the fashion of the famous John Trumbull painting of *George Washington before the Battle of Trenton*. No allusion was forgotten— from the general's full frontal stance, to the rarely worn formal uniform, to the aide in the background holding a spirited white horse, to the field glasses he held (Washington held a spyglass). On November 17, Grant wrote from Chattanooga to his good friend Russell Jones in Chicago that Antrobus had just left, "w[e]ll pleased with his success." Acknowledging Jones's interest in the painting, Grant continued, "I hope you will be equally pleased."[25]

About that time, Grant relocated his headquarters from Vicksburg to Nashville. He told Julia he chose that city because its strategic railroad hub made it convenient for her to travel to him from St. Louis, where she had placed their children in school. As Grant summoned Julia to Nashville, he sent his thirteen-year-old son home. A very ill young Fred arrived at Wish-ton-Wish just as Julia was leaving. For more than a month, the two Grant men at the Vicksburg front had suffered badly from dysentery. Grant recovered, but Fred was still not well. Troubled by Fred's illness, Julia hesitated to leave him, but young Ulysses urged her to go on to his father. Buck insisted that he could take care of his revered older brother (with the help of extended family and staff, of course). Reluctantly, Julia assented.[26]

While Grant tended to the business of war, Julia filled her spare time in Nashville visiting the consequences of his work, the constant stream of wounded men who flowed into the city's military hospitals. If her poor eyesight kept her from supporting the war effort by sewing and knitting, her personality perfectly fitted her for bringing loving cheer to wounded soldiers. She was a devoted and regular visitor to the hospitals, deeply touched by all she saw, and she regularly brought home tales of the men's stoicism despite their dreadful injuries. Those patients sentient enough to grasp that she was the wife of their commanding general plied her with requests for leave, for family visits, and for discharges from the army. With her tender heart, she felt duty bound to pass those along to Grant. In short order, he forbade her to visit the hospitals, not at all out of meanness to the men, but out of his own desperate need for an oasis within the slaughterhouse of war. "I hear of these (petitions) all day," he finally,

Carte de visite of Lieutenant
General Grant, c. 1864, when
he was approximately forty-two
years old. (*Author's collection*)

LIEUT. GEN GRANT

wearily told her. Then he spelled out precisely, in plain language, what he had always sought from her. "I sent for you to come that I might have a rest from all this sad part. I do not want you to know about these things. I want you to tell me of the children and yourself. I want and need a little rest and sunshine." Julia ceased her hospital visits at once; the greatest good she could do for her country was to supply Grant with the sunshine he needed.[27]

In late January 1864, Julia received a telegram urging her immediate return to St. Louis. Fred had taken a severe turn for the worse. Word was also sent to Grant, who was then in Chattanooga, and he immediately sought leave to meet them in St. Louis. Julia hastened to St. Louis on her own, with young Jesse and Jule in tow. She was in such a rush to get to Fred that she did not consider the possible consequences to Jule of returning to Missouri, but it was soon clear that Jule had not failed to consider them. When Jule had gone to Mississippi with the Grants, the Emancipation Proclamation had freed her, but because the proclamation had no effect in the border states, she would have been at risk of being enslaved again if she entered Missouri. "At Louisville," Julia wrote, "my nurse (a girl raised at my home) left me, as I suppose she feared losing her freedom if she returned to Missouri," she recalled. "I regretted this as she was a favorite with me." Grant may not have shared her regrets at Jule's departure. He made no efforts to recover her, but he quickly dispatched a staff officer to help Julia and Jesse continue to St. Louis. We know nothing of Jule's life once she left Julia, except for one tiny but satisfying fact. In her memoirs, after describing Jule's disappearance, Julia wrote: "However, she married soon afterwards."[28]

When Julia arrived at her son's bedside, it appeared that Fred might not live through the illness he had contracted at Vicksburg, often described as typhoid pneumonia. Julia thought of the Shermans' young son Willy, who had died from typhoid contracted in the camp near Vicksburg. She recalled her inability to comfort Ellen in that tragedy, and both Julia and Ulysses knew how inconsolable Sherman had been in the wake of his beloved Willy's death. As Grant rushed to be with his son in what he believed to be the boy's final hours, a new doctor prescribed a new medicine, which, Julia said, "acted like a charm." By the time the distraught general arrived at Fred's bedside on January 27, the young veteran's crisis had passed, and he recognized his father through tired but bright eyes.[29]

Julia's own eyes had begun to bother her earlier in the year. When Grant returned to Nashville on February 1, she remained in St. Louis with Fred, and several of Grant's letters during this time reflect his concern for her eyes. On February 14, for example, Grant was solicitous: "I hope your eyes are better than when you wrote." He missed her and urged her, if she could travel, to board a steamer quickly with Fred to be with him. "The spring campaign will open probably in the early part of Apl. after which there is no assurance when we will meet again." Grant then speculated about the most important personal benefit that might accrue from the tremendous honor he was about to receive: "The passage of the Lieut. Gen bill, if it does pass, may effect a change however in this respect. With such a change it might be necessary for me to pass from West to East occationally when of course we would meet."[30]

For once, though, Julia did not hurry to join Grant in camp. The prospect of her husband's rise to the historic grade of lieutenant general renewed her self-consciousness about her eyes. It was during this stay in St. Louis that Julia took the opportunity to consult with the famous surgeon about "straitening" them and learned with regret that it was "too late." On February 25, Grant renewed his request for her to join him, recognizing that "you have had a terrible time with your eyes," and hoping that "they have improved sufficiently for you to travel." Apparently, they had not, for on March 1, Grant wrote to his father from Nashville that Fred had so "fully recovered" that Grant had him in camp with him. "The balance of the family are all well."[31]

In the same letter, Grant told his father what he had been telling more than a few of his friends—and Lincoln, at the president's request—that he did not want to be president. "I have no ambition outside of my profession," Grant wrote to the father who had once despaired of his son's future, "and in that only to see our arms every where successful." As the presidential election year of 1864 opened with acclaim for Grant and calls for his promotion to lieutenant general, Lincoln sought assurance that Grant had no desire to replace him in the White House. Two of Lincoln's other generals, Frémont and McClellan, were openly being urged to compete for his job. The president was not anxious to crown Grant with laurels if they would encourage his ambition. So frequently and firmly did Grant express his lack of interest in any job but the one he had that Lincoln was finally convinced. When Congress approved Washburne's bill creating the grade of lieutenant general in mid-February, the president readily signed it. Though the legislation did not specify a recipient for the honor, there was no mystery about who would fill it, only—perhaps—about when it would happen. Immediately, it turned out; Lincoln intended to waste no time putting Grant to work saving the Union. On February 29, Halleck telegraphed Grant to present himself in Washington as soon as possible to accept the commission. Grant would meet the president of the United States for the first time in a ceremony in which the commander in chief would bestow upon him the nation's highest military office.

As a boarding school debutante, Julia had dreamed of marrying a dashing lieutenant. Now the thirty-eight-year-old matron found deep satisfaction in her forty-one-year-old husband's rise to the grade first (and last) held by the father of her country. The Antrobus painting had proven prophetic, it seemed. Julia's supreme, tenacious confidence in Grant had proven equally well founded. "Dudy" was not yet president, as she had predicted, but he was close enough to it to astound every other person of long acquaintance with him. Although neither Grant nor Lincoln could be satisfied until the Confederacy was defeated and the country reunited, Grant's personal ambition would be more than fulfilled when he was commissioned lieutenant general of the U.S. Army.[32]

Grant was well aware that tales of his determination and his modesty were spread across the land in equal measure with slurs against excessive drinking and butchery. From the beginning of the war, Grant had never lacked for supporters and detractors within the populace, the press, politicians, and his own family. All the good and bad in his life up to this point, though, was merely a rehearsal for the trials and glory and glare of attention to come. He had need of all of the help and encouragement his family and friends could give. Supported by Julia's love and unshakable optimism, fueled by his resolve, strengthened by his rising self-confidence, and reinforced by his logistical and battlefield experience, Lt. Gen. Ulysses S. Grant would be a new kind of general-in-chief. He was the general Lincoln had been seeking for three years. Destruction of the enemy's forces would be his sole object. Actions would speak louder than words.

CHAPTER 27

Lieutenant General's Wife

On a cold, damp, dreary Saturday morning in late February 1864, the president of the United States traveled down Pennsylvania Avenue to see the man he was about to commission lieutenant general of the United States. Lincoln was not going to see Grant in the flesh; he made the trip, along with a throng of curious citizens, to view the magnificent painting by John Antrobus, which was temporarily on display in House of Representatives committee room. If the president knew that the canvas had been previously exhibited in Chicago to raise money for the city's Soldiers' Home, he would have approved. Since the spring of 1862, the president had spent his summers in a cottage on the grounds of the Soldiers' Home in Washington, and he knew how vital such an institution was. Situated high on a hill four miles due north of the White House, the cottage was more of a real home to the Lincoln family during his presidency. It was where Lincoln, Mary, and Tad (and Robert, when he was not in school) spent their most private family time during the Civil War. Though relatively quiet (by White House standards), the cottage brought the war to Lincoln with a vividness that even his trips to military camps did not. The grounds of the nation's first military retirement home also accommodated a vast military hospital and one of the first national veterans' cemeteries. From the cottage, Lincoln could see the work he ordered to complete the dome of the Capitol even as he watched the nearby hospital and cemetery expand on almost a daily basis.[1]

Perhaps Lincoln made the trip to see the painting to size up the man who was fast becoming legend. Or perhaps, knowing that he would meet Grant for the first time in just a few days, Lincoln did not want to make the same mistake Stanton had made in Indianapolis five months before, when Stanton mistook another man in Grant's party for the general. Whatever the reason, Lincoln's journey to view the painting was a gesture that bound the president even more publicly to Grant. Seven months earlier, Lincoln had said that if Grant took Vicksburg, "why Grant is my man and I am his the rest of the war."[2]

The city of Washington breathlessly awaited the general's arrival. Or so it seemed—until the afternoon of March 8, when Grant arrived in Washington. Despite all the interest swirling around Grant, there was no one to greet him at the train station. Whether this was by design (for security reasons) or by mistake, Grant and Fred made their own way, unheralded, through the blustery, dusty streets to the Willard Hotel. There, as quickly became apparent, the desk clerk had not been one of those in the crowds to view the Antrobus painting at the Capitol:

> [He] glanced up to find an officer accompanied by a boy of thirteen facing him across the polished oak of the registration counter and inquiring whether he could get a room. "A short, round-shouldered man in a very tarnished major general's uniform," he seemed to a bystanding witness to have "no gait, no station, no manner. . . ." [T]he clerk was no more awed by the stranger's rank than he was attracted by his aspect. . . . Still, bright or tarnished, stars were stars. . . . [T]he clerk replied at last that he would give him what he had, a small top-floor room, if that would do. It would, the other said, and when the register was given its practiced half-circle twirl he signed without delay. The desk clerk turned it back again, still maintaining the accustomed, condescending air he was about to lose in shock when he read what the weathered applicant had written: "U.S. Grant & Son—Galena, Illinois."[3]

That version of that scene is by Shelby Foote, one of countless historians who have described in detail Grant's arrival at the Willard Hotel that day, seeking to understand and explain Grant's ordinary magic. The iconic image of the humble General Grant is powerfully embedded in our national memory. That scene, which includes the subsequent roar of cheers from thrilled hotel patrons in the lobby, also highlights the moment when tired, jaded Easterners under the protection of the Army of the Potomac—which itself had plenty of reasons by then to be tired and jaded—embraced the unassuming man from Illinois as their savior. What raised Grant's unheralded appearance at the Willard Hotel from the merely theatrical to the poignantly dramatic, however, is the presence of the young boy at his side. Fred, the young veteran of campaigns from Springfield to Vicksburg, was Grant's sole companion; Julia could not be there because her eyes continued to bother her.

Soon after the crowd in the lobby recognized Grant, Secretary Seward arrived to take charge of the celebrity general. After Grant put Fred to bed in the large suite that the clerk had miraculously found for him, Seward escorted him to the Executive Mansion, where Mary Lincoln's regular Tuesday evening reception was in progress. Primed by his trip to the Capitol, Lincoln recognized the general as soon as the shorter man made his way through the crowd. Greeting him warmly, Lincoln introduced him to his wife. In short order, the excited, unruly throng forced Grant to mount a sofa to increase his visibility and to avoid being crushed. In this moment of the trip, Julia's absence had consequences. Had Julia been with Grant that evening, she would have been introduced then to the first couple, and the relationship between the two wives might have developed differently than it did when they finally met several weeks later.

The next morning, Grant and his son walked the two blocks from the Willard to the White House for the historic commissioning ceremony. Brigadier General Rawlins accompanied them into the room where Lincoln and his Cabinet and his secretaries Hay and Nicolay waited, along with the soon-to-be-superseded Major General Halleck. Though the group's attention would naturally have been riveted upon Grant, it is likely that Lincoln's gaze turned to the young man. Fred, who had survived two bouts of typhoid, was precisely the same age that Lincoln's beloved Willie would have been if the same disease had not claimed him. The president's careful gaze and his fatherly sensibilities would have deduced the close bond between father and son. Lincoln could see that Grant was not merely the general he needed; he was a man whose priorities he shared.

After the brief ceremony, Grant and his small party quickly departed the city, heading southwest toward the Brandy Station, Virginia, headquarters of Gen. George Meade, commander of the Army of the Potomac. Though Lincoln expressed disappointment that Grant would not stay in Washington for a dinner in the new lieutenant general's honor that evening, the commander in chief must have been heartened by Grant's determination to get down to business. Grant's visit with Meade was also brief, but highly satisfactory to Meade, who had been convinced Grant would relieve him. In point of fact, Grant was relieved and pleased with his assessment of Meade's competence and of the fitness of the troops. As a result of that meeting and of his general distaste for Washington, Grant determined to establish his headquarters in the field for the duration of the war, traveling with Meade and the army. Insofar as possible, he would avoid the society, intrigue, and interference of politicians resident in the nation's capital, unlike his predecessors Scott, McClellan, and Halleck. The latter remained in Washington, now subordinate to Grant as chief of staff. Lincoln's confidence in his new military lineup is apparent in the records of the Library of Congress. On March 24, Lincoln returned Halleck's book on military science that he had borrowed two years earlier.[4]

Soon after his meeting with Meade, Grant and Fred returned to Nashville to wrap up his affairs, including elevating Sherman to command of the western armies. Grant returned east again, this time taking Julia and Jesse to Washington with him. Sherman rode with them much of the way, and Julia recalled somewhat fuzzily being privy to one of the most important strategy sessions of the war. The two men, she wrote, "had long conversations, I think in reference to Sherman's subsequent march to the sea." Because of the timing of this trip, that is unlikely. Discussion of the march was more than six months in the future, but it was on this trip that Grant divided the responsibilities for the war between himself and his favorite general. Johnston's army was Sherman's target; Lee's was Grant's. The two men probably also discussed Sherman's campaign for Atlanta in Julia's presence.[5]

If Julia incorrectly recalled the precise challenge facing Sherman at that moment, her memory was sharper when it came to recalling the challenges she was about to face in the nation's capital. As Sherman and Grant contemplated death and destruction, Julia decided to seek the redhead's recommendations regarding Washington society: "[K]nowing that General Sherman had often been there, I asked his advice as to etiquette, saying, 'General, tell me what I must do when we reach Washington.' He stopped suddenly, looked a trifle annoyed—I think I interrupted his thinking on some great war problem—repeating the question, he said: 'What shall you do in Washington? Why, return all of your calls, every one of them, and promptly, too, and you will be all right.'"

Supplied with a strategy for dealing with the capital and the host of strangers who would gaze critically upon every aspect of her appearance and behavior, Julia then secured what she most needed to meet the challenge—a proper suit of armor. "I was glad when we stopped for a day at Philadelphia, as my wardrobe, necessarily always simple, was now quite depleted," Julia noted. "[T]he few additions I was enabled to make at Philadelphia gave me both comfort and peace of mind." Julia's fashion sense exemplified Ralph Waldo Emerson's observation that "I have heard with admiring submission the experience of the lady who declared that the sense of being perfectly well-dressed gives a feeling of inward tranquility which religion is powerless to bestow." In Julia's case, beautiful material and workmanship in her clothing might also divert a viewer's attention from her flawed eyes.[6]

Julia soon found that neither measure was foolproof protection against wartime Washington's challenges. As she and her husband sat down to breakfast in the Willard dining room the morning after they arrived, Julia "experienced my first shock," she wrote, with evident distress. "My *vis-à-vis* at the table, a stout but not an old lady, with a bunch of hard, black curls on each side of her forehead, great heavy black eyebrows, and a very white face, deliberately raised her glasses and stared me out of countenance." Julia's new sartorial shield failed to deflect the woman's rude visual assault. "So annoyed was I that I asked the General to take me to my room." Thereafter, Julia "hardly ever went to table d'hote." Nor, as it happened, could she "return all her calls," since a "young staff officer, who had kindly volunteered his services as escort," was soon ordered to headquarters. Deprived of logistical assistance in a strange city, Julia moaned, "This broke up all my plans, and the one valuable maxim given me by General Sherman was never carried out."[7]

If she did not meet all of her social obligations, she did finally meet the president and First Lady. The Grants were invited to the Lincolns' last reception of the season at the White House, on April 19, but as "the General had already gone to the front," Julia found a "sufficient escort in Admiral [David G.] Farragut, who was just then being tremendously lionized by society." On his arm, she made her way into the White House: "After entering the Red Room, we soon reached the President. He at once recognized the Admiral, who presented me. Mr. Lincoln repeated: 'Mrs. General Grant?' greeted me in the most cordial manner, taking both my hands in his, expressed great pleasure at meeting me, . . . and presented me to his wife, who, after a few pleasant words of welcome, asked me to stand near her and see the company pass, but feeling a little shy, I did not accept, and the crowd pressing a little, we moved on."[8]

Julia's physical appearance would have struck both Lincolns forcefully, more so than most of their guests. Their firstborn son, Robert Todd Lincoln, had been born with strabismus, and they would have immediately recognized her condition. Having lived with Robert's distress over his deformity—the young boy had been taunted as "cock-eyed" by neighborhood toughs—Mary might have instinctively grasped that Julia would have found the gawking crowd and its attentions unnerving and sought to put her at ease.[9]

Almost exactly a year later, the two women would meet again under circumstances that have always reflected unfavorably on Mary Lincoln. In this first meeting, however, Mary extended her friendship and offered Julia a safe harbor next to her in the crowded ballroom. Julia moved on, though. No doubt, she reacted as she did out of shyness, as she said, and perhaps out of concern that she would be even more an object of public scrutiny were she to remain at the First Lady's side. What happened next was nevertheless the result of Julia's rebuff of Mary's offer: the popularity of the Farragut-Grant duo soon eclipsed that of the Lincolns on their home turf. "Hardly had we taken position [in the Green Room]," according to Julia, when the guests who had surrounded the Lincolns in the adjacent parlor did an about-face and began swarming in her direction. "[C]abinet ministers, senators, foreign ministers, judges of Supreme Court, army and navy officers, with a hundred or more of the belles and beaux of Washington, passed before Admiral Farragut and the wife of General Grant," Julia recalled.[10]

If Julia could recall that sequence of events so clearly when she wrote her memoirs decades after the fact, it was likely fresh in Mary's mind a year later, when the two women met again at Grant's headquarters at City Point, Virginia. Whatever sympathy Mary might initially have had for shy, disfigured Julia would have been sorely tested by Julia's unwitting snub and by this proof of the public's attraction to military heroes and their wives. Mary's personal jealousy and her keen political instincts for her husband's future must have been aroused. By all accounts, however, Julia enchanted Mary's husband that first evening. This happened even though Lincoln had been thoroughly, even sometimes spitefully, briefed years in advance by Grant's detractors on Julia's shortcomings as a slave owner with suspected "secesh" tendencies and on her role as guardian of his lieutenant general's sobriety.

The president reacted with delight when he heard of Julia's response to the burning question of whether her husband would take Richmond. "Yes, before he gets through," she replied firmly to an inquiring guest at the reception. "Mr. Grant always was a very *obstinate* man." Delighted not only with Julia's insight into her husband's nature but also with her charming modesty, Lincoln referenced her remark shortly thereafter, when Stanton questioned Grant's authority to order troops from the Washington defenses to the field. The lieutenant general and the secretary of war took the dispute to Lincoln, who heard them out. "You and I, Stanton, have been trying to boss this job, and we have not succeeded very well with it," the president concluded. "We have sent across the mountains for Mr. Grant, as Mrs. Grant calls him, to relieve us, and I think we had better leave him alone to do as he pleases."[11]

If Julia's success in Washington was recorded in the memories of those present at the White House reception, compliments on her actions several weeks later in New York were trumpeted to the world. Whether by design or accident, Julia found herself in a face-off against Nelly McClellan and Jessie Frémont, the three women vying on nominally feminine turf as surrogates for their husbands in what was actually a deadly serious contest. Grant had encouraged his wife to return from Washington to St. Louis via New York City, where she could visit their old friends, the Hillyers. While she was there, Colonel Hillyer accompanied Julia and his wife to "the great Sanitary Fair," which was in full swing in the city. There, she and her friends encountered a crowd of gawkers—and Jessie and Nelly, too. Julia later recalled that "A magnificent jewel-hilted sword was being voted for, to be given to the favorite general. . . . Colonel Hillyer said: 'Mrs. Grant, here is the famous sword. Wouldn't you like to cast a vote?' 'Of course I would,' and paying my fee, one dollar, I quietly wrote my name under that of General McClellan."[12]

When Colonel Hillyer voiced his shock, Julia sweetly replied, "Of course, I wish my husband to get the sword, but Colonel, it would not be in good taste for me to vote for my husband, would it? You see this is a very nice question," she said. "I never voted save at school for our May Queen, and I am sure the etiquette on such occasions should be that rival queens vote for each other. Any other course there would have been looked on as selfish and dishonorable, and, Colonel, I voted upon that precedent." Anyone who thought Julia's action naive and her rationale simplistic was fooled.[13]

There was an undercurrent to voting on the sword that was, perhaps, as significant as the charitable cause for which it was gathering contributions. Every visitor to the fair knew it was not merely women's play. From the start, the real contest was between McClellan and Grant, though there was a "scattering" of votes for other generals (surely there was at least one for Frémont, cast by Jessie). Not only did this election allow expression of preference for the very different fighting styles of the generals, but with the presidential election of 1864 looming, a vote to award the sword to Grant was also a vote for Lincoln. A vote for McClellan was, well, a vote for McClellan. The significance of this popularity poll was not lost on the public: "The voting at the polls was mostly done by ladies," according to the official *Record of the Metropolitan Fair*, "but the end showed that all the while the lords of creation were getting more and more interested, and were only preserving a strategic inactivity."[14]

Nor did its significance escape the generals' wives. Volunteer army nurse Adelaide Smith, who was working at the Department of Arms and Trophies at the fair on the day of Julia's visit, recalled the scene in her fascinating memoirs: "Here was to be decided the 'sword test', that would indicate the most popular general by the number of votes cast at one dollar each. . . . How these ladies worked for their favorites! Mrs. Grant, a noble-looking woman, accepted graciously, but without solicitation, all who offered votes for General Grant, of whom she invariably spoke as 'Mr. Grant'. Mrs. McClellan, with elegant society manner, lost no opportunity in gaining a vote for General McClellan; her vivacity, personal charm, and courteous flattery won many a vote for her husband."[15]

Although Nelly had ignored the Sanitary Commission's request for help during McClellan's active military command in 1862, she was front and center at the fair in 1864, in order to bolster her husband's presidential ambitions. Nelly's beauty was a tactical advantage in lobbying for votes that Julia knew she could not overcome, so she shrewdly maneuvered to her advantage. Claiming the high ground of chivalry, Julia hoped to inspire the crowd to support her husband in compensation for her plain modesty. Proof of her success was quick in coming. "The next day, the papers were full of praise of this little act," she recalled. "Public opinion said it was right and savored of the days of knighthood."[16]

Even without his wife's vote, Julia's husband garnered enough $1 bids to win the sword. Testifying to the significance of the poll in the eyes of politically active men, a last-minute telegram from the Union League Club of Philadelphia ordered "five hundred votes for Grant," which overcame McClellan's lead. Grant was less enthusiastic about his wife's action than was the press, though not because of how she voted. He was unhappy that she voted at all. According to Rawlins's recollection, Grant thought she should have declined to cast a vote to avoid unnecessary publicity. Indeed, Grant wrote Julia that he regretted "that my name has been mixed up in such a contest."[17]

Grant also warned her to watch young Jesse or "you might loos him in the streets in all the excitement[.] New York is a big place and you might not find him." He urged them both to return quickly to St. Louis and the rest of the children. Julia was slow to take his advice; instead, she stayed in the city, using the opportunity to visit Mathew Brady's photographic studio, where she had her portrait taken in one of her new gowns. Much like her husband's photograph documenting his rise to a fully uniformed brigadier general in Cairo in the fall of 1862, Julia recorded her rise to wife of lieutenant general of the United States Army in a perfectly dressed and carefully posed three-quarters profile portrait.[18]

Of her weeks in New York and later in St. Louis, Julia noted, "Mr. Stanton kindly sent me all telegraphic reports from the seat of war," but she did not mention at all what those reports contained. Once again, what Julia omitted from her memoirs were memories too painful to recall, even decades later. As Sherman began his march from Chattanooga toward Atlanta, Grant began his pursuit of Robert E. Lee in what is known as the Overland Campaign. Moving with the Army of the Potomac under Meade's field command, he struck out toward Richmond. Hoping to draw Lee into battle on favorable ground, he badly miscalculated more than once Lee's willingness to go on the offensive, but he never let up. The battles of the Wilderness (May 5–7), Spotsylvania Courthouse (May 8–21), North Anna (May 23–26), and Cold Harbor (June 1) produced horrific casualties that shocked the country and grieved Lincoln beyond any calamity yet in the war.[19]

Julia Dent Grant in 1864. "This was taken by Mathew Brady in New York when I was on my first visit to N.Y. the spring that General Grant first came East." (*Courtesy of the Ohio History Connection [AL04539, P397]*)

"After the Wilderness a roar of rage rose all over the North; it was declared that Grant was destroying the army with his butcheries, that he had no plan, and that the Union downfall was at hand," recalled the *New York Times* on the fiftieth anniversary of the Civil War. That was the memory Julia suppressed when she wrote her memoirs. She never mentioned any of the battles of the Overland Campaign, nor did she resume her narrative of the war until Grant began his siege of Petersburg. Instead, she wrote of her efforts to find a home in Philadelphia, as instructed by Grant, who thought the schools there were good and the distance from Washington agreeable.[20]

Although the Republican Party easily nominated Lincoln as its candidate on June 8 (replacing Hannibal Hamlin, Lincoln's first-term running mate, with Andrew Johnson), the rising casualties spawned by Grant's dogged summer campaign made McClellan's candidacy a serious concern and Frémont's third-party effort worrisome. Lincoln's political advisers fretted over his chances for reelection. So did his wife. In Grant's escalating casualty list Mary saw a threat to her husband's second term in the Executive Mansion. Two years before, she had urged her husband to fire McClellan because he was not fighting hard enough. Now she pressed Lincoln to fire Grant because he was fighting too hard. Elizabeth Keckley vividly remembered one of many such conversations, which echoed the clamor in the public and the press: "Mrs. Lincoln could not tolerate General Grant. 'He is a butcher,' she would often say, 'and is not fit to be at the head of an army. . . . He loses two men to the enemy's one. . . . Grant, I repeat, is an obstinate fool and a butcher.'"[21]

Despite public and private outcry over Grant, Lincoln stood by him. The president knew that eventually the human and technological resources of the United States would triumph over the Confederate States—if his generals would fight and if Northerners would give them time. Lincoln did the math in December 1862, after the Battle of Fredericksburg, when General Burnside threw the Army of the Potomac against Confederates entrenched in the hills above the town and suffered a disastrous defeat. Calculating the damage on a relative basis, though, the Confederates suffered worse. Stoddard recalled how Lincoln crunched the Fredericksburg numbers when he heard of the fiasco. "We lost fifty per cent more men than did the enemy, and yet there is sense in the awful arithmetic propounded by Mr. Lincoln. He says that if the same battle were to be fought over again, every day, through a week of days, with the same relative results, the army under Lee would be wiped out to its last man, the Army of the Potomac would still be a mighty host, the war would be over, the Confederacy gone, and peace would be won at a smaller cost of life than it will be if the week of lost battles must be dragged out through yet another year of camps and marches, and of deaths in hospitals rather than upon the field."

In one of the most famously prophetic statements attributed to Lincoln, Stoddard related the president's conclusion: "No general yet found can face the arithmetic, but the end of the war will be at hand when he shall be discovered." Of course, Lincoln preferred victories—the people needed victories, his reelection needed victories—but he knew in 1862 that even losses on the tragic scale of Fredericksburg served the purpose of the Union war machine. By the spring of 1864, Lincoln recognized in Grant the general who could "face the arithmetic." He knew it because after the Battle of the Wilderness, Grant had done something that none of his other generals had ever done. According to Gen. Carl Schurz, "It had been the habit of the Generals commanding the Army of the Potomac to cross the Rappahannock, to get their drubbing from Lee, and then promptly to retreat and recross the Rappahannock again. Grant crossed the Rappahannock, got his drubbing from Lee, but did not recross the Rappahannock again in retreat." Instead, Grant turned the Army of the Potomac south, in pursuit of Robert E. Lee.[22]

While Grant waged bloody war, Julia spent an enjoyable summer in St. Louis, where, no doubt, her husband's rise to lieutenant general silenced her previously annoying "Southern neighbors." As the school year loomed, Julia took the children and headed to Philadelphia, as Grant had urged, to find a home and good schools. But Julia could not find suitable, affordable housing in the city, so with the help of her brother, Frederick Dent, now a brigadier general on his former roommate's staff, she traveled about twenty miles northwest of Philadelphia, to the predominantly Quaker town of Burlington, New Jersey. There, they found good accommodations and good schools. Over the next several months, Grant made brief side visits to his family during infrequent trips to Washington.

In mid-June, Grant established headquarters for the siege of Petersburg, Virginia, on the outskirts of that city, on a tip of land called City Point, near the town of Hopewell. Along with a letter to his wife from there on June 19, Grant enclosed a gift: "Dear Julia, I send you three sterioscopic views taken at Mattaponix [Massaponax] Church, near Spotsylvania Court House. [Mathew] Brady is along with the Army and is taking a great many views and will send you a copy of each. To see them you will want a Sterioscope. Send to Covington for Buck's or buy one." Grant could not have known his loving intentions would be thwarted by Julia's strabismus, which would have prevented her from experiencing the three-dimensional effect of the stereoscope. Indeed, it is likely that Julia herself never knew what she was missing. Even if her eyes had lined up the two photos more or less into one, it is almost certain that the one she saw was still two-dimensional.[23]

In the same letter, Grant wrote: "There are no buildings here to live in and no place for you and the children to stay or I might send for you." He said he would try to find accommodations for her nearby, but they did not prove satisfactory. Instead, Julia made short but frequent trips to see her husband. The lieutenant general "always sent a ship or boat to meet me and allowed me to invite friends to accompany me," she explained. "He would come down the James River in his own boat and meet us at Fortress Monroe, and taking the party on his boat, we would arrive at City Point the next morning." Grant was not satisfied with these brief, intermittent visits. As always, he wanted Julia with him constantly, and the children, too, when they were not in school.[24]

As Grant sought to find a way to keep Julia near him at City Point, she was trying to arrange for his comfort in Burlington after the war, which she was confident her husband would soon bring to an end. She sought to bring east a young woman who had been their cook when they lived in Galena, and in this she received Grant's enthusiastic endorsement. "By all means send to Galena for the girl you had there if you want her," he encouraged her. "I want of all things good cooking when I get back home. It makes the greatest difference in my feeling well."[25]

Julia proceeded to write to Congressman Washburne, seeking his help in finding and transporting her cook. Washburne saved this letter, which offers rare insight into how Julia expressed herself, both literally (misspellings and all) and figuratively (quite charming, and in her reference to Richmond, quite conscious of her husband's reputation). On December 20, Julia wrote to the man who had become a close family friend:

> I am going to ask a favor of you, an infliction you must by this time have become accustomed to. I want you whilst in Galina make enquery for one *Maggie Cavinaugh*. She lived with me whilst I was in Galina. I want to get her to come here & live with me, here. I will fully satisfy her as to wages & will pay her expenses here of course. I am getting to be such an old scolder (since I have such an indifferent cook) that I really fear for The Genl's peace of mind when he comes home (After Richmond is taken) & beg for his sake you will put some one on Maggie's track & have her looked up & carefully shipped to your friend & admirer. . . . Let me wish you a happy Christmass with your family—Fred is going to City Point.[26]

By Christmas 1864, Lincoln had been reelected, owing in large part to victories by forces under the command of Sherman at Atlanta, Sheridan in the Valley, and Farragut in Mobile Bay. Only the army in Grant's immediate vicinity still lacked a strategically significant victory. But Grant was closing in on Lee, who had more than once expressed the opinion that a siege of Petersburg and Richmond was the military tactic he most feared. "This army cannot stand a siege," Lee had told Beauregard on May 11. To many heretofore-dissatisfied observers in the North, it looked like the end was in sight.[27]

Early in 1865, Grant's living quarters at City Point had improved sufficiently for him to request that Julia "make him a prolonged visit." Julia and Jesse set off for Grant's headquarters, where they and Fred would spend the final days of the war; their other children stayed with her brother Fred's wife at the Grants' New Jersey house. For the next four months, Julia's home was a small cabin, which replaced the tent Grant had previously occupied. "The Quartermaster [Rufus] Ingalls built this for the General so I could be with him he said," according to Julia. "They all flattered me by saying that I must stay with him and

General Grant, son Jesse, and Julia, in front of their cabin at Grant's headquarters at City Point, Virginia, spring 1865. (*Courtesy of the Library of Congress*)

that at headquarters they missed me. And so for the rest of this eventful winter, I was domiciled in this little cabin, enjoying not only the society of the Commanding General but of all the distinguished men and generals that visited headquarters that winter."[28]

The cabin, one of several erected for the officers, perched "on the point," the tip of the spear-shaped peninsula where the James and the Appomattox Rivers meet. Sitting on the bluff high above the rivers' convergence, the cabins afforded sweeping vistas of land across the broad expanses of water and of what had become "one of the busiest ports in all America" in less than a year. An officer of the 32nd Massachusetts Volunteers described the scene in the spring of 1865: "Beyond the masts and rigging and the smoke stacks and steam of the water craft, were seen groups of tents, long ranges of whitewashed barracks, log-huts and shanties of every shape bearing the signs of sutlers and licensed traders . . . such was the busy bustling life of the place which was the base of supplies for the army."[29]

Neither Colonel Parker's nor Julia's description of City Point mentioned the impressive and graceful Appomattox Manor, which still stands, less than one hundred yards from where the Grants' tiny cabin was constructed. The mansion had been the heart of a 2,300-acre working plantation, named Appomattox, until Union gunboats appeared on the nearby rivers in 1862. The Eppes family fled their home in panic, and the property soon came under Federal control. General Ingalls, who arrived at City Point in June 1864 to establish the logistical base for the siege of Petersburg, claimed use of the comfortable mansion for his large quartermaster's staff. When Grant appeared on the scene shortly thereafter, he refused to occupy the grand home, preferring instead to live in much smaller and cruder quarters—first a tent, then the small cabin. Sherman, who sat with Grant and Julia in their cabin when he visited in the spring of 1865, referred to the officers' living quarters as "a pretty group of huts."[30]

The incongruity of Julia's situation could not have been lost on her. As a child, she had grown up in a house very much like Appomattox Manor. Now, as the wife of the most powerful military man in the United States, Julia lived in conditions that were physically closer to those of the slaves her husband's success would free. She never breathed a word of dissent or regret. Indeed, Julia seemed truly content at City Point, even in a log cabin more humble than Hardscrabble, which she had openly despised. In a letter to a friend, Julia said, "I am snugly nestled away in my husband's log cabin. Headquarters can be as private as a home. . . . Am I not a happy woman?"[31]

Testifying to the couple's happiness there, Grant's aide Brig. Gen. Horace Porter recalled: "They would sit with her hand in his, manifesting the most ardent
devotion; and if a staff-officer came accidentally upon them they would look as
bashful as two young lovers spied upon in the scenes of their courtship." According to Porter, Julia "had learned perfectly how to adapt herself to camp life."
In addition to visiting the sick, she consulted with the camp cook on "delicacies
for their comfort." She took her meals with her husband and his staff, "kept up a
pleasant run of conversation at the table, and added greatly to the cheerfulness of
headquarters," in Porter's view. Julia "was noted for her amiability, her cheerful
disposition, and her extreme cordiality of manner," Porter remembered.[32]

Julia was not the only woman at City Point headquarters during this time.
She was, rather, the reigning queen, due to her husband's status, of a small
but merry society of officers' wives. Indeed, the size of the military city, the
ease of transportation to it from many Northern points, the large collection of
senior officers, and Julia's presence encouraged other wives to visit. Although
Rawlins did not favor wives in camp, he tolerated Julia's presence because it
enabled him to relax his sobriety patrol, and he did not have authority to forbid other officers the family privileges enjoyed by their commander. In fact, by
November 1864, when Grant requested Julia to join him at City Point, Rawlins
was also ready to have his wife with him in camp. "I wish you would write
to Mrs. Rawlins and ask her to come with you," Grant wrote to Julia. "Gen.
Rawlins would be pleased if you would do so and would regard it as a compliment." Though most women stayed shorter periods than did Julia, the wives
of Generals Edward C. Ord, George Meade, Charles Griffin, and others spent
time at City Point, as did Mrs. Stanton, who traveled from Washington with
her husband and their son.[33]

For two and a half years, Julia had been a cheerful but low-key presence in
western military camps. During her stay at City Point, surely, she intended no
different role for herself. Necessarily, though, in the closing days of the war,
Grant's headquarters became the epicenter of great events, and as a result,
Julia was pulled further into the maelstrom of history. On one occasion, Julia
found herself much closer to enemy action than she should have been, when a
Confederate ram steamed toward Grant's headquarters to shell the bluff. She
was disappointed when the Federals' river obstructions disabled it. "No roar
of cannon, no bursting of shell, no military pageant for me!"[34]

The president visited Grant's base of operations twice while Julia lived at
City Point. Each time, he came in response to a telegram from Grant, and both
of those visits were in some measure prompted by Julia. The first time was in

late January 1865, when Jefferson Davis sent three officials to see if a brokered peace could be arranged to end the war. The delegation, led by Vice President Alexander H. Stephens, arrived without advance notice at Grant's front lines under a flag of truce. Although Grant was nearer Petersburg at the time, he sent word to his staff for the commissioners to be escorted to his headquarters and shown every courtesy. As he hurried to City Point, he wired Washington for instructions as to how to proceed. Arriving before he received a response, he hosted the men to dinner on his headquarters boat, the *Mary Martin,* with his staff and his wife.

Julia was openly delighted with the prospect of peacefully settling the long, bloody war and also saw an opportunity to press a personal matter. "I had quite an interview with the commissioners, telling them they held a brother of mine as a prisoner and that he was a thorough rebel if there ever was one," according to Julia. Most likely, the Confederate peace commissioners were initially heartened by the thought that the Union general's wife could be an ally in their cause. Their smiles would have quickly dissolved, though. In response to their suggestion that her husband exchange a Confederate prisoner for her brother, Julia informed them that Grant had already flatly refused to do so. No doubt, such an unyielding posture toward Confederate sympathies within his own family disabused the commissioners of any notion that Grant would look leniently upon their petition. Indeed, in accordance with a telegram that came that evening from Washington, Grant quickly advised them that he had no authority to deal with any issues beyond the strictly military.[35]

When Grant learned that Lincoln intended the delegation should be sent back to Richmond without discussion with any official of the United States, however, the general urged the president to reconsider. He spoke not at all to the substance of the delegation's proposals but to the public relations impact—on the men of his army who had watched with great interest the delegation cross their picket lines and on the civilian population who would read about it in the newspapers—of a refusal to even meet with such a high-ranking delegation. Grant telegraphed his concerns to Stanton that "their going back without any expression from any one in authority will have a bad influence. . . . I am sorry however that Mr. Lincoln can not have an interview with the two named in this dispatch if not all three now within our lines." Grant's telegram convinced the president, who took a fast boat to Fort Monroe and there had a serious but predictably unsatisfactory meeting. More than one historian has seen Julia's influence in the handling of the peace commissioners. John Simon reasoned that the combination of Grant's well-known closeness to Julia and the warnings Lincoln had received early on about her "secesh tendencies" spurred Lincoln to limit Grant's interaction with the commissioners at the start. It seems more likely, as historian Michael Burlingame, among others, has held, that "[t]he general's wife had prodded him to do something to break the logjam," and that Lincoln trusted Grant's instincts in the matter.[36]

If Julia's "secesh tendencies" had been a concern of the president, Julia herself soon put his fears to rest. After his visit with the Southerners ended in failure—as he knew from the start that it would—Julia recalled that she accosted the president, expressing her dismay. "Why, Mr. President, are you not going to make terms with them? They are our own people, you know." Lincoln replied, "Yes, I do not forget that," and [according to Julia], "quietly taking from his pocket a large paper, he read aloud the terms he proposed to them, which were most liberal, I thought." When Lincoln told her they had rejected the terms, Julia "wrathfully" denounced the commissioners, and the president "smiled and said: 'I thought when you understood the matter you would agree with us.'" Although the peace commission met with failure, Lincoln had talked with the men in good faith and later made clear to the country the terms they refused to countenance, foremost among them reunion and the end of slavery.[37]

Lincoln returned to City Point in late March, this time as a direct result of Julia's insistence that the president take refuge from the stress and cares of the capital city. "[T]he papers daily announced the exhausted appearance of the President," she recalled. Reporters commented on Lincoln's ravaged features as he was sworn into office on the steps of the Capitol on March 4. At the Inaugural Ball, according to the New York Times, "Mr. LINCOLN was evidently trying to throw off care for the time; but with rather ill success, and looked very old." A week later, Lincoln cancelled a Cabinet meeting because, according to the Times, he was "quite ill with influenza." Julia's tender heart sought a means of helping her husband's ailing commander in chief. "I petitioned the General with hospitable intent to invite Mr. and Mrs. Lincoln down to visit the army," according to Julia; "so many people were coming, and the weather was simply delightful." Grant repeatedly rejected her pleas. "If President Lincoln wishes to come down," Grant told Julia, "he will not wait to be asked." Instinctively, Julia protested that Lincoln would not come without Grant's specific invitation, "for fear of appearing to meddle with army affairs." For support, she turned to the newest member of Grant's military staff, Capt. Robert Todd Lincoln.[38]

Young Lincoln's presence at City Point was the result of a delicate compromise earlier that year among the president, the First Lady, and Grant, sparked by Robert's fervent sense that duty and honor called him to military service.

Mary Lincoln believed that the two sons she had already lost excused her from thrusting a third into harm's way. Lincoln then wrote to Grant, asking him, "Could he, without embarrassment to you, or detriment to the service, go into your Military family with some nominal rank, I, and not the public, furnishing his necessary means?" Grant readily assented, awarding Robert the grade of captain, and shortly after his father's inauguration, Robert had assumed his nominal duties at City Point. As a result, he was available for consultation on that spring day in 1865, when Julia asked him, "why his father and mother did not come down on a visit." According to Julia, he told her, "I suppose they would, if they were sure they would not be intruding."[39]

That was enough to spur Grant to telegraph the president on March 20: "Can you not visit City Point for a day or two? I would like very much to see you, and I think the rest would do you good." Within hours, Lincoln accepted his invitation. "Had already thought of going immediately after the next rain," his message read. "Will go sooner if any reason for it. Mrs. L. and a few others will probably accompany me. Will notify you of exact time, once it shall be fixed upon." Although an eyewitness to the visit later opined that "it was generally agreed that Grant was not particularly desirous of Mr. Lincoln's presence at City Point . . . during those trying days," he also noted, "General Grant never for a moment manifested any impatience, but gave to the President every possible consideration due to his exalted position." Grant proved more successful in maintaining his equilibrium during the visit than did Julia.[40]

It began well enough, though. On the evening of March 24, the steam paddle boat *River Queen,* carrying the president, Mary Lincoln, their youngest son, Tad, and Elizabeth Keckley, docked at City Point without fanfare. Robert hurried to the Grants' cabin to tell them of the arrival. Even had the president intended to visit City Point on his own, it made a difference that his favorite general had invited him; observers commented on the warmth of the men's greeting. The fact that Julia had triggered the visit also made a difference; it inspired her to take ownership of the situation:

> I suppose the President's arrival was kept quiet for a purpose, but I was not satisfied, not being able to divest myself of the idea that I was somehow hostess, and so I urged not only a flourish of trumpets, but a grand salute to these guests, so distinguished and so honored. Our gracious President met us at the gangplank, greeted the General most heartily, and, giving me his arm, conducted us to where Mrs. Lincoln was awaiting us. She received us most cordially, and as soon as a few words of greeting had passed, the President said:

"Now, I am going to leave you two ladies together while the General and I go for a few moments to my room where we can have a little talk without being interrupted. Eh, General?"[41]

Unfortunately, the women's cordial relationship did not last long. "[Mary Lincoln's] behavior during this period was not just erratic," according to biographer Catherine Clinton. "Several outbursts indicate that she was in a constant state of hyperanxiety." More than half a dozen eyewitnesses to Mary's visit concur in that assessment (including Grant, Sherman, General Porter, U.S. Navy Capt. John S. Barnes, Maj. Adam Badeau, and *Chicago Tribune* correspondent Sylvanus Cadwallader), although some were more reticent or forgiving than others in their tales of Mary's "capricious and disturbing" behavior. Captain Barnes, who suffered excessively from Mary's wrath, later wrote with great diplomacy: "She was at no time well; the mental strain upon her was great, betrayed by extreme nervousness approaching hysteria, causing misapprehensions, extreme sensitiveness as to slight, or want of politeness or consideration." Of Lincoln, he remarked that "his manner toward her was always that of the most affectionate solicitude, so marked, so gentle and unaffected that no one could see them together without being impressed by it."[42]

The most forgiving of those who chronicled the visit was, in fact, Julia herself, who bore the brunt of many of Mary's irrational outbursts. More than twenty years passed before Julia wrote about the events, and the passage of time may have tempered Julia's memories of Mary Lincoln. Also, during those intervening years, Julia experienced some of the same misfortunes that had unstrung Mary. During Grant's presidency, Julia suffered as her beloved hero was publicly disparaged and degraded; she herself was accused of dishonest dealings with moneymen; and when the twin curses of poverty and cancer struck Grant suddenly and almost simultaneously, she bore sorrowful witness to her husband's hideously painful death. Looking back on her own behavior at City Point, Julia may have wished to cleanse her conscience by going easy on Mary.

At that first meeting, according to Julia, after their husbands left the stateroom, "Mrs. Lincoln politely pointed to the little sofa from which she had arisen and invited me to be seated." Julia then proceeded to make an innocent but ultimately fatal error in dealing with Mary: she approached the First Lady as an honored guest, not as visiting royalty: "As I was standing near her, I seated myself beside her on this small sofa; then, seeing a look of surprise from Mrs. Lincoln, I immediately started up, exclaiming, 'I crowd you, I fear.' She kindly extended her hand to detain me, saying, 'not at all' . . . from this little incident . . . is woven the sensational story so recently published."[43]

Julia was referring to Grant aide Major Badeau's recollection of the meeting, which was quite different. "How dare you be seated, until I invite you," was his version of Mary Lincoln's imperious remark. Other reports support Badeau's account of the meeting and imply that Julia's written version shaded the truth. According to Julia's sister, Mary Lincoln expected Julia to back out of the room when she departed, as if the general's wife were in the presence of a reigning monarch.[44]

Whether Mary recalled their White House meeting a year earlier and determined explicitly to put Julia firmly in her place, or whether, in her disturbed mental state, Mary unconsciously expressed her innate sense of superiority, that meeting set the tone for subsequent interactions between the two women. Within a span of less than twenty-four hours, Julia twice found herself on the way to review troops, riding side by side with Mary in a military ambulance (as any light cart with a canvas covering stretched over iron ribs was called in those days, even if it did not transport the wounded). Each time, Grant and Lincoln traveled on horseback and arrived at the site of the review more quickly than their wives. Each time, unfortunately, Julia and Mary arrived not only late but wholly out of humor. The ambulance ride was always extraordinarily rough, causing Mary once to hit her head severely against one of the iron ribs. Even more distressing to her, Mary twice learned that somewhere up ahead was a woman who was or had been near her husband. Jealous, she attacked those women and Julia, too.

Sally Griffin was her first target. As Julia and Mary bumped along toward the first review, a woman mounted on horseback galloped by. Upon being told that she was the wife of Gen. Charles Griffin, whose troops they were to review, Mary might have recalled that she had attended the Griffins' wedding in Washington in December 1861. Instead, Mary took the occasion to comment unfavorably at seeing so many women in camp. Major Badeau then innocently remarked that Grant had ordered all of his commanders' wives evacuated from the front, but General Griffin's wife had been given special permission from the president to remain. "What do you mean by that, sir?" Mary demanded. "Do you mean to say that she saw the President alone? Do you know that I never allow the President to see any woman alone?" Mary grabbed at the ambulance driver to force him to speed up, which only made the ride bumpier and splashed mud onto the women's clothing. Frustrated beyond speech, Mary struggled to escape the carriage and walk to the review. Julia's frantic efforts to prevent the First Lady from sinking in the knee-deep mud of the road were met with the iciest of rebuffs. Only General Meade's sudden arrival and his unexpected diplomatic skills saved the day; he told Mary that it had been Stanton, not Lincoln, who gave Mrs. Griffin permission to remain at the front.[45]

Later that afternoon, the muddy ambulance pulled up to Gen. Edward O. C. Ord's camp. Inside were two dirty, sore, tired, and extremely unhappy ladies. They arrived an hour behind their husbands, who were already reviewing Ord's troops. The beautiful, fashionably dressed Mary Mercer Ord was riding with her husband—and with Julia's and Mary's husbands, too. Mary demanded of no one in particular and of everyone in earshot, "What does the woman mean by riding by the side of the President? And ahead of me? Does she suppose that *he* wants *her* by the side of *him?*" When Julia attempted to soothe the First Lady's rage, Mary Lincoln turned her anger on Julia. Out spilled a torrent of jealous fear and fury, revealing Mary's anxiety and hostility toward the Grants. "I suppose you think you'll get to the White House yourself, don't you?" she demanded. Julia answered Mary's question with far greater tact than truth, considering her long-standing belief that Grant would one day be president. Julia responded that she was quite content with her present station, and that it was far greater than she had ever imagined. More enraged than ever, Mary shot back, "Oh! you had better take it if you can get it. 'Tis very nice." This exchange, reported in Badeau's account, does not appear in Julia's memoirs.[46]

In the meantime, Mrs. Ord had seen the ambulance arrive and broke away from the men to pay her respects to the First Lady and Julia. Oblivious to the previous conversation about her, she was greeted by a torrent of abuse by Mary Lincoln, who "positively insulted her, called her vile names in the presence of a crowd of officers, and asked what she meant by following up the President," according to Badeau. "The poor woman burst into tears," but the First Lady's wrath did not let up the rest of the trip. She constantly prodded the president and every other member of the party to punish General Ord and his wife. Julia and Grant stood by the Ords, which only heightened Mary's rage and deepened Lincoln's distress at his wife's lack of emotional control.[47]

A few days later, Julia proceeded, albeit unknowingly, to commit the worst sin possible against Mary Lincoln: she paid the president a deft compliment in front of his wife. According to Elizabeth Keckley, "if a woman desired to court Mary's displeasure, she could select no surer way to do it than to pay marked attention to the President." It happened on March 31, when Grant was away from City Point (he had left on March 29 to pursue Lee). Congressman Washburne had arrived at City Point, and Julia accompanied him to the *River Queen* to pay respects to the president and First Lady. There, a small party was gathered, which included the first couple, at least two senators and their wives, a Cabinet member, and a French count. The group was apparently in the midst of a lively discussion, for when Julia and Washburne entered, Mary turned to Julia, saying archly, "Suppose we ask Mrs. Grant . . . What should be done with the Confederate President Jefferson Davis in the event of his capture?" Julia "happened to catch the friendly glance of the President just then" and sought to respond in a manner that would earn the president's praise for herself as well as shine reflected light on her husband. "I would trust him," she answered adroitly, "I think, to the mercy of our always just and most gracious President." While "[t]he gentlemen all said it was a most diplomatic answer," it is unlikely that Mary tendered any of the many compliments that Julia later said she received for it.[48]

While Mary and Julia jousted verbally at City Point, their husbands made valuable use of Lincoln's time there. One of the early consequences of Lincoln's arrival in City Point was the meeting of Lincoln, Grant, Sherman, and Adm. David Porter in the *River Queen*'s stateroom on March 28. It was not a planned conference, as previously mentioned; Sherman was already on his way to Grant's headquarters to meet with the general when Grant sent his telegram to Lincoln. Had Lincoln not come as quickly as he did in response to Julia's invitation (had he waited until "after the next rains," for example), in all likelihood, he would have missed Sherman's visit completely, and that meeting and its impact on Sherman's treatment of Joseph Johnston would have been erased from history. Julia's kind heart, her desire to help forge a stronger bond between her husband and the president, and, no doubt, her delight in society (and the president was high society indeed) created one of the most significant meetings of the Civil War and—thanks to the famous G. P. A. Healy painting of the event—one of the most memorable tableaux as well.[49]

Petersburg fell during Lincoln's visit to City Point, and shortly thereafter, Navy Capt. John Barnes recalled that the president read to him "several dispatches from Mr. Stanton, expressing anxiety as to his exposing himself, and drawing contrasts between the duty of a 'general' and a 'president.'" Barnes noted that the president answered them from Grant's headquarters, "saying that he would take care of himself." Surely Stanton was more alarmed than comforted, though, when he received the following telegram:

City Point, April 3, 1865, 5PM

Hon. Edwin M. Stanton, Secretary of War:

Yours received. Thanks for your caution, but I have already been to Peters-burg. Staid with General Grant an hour and a half and returned here. It is cer-tain now that Richmond is in our hands, and I think I will go there to-morrow. I will take care of myself.

A. Lincoln[50]

"Thank God that I have lived to see this!" declared Lincoln on hearing the news of Richmond's fall on April 2. "It seems to me that I have been dreaming a horrid dream for four years, and now the nightmare is gone. I want to see Richmond." Given the secretary of war's distress over the president's vulner-ability at City Point, Lincoln surely would never have made the historic trip to the rebel capital had he not already been beyond Stanton's reach. Once again, Julia, whose suggestion led to Lincoln's presence in City Point, played a signal role in the events of the last weeks of Lincoln's life by making possible Lincoln's visit to Richmond on April 4.[51]

It was a dangerous, arduous, trip. Just getting the president and Tad to Rich-mond from City Point proved hazardous; according to several accounts, Lin-coln, Tad, and Admiral Porter nearly died in a close brush between their boat and a paddle steamer. When the small band finally docked at one of Richmond's wharves, no Federal troops were there to escort them, so they proceeded into the city on their own. Stanton would have trembled for his chief had he known that only a dozen sailors "armed with carbines" provided military escort into the still-smoldering rebel capital. A newspaper reporter, who had entered the city before the president's party, spied the familiar tall figure and called it to the attention of a few black men and women nearby. Soon, Lincoln was a magnet for hundreds of blacks, who surged to the riverfront from the city's charred, crumbling buildings. Reporter Charles Coffin described for his Boston readers "the enthusiastic bearing of the people—the blacks and poor whites who have suffered untold horrors during the war, their demonstrations of pleasure, the shouting, dancing, the thanksgiving to God, the mention of the name of Jesus— as if President Lincoln were next to the son of God in their affections. . . ." Lin-coln was deeply affected by all he saw and heard.[52]

Soon, Federal troops caught up with the president's party and led them to the Confederate White House, which had been hastily turned into Union Army headquarters. Tad was tired, and Lincoln was thirsty, so they went in-side. Lincoln sat in the study that had been Jefferson Davis's only two days earlier. Captain Barnes made his way from the wharf to the house in time to see Lincoln settle into the chair and ask for a glass of water. He saw in Lincoln "no triumph in his gesture or attitude." It was a long and emotionally draining day for the president, but before he left Richmond, he met with some local civic leaders and made a speech to a large gathering of blacks in the city's main square. Lincoln had seen the promised land, and he had visited it, too. If not for his trip to City Point, he would have died without having witnessed Richmond liberated from Confederate control. His concluding words at Capitol Square, as he sought to make his way through the crowd, were too sad and too prophetic. "There, now, let me pass on," he said to the grateful throng that lunged to touch him. "I have but little time to spare."[53]

Grant did not meet Lincoln in Richmond as he had in Petersburg, because by April 4, the general had Robert E. Lee almost cornered near Appomattox Court House. Julia and Jesse could not accompany Grant into certain battle, of course, so they remained on his headquarters boat docked at City Point, the *Mary Martin*. The Grant family had moved from the little cabin on the hill to the boat at some point during the Lincolns' visit. What was meant to make visiting with the Lincolns on the *River Queen* more convenient had, instead, produced even more friction between the wives. The *Martin* and the *River Queen* were steam paddle wheelers built on the same frame, and the City Point dock could accommodate only one of them at a time. In consequence, the other would be lashed to the ship at dock and its occupants forced to walk over the docked vessel to get to shore. Mary declared from the outset that "she would not go ashore if she had do so over Mrs. Grant's boat." Thus nearly every outing by "Mrs. Lincoln's boat" or "Mrs. Grant's boat"—as they came to be known derisively throughout City Point—resulted in "open discussions between their respective skippers [that] were sometimes warm," according to Captain Barnes, who added, "Of course, neither Mr. Lincoln nor General Grant took any notice of such trivialities."[54]

By this point in the visit, Julia recalled, "I saw very little of the presidential party now, as Mrs. Lincoln had a good deal of company and seemed to have forgotten us." "I felt this very deeply and could not understand it, as my regard for the family was not only that of respect but affection. The President had stood by my hero when dark clouds were in his sky, and I felt grateful. Richmond had fallen; so had Petersburg. All of these places were visited by the President and party, and I not a hundred yards from them, was not invited to join them."[55]

To satisfy her own burning curiosity about the rebel capital, Julia put together a party of ladies to steam to Richmond, where empty streets and shattered buildings turned her thoughts to "all the sad tragedies of the past four years. How many homes made desolate! How many hearts broken! How much youth sacrificed! And tears, great tears, fell from my eyes. For what, I could not tell," she wrote. In fact, though, she could tell, and she did: "Could it be that my visit reminded me of my dear old home in Missouri?"[56]

On her return to City Point, she learned Mary Lincoln had planned a large reception that evening to which she had not been invited. This open snub pushed Julia to the limits of her deference and overcame the rare self-restraint she had displayed during the president's visit. So it was with a trivial, even spiteful, act that Julia ended her interaction with the Lincolns at City Point. Commandeering "Mrs. Grant's boat" and securing the services of the head-quarters military band, Julia set off down the river for an evening excursion on her own. When she and her musical military escort aboard the *Martin* came within range of the *River Queen*, Julia instructed the band to play "Now You'll Remember Me." Steaming past the Lincolns' floating party for another hour, Julia learned on her return that "the kind President's boat had gone, and—well!—I regretted my ride up the river."[57]

Abraham Lincoln's time at City Point, inspired by Julia, had served to forge an even stronger bond between Grant and the president, but it carved a vast chasm between their wives. However favorably Julia may have impressed Lincoln during his visit, the president could not overcome his wife's jealous dislike of the lieutenant general's wife. The winning team of Lincoln and Grant was bringing the great national conflict to a close. It was clear the Confederacy was doomed, the terrible war all but over. As their husbands began relaxing their grip on the machinery of war, however, Mary and Julia were suiting up for combat on their own battlefield.

Even though Mary had lost friends and diminished her popularity through erratic and spiteful behavior, she was, nonetheless, the wife of the president. But Grant was the nation's rising man—the hero of the hour—and Julia the rising woman; their star power could not be underrated. Mary had seen proof of the couple's celebrity in her own house even before Grant conquered Lee's army. At City Point she had witnessed the deft social skills that belied Julia's otherwise plain, even dowdy exterior. Mary knew Julia was not to be underestimated. By the time the *River Queen* headed back to Washington on April 8 with the presidential party, Julia and Mary were undoubtedly already anticipating a nearly unending series of victory parties, rallies, receptions, galas, and banquets to which the two couples would be invited and at which they would be feted. The possibilities for social mischief, if not mayhem, given Mary's temperament, were nearly infinite. Mary would have instinctively resolved to dominate each and every venue, taking no prisoners. Julia would have been equally determined not to allow the First Lady to maneuver her into humiliating situations by continuing to snub her, and by inference, publicly demeaning her husband. Even before word of Lee's surrender at Appomattox, the two women had already begun jousting for social supremacy in postwar drawing rooms. Their brief City Point skirmish had ended in a draw. Their Washington campaign loomed on the horizon, and it was going to be a long, bitter fight. Or so they surely thought.

Tragically, though, it was heartbreakingly short.

CHAPTER 28

"I did not want to go to the theater"

Julia stayed at City Point despite an April 7 telegram from her husband, urging her to return to the children in Burlington. Grant believed the endgame with Lee was not yet quite in sight: "it may be 10 or 12 days before I return." Julia preserved the telegram, on which she proudly wrote: "I did not obey. I waited and returned with the victorious Genl's." It was one of her dearest souvenirs of those last days of the war. She and Mrs. Rawlins, also quartered on the *Martin,* would rejoice that they had disobeyed their husbands' orders to leave. Only days later they received word of the surrender, which took place on April 9. Julia and Mary Emma waited anxiously each evening for their husbands' return.[1]

The generals arrived so early on the morning of April 12 that Julia was asleep when Grant boarded the boat. At breakfast, one of Grant's staff encouraged him to visit Richmond, which he had not entered since the city fell. Grant refused, and Julia recalled, "When I urged him to visit Richmond, he leaned towards me and said: 'Hush, Julia. Do not say another word on this subject. I would not distress these people. They are feeling their defeat bitterly, and you would not add to it by witnessing their despair, would you?' I realized the delicacy and kindness of his decision and urged no more." Indeed, Grant so little liked to focus on the surrender that, according to Jesse, "in our family the final act of the drama was never discussed, either then or later."[2]

The City Point meeting of Lincoln, Grant, Sherman, and David Porter had convinced the officers that their commander in chief wished genuine magnanimity, not proud triumph, to be the essence of the coming victory. So firm was Grant's attitude in that regard, and so obediently did Julia emulate it, that she refused to accept one of the prized mementos from the surrender itself. General Ord joined the souvenir-hunting frenzy at the McLean house after Grant and Lee had departed, and emerged—after paying $40—with a small table from the parlor, which he presented to Julia. No doubt his gesture was in part an honor he paid to his superior officer. Surely, though, it also reflected Ord's gratitude to Julia for her defense of his wife against Mary Lincoln's unprovoked assault. Julia gracefully but firmly refused the souvenir, which she knew her husband would find offensive.[3]

Julia was thrilled to return to the nation's capital at her hero's side. The welcome she and Grant and his staff received on their arrival Thursday, April 13, was everything that she could have hoped for. "As we reached our destination that bright morning in our boat, freighted as she was with heroes, brave men, every gun in and near Washington burst forth—and such a salvo!—all the bells rang out merry greeting, and the city was literally swathed in flags and bunting." While Grant first went to the White House to confer with the president at his request, Julia "went with Mrs. Stanton to the War Department, where we were joined later by Mr. Stanton and General Grant." Preparations were being made for an "illumination" of the city that night, and Stanton laughingly remarked that the Navy Department had borrowed "two or three boxes of candles" from the army for its show.[4]

Illuminations were not new to the city by then. Noah Brooks observed that day that "[t]he national capital has certainly had a surfeit of illuminations." As an example, Brooks described in detail the illumination on April 11, which was, he wrote, exceedingly fine: "The whole effect, as witnessed from Arlington Heights, across the river, was very grand, the city being one blaze of light, while fountains of fire were continually spurting up into the cloud of light which seemed to hang over the capitol. . . . The War Department . . . had, among others, these mottoes: 'Our iron-clads are a terror to the nations,' 'U.S. Army, U.S. Navy, U. S. Grant . . . '"[5]

No doubt the April 13 illumination would be equally impressive, signifying the return of the general who had led the Army of the Potomac to victory over the Confederate general who bedeviled it for three bloody years. All of Washington, it seemed, planned to take to the streets that spring evening to enjoy it.

Mary Lincoln certainly intended to do so, even though her husband was not feeling well. What might have been a disappointment, in fact, became a singular opportunity for her to deal another blow in her tussle with Mrs. General Grant. Forgetting her past dislike for "Grant the Butcher," Mary Lincoln wrote a note and had it delivered to the Grants' suite at the Willard Hotel. "Mr. Lincoln is indisposed with quite a severe headache," it said, "yet would be pleased to see you this evening about 8 o'clock & I want you to drive around with us to see the illumination." Addressed only to General Grant, the message made no mention of Julia. When Julia told her husband she had just accepted the

Stantons' invitation to see the illumination and have dinner at their home, he urged her to join them, while he accompanied Mrs. Lincoln. Julia balked; she would not grant Mary the privilege of greeting the crowds in Washington with her famous husband before she did. "To this plan, I protested and said I would not go at all unless he accompanied me." Julia could tell that her tart response vexed Grant. "[W]ith a shadow of surprise," she recalled, he gave in to her desires. Grant agreed that he would attend the Stantons' dinner and then take Julia to see the illumination; afterwards he would call on the First Lady and accompany her. "This was all satisfactory to me," said Julia, "as it was the honor of being with him when he first viewed the illumination in honor of peace restored to the nation, in which he had so great a share—it was this I coveted."[6]

Despite her enjoyment of the evening, she desired a quick departure from Washington. "As soon as the General awoke in the morning, I asked him earnestly if we would not leave for Burlington today," Julia remembered, but Grant had promised to meet with the president at nine o'clock. He worried that the meeting might last too long for him to board the four o'clock train. His worries increased when a note arrived from the president, asking to delay Grant's audience so he might visit with his son Robert, who had just returned from the field. "Suppose you come at eleven o'clock, instead of nine," asked the president, and so, of course, eleven o'clock it was. Grant urged Julia to take Jesse and get on the train that afternoon, and he promised to do his best to join them.[7]

Grant was at the Executive Mansion with the president and his Cabinet when Julia witnessed the first in a series of strange and unsettling events over the subsequent twenty-four hours. A man presented himself at the door of her suite, "dressed in a light-colored corduroy coat and trousers and with rather a shabby hat of the same color." Julia noted his dress in detail, and "not liking either the looks of the messenger or his message," heard him say, "Mrs. Lincoln sends me, Madam, with her compliments, to say she will call for you at exactly eight o'clock to go to the theater." But Julia was no more inclined to bow to Mary's wishes on April 14 than she had been on April 13. "You may return with my compliments to Mrs. Lincoln," she told the caller, "and say I regret that as General Grant and I intend leaving the city this afternoon, we will not, therefore, be here to accompany the President and Mrs. Lincoln to the theater." The man then played what he must have thought to be his trump card: "Madam, the papers announce that General Grant will be with the President tonight at the theater." Julia would not be deterred. "You deliver my message to Mrs. Lincoln as I have given it to you," Julia insisted, showing the man to her door.[8]

Advertisements placed by Ford's Theatre, April 14, 1865. (*Washington Evening Star*)

Earlier in the day, the manager at Ford's Theatre had greeted with enthusiasm Mary's decision to secure a box at Ford's Theatre that evening for the Lincolns and the Grants. He informed the newspapers as a means of filling the house on Good Friday, an otherwise lackluster theater day. The *Evening Star*, in fact, carried two small items publicizing that evening's attractions, in which the play itself was definitely third fiddle. "LIEUT. GENERAL GRANT, PRESIDENT and Mrs. Lincoln have secured the State Box at Ford's Theater TO NIGHT, to witness Miss Laura Keene's American Cousin," read one. The other confirmed, "LIEUT GENERAL GRANT, ARRIVED in town last evening, on his way to Philadelphia will visit Ford's Theater THIS EVENING, in company with President and Mrs. Lincoln." There was no mention of Julia. If Julia had seen the papers, she might have guessed that Mary had taken the liberty of informing the newspapers as a fait accompli to force the result the First Lady intended. If that was Mary's intention, she failed.[9]

"As soon as I received the invitation to go with Mrs. Lincoln," Julia recalled, "I dispatched a note to General Grant entreating him to go home that evening; that I did not want to go to the theater; that he must take me home." So determined was Julia to leave Washington that she asked three of Grant's staff officers to go to the White House and "urge the General to go home that night." More than twenty years after that awful evening, she still wondered at her fierce determination: "I do not know what possessed me to take such a freak," she wrote, "but go home I felt I must." Grant recalled Julia's "freak" years later: "Lincoln had promised to go to the theater, and wanted me to go with him. While I was with the President, a note came from Mrs. Grant saying she must leave Washington that night. . . . Some incident of a trifling nature had made her resolve to leave that evening."[10]

When Grant told Lincoln that his wife insisted on leaving Washington that evening, Lincoln did not protest; both men understood the pressures their wives exerted on them. In fact, Stanton had already urged Grant not to go with Lincoln to the theater. Stanton always feared for Lincoln's safety in his theater outings. But it was Julia, not the secretary of war, who trumped the president in this instance. Mary spent much of the rest of the day asking and being rejected by a number of luminaries, including the Stantons, before she succeeded in securing guests for the evening: Clara Harris, the daughter of the New York senator, Ira Harris, and her stepbrother and fiancé, Maj. Henry Rathbone.[11]

Julia was also having a bad day. Her anxiety increased when she and Jesse sat at lunch in the dining room at the hotel with Mrs. Rawlins and her daughter. "[T]hese men came in and sat opposite to us," she recalled vividly. "They all four came in together. I thought I recognized in one of them the messenger of the morning, and one a dark, pale man, played with his soup spoon, sometimes filling it and holding it half-lifted to his mouth, but never tasting it. This occurred many times. He also seemed very intent on what we and the children were saying. I thought he was crazy. As we sat at the table, I said to Mrs. Rawlins in a low tone: 'Be careful, but observe the men opposite to us and tell me what you think.'"[12]

Mary Rawlins concluded that there was "something peculiar about them." Julia then speculated that they were "a part of Mosby's guerrillas," notorious rebel partisans who had roamed the outskirts of Washington for years, wreaking havoc on armed men and civilians alike. Julia feared for her family's safety in Washington that day, and considering her husband's position, she had reason to worry. Her husband had forced Lee's surrender, but Julia knew the war was not yet over. Indeed, over the previous months, she had heard fears expressed in high military councils that Confederate guerrillas might carry on the war. "Do you know," she told Mary Emma, "I believe there will be an outbreak tonight or soon. I just feel it, and am glad I am going away tonight."[13]

Her relief at Grant's return from the White House in time to take her to the train was palpable, but Julia was soon unsettled again as they made their way from the hotel to the train station in a carriage provided by Assistant Quartermaster Gen. Daniel Rucker. His wife sat inside with Julia, while Grant sat outside on top with the driver. "[A]s General Grant and I rode to the depot, this same dark, pale man rode past us at a sweeping gallop on a dark horse— black, I think. He rode twenty yards ahead of us, wheeled and returned, and as he passed us both going and returning, he thrust his face quite near the General's and glared in a disagreeable manner." The man's actions were so blatant that Julia "noticed the General draw back as the man returned and came so close." Grant recalled that Julia cried, "There is the man who sat near us at lunch to-day, with some other men, and tried to overhear our conversation." Later, under oath during the trial of the Lincoln assassination conspirators, a fellow actor, who was with Booth on the streets of Washington that afternoon, confirmed that Booth had "galloped off in pursuit" when the carriage carrying the Grants appeared. That was not the end of it, for there was an effort by another strange man to enter the Grants' private train car, when it paused briefly in Havre de Grace, Maryland, before they reached Philadelphia. The action of the train porters, who had locked the Grants' private car, preserved the family's security and peace of mind until the train stopped in Philadelphia.[14]

It was quite late when they arrived in that city, where they had to leave the train from Washington, take a ferry across the river, and board another train to their final destination. As the general had not had anything to eat since breakfast, they sought refuge in the dining room of a hotel near the ferry before their departure. They ordered some oysters for the general. Before the food arrived, however, Julia recalled, "a telegram was handed him, and almost before he could open this, another was handed him, and then a third." They were posted from the War Department in Washington and contained the worst possible news:

THE PRESIDENT WAS ASSASSINATED AT FORD'S THEATER AT 10:30 TO-NIGHT AND CANNOT LIVE. THE WOUND WAS A PISTOL SHOT THROUGH THE HEAD. SECRETARY SEWARD AND HIS SON FREDERICK WERE ALSO ASSASSINATED AT THEIR RESIDENCE AND ARE IN A DANGEROUS CONDITION. THE SECRETARY OF WAR DESIRES THAT YOU RETURN TO WASHINGTON IMMEDIATELY.[15]

As panic erupted in the nation's capital amid the shock of Lincoln's assassination, the attack on Seward, and rumors of Confederate plots, another telegram from Stanton advised Grant to pay close attention to his own safety as he made his way back to Washington. The general decided that he would lose little time if he first accompanied his wife the rest of the way to their New Jersey home before returning to the capital. Indeed, given the strange men in Washington and on the train and Stanton's admonitions to be extra careful, Grant's own peace of mind probably required that he personally insure that the rest of Julia's trip home and the home itself held no unpleasant surprises.

No sooner had he left Burlington early the next morning than a letter arrived at their home. Though it was addressed to her husband, Julia opened and read it, according to his instructions to review all messages in his absence. "General Grant, thank God, as I do, that you still live," the anonymous correspondent wrote, with evident relief. "It was your life that fell to my lot, and I followed on the cars. Your car door was locked, and thus you escaped me, thank God!" In Washington and elsewhere on the morning of April 15, rumors of Grant's assassination spread as part of the roiling public panic. Indeed, when the conspirators were rounded up for trial, in addition to charges of conspiracy to kill Lincoln, Johnson, and Seward, one of them was specifically charged with intent to kill Grant, when he was at Stanton's home on April 13, the night of the grand illumination: "Michael O'Laughl[e]n did then and there lie in wait for Ulysses S. Grant, then Lieutenant-General and Commander of the armies of the United States aforesaid, with intent then and there to kill and murder the said Ulysses S. Grant."[16]

CHAPTER 29

"the sunlight of his loyal love"

November 1868 brought the fulfillment of Julia's prophecy so many years earlier when she was mistress of Hardscrabble: Ulysses Grant was elected president of the United States. By all accounts, no woman has ever enjoyed being First Lady more than Julia Grant. She restored and redecorated the White House with delight. She hosted scores of parties and dinners. When she closed the grounds behind the White House to the public—because "Nellie and Jess, the latter just learning to ride on a velocipede, had no place to play"—some newspapers commented that the "Grants are getting a little too exclusive." But Julia finally had a grand home that reminded her of White Haven. "I love the dear old house. . . . Eight happy years I spent there—so happy!"[1]

Julia and Ulysses lost none of their attachment to each other as they entered their third decade of marriage during Grant's presidency. Every morning, Grant rose early and read the newspaper until Julia completed her toilette. "They invariably went down to breakfast arm in arm," according to White House usher William H. Crook. "Grant usually finished quickly . . . but Mrs. Grant lingered for another cup of coffee. However, he always waited for her and escorted her back to her sitting room, where they usually had another chat before he set out for his morning walk."[2]

Not that the Grants' White House years were all parties and gaiety. Grant made some terrible decisions, particularly in choosing and trusting advisers. Scandals erupted and even touched Julia at one point. Although Julia wanted a third term, it was not to be. After they left the Executive Mansion in 1877, the Grants' two-year trip around the world had all the trappings of a state visit. Her animated descriptions of all that she saw and ate and bought in Europe and Asia occupy more space in Julia's memoirs than either her Civil War or her White House years.

And then, tragedy struck.

Twice.

May 1884 brought the first, when Grant learned that the financial concern he had blithely entered (investing his friends' money as well as his own) with his son Buck and a shyster, Ferdinand Ward, collapsed without warning. "The failure of Grant and Ward came like a thunderclap," wrote Julia, leaving the Grants almost instantly destitute; Grant had neither a military nor a presidential pension. Friends rushed in with offers of help, but nearly all were refused. The couple liquidated almost everything, although they saved one of Ulysses's swords, which Julia later sent to the Smithsonian Institution. Grant began to write articles about his war experiences for *Century* magazine for much-needed income. Fate dealt them a second, fatal, blow in September of that same year. Living in reduced circumstances in their beach cottage at Long Branch, New Jersey, one day Grant bit into a peach, and howled from pain. It was the first symptom of the cancer that would kill him in less than a year.[3]

Julia told the story of her husband's last eleven months in the final three pages of her memoirs. During those months, Grant wrote more than one thousand pages. *The Personal Memoirs of Ulysses S. Grant,* published by Mark Twain almost as Grant died, was not merely an instant best seller; it has been hailed as one of the greatest books ever written. The story of Grant's last days is one of indomitable will applied to imperishable love. He would not leave Julia penniless, so he wrote her rich and himself immortal. Grant's agonized race to finish his memoirs, before death claimed him on July 23, 1885, inspired a tidal wave of admiration and support for him that echoed his popularity just after the Civil War. When he died, he was revered a hero and esteemed for his courage. His funeral was one of the grandest in American history, fueled by an outpouring of admiration, love, and sympathy.

Julia ended her memoirs with her husband's death, as if her life ended then, too, but she lived for seventeen years more. Though she wore black for the rest of her life, during those years, Julia spread sunshine from Europe to California as she followed her children and their children into the twentieth century. William Tecumseh Sherman remained one of her closest friends and became her financial adviser, while Absalom Markland, John Logan, and even Simon Bolivar Buckner Jr. assisted Julia and Fred in beating back an attempt by Adam Badeau to claim significant authorship of Grant's memoirs and royalties from it. The widow of General Grant called upon the widow of Jefferson Davis when they were both in New York, and the two became friends—a sort of post-Civil War odd couple. International royalty called upon Julia in New

York and in her final home in Washington, D.C. When the United States went to war against Spain in 1898, Mrs. General Grant led efforts to gather and ship supplies to U.S. soldiers in the Philippines. A year later, when Frederick Dent Grant's daughter married a Russian prince, the belle of White Haven added to her long list of accomplishments a princess granddaughter.[4]

By then, she had nearly finished her memoirs, most of which she dictated to Fred. Recalling the days she shared with her dashing lieutenant, Julia later said, was "a panacea for loneliness, a tonic for old age." It was also a chance to settle scores with those who had doubted her unshakable faith in her "Ulys" and an opportunity to document her remarkable life. From slave-owning debutante to hardscrabble farmer's wife to lieutenant general's wife to First Lady to world traveler, in the words of her biographer, "No American woman of her generation had traveled further or met more famous people than Julia Grant." Or, perhaps, had so many twists of fate.[5]

One of the most consequential was to be found in that strange series of events on April 14, 1865, which she recounted at length and in detail in her memoirs. Her account of those twenty-four hours has an anxious immediacy to it that sets it apart from the chatty tone of the rest of her story. There is a haunting quality to her description of how the specter of assassination—Lincoln's and quite possibly Grant's—followed them as she and Ulysses sped by rail through the night toward their home in New Jersey. They had left a capital city ringing with the joyful noise of peace, which plunged into darkness more profound than during the war's worst days. Relief, regret, and fear fought for attention in the Grants' minds as they headed into an unknown future on that terrible Good Friday.[6]

Even today, our minds reel in contemplation of the assassination. It is difficult not to think of the many contingencies that made Booth's success possible, nor of what might plausibly have occurred had any step in the chain of events been changed, even slightly. For Julia, surely, the contingency that mattered most was her utter refusal to allow her husband to accept Lincoln's invitation. Her memoirs dwell on the strange, threatening men who crossed the Grants' path from the Willard Hotel to Havre de Grace. When it was all over, she felt a sense of satisfaction that they had eluded them, an overwhelming sense of relief that her "freak," as she called it, had kept the Grants from going with the Lincolns to the theater. But had she spared her husband's life at the expense of Lincoln's? That is a thought that recurred to Grant over the rest of his life (as it recurred sorrowfully to Robert Todd Lincoln, who had also chosen not to accompany his parents). Nearly every Grant biographer notes that the general expressed the thought later in life that he might have saved the president had he been there. Julia, too, must have wondered at that possibility again and again.[7]

Return for a moment to that night, as Julia did at length in her memoirs. Consider another possibility that the Grants lived with until their deaths: What if they had been in the theater box with Lincoln and Mary, but Grant had been unable to prevent Lincoln's assassination? Then the ultimate outcome would have been the same—Lincoln dead, his guest alive. In projecting and examining that possibility, while Lincoln's story changes not at all, Grant's history alters perceptibly: the man who saved the Union failed to save his commander in chief. From that moment until this one, no one who ever heard the tale of that night at Ford's Theatre could divorce the image in their mind of Grant, aggressive savior of the Union, from that of Grant, powerless bystander to Lincoln's assassination.

On balance, the story of Grant's extraordinary life is, as Brooks Simpson so aptly called it, one of "triumph over adversity." But had Grant been with Lincoln that night yet failed to save him, the scales would tip, ever so slightly, perhaps, the other way. Grant may have regretted not going to the theater that night, and he may have regretted for twenty years the possibility that he might have saved the president if he had gone. That regret would have been nothing, though, compared to his anguish had he been in the president's box and not saved Lincoln. No matter how small the possibility of that sorrowful scenario, Julia saved her husband from its unceasing torment to his mind and heart. That Grant's legacy is less tragedy than triumph may, in fact, be Julia's legacy.

Julia Dent Grant's heart was always young, but it finally failed on December 14, 1902. At the age of seventy-six, she died in Washington, D.C., of heart and kidney disease. A week later, thousands attended her memorial service. Then she was laid to rest in a magnificent red granite sarcophagus next to her beloved Ulys.[8]

More than a century on, the love story of Ulysses and Julia Grant remains an inspiration. In 2002, Stephen Cushman wrote: "Whenever I smoke a cigar I think of Grant in the Wilderness." His elegiac poem is equally dazzling and haunting as prose: "I wonder what it takes to be happy in marriage and march through the woods making widows." Cushman answered his question even as he penned the verse, which included his elliptical reference to Julia, "the wife he couldn't stand to part from."[9]

What it took for Grant to make widows was, in fact, for him to be happy in his marriage, to have Julia with him. John Y. Simon, who devoted nearly every day of thirty-six years to collecting, cataloguing, annotating, and above all, reflecting upon twenty-eight volumes of Grant's papers, was convinced of Julia's centrality to her husband's being: "Through victories and defeats in battle, vicissitudes of command, burdens of administration, and crushing responsibilities, Ulysses's love for Julia provided his core of strength and stability."[10]

The little woman with the deformed eye, who hated numbers and could not balance her accounts, made it possible for Grant to do Lincoln's "awful arithmetic." As a young lieutenant, Grant had contemplated life as a mathematics instructor in order to win Julia's hand. As lieutenant general of the U.S. Army, he subtracted soldiers and multiplied widows until the sum of the nation's grief and glory equaled victory for the Union. Julia was essential to Grant. He was the man he was—the general that Lincoln needed—because of her.

Part of what made him that man, that general, was Julia's failure to write to him as much as he needed to hear from her. Ironic, then, that she should be the first First Lady to write (or at least, dictate) her memoirs. Part of what made him that man, that general, was the "sunshine" she radiated in Grant's presence. Ironic, then that he could not feel the warmth of her sunshine when they were separated by geography, though she felt his warmth always, even when separated by death. She concluded her memoirs with that thought: "For nearly thirty-seven years, I, his wife, rested and was warmed in the sunlight of his loyal love and great fame, and now, even though his beautiful life has gone out, it is as when some far-off planet disappears from the heavens; the light of his glorious fame still reaches out to me, falls upon me, and warms me."[11]

 CONCLUSION

"The woman who is known only through a man is known wrong"

Like so many other stories of the Civil War, this one begins and ends with Abraham Lincoln. It starts in his office in the White House at the outset of the Civil War, with his unprecedented open door to all, including women seeking redress or advantage for their husbands. It concludes in the Cabinet Room after his assassination, with the death of his hopes for a soft peace. In between those two points in American history lies this tale of how four women influenced the war by influencing their generals who fought it, in part because of what they thought about Abraham Lincoln.

Jessie Frémont, Nelly McClellan, Ellen Sherman, and Julia Grant were their generals' closest confidantes; no other person in the men's lives had as profound and persistent an impact upon the generals as did these women whom they loved and who bore their children. The generals wrote to their wives regularly, often daily, of their love, their hopes, their dreams, their fears—and their terrible, bloody work. When the wives responded, their letters were filled with talk of home, children, love, all that fighting men needed to hear. The women wrote about the war, and about the men charged with waging it. Sometimes they wrote about Lincoln; sometimes they wrote to him; sometimes they visited him.

The wives were known to change their opinions of Lincoln, and their shifting views of the president influenced their actions. Perhaps as early as the outset of Lincoln's presidency, Jessie Frémont thought the Railsplitter naive. Later, Jessie's view of Lincoln altered; she thought the commander in chief irrelevant, at least to her husband's management of the Western Department. She urged Frémont to issue his emancipation order without consulting with the president, who had spent so much of his political life wrestling very publicly with the issue of slavery. Next, she disdained Lincoln. Her hurried trip to Washington on her own initiative to rescue her husband's career ended badly. Lincoln listened to her carefully and asked her questions, and then—just as one can imagine he would have done if Jessie had been a man—he lost his temper when he heard her answers. Jessie proceeded to lose her temper, too, concluding her visit by challenging the authority of the president of the United States in her husband's name, by demanding the president's correspondence, by urging her husband to print more copies of the emancipation proclamation that the president had just told her was null and void, and by encouraging Frémont to arrest Frank Blair, Lincoln's "Vice Roy" in Missouri. Her disdain for Lincoln continued unabated for the rest of her life.

Only one man could engender more revulsion in Jessie's breast than did Abraham Lincoln: George Brinton McClellan. In a contest among the three men for the presidency, even her lifelong love affair with Frémont took a back seat to her fervent hopes for the end of slavery in the United States. Despite her enmity toward Lincoln, she had far more confidence in him in that regard than in McClellan. Jessie sacrificed much to defeat slavery. First, she sacrificed her husband's military career by urging him to issue—and later, against his commander in chief's direct orders, to distribute widely—his emancipation order. Then she sacrificed her husband's dream of the presidency to preserve his reputation as a champion against slavery. All her life, Jessie sacrificed for John Charles Frémont. Of that, there is little doubt.

There is some room for doubt, though, in the relationship between Nelly and George McClellan when it came to Nelly's opinions of and her interaction with Lincoln. It difficult to know for certain how much her unfavorable view of Lincoln, as expressed in her few extant letters and as echoed in her husband's, was her own and how much was influenced by Little Mac. The feistiness with which she had rejected a string of suitors and criticized Stanton supports a picture of a woman with strong opinions of her own. McClellan surely joined in her strong negative judgments of Lincoln, Stanton, and Halleck, which she then persistently reinforced in the couple's correspondence. The McClellans could always change a good opinion they had of someone, but never a bad one. Add Jessie's account of her meeting with the McClellans at Mary Lincoln's reception and you have another picture of Nelly's disregard for the president. Neither she (the "senior" woman of society in the small clutch of people gathered by Seward at Lincoln's request) nor Jessie attempted to break the very thick social ice as they stood under the gaze of the commander in chief, who held their husbands' fates in his hands. As the rules of Victorian manners decreed, even the most serious enemies should make an effort to appear above the fray in polite society, but Nelly made none. Though she was known for helping to smooth McClellan's actions on occasion, existing evidence shows that both in words and in deeds, Nelly bolstered her husband's arrogance toward Lincoln and his Cabinet.

When, later that same year McClellan brought Nelly, their daughter, and his mother-in-law to the Antietam battlefield to marvel at the site of his greatest victory, it is hard to imagine that Nelly would not have known that Lincoln and Halleck were frantically urging and ordering her husband back south toward Washington. It must have been obvious to her that McClellan was trying the patience of his superiors. Nonetheless, McClellan ignored them, and she allowed him to do so. Yes, she was still a relatively young woman, and he was an important military officer. Too, the apparent balance of power in a Victorian marriage tilted heavily in the husband's favor. Nevertheless, she could have found a way to subvert his ill-advised arrogance, just as Julia's "freak" forced Grant to refuse Lincoln's invitation to the theater.

Nelly's regrettable inaction was matched on occasion by regrettable actions, as when she urged her husband to defy Halleck's demands at the time of the Second Battle of Bull Run, when she coyly tried to get him to dart into Washington solely for the purpose of retrieving their silver, and when she encouraged him to resign from the army during the war. Even if there was no difference at all between Nelly's and McClellan's opinions of Lincoln, there was still room enough for good judgment to surface in the McClellans' relationship with the president, but between the two of them, it never did.

Good judgment is not the quality that immediately springs to mind when discussing Ellen Ewing Sherman. She is typically recognized for her religious zeal or her nagging, or both. Nonetheless, in her dealings with Lincoln on behalf of her husband, she is an exemplar of shrewdness and common sense. The emotional roller-coaster ride of the Shermans' wartime experience was extraordinary even by the standards of those four years. Rocketing from crisis to crisis—some coldly professional, some heartbreakingly personal—Ellen made intelligent and relatively dispassionate judgments about her husband's health, about what he should do, and about what she and the rest of his family should do on his behalf. In every case, she urged him to stay on the job and work through the crisis at hand. The earliest calamity during the war came at its outset, when Sherman was nearly felled by a charge of insanity. Wounded herself by the newspapers' bitter scorn for her husband and the shame and disgrace it visited upon her and her children, she nevertheless recovered quickly and marshaled the family resources.

Ellen's early independent judgment in support of Lincoln for president (when no one else in her family supported him) set the groundwork for her approach to Lincoln in crisis mode. Her letter to Lincoln contained superbly crafted arguments in favor of action on his part to erase the stain on Sherman's reputation, combining an honest assessment of her husband's state of mind with a blunt recounting of the charges against him and shrewd reference to his successor's failure to advance. Ellen's trust in Lincoln led her to accept Lincoln's verbal support, even in the absence of any positive action by him, as the best course for her husband, and she encouraged Sherman to trust Lincoln's judgment, too.

More than a year later, Ellen's anger led her to write to Sherman that the president ought to be impeached because of his support of McClernand over her husband after the battle of Chickasaw Bayou. She allowed herself to express her rage against Lincoln to Sherman, but that was a private moment. As far as can be determined, Ellen did not repeat that judgment in writing to anyone else; she did not appeal directly to the president to change his mind; she did not even hint to Sherman that he should leave the army. To the contrary, when her impatient, redheaded husband threatened to resign, she sternly accused him of contemplating desertion, essentially urging him to snap out of it. Even when Ellen did not approve of Lincoln's actions vis-à-vis her husband, she did not crusade against the commander in chief. She shrewdly never lost sight of the president's authority or his ability to help her family.

While Ellen's shifting perceptions of Lincoln were fairly straightforward, Julia Grant's feelings about Lincoln must have been quite complex. Lincoln and the civil war that his election sparked destroyed the mythical way of life Julia loved and forever idealized: White Haven—gone; "the comforts of slavery"— gone; her adored father's superior position in the social hierarchy—gone; her life as a pampered Southern belle—gone; her chivalric notions of war—gone. All were swept away in the tempest that was the Civil War. It was a war that her husband prosecuted industriously rather than romantically. It was a war that enabled her Ulys to rise out of boredom that starved his soul. It was a war that she encouraged him to fight. It was also a war that risked the lives of her husband, her children, and herself. It was a war that divided her family and elevated her former slaves to her political status.

Yet, there is no indication that Julia ever expressed dismay at Lincoln's policies toward slavery or at her husband's workmanlike approach to dismantling the infrastructure of her childhood in concert with his commander in chief. Julia did not merely lack anger against Lincoln, she felt warmly toward the man guiding the destruction of the society she mythologized. She risked much to be with Grant during the war and to bring him the "sunshine" he so desperately needed. It was Julia's natural tendency to spread "sunshine" that led her to urge Grant to invite the president to City Point at the end of March 1865. And it was only after Mary Lincoln rained on Julia's perpetually sunny disposition that Julia nerved herself to disappoint the president and insist that her husband refuse to attend the theater with the Lincolns.

Because they married these particular women, Frémont, McClellan, and Sherman had recourse to the reputations, if not the wisdom, of their wives' fathers for help in their darkest hours, when the generals' uncertain fates were in the hands of skeptical civilian and military leaders. Thomas Benton, Randolph Marcy, and Thomas Ewing were all brilliant and courageous men, whose political and/or military skills were renowned and whose reputations were not extinguished by their deaths. Frémont and McClellan ultimately failed to get satisfaction from Washington, despite the additional advantages of their own brilliant national reputations, early high military office, excellent political connections, and wide public celebrity. One of the many differences between them and Sherman—beyond his relative obscurity and his lack of overweening ambition—was Ellen's close relationship with her father. Ellen's strategic approach to rehabilitating Sherman, carefully coordinated with her formidable father, was distinctly different from the actions of Jessie and Nelly when their husbands encountered problems in Washington.

When Frémont's insubordination in California endangered his career in 1847, Thomas Hart Benton avoided telling his daughter about her husband's folly even as he sought to resolve it. He must have known that news of Frémont's situation would reach her ears eventually. His silence may have stemmed from his fear she would blunder in her eagerness to help her husband; he knew her stubbornness and her bluntness firsthand. Benton's fears were justified. Once Jessie learned of her husband's predicament, she initiated an unproductive encounter with President Polk, without the knowledge or approval of her husband or her father. She and her father worked at cross purposes again on Frémont's behalf shortly thereafter, when Jessie encouraged her husband to reject the presidential pardon that Benton had sacrificed so much to obtain for him.

Nearly fifteen years later, Jessie's famous father's name was her calling card when she sought a meeting with Abraham Lincoln late on an autumn evening in 1861. Her effort to rescue her husband and his ill-timed emancipation order from presidential purgatory was likely done without Frémont's enthusiastic support and most certainly would not have been approved by her father, had he still been alive. Though Benton and his daughter both desired a glorious career for Frémont, the Benton-Frémont team failed to work in concert. Jessie's avid support for her husband's third-party candidacy in 1856 severely ruptured her relationship with her father. In nearly every crisis, Jessie sided with her husband against her father, to Frémont's ultimate disadvantage. The one time Jessie constructively intervened on her husband's behalf was when she acted in the spirit of "Old Bullion" and secretly derailed her husband's presidential bid against Lincoln.

The McClellan-Marcy team's support for its general against the host of McClellan's real and imagined enemies was equally uncoordinated. While General Marcy covered for his son-in-law's failings more than once in dealing with Lincoln, Nelly encouraged her husband's disdain for and suspicion of the president. She even encouraged her husband to relinquish his high military position and its responsibilities in the middle of the war, a step that is difficult to imagine the dedicated Marcy condoning. Marcy's son-in-law undervalued the chief of staff's wealth of military experience and common sense. Even as Little Mac praised "that cool head," he did not hesitate to ignore Marcy's sage advice when it did not agree with his own inclinations.

In decided contrast to the fractured support systems that the Frémont-Benton and McClellan-Marcy families mounted during the Civil War, the Sherman-Ewing clan was largely a model team effort. Once she determined to rehabilitate her allegedly "insane" husband and his career, Ellen quickly shook off her own humiliation and despair and helped to launch and monitor the myriad moving parts of the family's defensive and offensive operations. She acted as her absent husband's eyes and ears within the family deliberations, reporting information from many sources. She spent countless hours writing and copying letters that kept Thomas Ewing, John Sherman, Philemon Ewing, Thomas Ewing Jr., and her husband informed of developments. She strategized in detail with her father and with John Sherman on various aspects of their fight. While she believed that Sherman had duplicitous rivals in the military, she did not leap from that conclusion to a more sweeping indictment of the president or his Cabinet, as did Jessie and Nelly in similar circumstances. Throughout, Ellen provided Sherman with judicious counsel from all members of her family, sent him reams of loving reassurance, and at times, tried to distract him from his troubles with lighthearted stories and endless questions. Ellen also personally and intelligently corresponded with an array of formidable men, including newspaper editors, General Halleck, and President Lincoln. Ellen's fierce, loving concentration on salvaging Sherman's future and her close collaboration with her father ensured that efforts of the Sherman-Ewing clan would persist until all were satisfied with Sherman's situation.

Grant never benefited from supportive collaboration between his wife and his father-in-law, nor was there even the barest possibility that he could. From the start, "Colonel" Dent had little regard for the man who ardently loved his favorite daughter and whom she loved so much in return. Indeed, Dent's (and the rest of her family's) pampering of Julia as a child was likely an important factor in her unintentional but persistent injury to Grant. Her careless failure to write faithfully to him was likely as much a result of her lack of self-discipline as it was of her deformed eye that spawned it. Grant's need for reassurance of Julia's love in the communication vacuum she created by her failure to write led to Julia's presence at City Point and thence to some of the most consequential events of Lincoln's final days. In the last year of the war, when Grant assisted Dent financially and managerially, and even later—when the old man became a fixture in the White House, entertaining, sleeping, and eating under Grant's roof—Dent derived the status and attention he always craved through the man whom he once vowed would never have a place at his table. It does not appear that Julia's delicate balancing act between her husband and her father ever endangered her relationship with either man (as did Jessie's), but had her father more respect for her choice of husband or more regard for the truly admirable man she married, Dent would have made his beloved daughter's life far easier than it was.

There was one great favor that Dent did for Grant, though the "Colonel" certainly did it unintentionally. Dent placed Grant in situations where the young man had the opportunity to learn firsthand about slaves and freedmen. Grant's responses to those situations helped to mold him; they also reveal much about him. From Dent, Grant acquired a slave, whom Grant later freed at a time when money from a sale instead would have netted him sorely needed cash. The slaves that Dent had given Julia as a child were an essential part of her robust support system, and Grant had solemnly pledged Dent he would sustain Julia's lifestyle at all costs. As a result, Grant lived with slaves, who were, at the very least, an embarrassment to him when he returned to the army. At worst, they provided an opening for his political and military detractors, as when the slave Jule traveled with Julia to be with Grant in camp. Only Lincoln's empathetic forbearance prevented the harm that others sought to do to Grant. Grant tolerated his wife's slaves, over whom he had no legal control, but it does not appear he made any effort to recover Jule when she escaped in 1864.

Dent's final favor to Grant in this regard was the land that Dent had given Julia as a wedding present, where Grant hewed Hardscrabble out of the forest with his own hands. There, Grant worked in the fields alongside black men and, to Dent's disgust, paid them more than the going rate for black laborers. In those fields, especially, Grant could take honest measure of them—their capabilities and their humanity. From that experience, Grant learned that black men would work without a lash and deduced they would fight, too. Once Lincoln made the decision to arm black soldiers, Grant had less reluctance than many generals to place them in combat units. The lessons that Dent's Southern lifestyle inadvertently imparted to Grant served Lincoln and the nation well during the Civil War.

There are other lessons to be learned from this story, too. Each of the wives is emblematic of the larger picture of women in the United States during the era of the Civil War. Jessie personifies conflicts within society that were rising along with the rising political aspirations of women. Jessie lived and breathed politics all of her life. She sought a noble end—the end of slavery—through her political machinations, but she also loved political intrigue (secret ciphers!) and the hurly-burly of election campaigning. She was a modern woman in nearly every way, except in her relationship with John Charles Frémont. Her marriage was marked by her desire for Frémont's success but also by an almost ruthless tendency to hijack tactical command of his career. Even so, she was extraordinarily deferential to his desires and his reputation. Just as she would not allow the possibility that her husband could be blamed for a McClellan presidency, she would not allow Frémont the embarrassment—in Victorian society—of having his wife publicly support women's suffrage.

In fact, three of the generals' wives publicly opposed female suffrage. Jessie believed women could manage men just as well without it, as she told Cady Stanton. Ellen enthusiastically led the Washington, D.C., campaign against suffrage, in line with the Catholic Church's view that giving women the vote would destroy the divinely established male hierarchy in marriage. Julia Grant also stayed within the bounds of Victorian society and refused to lend her name to the suffragette cause, even (or perhaps, especially) when her name carried the weight of her husband's White House. Of all of the wives, though, Jessie must have been the most torn between society's norms and her own aspirations. Jessie had been trained by her mother to be a good wife and by her father to be a savvy politician. In nineteenth-century America, where those roles were still considered by mainstream society to be mutually exclusive, that was a recipe for stress and frustration. Jessie is one of the most famous examples of that internal contradiction. Her meeting with Lincoln encapsulated that societal dilemma, and Jessie remains an icon of the American woman in society in that era.[1]

As the growing suffragette movement demonstrated, the years during and after the Civil War saw profound changes in women's roles in society. Even one of the "safest" places for women to expand their interests beyond the home became fraught with pitfalls. The church—the faith of any religion—has long been an approved outlet for women's interests and energies. In the run-up to the Civil War, though, a flood of Irish-Catholic immigrants spilled controversy even into that sanctuary. Catholicism became a focus of social and political prejudice; fierce local and national arguments over jobs and education and patriotism ignited nearly as much passionate debate as those over secession and slavery. The era's religious-political-economic-social ferment is writ large in the life of Ellen Ewing Sherman, as is the ability of gifted women to make signal contributions to their faith and their country without choosing between them.

Julia Grant's experience illustrates how the Civil War transformed the whole of American society and serves as a reminder that Confederate women were not the only ones to lose their way of life in the conflict. As disparate as the North and South might have appeared in 1860, the two halves of the country were, in fact, woven together by stout ties of family, history, and memory. Split asunder in 1861, the nation faced the daunting challenge of pulling itself together four years later. Americans were forced to decide how they would incorporate into their lives the changes wrought by the war. They could either dwell upon what they lost, or—like Julia—they could embrace what survived.

Nelly McClellan represents the cipher that so many women of the Victorian era remain to this day. All of these women bring to mind Henry Adams's observation on nineteenth-century women, but none more so than Nelly: "The woman who is known only through a man is known wrong, and excepting one or two like Mme. de Sévigné, no woman has pictured herself. The American woman of the nineteenth century will live only as the man saw her. . . ." Each of these general's wives "pictured herself" through her letters, memoirs, or other writings, but because so few of Nelly's wartime letters and none of her wartime diaries survived, she has become virtually invisible to the very historians who owe her an incalculable debt for saving McClellan's letters. Just a few of her letters were saved, and no biography of her exists; she is known "only as the man saw her." Even so, echoes of her letters in those from "the man" are tantalizing. In them, she appears an obedient Victorian woman, fully in accord with every thought of her husband. There are, nevertheless, intimations that she was also an independent, even somewhat detached, wife.[2]

Her postwar diaries tell us a bit more about her travels and her health, but not of her thoughts—except for one brief entry five years after the end of the

Civil War. It had to do with that issue so much on the minds of smart, independent women in the late 1800s—whether women should be allowed to vote. In contrast to what we know about the other wives' public opposition to women's suffrage, there is no record of Nelly's stand on the subject, even though her husband pursued national and state political offices and the question must have been put to her at some point. Yet, there is a hint about how she felt, or rather—as is the case so often in Nelly's writing—there is a statement that can be interpreted in more than one way. In the summer of 1870, the McClellans were enjoying one of the marvels of the nineteenth century; they were rocketing westward across the United States at speeds up to thirty-five miles per hour on the brand-new Transcontinental Railroad. In her small, elegant diary Nelly wrote on August 14: "Cheyenne, Wyoming. Where the women vote!" That exclamation might be envy or it might be scorn. I like to think that quiet, outwardly obedient, but still secretly feisty Nelly wanted to vote.[3]

The reader of Civil War history cannot help but be struck by the symmetry of the story of these two sets of U.S. Army generals. The first set, John Charles Frémont and George Brinton McClellan, were like meteors. They blazed at first sight, raced high in the public's eye, left chaos in their wake, then faded from view. The second set, William Tecumseh Sherman and Ulysses S. Grant, were like stars. In the fading light of dusk they were only dimly perceived, but their brilliance emerged as night fell. In the darkest hours, they shone brightly enough to light a path home, and they endured.

There is symmetry, too, in the wives' stories. Jessie Benton Frémont and Mary Ellen McClellan both displayed the most conventional nineteenth-century wifely attribute—uncritical, worshipful endorsement of their husbands' every instinct. But their support for the slender reeds that were their husbands proved disastrous to the generals and nearly so to the nation. They provided emotional strength that enabled their husbands to persist in their incompetence and delusion and to reject the advice and friendship of their commander in chief, whom both wives equally disdained. In the end, Jessie and Nelly contributed most to the Union war effort by accelerating their husbands' removal from active command.

Ellen Ewing Sherman and Julia Dent Grant were no less smart or socially polished than Jessie and Nelly. Their husbands loved them, and they loved them in return, but Ellen and Julia did not hesitate to take issue with the generals when they believed their actions to be wrong or their judgments ill advised. Their belief in their husbands' character and potential was ardent, but it was not unbounded. They intelligently supported their husbands' best instincts—

including trust in and admiration for Lincoln—and rebuffed their worst. In military terms, Ellen and Julia were their husbands' centers of gravity, the source of the strength that Sherman and Grant used to win the Civil War.

Acknowledgments

In 2008, I graduated from The George Washington University with a master's degree in history but no idea how to begin my second career as a historian. My first thought was to write a journal article about Civil War generals' wives who sought Lincoln's help for their husbands' careers. Seeking advice, I talked with two men whose military history expertise and judgment I respect. Both thought the topic compelling, but each independently told me there was a book, not just an article, in it. I've almost forgiven Ron Spector and Jim Morton for launching me into this lengthy project, even as I now thank them. My longtime friend, Matthild Schneider Morton, and one of my newest friends, Dianne Spector, contributed, too, generously reviewing drafts of the manuscript along the way, always improving it. I have so many people to thank but none to blame for any errors. Those are all mine.

My earliest readers, Evan Laney and Michael Keeling Jr., provided consistent insight and encouragement, as have my talented writing friends—Mary Ann Foxley, Minoa Uffelman, Ginger Pape, Delphine Lowe, Victoria Ross, Kathleen Murphy, Susan Bischoff, and Erica Martin. Alice Gorman's advice and support have helped beyond measure. Along the way, I was fortunate to encounter eminent historians who were generous with their time and insights, even when they disagreed with my conclusions. They include Graham Cosmas, Tom Long and his wife Susan, Tyler Anbinder, Andrew Zimmerman, Adele Alexander, Catherine Clinton, Carol Reardon, Carol Berkin, Brooks Simpson, Gary Gallagher, Stephen W. Sears, Margaret Vining, and John Shy. Bruce Vandervort and his late wife Wendy were among the first to praise my scholarship, albeit on another topic. I'll never forget their generosity of spirit to a brand-new scholar.

Like so many historians, I found researching the book to be the most enjoyable part of the project. The Library of Congress is the true treasure chest of our nation, and its experts are treasures, too. Michelle Krowl, Civil War and

Reconstruction specialist in the Manuscript Division, has been a consistent source of information, good advice, and encouragement over many years. I am in her debt. Manuscript Reference Librarian Bruce Kirby assisted me in my countless requests for papers and pointed me toward some of the Library's true Civil War gems. The Ulysses S. Grant Presidential Library's collection of the Papers of Ulysses S. Grant is pure gold, as are the people who care for them and share them with the world. Meg Henderson has been a pleasure to work with in her dual capacity at the Library and with the Ulysses S. Grant Association.

John Marszalek, president of the Library and editor of the Grant Papers, first came to my attention with his biography of Sherman, and has continued to astound me with the depth and breadth of his scholarship—and his generosity. When I brashly asked if he and his wife Jeanne would read my manuscript, they agreed. It was only when I received their helpful, comprehensive, and detailed notes that I realized what an unreasonable request I had made— and how generous they were to say yes. It is not an overstatement to say that without their willingness to help an aspiring scholar, this book would not have found a publisher. The Sherman House Museum in Lancaster, Ohio, part of the Fairfield Heritage Association, should be required visiting for every Civil War scholar. During my all-too-brief stay, Laura and Frank Bullock conveyed to me the importance of Lancaster in Ellen's and Cump's lives in ways I would never have otherwise appreciated. Senior Librarian Toni Vanover and Library Associate Mary Knight Vickers of the Johann Fust Community Library in Boca Grande, Florida, were both invaluable in securing books I needed. And Riche Sorenson at the Smithsonian Institution helped me through the process of securing permission to use the image of Ellen Sherman by G. P. A. Healy that Cump felt most perfectly represented her. Marilyn Van Winkle of the Autry Museum of the American West and Lily Birkhimer at the Ohio History Connection provided key illustrations, and my great friend Deanna Horton found the lovely engraving of Nelly's "secession colors" dress.

The University of Notre Dame Archives holds the vast collection of The William T. Sherman Family Papers and has digitized much of it. I was grateful that the online resources of the Archives enabled me to research the collection wherever I happened to be. I was also pleased to spend a week in the Archives, where archivists Kevin Cawley, Joseph Smith, and Charles Lamb patiently answered my many questions and guided me toward valuable information. My week at Notre Dame was made possible by a travel grant from the Cushwa Center for the Study of American Catholicism, for which I am grateful. Dr. Kathleen Sprows Cummings, director of the Center, also helped immensely in my efforts to understand the many dimensions of Ellen Sherman's Catholic faith. I found Dr. Cummings through my longtime friend Mimi Feller. Mimi is part of a book club that has been an important part of my life for the past twenty-five years. Along with Chris Vaughn, Gail Wilkins, Maxine Champion, Jane Nuland, and Mary Howell, Matthild and Mimi and I have absorbed and dissected all manner of novels and nonfiction. I remember clearly the evening in September 2010 when I screwed up my courage to tell the group I was "writing a book." They will be my most valued critics.

In 2012, the Friends of Boca Grande Community Center held its first week-long "Civil War Reflections." At the suggestion of Barbara Edgerton, conference chairman Roger Lewis invited me to be a part of it. That first opportunity to talk about my research to my neighbors reenergized me at a time when my spirits were flagging. One of those neighbors, John Cleghorn, also generously reviewed this work. The Sarasota Civil War Symposium has brought experts in the field together every January for more than twenty years. In 2014, its founder, Bob Maher of the Civil War Education Association, invited me to speak on the subject of this book. That was quite a leap of faith, considering the caliber of historians Bob entices to Sarasota, and I appreciate his invitation to this day. Among those regulars is another well-known Civil War historian whom I asked to read my manuscript. Richard McMurry made many invaluable suggestions—including altering the course of the Tennessee River to reflect reality—and I am indebted to him. Joseph Reinhart and Thomas Tate, whom I met in Sarasota, have been of great help. I am honored to serve on the Board of Directors of President Lincoln's Cottage at the Soldiers' Home, and there, I've had the great fortune to be inspired by renowned Civil War scholars, including Edna Greene Medford, Douglas Wilson, Matthew Pinsker, and Harold Holzer, as well as its knowledgeable director, Erin Carlson Mast. Visiting the Cottage always sparked creative thought by carrying me back in time to the world my characters inhabited 150 years ago.

In the midst of this project, Clay Risen of the *New York Times* published a piece I wrote about Julia Grant for his celebrated *Disunion* series, and in 2014 the renowned independent bookstore Politics and Prose published my first poem—about the Civil War—in its *District Lines* anthology. I thank them both. My appreciation also goes to editor Bruce Vandervort for publishing an article and inviting me to review several books for the distinguished *Journal of Military History*. While trying to land the whale of the book I was writing, it meant so much to have these expressions of confidence from such prestigious publications.

In order to better understand the physical and mental health of the wives and their husbands, I turned gratefully to several medical experts, including doctors Susan R. Barry, Barbara Morris, Karen Myers, and Mindy Schwartz. And at an early stage in my research and reflection on why Nelly Marcy finally agreed to marry George McClellan, Colleen Konheim offered a range of thoughtful insights to guide my thinking. Cartographer Scott Zillmer of Terra Carta was a pleasure to work with again. His creation of the Julia Grant map from my map points and our telephone discussions pushed the envelope in his field and in mine. Our maps in this book tell a new story of the Civil War. My friend Mary Scanlon was a constant inspiration in this tale of military wives. During the course of this project, her husband Dennis deployed twice to Afghanistan. Lt. Col. Casey Doss, who returned from Afghanistan in 2014, and his wife Martha were similarly inspirational as were three of my most well-read friends, Mac Carey, Bud Konheim, and the late Landon Rowland. And through all these years, Karol Scott, Heather Gradison, Gail Bell, Geraldine Conrad, and Sylvia Pinto were helpful and supportive in more ways than I can possibly acknowledge. Writing is solitary and sedentary work, and I am also grateful to Bisbee, my ageless canine companion, who faithfully walks me every day.

Where the rubber meets the road in writing is in publishing, and my debts in this regard are huge. First in line is Pete Veru, my fellow graduate history colleague at The George Washington University. He encouraged me and introduced me to his friend, Cheryl Pientka, director of foreign and subsidiary rights and agent at Jill Grinberg Literary Management LLC. I am indebted to her for agreeing to take me on as a client when this project was in its earliest stages—little more than an idea by an unpublished author in a vast field of books by giants. Cheryl navigated the twists and turns of this multi-year adventure, never losing her enthusiasm and providing encouragement and expertise throughout. She moved the project along with unfailing grace and determination. I cannot thank her enough. Cheryl also introduced me to Rosemary Ahern. Every author needs a good editor, and in Rosemary I found a great one, who grasped what I was trying to accomplish and helped me achieve it. Working with her was truly an exhilarating experience. In the end, though, this book would not have happened without the support of Joyce Harrison, acquiring editor for the Kent State University Press. From my first discussion with her at the Society of Civil War Historians in Lexington, Kentucky, Joyce grasped how this book is different from all others and encouraged me to pursue the wives' stories. She maneuvered the manuscript through the readers' reviews and my multiple revisions with patience and optimism. Joyce and her hardworking, creative coworkers, including Mary Young, Christine Brooks, and Susan Cash, have been a pleasure to work with. Valerie Ahwee made innumerable, valuable contributions through her careful copyediting.

This book is the product of eight years of research and writing—and sixty-five years of living. No doubt the fact that I was born into a military family had more than a little to do with my interest in how military wives affect their husbands' careers. My father was a U.S. Navy Hospital Corpsman, who retired a master chief. As a result, my mother had what is called "the toughest job in the Navy"—a Navy wife. Richard and Betty Shy will always be an inspiration to me. My sisters Linda Moats and Melody Bobisuthi and my brother Richard Shy share the close bonds of a nomadic military family, and I am fortunate to have had their support all my life.

My greatest appreciation goes to Lindsay, my husband of more than thirty years. He has come to know Jessie, Nelly, Ellen, and Julia nearly as well as I do. They were our constant dinner companions for eight years and would also appear at odd moments—on a drive in Montana or during a dive in the Galapagos—when something I saw or heard sparked a random thought. He read the manuscript many, many times as it evolved and always made valuable suggestions. Most of all, Lindsay believed in me. He made it possible for me to write this book. I am grateful to have this opportunity to thank him in these pages.

Notes

Introduction

1. Readers who wish to know more about women's lives during this era have many sources they can tap. Literature on the roles of men and women in nineteenth-century America and how the Civil War changed them is substantial: Silber, *Gender and the Sectional Contest* and Clinton and Silber, eds., *Battle Scars*. See, especially, the introduction by Silber, "Colliding and Collaborating: Gender and Civil War Scholarship," 3-18. Varina Davis's quote is from Cashin, *First Lady of the Confederacy, 99*.

2. Insight into Southern women in this era continues to expand and evolve. Two excellent studies are by Faust, *Mothers of Invention,* and Varon, *We Mean to Be Counted.* For more on differences and similarities across the North-South cultural divide in this era, see Howe, "American Victorianism as a Culture," 519. For more about Northern women, the standard is Silber, *Daughters of the Union,* esp. 70-71, 97-99. See also Varon, "Gender History and Origins of the Civil War," 19-23. Other works on the experience of Northern women in the war include the thoughtful treatment of Dr. Mary Walker in "Mary Walker, Mary Surratt, and Some Thoughts on Gender in the Civil War," in Clinton and Silber, *Battle Scars,* 104-19; and Giesberg, *Army at Home,* which focuses on working-class women and the challenges they faced during the war. A fascinating study of women before, during, and after a battle in their town can be found in Creighton, *The Colors of Courage.*

3. For a discussion of the dominance of print culture in Victorian America, see Howe, "American Victorianism," 521. Washington's micromanagement of the war is examined by Tap, "Amateurs at War," 1-18. Regarding separate spheres, see, for example, Bleser and Gordon, eds., *Intimate Strategies of the Civil War,* xi; Howe, "American Victorianism"; and Stanton, Anthony et al., *History of Woman Suffrage, 1876-1885.* Erosion of the spheres is discussed in Silber, *Gender,* 35. Wives' petitions to Lincoln began even before he took office, when wives of several officers in Fort Sumter left the fort in late January, then proceeded to Washington to "funnel information to" President James Buchanan and president-elect Abraham Lincoln. Goodheart, "Women and Children First."

4. Williams, *Lincoln & His Generals,* 11.

5. *Harper's Weekly,* Feb. 23, 1861, 123.

6. Denton, *Passion and Principle,* 248.

7. Wilson and Clair, *They Also Served,* 93.

8. Among the best are Marszalek, *Sherman;* Simpson, *Grant;* Bleser and Gordon, *Intimate Strategies;* and Berkin, *Civil War Wives.* For Frémont, see also Denton, *Passion.*

An earlier work that brings a Confederate general's wife to the foreground is Gordon, *General George E. Pickett in Life and Legend*.

9. It is often said that Lincoln is second only to Jesus in the number of biographies. Among the classic and more recent Lincoln biographies are Donald, *Lincoln;* Burlingame, *Lincoln: A Life;* and Goodwin, *Team of Rivals*. Lincoln biographical information contained herein is largely drawn from those sources.

10. Quoted in Brooks, *Lincoln Observed,* 79–88.

11. Wilson, *Under the Old Flag,* 349.

12. Adams, *The Education of Henry Adams,* 131. Mrs. Speed gave Lincoln an Oxford Bible, which he kept through his life; Mrs. Browning was a favorite correspondent and the recipient of Lincoln's famous April Fools' Day letter describing his courtship of Mary Owens in thinly disguised farce.

13. See examples in Ross, *Proud Kate,* and Keckley, *Behind the Scenes*.

14. But even within the Cabinet officers' families, not all women were tolerated (for example, Secretary Chase's beautiful daughter Kate was persona non grata to Mary), nor all military officers' wives—as will be discussed, Julia Grant witnessed one of Mary's most famous jealous rages, aimed at the wife of Gen. Edward O. C. Ord. Behn, "Mr. Lincoln and Friends," http://www.mrlincolnandfriends.org/inside.asp?pageID=12&subjectID=11.

15. Notable biographies of the men and women are listed in notes at the beginning of each part. The quote is from Adams, *Education of Henry Adams,* 264.

16. Statistic from Wagner, Gallagher, and Finkelman, eds., *Civil War Desk Reference,* 860.

1. "the place a son would have had"

1. This chapter's quotes and details of Jessie's California trip are from J. B. Frémont, *A Year of American Travel,* 46. Passenger manifest for SS *Crescent City,* http://www.sfgenealogy.com/californiabound/cb077.htm.

2. One of the hallmark books in the growing field of Civil War masculinity studies begins with the story of a Southern man who undertook Jessie's same journey at almost the very same time, introducing the term "éclat-based culture," which the author uses throughout the book to describe the "flamboyant" combination of ambition, determination, romanticism, and ardor that he said composed Southern masculinity in that era. That makes Jessie's (and later Ellen Sherman's) decision to undertake that round-trip more than once truly remarkable. Berry, *All That Makes a Man*.

3. Nevins, *Pathmarker*. First published in 1939, and based on Nevins's earlier two-volume biography of Frémont, this remains the most comprehensive biography of the man, whom, you will notice, Nevins did not call "Pathfinder." Much of the information about Frémont contained herein is taken from that source. Other sources include Williams, *Lincoln & His Generals;* Chaffin, *Pathfinder;* Denton, *Passion;* and Frémont and Frémont, *Memoirs of My Life,* which Jessie had a hand in crafting.

4. "A History of U.S. Topographical Engineers, 1818–1863," http://www.topogs.org/History2.htm.

5. See Roosevelt Jr., *Thomas Hart Benton*.

6. Nevins, *Pathmarker,* 83.

7. J. B. Frémont, *Year of American Travel,* 44. Stone, *Immortal Wife,* 22.

8. Sides, *Blood and Thunder,* 48. Herr and Spence, eds., *Letters,* 4.

9. Among the many books about Jessie are, notably, Phillips, *Jessie Benton Frémont;* Denton, *Passion;* and Herr, *Jessie Benton Frémont.* Most biographical details contained herein are taken from those works and Herr and Spence, eds., *Letters.* The quote is from the title of Denton's book.

10. Phillips, *Jessie Benton Frémont,* 16. JBF to Lydia Maria Child, in Herr and Spence, eds., *Letters,* 122.

11. Roosevelt Jr., *Thomas Hart Benton,* 364. J. B. Frémont, *Year of American Travel,* 43.

12. Phillips, *Jessie Benton Frémont,* 50, 51.

13. Frémont and Frémont, *Memoirs of My Life,* 66, 67.

2. *"Be sure you're right and then go ahead"*

1. Quoted in "Jessie Benton Frémont in Her Girlhood Days," *Press and Horticulturist,* 3.

2. Phillips, *Jessie Benton Frémont,* 55-58. According to more than one account, the Bentons had learned about the elopement before John and Jessie told them.

3. *Washington Globe,* Nov. 27, 1841. The quote is from Galusha Grow in "Jessie Benton Frémont in Her Girlhood Days." Phillips, *Jessie Benton Frémont,* 65. Some accounts say she was fifteen when she married; Jessie may have spread that tale in later years to make her seem younger: *New York Times,* Dec. 29, 1902, from Los Angeles, Dec. 28: "Gen. Frémont's Widow Dead—Had Been an Invalid for Two and a Half Years—Eloped with Lieut. Frémont at the Age of Fifteen."

4. Herr and Spence, eds., *Letters,* 7, 8. Nevins, *Pathmarker,* 118-20.

5. Nevins, *Pathmarker,* 86-88.

6. Ibid., 94-96. See Sides, *Blood and Thunder,* which offers a remarkable portrait of Carson, including his relationship with Frémont, whom Carson credited with saving his life on one of the expeditions.

7. Nevins, *Pathmarker,* 124. Longfellow and Longfellow, eds., *Life of Henry Wadsworth Longfellow,* 65, 66.

8. Nevins, *Pathmarker,* 127-29.

9. Ibid., 130.

10. Herr, *Jessie Benton Frémont,* 89-91 (emphasis in the original).

11. Ibid., 90-91.

12. Ibid., 91.

13. Laas, ed., *Wartime Washington,* provides an excellent biography of Francis Preston Blair Sr. in the introduction to his daughter's letters.

14. J. C. Frémont, "The Conquest of California," *Century Magazine,* 920.

15. An excellent description of what is most often called the "Bear Flag Revolt" can be found in Nevins's chapter titled "The Bear Flag Outbreak," in *Pathmarker,* 253-86. Quoted in Nevins, *Pathmarker,* 301. JBF to JCF, June 16, 1846.

16. An excellent account can be found in Nevins, *Pathmarker,* 305-26.

17. Phillips, *Jessie Benton Frémont,* 111. It is unclear precisely when Jessie read the newspaper report. Phillips says it was in mid-March; Nevins places the meeting with President Buchanan in June, per President Polk's diary entry (see note 18 below).

18. Carson quoted in Phillips, *Jessie Benton Frémont,* 116. Carson's autobiography makes no reference to Jessie's role or her presence in the meeting with President Polk. Carson, *Kit Carson's Autobiography,* 119-20. Polk diary entry of June 7, 1847, quoted in Nevins, *Pathmarker,* 328.

19. Herr and Spence, eds., *Letters,* 36.

20. Borneman, *Polk,* 278-85. Polk had so admired Senator Benton that in 1846, he promoted legislation to create the rank of lieutenant general in order to bestow it upon Old Bullion, but that did not happen. Less than a year later, Polk wrote in his diary: "I meet Colonel Benton almost every Sabbath at Church, he never speaks to me as he was in the habit of doing before the trial of Colonel Frémont" (285).

21. Nevins, *Pathmarker,* 343.

22. Ibid., 343-46.

23. Phillips, *Jessie Benton Frémont,* 130.

3. *"Frémont and Our Jessie"*

1. Nevins, *Pathmarker,* 347-71.

2. Ibid., 393.

3. J. B. Frémont, *Year of American Travel,* 143-46.

4. Sherman, *Memoirs,* 114. Roosevelt Jr., *Thomas Hart Benton.* Kennedy, *Profiles in Courage.*

5. Quote from J. B. Frémont, *Year of American Travel,* 151. Nevins, *Pathmarker,* 388-90.

6. Nevins, *Pathmarker,* 391.

7. Phillips, *Jessie Benton Frémont,* 175.

8. Nevins, *Pathmarker,* 404-7.

9. Ibid., 409.

10. Infant mortality statistics, http://eh.net/encyclopedia/article/haines.demography. Phillips, *Jessie Benton Frémont,* 191.

11. Nevins, *Pathmarker,* 407-10.

12. Nevins, *Ordeal of the Union,* 156.

13. Phillips, *Jessie Benton Frémont,* 193.

14. Quoted in Nevins, *Pathmarker,* 423.

15. An excellent, brief summary of the creation of the Republican Party and of the 1856 election can be found in Herr and Spence, eds., *Letters,* 64-69.

16. Ibid., 65, 66.

17. Ibid.

18. Ibid., 67.

19. Quoted in Herr, *Jessie Benton Frémont,* 261.

20. JBF to Elizabeth Blair Lee (EBL), Apr. 18, 1856, in Herr and Spence, eds., *Letters,* 98. The manner in which the Republican Party used Jessie's image and talents for its purposes in the 1856 election is examined in detail, with emphasis on the larger questions of gender politics, in Pierson, *Free Hearts and Free Homes.*

21. Herr and Spence, eds., *Letters,* 68.

22. JBF to EBL, Apr. 18, 1856. Ibid., 98. *New York Tribune,* Aug. 18, 1856.

23. Nevins, *Pathmarker,* 455.

24. Phillips, *Jessie Benton Frémont,* 213. Citing JBF to JCF, Sept. 23, 1857, in Herr and Spence, eds., *Letters,* 171.

25. Quoted in Phillips, *Jessie Benton Frémont,* 261.

26. Herr and Spence, eds., *Letters,* 233n1. Another friend disputed the charge.

27. Nevins, *Pathmarker,* 475.

28. JBF to William Armstrong, June 10, 1861. Herr and Spence, eds., *Letters,* 240.

4. "quite a female politician"

1. According to historian T. Harry Williams, Lincoln's award of carte blanche referred to Frémont's authority to organize his department, not to the general's overall military authority. Williams, *Lincoln & His Generals,* 35.

2. Nevins considered the rent "moderate." *Pathmarker,* 494n22. Grant's quote is from Young, *Around the World with General Grant,* 264. *New York Times,* Sept. 9, 1861.

3. Quoted in Nevins, *Pathmarker,* 481.

4. Williams, *Lincoln & His Generals,* 36. Herr and Spence, eds., *Letters,* 245.

5. Nevins, *Pathmarker,* 501, 502.

6. Quote in JBF to Lydia Maria Child, in Herr and Spence, eds., *Letters,* 122.

7. Nicolay and Hay, *Abraham Lincoln,* IV:416, 417-18. Both quotes are from Burlingame, *Lincoln,* I:202.

8. Lincoln explained his reasoning about Frémont's emancipation order in a letter to a close friend less than two weeks after he had revoked it: Abraham Lincoln to Orville H. Browning, Sept. 22, 1861. Lincoln, *The Abraham Lincoln Papers,* Library of Congress, Series I.

9. Lester, *Charles Sumner,* 360 (emphasis in the original).

10. Abraham Lincoln to JCF, Sept. 2, 1861. Nicolay and Hay, *Abraham Lincoln,* IV:418. Hay, *Inside Lincoln's White House,* 24.

11. Nevins, *Pathmarker,* 515.

12. JBF to EBL, July 17, 1861. Herr and Spence, eds., *Letters,* 255.

13. Ibid., 264-67. According to Herr and Spence, who document the three written versions of the meeting, none of Jessie's written accounts were contemporaneous, or even earlier than Lincoln's recollection, recorded by Hay in his diary in 1863. A recent work about the Frémonts says that Jessie wrote a contemporaneous account (Denton, *Passion and Principle,* 420n320). Frémont's biographer, Allen Nevins, cites an "undated" written account by Jessie of the meeting.

14. Nicolay and Hay, *Abraham Lincoln,* 414-15.

15. Herr and Spence, eds., *Letters,* 264.

16. Ibid., 265. Her version is contained in an excerpt from her unpublished memoir, "Great Events," which is reprinted in Herr and Spence, eds., *Letters,* 264-67.

17. http://www.thelincolnlog.org; see entries for June–Nov. 1856.

18. Quoted in Brooks, *Lincoln Observed,* 84-86.

19. Phillips, *Jessie Benton Frémont,* 249. Herr and Spence, eds., *Letters,* 264-68.

20. Secretary of War Simon Cameron (Dec. 1861) and Gen. David Hunter (May 1862) each distributed emancipation proclamations of sorts without prior consultation with the president, though, given their intimate involvement in the Frémont proclamation revocation, they certainly should have known better. When Lincoln ordered the men to withdraw their unauthorized proclamations, they did so with as little grace as had Frémont.

21. Quoted in Herr and Spence, eds., *Letters,* xix. JBF to E. C. Stanton, Apr. 22, 1866. Ibid., 396. Lincoln had courageously supported legislation to give women the vote in his unsuccessful reelection campaign for the Illinois House of Representatives in 1836. Burlingame, *Lincoln,* 1:136.

22. Herr and Spence, eds., *Letters,* xvii.

23. Miers and Powell, eds., *Lincoln Day by Day,* 65. For the weather statistics, http://www.accuweather.com/en/us/washington-dc/20006/september-weather/327659, www.currentresults.com/Weather/US/humidity-city-september.php.

24. JBF to Thomas Starr King, Dec. 29, 1861, and Oct. 16, 1863. Herr and Spence, eds., *Letters,* 304, 356.

25. JBF to Charles Wentworth Upham, May 31, 1856. Upham had prepared a sort of official campaign biography of presidential candidate Frémont and had the temerity to write of Jessie: "All that it would be proper to say of her in this work, is all that could be said of any woman,—she is worthy of her origin and of her lot." Ibid., 102, 103n1 and 4.

26. Grinnell and Parker, *Men & Events,* 174.

27. In the nineteenth century, to "try titles" was a phrase that meant a challenge—legal or physical—to another's position or authority. See Brown, "Pleasant Valley: A History of Elizabethtown," for an account of a wrestling match "to try titles." Nevins, *Pathmarker,* 516.

28. The Cowle story is in Herr and Spence, eds., *Letters,* 266-67, citing Jessie's still unpublished memoir, "Great Events," 269-72. Lincoln to JBF, in Nicolay and Hay, *Lincoln,* IV:414.

5. *"It is your Lerida"*

1. Herr and Spence, eds., *Letters,* 269. The reference to the *New York Times* article argues for dating the telegram on the 10th, before her meeting with the president.

2. *New York Times,* Sept. 10, 1861.

3. Herr and Spence, eds., *Letters,* 266-68. The editors have deciphered most of the code words. "Lerida" is the site in Spain of Julius Caesar's victory in 49 B.C. over Pompey, his former co-consul turned political rival. "Salem witch" was a phrase meaning "be silent" within the family, and Bronte was the Frémonts' dog. Frederick Billings was their lawyer. The "General Washington" reference remains unclear but may refer to something that Judge Cowles had told her on the way back from the White House, an allusion to Gen. Horatio Gates, who was accused of plotting against Gen. George Washington. Quoting from "Great Events," Cowles said, "Mrs. Frémont, the General has no further part in this war. He will be deprived of all of his part in the war; it is not the President alone, but there is a faction which plans the affairs of the North and they will triumph, and they are against the General. It will be like General Gates, it will be thirty years before he is known and has justice." Gates was ultimately relieved of command and according to some historians never given an opportunity to clear his name.

4. EBL to Samuel Phillips Lee, Sept. 17, 1861, marked "Confidential." Laas, ed., *Wartime Washington,* 79.

5. An investigation was later opened in Congress, which sorted through everything from the fancy uniforms of the cavalry unit named General Frémont's Body Guard to his construction of forts. Even though he was ultimately cleared of charges of personal corruption, Frémont, a poor manager of his own business affairs all of his life, was wholly unsuited to managing the vast Western Department. Frémont's letter reprinted in Joint Committee on the Conduct of the War, *Report of the Joint Committee on the Conduct of the War,* 136. "General Jessie" quote in Nevins, *Pathmarker,* 519.

6. *New York Times,* Oct. 31, 1861.

7. Quoted in Burlingame, *Lincoln,* 2:209.

8. JBF to John Greenleaf Whittier, Oct. 17, 1863. Herr and Spence, eds., *Letters,* 357.

9. Quoted in Phillips, *Jessie Benton Frémont,* 252.

10. Quoted in Nevins, *Pathfinder,* 551.

11. This ruse demonstrated Frémont's supreme emphasis on isolation and his staff's recognition of it. Declining to interrupt the general even for valuable enemy intelligence,

his staff forced the "farmer" to wait more than six hours before finally showing him into Frémont's tent. Williams, *Lincoln & His Generals,* 40.

12. The quote "irreparable harm" is from Nevins, *Pathmarker,* 519.

13. Ibid., 553.

14. Ibid.

6. *"There is a time to do and a time to stand aside"*

1. Details of John's western Virginia assignment and Jessie's role there are drawn from Herr, *Jessie Benton Frémont,* 358–62, and Nevins, *Pathmarker,* 553–55.

2. Nevins, *Pathmarker,* 554–55.

3. Valley campaign description in ibid., 556. JBG quoted in Herr, *Jessie Benton Frémont,* 361–62.

4. JBF to George Julian, Mar. 3, 1863. Herr and Spence, eds., *Letters,* 349. Quoted in Herr, *Jessie Benton Frémont,* 366.

5. Herr and Spence, eds., *Letters,* 244, 370.

6. Waugh, *Reelecting Lincoln,* is the source for much of the material in this chapter on the 1864 presidential election and the machinations surrounding Frémont's candidacy and withdrawal.

7. McClellan's letter resigning from the army is dated Nov. 8, 1864, in which he asks that it "take effect today." Lincoln Log, Nov. 8, 1864.

8. Quoted in Waugh, *Reelecting Lincoln,* 264. There was even talk of Grant stepping into the race and Frémont and Lincoln stepping out of it. Nevins, *Pathmarker,* 578.

9. Nevins, *Pathmarker,* 578–80. There is no clear explanation as to why Jessie did not play a more prominent (or even a barely prominent role) in the 1864 presidential election. It is unfortunate that Michael Pierson, who examined the different ways in which the Republican Party used Jessie in 1856 and Mary Lincoln in 1860 to further its aims, did not extend his study to 1864, when those two women (and Nelly McClellan) faced off against each other, at least in a metaphorical sense. He ends his study after the 1860 race. Pierson, *Free Hearts and Free Homes.*

10. Burlingame, *Lincoln,* 2:690–95.

11. Phillips, *Jessie Benton Frémont,* 269.

12. JBF to John Greenleaf Whittier, Nov. 19, 1889. Herr and Spence, eds., *Letters,* 529.

13. See Waugh, *Reelecting Lincoln;* Flood, *Lincoln at the Gates of History;* Burlingame, *Lincoln,* vol. 2; Denton, *Passion;* Nevins, *Pathmarker.*

14. Quoted in Phillips, *Jessie Benton Frémont,* 270.

15. JBF to John Greenleaf Whittier, Aug. 22, 1864. Herr and Spence, eds., *Letters,* 382.

16. After Jessie's death, Lily destroyed almost all of her parents' letters. Herr, *Jessie Benton Frémont,* 449, 450.

17. JBF to Alexander K. McClure, June 25, 1877. JBF to Samuel Pickard, May 28, 1893. Herr and Spence, eds., *Letters,* 433, 549.

18. Herr, *Jessie Benton Frémont,* 387–91, discusses the Memphis, El Paso, & Pacific Railroad bankruptcy. Ibid., 388–90. Herr cites letters from JCF to Ream, calling her "darling" and describing one of his letters to her as "a love letter" but concludes that Frémont's relationship with Ream was an essentially innocent one, one of several she had with "susceptible older men." According to Herr, though, "Jessie was too perceptive a woman not to have sensed his infatuation." Denton, *Passion,* 424n350, also concludes that Frémont's attraction to Ream was intense, but "a romantic entanglement seems unlikely."

19. Herr, *Jessie Benton Frémont,* 402–9.

20. Quoted in Nevins, *Pathmarker,* 569.

7. *"you are fond of attention and gaiety"*

1. "History of the Maryland Flag," Maryland Office of the Secretary of State, http://www.sos.state.md.us/services/FlagHistory.aspx. Mary Ellen Marcy, whose mother's name was also Mary, was sometimes called Ellen, but mostly Nelly or Nell. In order to avoid confusion with Ellen Sherman—named Eleanor, but always called Ellen—Mrs. George Brinton McClellan will be "Nelly" throughout.

2. Letter from Mary Ellen McClellan (MEM) to George Brinton McClellan (GBM), summer of 1862, quoted in Sears, *Young Napoleon,* 236.

3. Wilson and Clair, *They Also Served,* 93. This slender volume contains the only published biography of Nelly (four pages long), which provides some interesting details about her early life, but—like so many other historians' references to her—gets her name wrong. Even worse mistakes regarding Nelly can be found in the many online references to her being born in 1830. Her father did not graduate from West Point until 1832. The other major work that contains biographical information on Nelly is Sears, *Young Napoleon.*

4. Over the years, examinations of George McClellan's life and war fighting have tended to line up very explicitly for him or against him. For many years, the standard biography has been Sears, *Young Napoleon,* but Ethan Rafuse has recently made a strong bid to challenge that excellent work's iconic standing with his critical analysis of the man and method of warfare in *McClellan's War.* Most of the biographical and battle information has been sourced from those two books.

5. Quoted in Sears, *Young Napoleon,* 41.

6. Quoted in Hassler, *A. P. Hill,* 17.

7. Quoted in ibid., 19.

8. RBM to MEM, June 12, 1856. Ibid., 19. The 1856 equivalent of $10,000 was worth approximately $260,000 in 2014, according to a currency inflation calculator (http://www.westegg.com/inflation/infl.cgi), a not insubstantial sum for the time, which gives insight into the dimensions of the Marcys' aspirations for their daughter.

9. GBM to MEM, July 1856, quoted in Sears, *Young Napoleon,* 61.

10. Quoted in Hassler, *A. P. Hill,* 20.

11. A. P. Hill to RBM, May 29, 1857. Ibid., 20, 21.

12. Ibid., 21.

13. Hill's health is discussed in Waugh, *The Class of 1846,* and in Robertson Jr., *A. P. Hill.*

14. GBM to Mary Marcy, July 22, 1865. George Brinton McClellan Papers (hereafter GBM Papers), Library of Congress (hereafter LoC).

15. Waugh, *Class of 1846,* 171.

16. Extracts of letters from GBM to MEM, cited in ibid., 551n44. Sears, *Young Napoleon,* 63.

17. Steckel, "The Age at Leaving Home in the United States, 1850–1860."

18. Ross, *Proud Kate,* 91.

19. The man who graduated first that year was Charles Seaforth Stewart, colonel in the Army Corps of Engineers during the Civil War. An excellent account of that West Point graduating class can be found in Waugh, *The Class of 1846.*

20. "Catharine Beecher," http://150.mansfield.edu/beecher.htm.

21. For this discussion of homeopathy and McClellan's turn to it because of Nelly, I

am indebted to Rafuse, "Typhoid and Tumult." Meade's reference to McClellan's "claimed extraordinary judgment" provides additional insight into how McClellan was perceived by his peers.

22. *Punch* magazine, Jan. 26, 1862.

23. GBM to MEM, July 30, 1861. McClellan, *McClellan's Own Story,* 82–83. Rafuse, *McClellan's War,* 81. Rafuse describes how McClellan's father, who had been raised Presbyterian, changed his religion to Episcopalian upon his marriage; this may have eased McClellan's generally inflexible mind about changing his religion back to Presbyterian to agree with that of his beloved Nelly. GBM to MEM, 1859–60. Sears, *Young Napoleon,* 63 (emphasis in the original).

24. Sears, *Young Napoleon,* 125. GBM to MEM, Aug. 9, 1861. McClellan, *McClellan's Own Story,* 85. GBM to MEM, Oct. 31, 1861. Ibid., 172.

25. Rafuse, "Typhoid and Tumult," 12. Quote from Sears, *Young Napoleon,* 141–44. Interestingly, McClellan's visit with the *Herald* had been arranged by Secretary Stanton (Rafuse, *McClellan's War,* 174). Hay, *Inside Lincoln's White House,* 31, 32.

26. GBM to MEM, May 10, 1862, cited in Sears, ed., *Papers,* 262, 263. GBM to MEM, July 10, 1862. Ibid., 348.

27. Catton, *Mr. Lincoln's Army,* 219. See also Williams, *Lincoln and His Generals,* 26, and McClellan, *McClellan's Own Story,* 56.

28. Glatthaar, *Partners in Command,* 237–41.

29. In a letter to his brother after the Red River expedition, McClellan was upset that Marcy had not given him as much credit as he thought he was due. He vowed he would get back at him sometime, perhaps even have Marcy serve under him.

8. *"Flora McFlimsey"*

1. Sears, *Young Napoleon,* 72.

2. *New York Times,* July 16, 1861.

3. McClellan, *McClellan's Own Story,* 51.

4. MEM to Elizabeth B. McClellan, June 28, 1861. GBM Papers, LoC, 83.

5. GBM to MEM, July 30, 1861. McClellan, *McClellan's Own Story,* 82. GBM to MEM, July 27, 1861. Ibid. GBM to MEM, Aug. 4, 1861. Ibid., 84. Earlier that month, McClellan traveled to Philadelphia to be presented with a magnificent jeweled sword by the city fathers. *New York Times,* Nov. 25, 1861.

6. GBM to Simon Cameron, Oct. 31, 1861. Sears, ed., *Papers,* 115.

7. GBM to Elizabeth B. McClellan, Nov. 9, 1861. Ibid., 129.

8. Description of Georgetown from Stoddard, *Inside the White House,* 157. Sherman, *Memoirs,* 219–20.

9. McClellan mentions both simple fare and lavish meals at Wormley's during this time. Ross, *Proud Kate,* 100. Dana, "Reminiscences," 22.

10. Ellen Ewing Sherman (EES) to William Tecumseh Sherman (WTS), Feb. 24, 1862. William T. Sherman Family Papers Collection (CSHR) 2/92, Univ. of Notre Dame Archives (UNDA).

11. GBM to Elizabeth McClellan, Jan. 23, 1862. GBM Papers, LoC.

12. Stoddard, *Inside the White House,* 175.

13. The description of Kate Chase is from Ross, *Proud Kate,* 99. It takes one to know one; apparently, Kate had given an equally lavish party herself at just about the same time. Meade's and Nelly's quotes are from Sears, *Young Napoleon,* 135.

14. McClellan, *McClellan's Own Story,* 238. Even then, he was not sure he had enough.

15. Julian, *Political Recollections,* 203.

16. Abraham Lincoln, Executive Order—Special War Order No. 1, Jan. 31, 1862, http://www.presidency.ucsb.edu/ws/index.php?pid=69788#axzz1JYf1qliC. *Harper's Weekly,* Mar. 8, 1862, 147.

17. At least one historian has described "Quaker guns" as a routine part of an effort to fool the enemy during a well-planned retreat. Hassler, *McClellan, Shield of the Union.*

18. Mrs. John Sherwood to MEM. GBM Papers, LoC (emphasis in the original).

19. GBM to MEM, telegram, Mar. 12, 1862. Ibid.

20. *New York Times,* Mar. 27 and May 13, 1862.

21. Letter from GBM to Maria E. McClellan, June 9, 1862. Sears, *Papers,* 294.

22. Sears, *To the Gates of Richmond,* 58.

23. GBM to Abraham Lincoln, Apr. 20, 1862. Sears, ed., *Papers,* 244. Interestingly, this letter is not included in *McClellan's Own Story,* although other letters to Lincoln during that time are included.

24. MEM to GBM, July 31, 1862. GBM Papers, LoC.

25. MEM to GBM, Aug. 6, 1862. Ibid.

26. GBM to MEM, Aug. 31, 1862. McClellan, *McClellan's Own Story,* 532.

27. Henry Halleck to GBM, Oct. 1862. Scott, ed., *The War of the Rebellion,* ser. 9, vol. 1, part I, ch. 31 (1887), 72.

28. AL to GBM, Oct. 7, 1862. Quoted in Tarbell, *The Life of Abraham Lincoln,* II:351.

29. *New York Times,* Oct. 16, 1862.

30. GBM to Samuel Barlow, Oct. 17, 1862. Sears, ed., *Papers,* 500.

31. Abraham Lincoln to GBM, Oct. 13, 1862. Quoted in Tarbell, *Abraham Lincoln,* 131. *New York Times,* Oct. 15, 1862.

32. AL to GBM, telegram, Oct. 24, 1862. Scott, ed., *The War of the Rebellion,* ser. 1, vol. 19, ch. 31, 485.

33. GBM to MEM, Nov. 7, 1862. McClellan, *McClellan's Own Story,* 660.

9. *"don't send any politicians out here"*

1. GBM to Samuel Barlow, Jan. 20, 1863. Sears, ed., *Papers,* 535.

2. GBM to MEM, Feb. 28, 1863. Ibid., 541. *New York Times,* Feb. 14, 1915.

3. JBF to Thomas Starr King, Jan. 1864, quoted in Herr and Spence, eds., *Letters,* 360. According to Herr and Spence, the two women—with the rest of their powerful committee—were able to "collect an impressive array of weaponry, flags, and military accoutrements for display during the event, ranging from the original Bowie knife to George Washington's uniform, cane and sword" (360n). GBM to Elizabeth M. McClellan, Mar. 13, 1864. Sears, ed., *Papers,* 571.

4. Waugh, *Reelecting Lincoln,* 342, 343.

5. For example, see GBM to William C. Prime, Sept. 28, 1864, and GBM to Charles Mason, Oct. 3, 1864. Sears, ed., *Papers,* 606, 609. Letter from William O. Bartlett to Abraham Lincoln, Sept. 3, 1864. Abraham Lincoln Papers, Library of Congress, Series I, General Correspondence, 1833–1916 (emphasis in the original).

6. Colonel quoted in Waugh, *Reelecting Lincoln,* 342. McClellan quoted in Sears, ed., *Papers,* 614.

7. Ibid., 617n1.

8. GBM to Elizabeth B. McClellan, Nov. 11, 1864. Ibid., 619.

9. GBM to Samuel Barlow, Nov. 10, 1864. Ibid., 618.

10. "Departure of Gen. McClellan for Europe." *New York Times,* Jan. 26, 1865. GBM to Manton Marble. Sears, ed., *Papers,* 624.

11. GBM to William Adams, May 4, 1865. Ibid., 631.

10. *"you have quite enough else to attend to"*

1. Williams, *McClellan, Sherman and Grant,* 15.

2. Quoted in Sears, *Young Napoleon,* 131-33, 236. Edwin Stanton, who had been unimpressed with Lincoln's intelligence and skill when he tried a case with Lincoln in Illinois in the 1840s, may have been one of the first to call Lincoln a "gorilla." But Stanton's opinion of Lincoln improved markedly as he became better acquainted with the president. McClellan never altered his first unfavorable opinion of Lincoln. GBM to MEM, Nov. 17, 1861. Sears, ed., *Papers,* 135, 136.

3. GBM to MEM, Oct. 31, 1861. Ibid., 113, 114.

4. GBM to MEM, Aug. 4, 1862. Ibid., 385.

5. GBM to MEM, Apr. 30, 1862. McClellan, *McClellan's Own Story,* 316 (emphasis in the original).

6. GBM to MEM, Apr. 23, 1862. Ibid., 318. MEM to GBM, June 22, 1862. GBM Papers, LoC.

7. GBM to MEM, Aug. 30. GBM Papers, LoC.

8. GBM to MEM, Sept. 9, 1862. Sears, *Papers,* 441. GBM to MEM, Sept. 20, 1862. Ibid., 473.

9. For a detailed examination of McClellan's missed opportunities, see Catton, *Lincoln's Army.*

10. Wilson and Clair, *They Also Served.* MEM to GBM, Aug. 31, 1862. GBM Papers, LoC.

11. National Park Service, http://www.nps.gov/nr/travel/national_cemeteries/Death.html.

12. GBM to MEM, July 26, 27, 28, 1862. McClellan, *McClellan's Own Story,* 455-57.

13. GBM to MEM, Aug. 9(?), 1862 (no precise date given, but Prime placed it between letters of Aug. 8 and 10). Ibid., 464, 465.

14. GBM to MEM, Sept. 2, 1862. Ibid., 566.

15. GBM to MEM, July 12, 1862. Ibid., 447. "alter ego," quoted in Sears, *Young Napoleon,* 62.

16. Manning, "Civil War Letters," http://teachinghistory.org/best-practices/examples-of-historical-thinking/25048.

17. Sears, *Young Napoleon,* 236.

18. MEM to GBM, Aug. 3, 1862, and MEM to GBM, Aug. 23, 1862. GBM Papers, LoC.

19. GBM to MEM, Nov. 1, 1861, quoted in Sears, *Young Napoleon,* 125. GBM to MEM, May 8, 1862. McClellan, *McClellan's Own Story,* 396.

20. Ibid., 363 (emphasis in the original).

21. MEM to GBM, Aug. 3, 1862. McClellan Papers, LoC. GBM to MEM, July 13, 1862, quoted in McClellan, *McClellan's Own Story,* 447, 448.

22. McMurry, *Atlanta 1864,* 97.

23. Ibid., 73.

24. GBM to MEM, May 25, 1862. Sears, ed., *Papers,* 275. The 5 P.M. portion of the letter quoted was not included in McClellan, *McClellan's Own Story,* 396; 5 P.M. portion in Sears, ed., *Papers,* 275.

25. GBM to MEM, July 17, 1862. McClellan, *McClellan's Own Story,* 449, 450. GBM to MEM, July 30, 1862. Sears, ed., *Papers,* 367. GBM to MEM, Nov. 7, 1862. McClellan, *McClellan's Own Story,* 660.

11. *"I almost wish . . . they would displace you"*

1. GBM to MEM, July 17, 1862. Sears, ed., *Papers,* 362. GBM to MEM, July 18, 1862. McClellan, *McClellan's Own Story,* 450.

2. GBM to MEM, July 20, 1862. McClellan, *McClellan's Own Story,* 452.

3. GBM to MEM, Aug. 10, 1862. Ibid., 389.

4. MEM to GBM, Aug. 4, 1862. GBM Papers, LoC. MEM to GBM, Aug. 23, 1862. Ibid.

5. Mary Todd Lincoln to Abraham Lincoln, Nov. 2, 1862. Abraham Lincoln Papers, LoC. In *Mrs. Lincoln,* Catherine Clinton reveals that during the 1864 campaign period, Mary Lincoln did not directly advise her husband on political strategy; this kind of indirect advice may have been as close as she came at that time.

6. Aspinwall letter cited in Sears, ed., *Papers,* 366n1. GBM to MEM, July 24, 1862. McClellan, *McClellan's Own Story,* 455.

7. GBM to MEM, Oct. 5, 1862. McClellan, *McClellan's Own Story,* 655.

8. Waugh, *Lincoln and McClellan,* 217, 218.

9. GBM to Abraham Lincoln, Apr. 23, 1862. Sears, ed., *Papers,* 246. GBM to MEM, May 3, 1862. McClellan, *McClellan's Own Story,* 317.

10. GBM to MEM, Apr. 19, 1862. McClellan, *McClellan's Own Story,* 312. Elizabeth Blair Lee to Stephen Lee, Apr. 23, 1862. Laas, ed., *Wartime Washington,* 132.

11. GBM to MEM, July 17, 1862. McClellan, *McClellan's Own Story,* 449.

12. RBM to GBM, July 15, 1862. Sears, ed., *Papers,* 359. GBM to RBM, July 15, 1862. Ibid.

13. Sears, *Young Napoleon,* 149.

14. Ibid., 226.

15. Quoted in Burlingame, *Lincoln,* 2:197. McClellan's habit of sleeping late had been noted earlier by Marcy. In a letter to his daughter on November 18, 1861, Marcy wrote: "McClellan would send you his love but he's not up yet." RBM to MEM, Nov. 18, 1861. GBM Papers, LoC. Burlingame, *Lincoln,* 2:197. Time and propinquity may well have altered General Marcy's opinion of McClellan from his early, unbounded admiration, particularly since McClellan gave him virtually no authority, despite McClellan having petitioned the president personally to have Marcy as his chief of staff. Adding injury to insult, such close quarters also resulted in Marcy contracting typhoid along with McClellan in late December 1861. Sears, *Young Napoleon,* 112, 136.

12. *"how the mighty are fallen"*

1. Twain acknowledged his debt to Prime's book at the end of *Innocents Abroad:* "I am aware that this is a pretty voluminous notice of Mr. Grimes's book. However, it is proper and legitimate to speak of it, for 'Nomadic Life in Palestine' is a representative book—the representative of a class of Palestine books—and a criticism upon it will serve for a criticism upon them all. And since I am treating it in the comprehensive capacity of a representative book, I have taken the liberty of giving to both book and author fictitious names. Perhaps it is in better taste, any how, to do this." Twain, *Innocents Abroad,* 536.

2. "Why Lincoln Closed the JoC," *Journal of Commerce,* http://www.joc.com/sites/default/files/joc_inc/history/p8.html.

3. GBM to Samuel Barlow, Jan. 29, 1876, quoted in Sears, *Young Napoleon,* 394. Stephen W. Sears has unraveled the steps in the publishing of *McClellan's Own Story* in "The Curious Case of General McClellan's Memoirs."

4. Sears, *Young Napoleon,* 398. McClellan's letter book containing his chosen extracts from his letters to Nelly also escaped the warehouse fire."The Report of Gen. McClellan," *New York Times,* Jan. 6, 1864. As presented to the War Department for publication, the "Report" consisted of a primary document of 756 pages and 263 additional individual reports of McClellan's subordinates. Sears, *Young Napoleon,* 356. After much bickering, Congress ordered a truncated version of 242 pages printed. A *New York Times* editorial savaged it as "nothing less than the *Military Memoirs of George B. McClellan,* printed at the expense of the Government" and claimed its purpose was not military but political.

5. *New York Times,* Oct. 30, 1885, and Nov. 2, 1885.

6. Ibid., Nov. 12, 1885.

7. Sears, "Curious Case," 101. Quote is from Twain, *Innocents Abroad,* 532.

8. Prime, "Biographical Sketch" in McClellan, *McClellan's Own Story,* 2.

9. On Victorian privacy sensibilities, see Summerscale, *The Suspicions of Mr. Whicher,* 109–10. Nicolay and Hay, "Abraham Lincoln: A History," 394.

10. Sears, *Controversies & Commanders,* 6.

11. Prime, "Biographical Sketch," in McClellan, *McClellan's Own Story,* 24.

12. Pickett, *Pickett and His Men;* Elizabeth Bacon Custer wrote three books: *Boots and Saddles, Tenting on the Plains,* and *Following the Guidon;* among the many books Jessie wrote to burnish her husband's reputation is *The Story of the Guard.* See Secrest, *Shoot the Widow: Adventures of a Biographer in Search of Her Subject.*

13. Sears, "Curious Case." Sears finds no fault with Nelly.

14. See Gordon's *Pickett* for a portrayal of a Civil War widow at the other extreme of the spectrum: La Salle Corbell Pickett manufactured much of her story of their life together and may even have manufactured letters by her husband to create the heroic legacy she wanted associated with her husband. Though filled with inaccuracies, her book was a best seller.

15. GBM to MEM, June 12, 1862. Sears, ed., *Papers,* 297. GBM to MEM, July 22, 1862. McClellan, *McClellan's Own Story,* 453. GBM to MEM, Apr. 27, 1862. Sears, ed., *Papers,* 250. GBM to MEM, July 20, 1862. Ibid., 367.

16. Prime, "Biographical Sketch," in McClellan, *McClellan's Own Story,* 23, 24. GBM to MEM, Sept. 8, 1861. Ibid., 90. GBM to MEM, July 27, 1862. Sears, *Papers,* 373. Prime did not include this portion of the letter in *McClellan's Own Story.*

17. GBM to MEM, July 29, 1862. McClellan, *McClellan's Own Story,* 457, 458.

18. Sears, "Curious Case."

19. Letter of July 13, 1862, in McClellan, *McClellan's Own Story,* 447, 448.

20. Cited in Sears, ed., *Papers,* 354.

21. Diary of Mary Ellen McClellan for May 5, 1866-December 31, 1867. GBM Papers, LoC. McClellan might have vowed to forget his "unpleasantness" with Lincoln in the wake of the assassination, but he had not, after all.

22. *New York Times,* Oct. 30, 1885.

23. GBM to MEM, Sept. 20, 1862. McClellan, *McClellan's Own Story,* 613, 614.

24. Ibid., ii, 2. Or perhaps she saw it and did not care enough to correct it.

25. Find a Grave, http://www.findagrave.com/cgi-bin/fg.cgi?page=gr&GRid=8215496. Prime was not alone in misspelling Nelly's name. The *New York Times* produced an even worse travesty of her name in its obituary notice for "Mrs. George B. McClellan" on March 13, 1915: "The body of Mrs. Elton Mary McClellan, widow of General George B. McClellan, the famous Union Commander in the Civil War, was buried in Riverview Cemetery here this afternoon." And the title of the only published biography of Nelly that exists, part of the small collection of biographies of Civil War wives, *They Also Served*, is, sadly, "Ellen Mary Marcy McClellan."

13. *"It is high or low tide with us ever"*

1. This story is told in Burlingame, *Lincoln*, 1:294–307, including speculation that Ewing might have deliberately ignored favorable written references supporting Lincoln's quest to become land commissioner.

2. Newspaper report in Brooks, *Downfall of American Slavery*, 116. Telegram from Abraham Lincoln to Thomas Ewing, Sept. 27, 1849. Thomas Ewing Family Papers, LoC. Mary Lincoln quote in Brooks, *Downfall of American Slavery*, 116.

3. Quote is from a letter from Ellen Ewing (EE) to William Tecumseh Sherman (WTS), May 22, 1849. William T. Sherman Family Papers Collection (CSHR), Box 2, Folder 60 (2/60) Univ. of Notre Dame Archives (UNDA). First published in 1875, *The Personal Memoirs of Genl. W. T. Sherman* is essential to understanding the man. He revised his memoirs in 1885, adding more detail about his family history. The standard biography of Sherman is John Marszalek's *Sherman*. Other interpretations of his complex character can be found in Fellman, *Citizen Sherman*; Lewis, *Fighting Prophet*; Flood, *Grant and Sherman*. The biographical details contained herein are largely derived from these sources.

4. Ellen Ewing Sherman (EES) to Thomas Ewing Sr. (TESr.), Feb. 18, 1869. CSHR 1/93, UNDA.

5. Sherman, *Memoirs*, I:14.

6. Ibid.

7. Ibid., 11.

8. WTS to EES, July 16, 1861. CSHR 1/138, UNDA.

9. WTS to EE, May 13, 1837. CSHR 1/100, UNDA.

10. WTS to EE, June 14, 1844. CSHR 1/104, UNDA.

11. EE to WTS, July 2, 1844. CSHR 2/58, UNDA.

12. Fellman, *Citizen Sherman*, 30. "The Rathbone Tragedy." *New York Times*, Dec. 29, 1883.

13. Sherman, *Memoirs*, I:89–111.

14. Father Josue M. Young (Fr. Young) to Bishop John Baptist Purcell (Bishop Purcell), Jan. 23, 1845. The Archdiocese of Cincinnati Collection (CACI) II-4-I, UNDA. Fr. Young to Bishop Purcell, Jan. 19, 1847. CACI II-4-j, UNDA.

15. Those remedies were modern medicine, though, compared to the historical "cure" for the disease, which gave rise to the phrase "the royal touch." Beginning in the thirteenth century, it was believed that the touch of a monarch could cure scrofula, and the natural tendency of the lesions to subside (temporarily, at least) gave credence to the practice. Until the early 1700s, the Anglican Church's Book of Common Prayer included a "Royal Touch Ceremony," and Shakespeare described one such ceremony in his play *Macbeth*. By the mid-1800s, however, the royal cure had largely been abandoned. Gosman, MacDonald, and Vanderjagt, eds., *Princes and Princely Culture, 1450–1650*, vol. I.

The term "the royal touch" continued in popular use. Indeed, Lincoln characterized the Thirteenth Amendment to the Constitution, which outlawed slavery, "a King's cure for all the evils," that would immediately and permanently ensure the abolition of slavery. Basler, ed., *Collected Works of Abraham Lincoln,* 8:255.

16. EE to WTS, May 22, 1849, CSHR 2/60, UNDA; EES to WTS, May 28, 1860, CSHR 2/81, UNDA; EES to WTS, Nov. 30, 1860, CSHR 2/84, UNDA. Excellent narratives of Ellen's youth and the early days of the Shermans' marriage can be found in Marszalek, *Sherman,* and in McAlister, *Ellen Ewing Sherman.* Unless otherwise noted, my account is based on those sources. Ellen is long overdue for a modern biography.

17. EE to WTS, Jan. 19, 1849. CSHR 2/60, UNDA.

18. WTS to EE, Mar. 27, 1849. CSHR 1/112, UNDA.

19. "[The wedding] occurred at the house of Mr. Ewing, the same now owned and occupied by Mr. F. P. Blair, senior, on Pennsylvania Avenue, opposite the War Department." Sherman, *Memoirs,* I:112.

20. Burton, *Three Generations,* 61. "Irish-Catholic Immigration to America," http://www.loc.gov/teachers/classroommaterials/presentationsandactivities/presentations/immigration/irish2.html. EE to WTS, July 2, 1844. CSHR 2/58, UNDA.

21. WTS to EE, Apr. 7, 1842. CSHR 1/103, UNDA.

22. Fr. Young to Bishop Purcell, May 30, 1848. CACI II-4-k, UNDA. Sherman, *Memoirs,* I:13.

23. EES to WTS, Mar. 7, 1862. CSHR 1/143, UNDA.

24. WTS to EE, Jan. 22, 1839. CSHR 1/102. WTS to EE, Apr. 7, 1842. CSHR 1/103, UNDA.

25. EES to WTS, Jan. 29, 1861. CSHR 1/143, UNDA.

26. EES to TESr, June 20, 1860. CSHR 1/83, UNDA.

27. EES to WTS, Aug. 7, 1862. CSHR 2/98, UNDA.

28. Flag incident from McAlister, *Ellen Ewing Sherman,* 330; Marszalek, "General and Mrs. William T. Sherman: A Contentious Union," 138.

14. "You will never be happy in this world unless you go into the Army again"

1. Philemon Tecumseh Sherman, *Reminiscences of Earlier Days.* CSHR, 7/01, UNDA (emphasis in the original).

2. "Jonah of banking" from WTS to John Sherman (JS), Oct. 12, 1857, quoted in Marszalek, *Sherman,* 113.

3. EES to WTS, May 1, 1860. CSHR 2/81, UNDA.

4. Sherman, *General W. T. Sherman as College President,* 350.

5. "After the battle of Shiloh, I found among the prisoners Cadet Barrow, fitted him out with some clean clothing, of which he was in need, and learned that Cadet Workman was killed in that battle." Sherman, *Memoirs,* I:183. Quoted in Marszalek, *Sherman,* 139.

6. EES to WTS, Jan. 16, 1861, CSHR 2/86; WTS to EES, Jan. 20, 1861, CSHR 2/86; EES to WTS, Jan. 29, 1861, CSHR 2/86, UNDA.

7. Sherman, *Memoirs,* 195, 196. WTS to David French Boyd, Apr. 4, 1861. Simpson and Berlin, eds., *Sherman's Civil War,* 65.

8. WTS to JS, April 22, 1861. Simpson and Berlin, eds., *Sherman's Civil War,* 206.

9. Kennett, *Sherman: A Soldier's Life,* 113.

10. Sherman, *Memoirs,* I:199-200.

11. EES to TESr., May 11, 1861. CSHR 1/83, UNDA.

12. WTS to EES, July 28, 1861. CSHR 1/138, UNDA.

13. Sherman, *Memoirs*, I:218-92.

14. Sherman quote from a speech in 1873, quoted in Marszalek, *Sherman*, 152. WTS to EES, July 24, 1861. CSHR 1/138, UNDA.

15. Sherman, *Memoirs*, I:219-220.

15. *"releive my husband from the suspicions now resting on him"*

1. Sherman, *Memoirs*, I:220. In addition to Sherman, Anderson selected brigadier generals George H. Thomas, Ambrose Burnside, and Don Carlos Buell to accompany him (though the last was then posted in California and would take months to come east).

2. Ibid., 221.

3. EES to WTS, Aug. 18, 1861, CSHR 2/87; WTS to EES, Aug. 3, 1861, CSHR 1/139, UNDA.

4. McAllister, *Ellen Sherman*, 193. EES to WTS, Sept. 21, 1861. CSHR 2/88, UNDA.

5. Sherman, *Memoirs*, I:227.

6. Marszalek, *Sherman*, 160.

7. Sherman, *Memoirs*, I:228-31.

8. WTS to JS, Oct. 26, 1861. Simpson and Berlin, eds., *Sherman's Civil War*, 153.

9. *New York Times,* Oct. 31, 1861.

10. Ibid., Oct. 16, 1861. For a more complete understanding of the relationship between Sherman and the press, see Marszalek, *Sherman's Other War.*

11. WTS to EES, Nov. 1, 1861. CSHR 1/140, UNDA.

12. EES to Jane Latimer, Nov. 29, 1871. CSHR 1/69, UNDA.

13. Ellen Ewing Sherman, "Recollections for my Children," Oct. 28, 1888. CSHR 4/65, UNDA.

14. EES to WTS, Apr. 29, 1855. CSHR 2/61, UNDA.

15. EES to WTS, May 13, 1855. CSHR 2/62, UNDA.

16. EES to WTS, Sept. 21, 1861, CSHR 2/88; EES to WTS, Sept. 29, 1861, CSHR 2/88, UNDA.

17. EES to WTS, Oct. 4, 1861, CSHR 2/88, UNDA; EES to WTS, Oct. 10, 1861, ibid.

18. *Chicago Tribune,* quoted in Marszalek, *Sherman's Other War,* 74. Villard, *Memoirs,* 211.

19. EES to WTS, Oct. 10, 1861, CSHR 2/88, UNDA; WTS to EES, Oct. 12, 1861, CSHR 1/140, UNDA.

20. WTS diary, 1861. CSHR 5/04, UNDA. Lewis, *Fighting Prophet*, 191.

21. WTS to EES, Nov. 1, 1861. CSHR 1/140, UNDA.

22. Marszalek, *Commander*, 18, 55-56.

23. EES to JS, Nov. 10, 1861. Simpson and Berlin, eds., *Sherman's Civil War*, 156n1. EES diary, 1861. CSHR 5/15, UNDA.

24. EES diary, 1861, CSHR 5/15; EES to WTS, Nov. 18, 1861, SHR, UNDA.

25. *New York Times,* Dec. 9, 1861.

26. EES diary, 1861. CSHR 5/15, UNDA.

27. *Cincinnati Commercial,* Dec. 11, 1861.

28. EES to WTS, Dec. 19, 1861. CSHR 2/89, UNDA. "Papa was crazy" and WTS letter to TESr., quoted in Lewis, *Fighting Prophet,* 201.

29. McAllister, *Ellen Sherman,* 202. TESr to WTS, Dec. 22, 1861. CSHR 1/38, UNDA (emphasis in the original).

30. John Sherman (JS) to EES, Dec. 14, 1861. CSHR 4/01, UNDA.

31. EES to WTS, "end of December" 1861. CSHR 2/89, UNDA.

32. Marszalek, *Sherman*, 166, 167. Halleck had, however, used the term in a letter to his wife. EES to WTS, Dec. 22, 1861. CSHR 2/89, UNDA.

33. WTS to EES, Jan. 1, 1862, CSHR 1/141; EES to WTS, Jan. 8, 1862, CSHR 2/90, UNDA.

34. EES to Abraham Lincoln, Jan. 9, 1862. Lincoln Papers, LoC. The misspellings and the emphasis in this letter are in the original.

35. EES to WTS, Jan. 15, 1862. CSHR 2/90, UNDA. It is possible that Lincoln learned about Thomas Ewing's intention to seek a meeting with him and decided that he would address Ellen's letter in that context.

36. See WTS to EES, Jan. 29, 1862, CSHR 1/141; EES to WTS, Jan. 22, 1862, CSHR 2/91, UNDA.

37. EES to WTS, Jan. 23, 1862, CSHR 2/91; WTS to EES, Jan. 29, 1862, CSHR, 1/141 UNDA.

38. EES to WTS, Jan. 29, 1862. CSHR 2/91, UNDA.

39. The Lincoln Log, Jan. 29, 1862.

40. On September 17, 1861, in the wake of Frémont's emancipation order, Thomas Ewing had written to Lincoln a frank and negative assessment of Frémont, based on Ewing's service with him in the Senate. Not long before the *Cincinnati Commercial* article appeared, Lincoln sought Ewing's advice on what had become known as "The Trent Affair," when a U.S. Navy captain—on his own initiative—stopped a British ship in the Caribbean Sea and seized Confederate agents James Mason and John Slidell. The furor threatened to pull the North into war with England, and Ewing counseled the president to "surrender [Mason and Slidell] and say in our diplomatic note that we do so because we are satisfied, some precedents to the contrary notwithstanding that the law of nations did not justify the seizure." TESr to Abraham Lincoln, Lincoln Papers, LoC.

41. Joshua Speed to Abraham Lincoln, Oct. 7, 1861. Lincoln Papers, LoC.

42. Abraham Lincoln to Samuel Curtis, Dec. 12, 1861. *Collected Works of Abraham Lincoln*, 5:66.

43. EES to WTS, Jan. 29, 1862. CSHR 2/91, UNDA.

44. Sherman, *Memoirs*, I:248.

45. WTS to Ulysses S. Grant (USG), Feb. 15, 1862. The Papers of Ulysses Grant (Grant, *Papers*), 4:215, editor's note.

46. Sherman, *Memoirs*, I:249. Welles, *Diary*, 92.

47. Sherman, *Memoirs*, I:254-57. Shiloh means "place of peace."

48. EES to WTS, Feb. 28, 1862, and Feb. 22, 1862. CSHR 2/92, UNDA.

49. EES to WTS, Mar. 17, 1862. CSHR 2/93, UNDA.

50. Of the many accounts of the Battle of Shiloh from which this description is drawn are those in the memoirs of Sherman and Grant, as well as those of historians Marszalek, Simpson, and Flood.

51. USG, *Memoirs*, 1:343. Thanks to the marvels of technology, it is possible to search the *Memoirs* for specific words—and even punctuation marks.

52. Smith, *Grant*, 201, quoting from the *Army and Navy Journal*, Dec. 30, 1893, which quoted in turn from a *Washington Post* interview with Sherman. Later, on page 336 of his book, Smith wrote that Grant never said that phrase. It remains, however, one of the most famous exchanges of the war—just too good not to repeat.

53. This account relies upon Marszalek, *Sherman's Other War*, 90-100.

54. EES to WTS, Apr. 26, 1862. CSHR 2/94, UNDA.

55. Schenker Jr., "Ulysses in His Tent," 175-221. My thanks to Dr. John Marszalek for pointing me to this article and its perceptive take on Halleck's behavior during this time.

56. The National Park Service gives its name also as the Battle of Walnut Hills or the Battle of Chickasaw Bluffs, http://www.nps.gov/hps/abpp/battles/ms003.htm.

57. For a more detailed account, see Marszalek, *Sherman's Other War,* 131-40.

58. EES to WTS, Feb. 14, 1863. CSHR 2/103, UNDA.

59. EES to WTS, Feb. 22, 1863, CSHR 2/103; WTS to EES, Feb. 26, 1863, CSHR 2/01, UNDA.

60. EES to WTS, June 1, 1862. CSHR 2/96, UNDA.

16. *"I have never dared to murmer at God's decree"*

1. EES to Maj. General Hurbut, Mar. 16, 1863, http://www.civilwarautographs.com/search.php. EES to WTS, 26 July 1863. CSHR 2/108, UNDA.

2. Minnie Sherman Fitch, "Album of the Heart." CSHR 7/04, UNDA.

3. Marszalek, *Sherman,* 237.

4. EES to WTS, Nov. 9, 1863. CSHR 2/110, UNDA.

5. Sherman, *Memoirs,* I:376. Sherman sometimes spelled his son's name Willie; most of the time, he wrote "Willy," as did Ellen.

6. Ibid., 377.

7. WTS to JS, Oct. 24, 1863. Simpson and Berlin, eds., *Sherman's Civil War,* 567. WTS to Philemon B. Ewing, Oct. 24, 1863. Ibid., 563.

8. WTS to EES, Oct. 6, 1863. CSHR 2/07. WTS to Thomas Ewing Sherman, Oct. 4, 1863. CSHR 2/07, UNDA.

9. EES to WTS, Feb. 24, 1864. CSHR 2/111, UNDA.

10. For accounts of the Lincolns' reaction to their Willie's death, see Clinton, *Mrs. Lincoln,* and Donald, *Lincoln.*

11. Keckley, *Behind the Scenes,* 104.

12. EES to WTS, Oct. 6, 1863. CSHR 2/07, UNDA.

13. EES to WTS, Jan. 29, 1864. CSHR 2/111, UNDA.

14. EES to WTS, Feb. 2, 1864, CSHR 2/111; EES to WTS, Feb. 26, 1864, CSHR 2/111, UNDA.

15. WTS to EES, July 13, 1864. CSHR 2/16, UNDA. Sherman reiterated this thought in letters to Philemon Ewing and Hugh Ewing the same day.

16. WTS to EES, Jan. 11, 1864. CSHR 2/10, UNDA.

17. *"for the privilege of whipping negro wenches"*

1. EES to WTS, Aug. 30, 1862. CSHR 2/99, UNDA.

2. EES to WTS, July 10, 1862, CSHR 2/97; EES to WTS, Dec. 31, 1860, CSHR 2/85, UNDA.

3. EES to WTS, Dec. 19, 1861, CSHR 2/85; EES to WTS, Jan. 19, 1861, CSHR 2/86; EES to WTS, Feb. 6, 1861, CSHR 2/87, UNDA.

4. EES to WTS, Aug. 7, 1862. CSHR 2/98, UNDA.

5. Hussey, *Archbishop Purcell.* EES to WTS, Oct. 18, 1864, CSHR 2/117; EES to WTS, Oct. 19, 1864, CSHR 2/117, UNDA.

6. EES to WTS, Jan. 29, 1861, CSHR 2/86; EES to WTS, Feb. 6, 1861, CSHR 2/87, UNDA. Many people, North and South, blamed abolitionists for causing the war.

7. EES to WTS, Apr. 23, 1862, CSHR 2/94; EES to WTS, June 1, 1862, CSHR 2/96, UNDA.

8. Donald, *Lincoln,* 529.

9. Simpson and Berlin, eds., *Sherman's Civil War,* 708, 709.

10. EES to WTS, Sept. 17, 1864, CSHR 2/116; EES to WTS, Apr. 23, 1862, CSHR 2/94, UNDA.

11. WTS to JS, May 20, 1861, while Sherman was still with the St. Louis RR Co. Simpson and Berlin, eds., *Sherman's Civil War,* 87.

18. *"the Government requires sacrifices from wives"*

1. WTS to Ulysses S. Grant (USG), Sept. 23, 1864. Simpson and Berlin, eds., *Sherman's Civil War,* 724.

2. Sherman, *Memoirs,* II:249. WTS to USG, Oct. 11, 1864. Simpson and Berlin, eds., *Sherman's Civil War,* 733.

3. USG to WTS, telegram, Nov. 2, 1864. Grant, *Papers,* 12:373.

4. Sherman, *Memoirs,* II:169. WTS to EES, telegram, Nov. 12, 1864. Andre de Coppet Collection, Box 31, File 4, Princeton Univ. Library. There are a number of reasons to believe this was a telegram rather than a letter, including that it is addressed to "Mrs. W. T. Sherman" and not to "Dearest Ellen," his usual salutation. Sherman, *Memoirs,* II:169.

5. Sherman, *Memoirs,* II:221.

6. EES to WTS, July 9, CSHR 2/114; Aug. 22, CSHR 2/115; Sept. 17, CSHR 2/116; Oct. 31, 1864, CSHR 2/117, UNDA.

7. EES to WTS, Oct. 31, 1864. CSHR 2/117, UNDA.

8. WTS to EES, Dec. 16, 1864, CSHR 2/19; WTS to EES, Dec. 25, 1864, CSHR 2/119, UNDA.

9. WTS to EES, Dec. 30, 1864. CSHR 2/19, UNDA.

10. EES to WTS, Dec. 29, 1864. CSHR 2/118, UNDA.

11. EES to WTS, Oct. 19, 1864, CSHR 2/117; EES to WTS, Dec. 29, 1864, CSHR 2/118, UNDA.

12. Lewis, *Fighting Prophet,* 458, 459.

13. EES to WTS, Dec. 29, 1864, CSHR 2/118; WTS to EES, Dec. 31, 1864, CSHR 2/19; EES to WTS, Feb. 6, 1865, CSHR 2/120, UNDA.

14. Marszalek, *Sherman,* 315. WTS to EES, Dec. 31, 1864. CSHR 2/19, UNDA.

15. Sherman, *Memoirs,* II:269-79.

16. EES to WTS, Feb. 15, 1865. CSHR 2/120, UNDA.

17. WTS to EES, Mar. 23, 1865. CSHR 2/21, UNDA.

18. *New York Times,* July 1, 1865, quoting a letter from clergymen to EES of June 7.

19. *"my opinion of you is unaltered"*

1. Sherman, *Memoirs,* II:322-24, which includes the March 22 letter from Grant.

2. Porter, *Campaigning with Grant,* 418-20.

3. Grant re: Mary Lincoln quoted in Porter, *Campaigning,* 419. Sherman, *Memoirs,* II:326.

4. "Admiral Porter's Account of the Interview with Mr. Lincoln," in Sherman, *Memoirs,* II:328-31.

5. Porter, *Campaigning with Grant,* 423, 424.

6. Sherman, *Memoirs,* II:325-28.

7. Ibid.

8. WTS to EES, Mar. 31, 1865, CSHR 2/21; WTS to EES, Apr. 22, 1865, CSHR 2/23, UNDA.

9. WTS to TESr., Apr. 5, 1865. Simpson and Berlin, eds., *Sherman's Civil War,* 842. EES to WTS, Apr. 1865. CSHR 2/121, UNDA.

10. Sherman, *Memoirs,* II:344.

11. Ibid., 347.

12. Ibid., 347-48. Flood, *Grant and Sherman,* 331. In the trial of the Lincoln conspirators, a witness testified to finding a letter "floating in the water" at the wharf at Morehead City, N.C., on May 2 that read:

> WASHINGTON, April the 15, '65.
> DEAR JOHN,—I am happy to inform you that Pet has done his work well. He is safe, and Old Abe is in hell. Now, sir, All eyes are on you. You must bring Sherman: Grant is in the hands of Old Gray ere this. Red Shoes showed lack of nerve in Seward's case, but fell back in good order. *Johnson* must come. Old Crook has him in charge. . . ." (quoted in Poore, *The Conspiracy Trial,* III:267)

13. Ibid., 351.

14. Ibid., 353.

15. Ibid., 355, 356.

16. WTS to USG, Apr. 18, 1865. Ibid. WTS to HWH, Apr. 18, 1865. Sherman, *Memoirs,* II:354.

17. EES to WTS, Apr. 10, 1865, CSHR 2/121; WTS to EES, Apr. 18, 1865, CSHR 2/23; WTS to EES, Apr. 22, 1865, CSHR 2/23, UNDA.

18. WTS to EES, Oct. 27, 1864. CSHR 2/18, UNDA.

19. Marszalek, *Sherman,* 350.

20. Welles, *Diary,* 295.

21. *New York Times,* Apr. 24, 1865.

22. Sherman, *Memoirs,* II:366.

23. HWH to Edwin Stanton, Apr. 26, 1865, quoted in ibid., II:860.

24. Burton, *Three Generations,* 163. EES to WTS, Apr. 26, 1865. CSHR 2/121, UNDA.

25. Quoted in Marszalek, *Sherman,* 351. Sherman, *Memoirs,* II:373. Marszalek, *Sherman,* 353.WTS to HWH, May 10, 1865. Simpson and Berlin, eds., *Sherman's Civil War,* 895, 896.

26. Marszalek, *Sherman,* 350.

27. WTS to John Rawlins, May 19, 1865. Simpson and Berlin, eds., *Sherman's Civil War,* 902. This echoes, too, Coriolanus, who was banished outside Rome for his perceived treachery. Lewis, *Fighting Prophet,* 567.

28. EES to WTS, May 17, 1865. CSHR 2/122, UNDA.

29. Sherman, *Memoirs,* II:378.

30. Marszalek, *Sherman,* 357.

20. "No greater glory than to fill a patriot's grave"

1. EES to TESr., Feb. 18, 1869. CSHR 1/93, UNDA.

2. Flood, *Grant and Sherman,* 394, 395.

3. Quoted in Ellen Sherman, *Memorial of Thomas Ewing of Ohio.* CSHR 20/63, UNDA

4. Ibid.

5. EES to Archbishop John Baptist Purcell, July 17, 1874. CACI II-5-f, UNDA.

6. McAllister, *Ellen Ewing Sherman,* 366.

7. Burton, *Three Generations,* 251. The wool coat later had to be burned because of moths, but the brass buttons can still be seen in a small box in the William T. Sherman Family Collection in the Archives at the University of Notre Dame.

8. Quoted in Lewis, *Fighting Prophet,* 638. Flood, *Grant and Sherman,* 395.

9. Kennett, *Sherman*, 324. Fellman, *Citizen Sherman*, 355–65. Kennett, *Sherman*, 331. Marszalek, *Sherman*, 416, 421.

10. McAllister, *Ellen Ewing Sherman*, 354.

11. EES to WTS, May 3, 1887. CSHR 2/163, UNDA.

12. McAllister, *Ellen Ewing Sherman*, 367.

13. Sherman quoted in Burton, *Three Generations*, 269. WTS to John Tourtelotte, Dec. 6, 1888. CSHR 1/175, UNDA.

14. Letters received by WTS on death of Ellen Sherman. Sherman Family Papers, CSHR 7/10, UNDA.

15. WTS to Walter George Smith, Dec. 8, 1885. CSHR 7/10-30, UNDA. Marszalek, *Sherman*, 491.

16. Dickens, *Great Expectations*, 5.

17. In ibid., 489.

18. Excerpted from the oath that graduates of West Point take upon being commissioned as second lieutenants, and which U.S. Army officers take at each grade promotion, http://www.history.army.mil/html/faq/oaths.html. Marszalek, *Sherman*, 492.

19. Quoted in Marszalek, *Sherman*, 493.

20. EES to WTS, Sept. 10, 1862, CSHR 2/100; EES to WTS, June 14, 1862, CSHR 2/96, UNDA.

21. *"sunshine"*

1. Emerson, "Grant's Life in the West," 419 (emphasis in the original).

2. Julia Dent Grant (JDG), *Memoirs*, 97.

3. Allen, *Memorial*, 16.

4. Scott, ed., *The War of the Rebellion*, ser. I, 7:586.

5. Quoted in Smith, *Grant*, 164.

22. *"this, to me, most delicate subject"*

1. Biographical information on Grant is vast and deep. Among the best biographies are those of Simpson, *Grant;* Smith, *Grant;* and McFeely, *Grant*. Although Grant's own two-volume *The Personal Memoirs of U. S. Grant* provide less personal than military information, they are essential reading. Biographical details on Grant contained herein are from those sources, unless otherwise indicated.

2. "Reminiscences of General Frederick Dent Grant." *U. S. Grant Association Newsletter.* The article quoted first appeared in *New York World Sunday Magazine,* Apr. 25, 1897.

3. "Juleps" quote from Catton, "Introduction," in JDG, *Memoirs*, 2. Biographical information about Julia is also widely available. In addition to her fascinating *Personal Memoirs of Julia Dent Grant,* the most complete—and completely flattering—biography is Ross, *The General's Wife.* More recently, Berkin's *Civil War Wives* provides valuable insight into Julia and her times. See also Simon, "A Marriage Tested by War." Major modern biographies of Grant pay close attention to Julia, testifying to her importance in his life. It is not clear whether the slave Jule ever legally belonged to Julia. Historians still debate whether Dent retained legal title to the four slaves she claimed her father had given her.

4. Ross, *The General's Wife,* 9. JDG, *Memoirs,* 34.

5. JDG, *Memoirs,* 47.

6. USG to Julia Dent (JD), Feb. 4, 1848. Grant, *Papers,* 1:152.

7. JDG, *Memoirs*, 126, 127.

8. Barry, *Fixing My Gaze*, 173. In her book, neuroscientist Sue Barry tells of her three surgeries before the age of eight to correct her eye alignment, the result of infantile strabismus. The surgeries were all performed by one of the most prominent eye surgeons in the United States, with the best science and latest equipment available in the middle of the twentieth century. The operations did make her look less cross-eyed, but they did not improve her vision. Even today, such surgery rarely ever corrects the underlying vision problem. In fact, Barry was in college "before I learned that I didn't see the way other people did." A professor of neurobiology astounded her in class one day when he lectured about vision and the brain, concluding, "many strabismics don't see in 3D. They're virtually stereoblind."

9. Ibid., 3. Ross, *General's Wife*, 329.

10. JDG, *Memoirs*, 35–38.

11. Ibid., 38.

12. Ross, *The General's Wife*, 329. Quote from JDG, *Memoirs*, 110, 194.

13. JDG, *Memoirs*, 61.

14. Ross, *General's Wife*, 37.

15. JDG, *Memoirs*, 105.

16. Simpson, *Grant*, 10–12.

17. USG, *Memoirs*, 1:46, 47.

18. "Mrs. Orvil Grant," *Troy Intelligencer*, Apr. 17, 1892, from the Ulysses S. Grant homepage, http://www.granthomepage.com/intmrsorvilgrant.htm.

19. McFeely, *Grant: A Biography*, 24. "Homeliness" from Berkin, *Civil War Wives*, 228.

20. Barry, *Fixing My Gaze*, 17. Julia's earliest memory is of her delight as a toddler when her father "caught me up and held me high in the air." JDG, *Memoirs*, 33.

21. JDG, *Memoirs*, 48. Their horseback courtship is so iconic that in 2011, when the U.S. Mint commissioned a coin for Julia in its "First Spouse Gold Coin Series," the reverse side of the coin was a representation of the couple on horseback. According to the Mint's description, "[t]he design captures the courtship of a young Julia Dent and future Civil War general and president, Ulysses S. Grant, horseback riding at her family's plantation, White Haven" (www.firstspousecoins.us).

22. Ibid., 49–50.

23. Excerpts from USG to Julia Boggs Dent (JBD) of June 4, July 28, Aug. 31, Sept. 7, 1844, and Jan. 12, 1845. Grant, *Papers*, 1:26, 30, 33, 37, 40.

24. JDG, *Memoirs*, 51.

25. Ibid., 51.

26. Ibid.

27. Excerpts from USG to JBD of July 28, 1844; June 25, 1845; July 17, 1845; Feb. 5, 1846, from Camp Salubrity to Corpus Christi, Texas. Grant, *Papers*, 1: 29, 45, 52, 70.

28. USG to JBD, May 11, 1846. Ibid., 1:147.

29. Ibid.

30. USG, *Memoirs*, 192.

31. Quote from Smith, *Grant*, 56, 634n101. USG, *Memoirs*, 159.

32. Quote from USG, *Memoirs*, 53. Smith, *Grant*, 69.

23. *"how forsaken I feel here!"*

1. Ross, *General's Wife*, 45, 46.

2. JDG, *Memoirs*, 55–56, 64n30. Julia named Sidney Smith as a groomsman, but he

had died in the Mexican War. Ross and most Grant biographers claim Longstreet as the other groomsman and likely Grant's best man.

3. Ibid., 57.

4. Ibid., 58.

5. USG to Bvt. Maj. Oscar Fingal Winship, Feb. 10, 1849. Grant, *Papers*, 1:173.

6. JDG, *Memoirs*, 60.

7. Ibid., 65-66. Gregory left a year later, enticed by higher wages offered by a neighbor.

8. Ibid., 84.

9. Excerpts from letters of May 21, 1851, and June 29, 1851, Detroit, Michigan, and Sacket's Harbor, New York. Grant, *Papers*, 1:209, 210, 214, 215.

10. JDG, *Memoirs*, 69.

11. Smith, *Grant*, 78, 637n51. Grant's ghastly firsthand experience of the isthmus crossing made him a lifelong proponent of a canal through it. As president, he ordered the earliest U.S. surveys for a route. McCullough, *Path between the Seas*, 26.

12. Excerpts from USG to JDG, Aug. 20, Sept. 14, Sept. 19, Oct. 7, Oct. 26, 1852. Grant, *Papers*, 1:269, 270.

13. Excerpts from USG to JDG, Dec. 3, Dec. 19, 1852, June 28, 1853. Ibid., 1:274, 278, 303.

14. Simon, "A Marriage Tested by War," 126; McFeely, *Grant: A Biography*, 50. USG to JDG, June 5, 1846. Grant, *Papers*, 1:90.

15. Ross, *General's Wife*, 70, 72.

16. Smith, *Grant*, 85n105; McFeely, *Grant*, 55n36. The McClellan story is in Smith, *Grant*, 83n91. Garland, *Ulysses S. Grant*, 127.

17. Grant, *Papers*, 1:328, 329.

18. USG, *Memoirs*, 1:210. Eaton and Mason, *Grant, Lincoln, and the Freedmen*, 100. John Eaton was chaplain on Grant's staff in 1862, when Grant had placed him in charge of contrabands who came into his army's lines.

19. McFeely, *Grant: A Biography*, 55.

20. USG to JDG, May 2, 1854. Grant, *Papers*, 1:332.

21. Simpson, *Ulysses S. Grant*, 64n2.

22. Frederick D. Grant, "General Grant's Home Life," *Independent*, Apr. 29, 1897, 535. Ross, *General's Wife*, 73.

23. JDG, *Memoirs*, 71, 75.

24. Ibid., 75.

24. "Is this my destiny?"

1. JDG, *Memoirs*, 80.

2. Ibid., 76, 77.

3. Ibid., 77, 78. She claimed that this episode of despair was greater than that which accompanied the failure of the firm Grant & Ward that bankrupted Julia and Grant.

4. Interview with Mary Robinson, *St. Louis Republican*, July 24, 1885.

5. JDG, *Memoirs*, 91, 92.

6. USG, *Memoirs*, 1:214, 215.

7. USG to Jesse Grant. Grant, *Papers*, 1:337. Pawn ticket, Dec. 23, 1857. Ibid., 1:339.

8. USG, *Memoirs*, 1:211.

9. Ross, *General's Wife*, 93, 99.

10. McFeely, *Grant: A Biography*, 64.

11. JDG, *Memoirs*, 82.

12. The house that the Grants rented in 1860 is not the grand Italianate house that the town fathers gave them after his presidency, which is now a museum, http://www.granthome.com.

13. JDG, *Memoirs*, 85–86.

14. Porter, "Eulogy of General Grant," in Shurter, ed., *Masterpieces of Modern Oratory*, 262.

15. "Chronology." Grant, *Papers*, 1:425, 426.

16. My thanks to William McFeely for sparking this line of thought by including this quotation at the start of his chapter, "Galena." McFeely, *Grant: A Biography*, 58.

25. *"secesh wives with their own little slaves"*

1. JDG, *Memoirs*, 87, 92.

2. USG to Frederick Dent, Apr. 19, 1861. Grant, *Papers*, 2:3, 4. USG to Jesse Grant, Apr. 21, 1861. Ibid., 2:6, 7. USG to Jesse Grant, May 6, 1861. Ibid., 2:22.

3. USG, *Memoirs*, 1:230.

4. Young, *Around the World with General Grant*, 263. McClellan, *McClellan's Own Story*, 47. USG, *Memoirs*, 1:123.

5. USG to JDG, May 10, 1861. Grant, *Papers*, 2:26. USG to Frederick Dent, Apr. 19, 1861. Grant, *Papers*, 2:3, 4.

6. Regarding sewing, see Ross, *General's Wife*, 37, and Barry, *Gaze*, 42. JDG, *Memoirs*, 89.

7. This was the boast of Sen. James Chesnut, husband of famed Civil War diarist Mary Chesnut, quoted in McPherson, *Battle Cry of Freedom*, 238.

8. JDG, *Memoirs*, 92.

9. Catton, *Grant Moves South*, 5. USG to JDG, June 26, 1861. Grant, *Papers*, 2:50.

10. JDG, *Memoirs*, 92. Ross, *General's Wife*, 110, 113, 126.

11. Quoted in Simpson, *Ulysses S. Grant*, 89.

12. USG to JDG, Aug. 10, 1861. Grant, *Papers*, 2:96, 97.

13. USG to Jesse Grant, July 13, 1861. Ibid., 2:66, 67.

14. USG to JDG, July 7, 1861. Ibid., 2:59. USG, *Memoirs*, 1:248. JDG, *Memoirs*, 92. USG to JDG, Aug. 1861. Grant, *Papers*, 2:141.

15. USG to JDG, July 19, 1861. Grant, *Papers*, 2:73. USG to JDG, Aug. 26, 1861. Ibid., 2:141. USG to JDG, Sept. 29, 1861. Ibid., 3:327.

16. USG to JDG, Aug. 10, 1861. Ibid., 2:96. Catton, *Grant Moves South*, 68. Biographical information about Rawlins is contained in the same book and in McFeely, *Grant: A Biography*, 85, 86.

17. "Gen. Grant's Emphatic Word." *New York Times*, Feb. 7, 1885. USG to JDG, Aug. 26, 1861. Grant, *Papers*, 2:141.

18. Nevins, *Pathmarker*, 521. Catton, *Grant Moves South*, 39, 40.

19. "Proclamation to the Citizens of Paducah!" Frost, *The Rebellion in the United States*, 851. Markland, "A. H. Markland," 322.

20. JDG, *Memoirs*, 93.

21. Hooper, "The Two Julias."

22. JDG, *Memoirs*, 93–95.

23. Catton, *Grant Moves South*, 109.

24. Grant Papers, LoC.

25. Quoted in Johnson and Buel, eds., *Battles and Leaders*, I:352.

26. USG to Mary Grant, Oct. 25, 1861. Grant, *Papers*, 3:77.

27. JDG, *Memoirs*, 96.

28. Grant, *Papers*, 4:118–19, editor's note.

29. Marszalek, *Sherman's Other War*, 118.

30. Grant, *Papers*, 4:118, 119, editor's note.

31. Ibid.

32. Library of Congress Borrowing Ledgers, Receipt Book L, 1861–1863, LC Archives, Manuscript Division, Library of Congress.

33. USG, *Memoirs*, 1:287.

34. Frederick Grant quote in Johnson and Buel, eds., *Battles and Leaders*, I:352. JDG, *Memoirs*, 95.

35. USG, *Memoirs*, 1:311.

36. Halleck quoted in Catton, *Grant Moves South*, 188n12. Stanton quoted in Dana, *Recollections*, 10, 11.

37. Halleck to McClellan, Mar. 5, 1862. Smith, *Grant*, 173. Schenker, "Turning Point," 180, 181. Simpson, *Ulysses S. Grant*, 122. See also Grant, *Memoirs*, ch. XXII, "Relieved of the Command."

38. Catton, *Grant Moves South*, 206.

39. JDG, *Memoirs*, 96–99.

40. *New York Times*, Apr. 22, 1862.

41. USG to Jesse Grant, Apr. 26, 1862. Grant, *Papers*, V:78, 79. See editor's note, 79. JDG to Elihu Washburn, May 16, 1862, in Catton, *Grant Moves South*, 260, 261. Grant, *Papers*, 5:120, editor's note. This invites speculation as to whether Jesse pressured Julia to write the letter.

42. Marszalek, *Commander*, 122. Schenker, "Turning Point," 193, 194. Thanks to Charles Bracelen Flood for highlighting this particular example of Halleck's attention to detail. Flood, *Grant and Sherman*, 124. Schenker and Marszalek note that this was in keeping with Halleck's belief in the value of careful attention to regulations. USG, *Memoirs*, 1:144.

43. Ibid., 147. See Schenker, "Turning Point," for a detailed analysis of Halleck's behavior and motivations from Shiloh to Corinth.

44. USG, *Memoirs*, 147. HWH to USG, Apr. 30, 1862. Grant, *Papers*, 5:105, editor's note.

45. USG to JDG, Apr. 1862. Grant, *Papers*, 5:72.

46. USG to HWH, May 11, 1862. Ibid., 5:114. HWH to USG, May 12, 1862. Ibid., 5:115, editor's note.

47. USG to JDG, May 13, 1862. Ibid., 5:117.

48. USG to E. B. Washburne, May 14, 1862. Ibid., 5:119.

49. USG to JDG, May 31, 1862. Ibid., 5:135.

50. Sherman, *Memoirs*, 276.

51. When he wrote his memoirs, Sherman could not find the letter from Grant, but he included a copy of his reply, dated June 6. WTS to USG, June 6, 1862. Ibid., 276. USG to JDG, June 9, 1862. Grant, *Papers*, 5:140, 141.

52. Not until October 24, 1863, fifteen months later, did Grant ask her to "write soon." After that, for the remaining eighteen months of the Civil War, only seven of the seventy-three letters Grant wrote to Julia (more than one a week) remarked on her lack of writing, and those comments were quite mild, almost afterthoughts. The two shrill exceptions related to her failure to inform him where she was ("I have not even heard whether you have left St. Louis. . . . Why have you not written? . . . If I should be so neglectful I would get a regular c[ussn']"). His letters noted receipt of some from her now and then, but

other than one spate of "almost dayly" letters in mid-October 1864 (largely dealing with details of setting up the new household in Burlington), it appears that she did not write more frequently than before, although the mails were clearly more reliable. USG to JDG, Oct. 2, 1864. Grant, *Papers*, 12:262.

53. USG to JDG, Nov. 14, 1863. Ibid., 9:396. USG to JDG, Apr. 27, 1864. Ibid., 10:363. USG to JDG, Jan. 11, 1865. Ibid., 13:262.

54. Simon, "A Marriage Tested by War," 124.

26. *"Do stop digging at this old canal"*

1. Simon, "A Marriage Tested by War," 135.

2. USG to Jesse Grant, Nov. 23, 1862. Grant, *Papers*, 6:344. JDG, *Memoirs*, 113.

3. J. E. Johnston to S. Cooper, telegram, Aug. 2, 1863. Scott, ed., *Official Records*, ser. I, vol. XXIV, part 3, 1042.

4. JDG, *Memoirs*, 105.

5. "Airliewood," http://www.airliewood.com/History/civilwar.html.

6. JDG, *Memoirs*, 106.

7. Ibid., 106, 107.

8. Simpson, *Ulysses S. Grant*, 164.

9. J. G. Deupree, "The Noxubee Squadron," 60-62. JDG, *Memoirs*, 107.

10. JDG, *Memoirs*, 107.

11. For an alternative story claiming she was captured, see Groom, *Vicksburg, 1863*, 201.

12. Dodge, *Personal Recollections*, 123. JDG, *Memoirs*, 109.

13. USG to JDG, Feb. 11, 1863. Grant, *Papers*, 7:311. JDG *Memoirs*, 110.

14. "Nail" from Winschel, *Vicksburg*, 14. "Key" in Fraser, *Vicksburg*, 3.

15. JDG, *Memoirs*, 111.

16. Letter from Maj. Gen. Charles S. Hamilton to U.S. Sen. James R. Doolittle (R-Wisconsin), Jan. 30, 1863. Grant, *Papers*, 7:308, editor's note. Cadwallader and Thomas, *Three Years with Grant*, 102-9. Simpson, *Grant*, 206-8. Catton, "Introduction" to JDG, *Memoirs*, 1, 3-5. Groom, *Vicksburg, 1863*. See in particular the thorough analysis by Michael Ballard in chapter 3: "River of Lies," in *Vicksburg*. My thanks to Dr. John Marszalek for directing my attention to this book.

17. Groom, *Vicksburg 1863*, 276.

18. JDG, *Memoirs*, 112.

19. *New York Times*, Apr. 22, 1863.

20. JDG, *Memoirs*, 119.

21. Abraham Lincoln to James C. Conkling, Aug. 26, 1863, http://www.abrahamlincolnonline.org/lincoln/speeches/conkling.htm. Abraham Lincoln to USG, July 13, 1865, cited in Waugh, *U. S. Grant*, 66.

22. One of the best descriptions of civilian life in Vicksburg during Grant's campaign can be found in Mary Webster Loughborough's memoir of that time. Published in 1864, under the title *My Cave Life in Vicksburg*, "by a lady," it is still in print.

23. Laas, ed., *Wartime Washington*, 5.

24. JDG, *Memoirs*, 123.

25. USG to J. Russell Jones, Nov. 17, 1863. Grant, *Papers*, 9:406. Jones may have intended the painting as part of a propaganda campaign to encourage Lincoln to give Grant the grade that Washington had last held by portraying him as a Washington look-alike. Holzer and Foner, *The Civil War in 50 Objects*.

26. JDG, *Memoirs,* 125.

27. Ibid.

28. Simon, "A Marriage Tested by War," 129. JDG, *Memoirs,* 126.

29. Ross, *General's Wife,* 158. JDG, *Memoirs,* 126.

30. USG to JDG, Feb. 14, 1864. USG to JDG, Feb. 17, 1864. Grant, *Papers,* 10:137-38.

31. USG to JDG, Feb. 25, 1864. Ibid., 10:155. USG to Jesse Grant, Mar. 1864. Ibid., 10:183.

32. Winfield Scott held the rank of brevet lieutenant general of the U.S. Army but was never officially raised to the grade of lieutenant general. There were many lieutenant generals in the Confederate States Army, as is the case in the current U.S. Army.

27. Lieutenant General's Wife

1. *Chicago Tribune,* Feb. 28, 1864. For a history of President Lincoln's Cottage at the Soldiers' Home and its importance in Lincoln's life and work, see Pinsker, *Lincoln's Sanctuary.* Designated a National Monument in 2000, you can visit it today: http://lincoln cottage.org.

2. Sword, *Mountains Touched by Fire,* 53. Lincoln quoted in Williams, *Lincoln & His Generals,* 272.

3. Foote, *The Civil War: A Narrative,* Vol. 3, *Red River to Appomattox,* 3.

4. My thanks to Michelle Krowl, Civil War and Reconstructionist specialist at the Library of Congress, for this brilliant piece of detective work. While historians have long noted that Lincoln borrowed Halleck's book from the library when he was alarmed at Mc-Clellan's immobility in early 1862, she was the first to check when he returned it—shortly after he made Grant general-in-chief. Library of Congress Borrowing Ledgers, Receipt Book L, 1861-1863, LC Archives, Manuscript Division, Library of Congress. Lincoln and Grant met at the White House that evening (*Chicago Tribune,* Mar. 25, 1864).

5. JDG, *Memoirs,* 128.

6. Ibid., 129. Emerson, *Letters,* 88. JDG, *Memoirs,* 129.

7. JDG, *Memoirs,* 129.

8. The last regular afternoon reception was on April 9 (the one on April 2 having been postponed), but it is more likely that Julia attended the Lincolns' last evening reception, on April 19, where there was "a large crowd," Lincoln Log, citing *Washington Chronicle,* Apr. 20, 1864. JDG, *Memoirs,* 129.

9. For discussions of Robert Lincoln's eye problems, see Clinton, *Mrs. Lincoln,* and Emerson, *Giant in the Shadows.*

10. JDG, *Memoirs,* 130.

11. Julia quoted in Kirkland, *The Pictorial Book of Anecdotes,* 554. Lincoln quoted in Flood, *Grant and Sherman,* 239, 240.

12. JDG, *Memoirs,* 130, 131.

13. Ibid.

14. New York Metropolitan Fair, ed. and pub., *A Record of the Metropolitan Fair,* 208, 209.

15. Smith, *Reminiscences,* 60, 61.

16. JDG, *Memoirs,* 131.

17. Smith, *Reminiscences,* 61. According to official records, voting for the sword raised nearly $45,000 for the Sanitary Commission. Grant won by almost sixteen thousand votes, many cast in blocks by political clubs. There were fears of corruption, and on the last day of voting, twenty-five New York City policemen were dispatched to the Arms

and Trophies Department to insure order. New York Metropolitan Fair, ed. and pub., *A Record of the Metropolitan Fair,* 208, 209. JDG, *Memoirs,* 144n15.

18. USG to JDG, May 31, 1864. Grant, *Papers,* 10:350.

19. JDG, *Memoirs,* 130.

20. "Grant and Lee, the Rival Chieftains," *New York Times,* Apr. 4, 1915.

21. Keckley, *Behind the Scenes at the White House,* 133, 134.

22. Stoddard, *Inside the White House,* 101. "Grant and Lee, the Rival Chieftains," *New York Times,* Apr. 4, 1915.

23. USG to JDG, June 19, 1864. Grant, *Papers,* 11:84, 85.

24. JDG, *Memoirs,* 132.

25. USG to JDG, Oct. 2, 1864. Grant, *Papers,* 12:262.

26. Editor's note, ibid., 12:262.

27. Quoted in Smith, *Grant,* 349.

28. JDG, *Memoirs,* 135.

29. Pfanz, *The Petersburg Campaign,* 1.

30. Appomattox Manor, http://www.nps.gov/nr/travel/jamesriver/app.htm. Gen. Dwight Eisenhower's decision to camp in a trailer outside beautiful Southwick Manor at Portsmouth, England, while preparing for the invasion of Normandy, is reminiscent of this decision by Grant. Sherman, *Memoirs,* 810.

31. JDG to Lillian Rogers, Feb. 7, 1865, quoted in Simpson, *Ulysses S. Grant,* 516n42.

32. Porter, *Campaigning with Grant,* 284.

33. USG to JDG, Nov. 25, 1864. Grant, *Papers,* 13:26. JDG, *Memoirs,* 139, 140.

34. JDG, *Memoirs,* 136, 137.

35. Ibid., 138.

36. USG to Edwin Stanton, Feb. 2, 1865. *Neale's Magazine,* July–December 1913, 58. Simon, "A Marriage Tested by War," 133. Burlingame, *Lincoln,* 2:754.

37. JDG, *Memoirs,* 137, 138. It is very possible that Julia's conversation with Lincoln about the peace commission took place during his next trip to City Point. McFeely's examination of the events argues that the president returned to Washington directly from Fortress Monroe and so would not have seen Julia, who remained at City Point. McFeely, *Grant: A Biography,* 208.

38. JDG, *Memoirs,* 141. *New York Times,* Mar. 8 and 15, 1865. JDG, *Memoirs,* 141.

39. Nicolay and Hay, "Abraham Lincoln," *Century Magazine,* vol. 17, 309. JDG, *Memoirs,* 142.

40. Ulysses S. Grant to Abraham Lincoln, Mar. 20, 1865, and AL to USG, Mar. 20, 1865. *Harper's Weekly,* December 1896, 358. Barnes, "With Lincoln," *Appleton's Magazine,* January–June 1907, 742.

41. JDG, *Memoirs,* 142.

42. Clinton, *Mrs. Lincoln,* 237. Barnes, "With Lincoln," 743.

43. JDG, *Memoirs,* 142.

44. Badeau, *Grant in Peace,* 362. Ross, *General's Wife,* 179.

45. "President and Mrs. Lincoln attend evening wedding of Capt. Charles Griffin and Sally Carroll, daughter of William T. Carroll, clerk of Supreme Court," *New York Herald,* Dec. 11, 1861. Badeau, *Grant in Peace,* 357. Clinton, *Mrs. Lincoln,* 238.

46. Badeau, *Grant in Peace,* 358, 359.

47. Ibid., 359. Julia's more subdued version of those events can be found on pp. 146 and 147 of her *Memoirs.*

48. Keckley, *Behind the Scenes*, 124. JDG, *Memoirs*, 149, 150.

49. In the bicentennial year of Lincoln's birth, 2009, the U.S. Postal Service issued a stamp, which purported to show the meeting at City Point and noted that the design of the stamp was taken from the G. P. A. Healy painting. It certainly was taken from it and was not a reproduction of it, for the image on the stamp excluded Admiral Porter.

50. Abraham Lincoln to Edwin Stanton, telegram, Apr. 3, 1865. Scott, ed., *The War of the Rebellion*, ser. 1, vol. 44, part III, ch. 58, p. 509.

51. Quoted in Burlingame, *Lincoln*, 2:790.

52. Ibid., 2:789, 790.

53. Barnes, "With Lincoln," 749. Lincoln quoted in Burlingame, *Lincoln*, 2:791, 792.

54. Barnes, "With Lincoln," 524.

55. JDG, *Memoirs*, 150.

56. Ibid.

57. Ibid., 150, 151, 167n3. She certainly regretted having missed a last opportunity to see the president, but she regretted more than that. In the final version of her memoirs, Julia began recounting the episode by acknowledging that "it reflects most severely on my amiability," and she ascribed the exquisite timing of the performance of that particular song to "bad luck," which was patently untrue. Indeed, she wrote an alternative version of the event in a draft of her memoirs in which she dissembled even more: "The dear, kind President's boat had left when I returned, and how unhappy and mortified I was when I learned that Mrs. Lincoln had been greatly disappointed at not having the band for her reception." Unhappy and mortified at Mary's disappointment? So manifestly untrue was the statement that Julia could not even bring herself to include it in the final version of her manuscript.

28. *"I did not want to go to the theater"*

1. USG to JDG, telegram, Apr. 7, 1865, and editor's note. Grant, *Papers*, 14:366.

2. JDG, *Memoirs*, 153. Grant and Granger, *In the Days of My Father*, 29.

3. Porter, *Campaigning with Grant*, 487. Ord had reason to feel indebted to Grant and Julia for standing up against Mary's attacks on Mrs. Ord. In a letter to his brother Placidus nearly a year earlier, Ord revealed that his beautiful wife had caused him much distress within his military family: "My enemies have made much use of the fact that my wife is a secessionist and related to their officers. . . . I have had this fact of my wife's family politics thrown in my teeth by generals' wives. . . . Should your wife still have her secessionist views, you had better at once quit the service and go into private business, for her politics will become known more rapidly than if she had the small pox—and officers will avoid having you with them for fear it will operate to their disadvantage—it is melancholy that this is so but it is true. . . ." Edward Ord to J. Placidus Ord, May 23, 1864. GTMGamms 146, Ord family papers, Georgetown Univ. Library Center for Special Collections.

4. JDG, *Memoirs*, 153, 154.

5. Brooks, *Mr. Lincoln's Washington*, 439, 440.

6. Titone, *My Thoughts Be Bloody*, 351. JDG, *Memoirs*, 154.

7. JDG, *Memoirs*, 154. The Grants did not know that the Lincolns would prove accomplices in getting Grant to the train on time. The day before, the president sent a note to his wife, suggesting that they take a carriage ride to the Navy Yard on Friday afternoon. Mary was delighted with her husband's tender gesture, and both Lincolns cleared their

calendars for what proved to be one of their most affectionate times together in all of their years in Washington.

8. JDG, *Memoirs*, 155. Her description of the messenger matches that of George Atzerodt, one of the assassination conspirators.

9. *Evening Star*, Apr. 14, 1865.

10. JDG, *Memoirs*, 155. Grant quoted in Young, *Around the World with General Grant*, 332.

11. In 1883, Colonel Rathbone murdered his wife and attempted suicide; he had been mentally unstable for years. The tragedy at Ford's Theatre was always considered the cause of his derangement. *New York Times*, Dec. 29, 1883.

12. JDG, *Memoirs*, 155, 156.

13. Ibid., 156.

14. Julia quoted in ibid. Grant quoted in Young, *Around the World*, 332. JDG, *Memoirs*, 157, 167n6.

15. Smith, *Grant*, 410.

16. JDG, *Memoirs*, 157. Jesse Grant recalled receiving a similar letter years later, when all of the conspirators were dead or in prison. Grant and Granger, *In the Days of My Father*, 40. Poore, ed., *The Conspiracy Trial*, 18.

29. *"the sunlight of his loyal love"*

1. JDG, *Memoirs*, 174.

2. Ross, *General's Wife*, 213.

3. Smithsonian Institution, *Annual Report of the Board of Regents of the Smithsonian Institution, 1887*, 11.

4. Ross, *The General's Wife*, 328. Julia did, sometimes, wear all white in the summer.

5. Julia quoted in "Foreword," by Simon, ed., in JDG, *Memoirs*, 20. Ross, *The General's Wife*, 335.

6. JDG, *Memoirs*, 155–57.

7. Perret, *Ulysses S. Grant*, 362.

8. Ross, *The General's Wife*, 328–32.

9. Cushman, "Whenever I Smoke a Cigar," included in Cushman, *Bloody Promenade*.

10. Weber, "John Y. Simon, Tireless Editor of Grant's Papers, Dies at 75," *New York Times*, July 10, 2008. Simon, in Bleser and Gordon, eds., *Intimate Strategies*, 135.

11. JDG, *Memoirs*, 331.

Conclusion

1. Ellen Sherman's stance in McMillen, *Seneca Falls*, 223. Julia's stance in "American President: Ulysses S. Grant. A Reference Page—Julia Grant," http://millercenter.org/president/grant/essays/firstlady/julia.

2. Adams, *The Education of Henry Adams*, 353.

3. Brown, *Hear That Lonesome Whistle Blow*, 140. Diary of Mary Ellen McClellan, 1870, Papers of George Brinton McClellan, LoC. The Territory of Wyoming allowed women to vote as early as 1869, as a means of attracting women residents, http://www.wyohistory.org/essays/right-choice-wrong-reasons-wyoming-women-win-right-vote.

Bibliography

Archival Collections

Georgetown University Library Center for Special Collections
    Ord Family Papers
Library of Congress, Manuscript Division
    Library of Congress Borrowing Ledgers
    Papers of Ulysses S. Grant
    Papers of Abraham Lincoln
    Papers of George Brinton McClellan
Princeton University Library
    Andre de Coppet Collection
University of Notre Dame Archives
    The Archdiocese of Cincinnati Collection
    William T. Sherman Family Papers

Published Collections and Memoirs

Adams, Henry. *The Education of Henry Adams: An Autobiography.* Cambridge, Mass.: Houghton Mifflin Company, 1918.

Brooks, Noah. *Abraham Lincoln and the Downfall of American Slavery.* New York: G. P. Putnam's Sons, 1894.

———. *Lincoln Observed: Civil War Dispatches of Noah Brooks.* Edited by Michael Burlingame. Baltimore: Johns Hopkins University Press, 1998.

———. *Mr. Lincoln's Washington; Selections from the Writings of Noah Brooks, Civil War Correspondent.* Edited by P. J. Staudenraus. South Brunswick, N.J.: T. Yoseloff, 1967.

Brown, George Levi. *Pleasant Valley: A History of Elizabethtown.* New York: Post and Gazette Print, 1905.

Cadwallader, Sylvanus, and Benjamin Platt Thomas. *Three Years with Grant.* New York: Knopf, 1955.

Custer, Elizabeth Bacon. *"Boots and Saddles"—Or, Life in Dakota with General Custer.* New York: Harper & Brothers, 1885.

———. *Following the Guidon.* New York: Harper & Brothers, 1890.

———. *Tenting on the Plains, Or, General Custer in Kansas and Texas.* New York: C. L. Webster & Company, 1889.

Dana, Charles A. *Recollections of the Civil War: With the Leaders at Washington and in the Field in the Sixties.* New York: D. Appleton and Company, 1913.

Dodge, Grenville M. *Personal Recollections of President Abraham Lincoln, General Ulysses S. Grant, and General William T. Sherman*. New York: Monarch Printing Company, 1914.

Frémont, Jessie Benton. *The Story of the Guard: A Chronicle of the War*. Boston: Ticknor and Fields, 1863.

———. *A Year of American Travel*. New York: Harper & Bros., 1878.

Frémont, John Charles, and Jessie Benton Frémont. *Memoirs of My Life: Including in the Narrative Five Journeys of Western Exploration, during the Years 1842, 1843–4, 1845–6–7, 1848–9, 1853–4*. Chicago: Belford, Clarke, 1887.

Frost, Mrs. J. Blakeslee. *The Rebellion in the United States, or The War of 1861*. Vol. II. Hartford: J. Blakeslee Frost, 1863.

Grant, Jesse Root, and Henry Francis Granger. *In the Days of My Father, General Grant*. New York: Harper & Brothers, 1925.

Grant, Julia Dent. *The Personal Memoirs of Julia Dent Grant (Mrs. Ulysses S. Grant)*. Edited by John Y. Simon. Carbondale: Southern Illinois University Press, 1975.

Grant, Ulysses S. *Personal Memoirs of U. S. Grant*. Vols. I and II. New York: Charles L. Webster & Company, 1885–86.

Grinnell, Josiah Bushnell, and Henry W. Parker. *Men & Events of Forty Years, Autobiographical Reminiscences of an Active Career from 1850 to 1891*. Boston: D. Lothrop, 1891.

Hay, John. *Inside Lincoln's White House: The Complete Civil War Diary of John Hay*. Edited by Michael Burlingame. Carbondale: Southern Illinois University Press, 1999.

Herr, Pamela, and Mary Lee Spence, eds. *The Letters of Jessie Benton Frémont*. Urbana: University of Illinois Press, 1993.

Joint Committee on the Conduct of the War. *Report of the Joint Committee on the Conduct of the War*. Washington, D.C.: Government Printing Office, 1863.

Julian, George Washington. *Political Recollections, 1840–1872*. Chicago: Jansen, McClurg & Company, 1884.

Keckley, Elizabeth. *Behind the Scenes: Or, Thirty Years a Slave and Four Years in the White House*. New York: G. W. Carleton & Co., Publishers, 1868.

Kirkland, Frazer. *The Pictorial Book of Anecdotes and Incidents of the War of Rebellion*. Hartford, Conn.: Hartford Publishing Co., 1866.

Laas, Virginia Jean, ed. *Wartime Washington: The Civil War Letters of Elizabeth Blair Lee*. Urbana: University of Illinois Press, 1991.

Lincoln, Abraham. *The Collected Works of Abraham Lincoln*. Edited by Roy P. Basler. New Brunswick, N.J.: Rutgers University Press, 1953.

Longfellow, Henry Wadsworth, and Samuel Longfellow, eds. *Life of Henry Wadsworth Longfellow: With Extracts from His Journals and Correspondence in Three Volumes*. Boston: Houghton, Mifflin, 1891.

Loughborough, Mary Ann Webster. *My Cave Life in Vicksburg with Letters of Trial and Travel*. New York: D. Appleton and Co., 1864.

McClellan, George Brinton. *McClellan's Own Story*. New York: C. L. Webster & Company, 1887.

New York Metropolitan Fair, ed. and pub. *A Record of the Metropolitan Fair: In Aid of the United States Sanitary Commission*. New York: New York Metropolitan Fair, 1864.

Pickett, La Salle Corbell. *Pickett and His Men*. Atlanta: Foote & Davies, 1899.

Porter, Horace. *Campaigning with Grant*. New York: Century, 1906.

———. "Eulogy of Ulysses S. Grant." In *Masterpieces of Modern Oratory*, edited by Edwin DuBois Shurter, 257–358. New York: Ginn and Company, 1906.

Scott, Robert N., ed. *The War of the Rebellion: A Compilation of the Official Records of the Union and Confederate Armies*. Washington, D.C.: Government Printing Office, 1880–1901.

Sears, Stephen W., ed. *The Civil War Papers of George B. McClellan: Selected Correspondence, 1860–1865*. New York: Ticknor & Fields, 1989.

Sherman, William T. *General W. T. Sherman as College President; a Collection of Letters, Documents, and Other Material, 1859–1861.* Edited by Walter L. Fleming. Cleveland, Ohio: Arthur M. Clark Company, 1912.

———. *Memoirs of General W. T. Sherman.* New York: Charles L. Webster & Co., 1891.

Simpson, Brooks D., and Jean V. Berlin, eds. *Sherman's Civil War: Selected Correspondence of William T. Sherman, 1860–1865.* Chapel Hill: University of North Carolina Press, 1999.

Smith, Adelaide W. *Reminiscences of an Army Nurse during the Civil War.* New York: Greaves Pub., 1911.

Smithsonian Institution. *Annual Report of the Board of Regents of the Smithsonian Institution, 1887.* Washington, D.C.: Government Printing Office, 1889.

Stoddard, William Osborn. *Inside the White House in War Times.* New York: C. L. Webster & Company, 1890.

Twain, Mark. *Autobiography of Mark Twain.* Vols. I and II. Oakland: University of California Press, 2010, 2013.

Villard, Henry. *Memoirs of Henry Villard, Journalist and Financier, 1835–1900.* Boston: Houghton, Mifflin, 1904.

Welles, Gideon. *Diary of Gideon Welles, Secretary of the Navy under Lincoln and Johnson.* Edited by Edgar Thaddeus Welles. Boston: Houghton Mifflin, 1911.

Wilson, James Harrison. *Under the Old Flag.* Vol. I. New York: D. Appleton and Co., 1912.

Books

Allen, Stephen Merrill, ed. *Memorial Life of General Ulysses S. Grant.* Boston: Webster Historical Society Publishers, 1889.

Badeau, Adam. *Grant in Peace, from Appomattox to Mount McGregor: A Personal Memoir.* Hartford, Conn.: S. S. Scranton & Co., 1887.

Ballard, Michael. *Vicksburg: The Campaign That Opened the Mississippi.* Chapel Hill: University of North Carolina Press, 2004.

Barry, Susan R. *Fixing My Gaze: A Scientist's Journey into Seeing in Three Dimensions.* New York: Basic Books, 2009.

Berkin, Carol. *Civil War Wives: The Lives and Times of Angelina Grimké Weld, Varina Howell Davis, and Julia Dent Grant.* New York: Alfred A. Knopf, 2009.

Berry, Stephen W. *All That Makes a Man.* New York: Oxford University Press, 2003.

Bleser, Carol K., and Lesley Gordon, eds. *Intimate Strategies of the Civil War: Military Commanders and Their Wives.* New York: Oxford University Press, 2001.

Borneman, Walter R. *Polk: The Man Who Transformed the Presidency and America.* New York: Random House, 2008.

Brooks, Noah. *Abraham Lincoln, and the Downfall of American Slavery.* New York: G. P. Putnam's Sons, 1894.

Brown, Dee. *Hear That Lonesome Whistle Blow: The Epic Story of the Transcontinental Railroads.* New York: Henry Holt and Company, 1977.

Burlingame, Michael. *Abraham Lincoln: A Life.* Vols. I and II. Baltimore: Johns Hopkins University Press, 2008.

Burton, Katherine. *Three Generations: Maria Boyle Ewing (1801–1864), Ellen Ewing Sherman (1824–1888), Minnie Sherman Fitch (1851–1913).* New York: Longmans, Green, 1947.

Carson, Kit. *Kit Carson's Autobiography. [With a Portrait and a Facsimile.].* Edited by Milo Milton Quaife. Chicago: R. R. Donnelley & Sons, 1935.

Cashin, Joan E. *First Lady of the Confederacy: Varina Davis's Civil War.* Cambridge, Mass.: Belknap Press of Harvard University Press, 2006.

Catton, Bruce. *Grant Moves South.* Edison, N.J.: Castle Books, 2000.

———. "Introduction." In Julia Dent Grant, *The Personal Memoirs of Julia Dent Grant (Mrs.*

Ulysses S. Grant), 1–7. Edited by John Y. Simon. Carbondale: Southern Illinois University Press, 1975.

———. *Mr. Lincoln's Army: The Odyssey of General George Brinton McClellan and the Army of the Potomac.* New York: Doubleday & Co., Inc., 1951.

Chaffin, Tom. *Pathfinder: John Charles Frémont and the Course of American Empire.* New York: Hill and Wang, 2002.

Clinton, Catherine. *Divided Houses: Gender and the Civil War.* New York: Oxford University Press, 1992.

———. *Mrs. Lincoln: A Life.* New York: HarperCollins, 2009.

Clinton, Catherine, and Nina Silber, eds. *Battle Scars: Gender and Sexuality in the American Civil War.* New York: Oxford University Press, 2006.

Creighton, Margaret. *The Colors of Courage: Gettysburg's Forgotten History: Immigrants, Women, and African Americans in the Civil War's Defining Battle.* New York: Basic Books, 2006.

Cushman, Stephen. *Bloody Promenade: Reflections on a Civil War Battle.* Charlottesville: University Press of Virginia, 1999.

Denton, Sally. *Passion and Principle: John and Jessie Frémont, the Couple Whose Power, Politics, and Love Shaped Nineteenth-Century America.* New York: Bloomsbury, 2007.

Dickens, Charles. *Great Expectations.* Cambridge, Mass.: Riverside Press, 1868.

Donald, David Herbert. *Lincoln.* New York: Simon & Schuster, 1995.

Eaton, John, and Ethel Osgood Mason. *Grant, Lincoln, and the Freedmen.* New York: Longmans, Green, and Co., 1907.

Emerson, Jason. *Giant in the Shadows: The Life of Robert T. Lincoln.* Carbondale: Southern Illinois University Press, 2012.

Emerson, Ralph Waldo. *Letters and Social Aims.* Boston: J. R. Osgood, 1876.

Faust, Drew Gilpin. *Mothers of Invention: Women of the Slaveholding South in the American Civil War.* Chapel Hill: University of North Carolina Press, 1996.

Fellman, Michael. *Citizen Sherman: A Life of William Tecumseh Sherman.* New York: Random House, 1995.

Flood, Charles Bracelen. *Grant and Sherman: The Friendship That Won the Civil War.* New York: Farrar, Straus and Giroux, 2005.

———. *Lincoln at the Gates of History.* New York: Simon & Schuster, 2009.

Foote, Shelby. *The Civil War: A Narrative.* Vol. 3, *Red River to Appomattox.* New York: Vintage Books, 1986.

Fraser, Mary Ann. *Vicksburg: The Battle That Won the Civil War.* New York: Henry Holt and Company, LLC, 1999.

Garland, Hamlin. *Ulysses S. Grant, His Life and Character.* New York: The MacMillan Company, 1920.

Giesberg, Judith Ann. *Army at Home: Women and the Civil War on the Northern Home Front.* Chapel Hill: University of North Carolina Press, 2009.

Glatthaar, Joseph T. *Partners in Command: The Relationships between Leaders in the Civil War.* New York: Free Press, 1994.

Goodwin, Doris Kearns. *Team of Rivals: The Political Genius of Abraham Lincoln.* New York: Simon & Schuster, 2005.

Gordon, Lesley J. *General George E. Pickett in Life and Legend.* Chapel Hill: University of North Carolina Press, 1998.

Gosman, A. MacDonald, and A. Vanderjagt, eds. *Princes and Princely Culture, 1450–1650.* Leiden, the Netherlands: Brill NV, 2003.

Groom, Winston. *Vicksburg, 1863.* New York: Alfred A. Knopf, 2009.

Guelzo, Allen C. *Lincoln's Emancipation Proclamation: The End of Slavery in America.* New York: Simon & Schuster, 2004.

Hassler, Warren W. *A. P. Hill: Lee's Forgotten General.* Richmond: Garrett & Massie, 1957.

————. *General George B. McClellan: Shield of the Union.* Baton Rouge: Louisiana State University Press, 1957.

Herr, Pamela. *Jessie Benton Frémont: A Biography.* New York: F. Watts, 1987.

Holzer, Harold, and Eric Foner. *The Civil War in 50 Objects.* New York: Viking, 2013.

Hussey, M. Edward. *Archbishop Purcell of Cincinnati.* Amazon.com Kindle: 2011.

Johnson, Edward Underwood, and Clarence Clough Buel, eds. *Battles and Leaders.* Vols. I–IV. New York: The Century Co., 1884.

Kennedy, John F. *Profiles in Courage.* Memorial ed. New York: Harper & Row, 1964.

Kennett, Lee. *Sherman: A Soldier's Life.* New York: Perennial, 2002.

Kimmel, Stanley. *Mr. Lincoln's Washington.* New York: Coward-McCann, Inc., 1957.

Lester, Charles Edward. *Life and Public Services of Charles Sumner.* New York: U.S. Publishing Company, 1874.

Lewis, Lloyd. *Sherman, Fighting Prophet.* New York: Harcourt, Brace and Company, 1932.

Markland, Absalom. "A. H. Markland." In *Reminiscences of Abraham Lincoln by Distinguished Men of His Time,* edited by Allen Thorndyke Rice, 315-29. New York: Haskell House Publishers Ltd., 1971. Originally published in 1888.

Marszalek, John F. *Commander of All Lincoln's Armies: A Life of General Henry W. Halleck.* Cambridge, Mass.: Belknap Press of Harvard University Press, 2004.

————. "General and Mrs. William T. Sherman: A Contentious Union." In *Intimate Strategies of the Civil War: Military Commanders and Their Wives,* edited by Carol K. Bleser and Lesley Gordon, 138-56. New York: Oxford University Press, 2001.

————. *Sherman: A Soldier's Passion for Order.* New York: Free Press, 1993.

————. *Sherman's Other War: The General and the Civil War Press.* Kent, Ohio: Kent State University Press, 1999.

McAllister, Anna Shannon. *Ellen Ewing Sherman, Wife of General Sherman.* New York: Benziger Brothers, 1936.

McCullough, David G. *The Path between the Seas: The Creation of the Panama Canal, 1870–1914.* New York: Simon & Schuster, 1977.

McFeely, William S. *Grant: A Biography.* New York: Norton, 1981.

McMillen, Sally. *Seneca Falls and the Origins of the Woman's Suffrage Rights Movement.* New York: Oxford University Press, 2009.

McMurry, Richard M. *Atlanta 1864: Last Chance for the Confederacy.* Lincoln: University of Nebraska Press, 2000.

McPherson, James M. *Battle Cry of Freedom: The Civil War Era.* New York: Oxford University Press, 1988.

Miers, Schenk, and Charles Percy Powell. *Lincoln Day by Day: A Chronology, 1809–1865.* Washington, D.C.: Lincoln Sesquicentennial Commission, 1960.

Nevins, Allan. *Frémont, Pathmarker of the West.* Lincoln: University of Nebraska Press, 1992.

————. *Ordeal of the Union: A House Dividing, 1852–1857.* Vol. 2. New York: Charles Scribner's, 1947.

Nicolay, John G., and John Hay. *Abraham Lincoln: A History.* Vols. I–X. New York: The Century Co., 1914.

Perret, Geoffrey. *Ulysses S. Grant: Soldier & President.* New York: Random House, 1997.

Pfanz, Donald. *The Petersburg Campaign: Abraham Lincoln at City Point, March 20-April 9, 1865.* Lynchburg, Va.: H. E. Howard, 1989.

Phillips, Catherine Coffin. *Jessie Benton Frémont, a Woman Who Made History.* San Francisco: J. H. Nash, 1935.

Pierson, Michael D. *Free Hearts and Free Homes: Gender and American Antislavery Politics.* Chapel Hill: University of North Carolina Press, 2003.

Pinsker, Matthew. *Lincoln's Sanctuary: Abraham Lincoln and the Soldiers' Home.* New York: Oxford University Press, 2003.

Poore, Benjamin Perley, ed. *The Conspiracy Trial for the Murder of the President.* Vol. III. Boston: J. E. Tilton and Company, 1866.

Rafuse, Ethan Sepp. *McClellan's War: The Failure of Moderation in the Struggle for the Union.* Bloomington: Indiana University Press, 2005.

Rice, Allen Thorndyke, ed. *Reminiscences of Abraham Lincoln by Distinguished Men of His Time.* New York: Haskell House Publishers Ltd., 1971. Originally published in 1888.

Robertson, James I., Jr. *General A. P. Hill: The Story of a Confederate Warrior.* New York: Random House, 1987.

Roosevelt, Theodore, Jr. *Thomas Hart Benton.* New York: Houghton Mifflin, 1886.

Ross, Ishbel. *The General's Wife: The Life of Mrs. Ulysses S. Grant.* New York: Dodd, Mead, 1959.

———. *Proud Kate, Portrait of an Ambitious Woman.* New York: Harper, 1953.

Sears, Stephen W. *Controversies & Commanders: Dispatches from the Army of the Potomac.* Boston: Houghton Mifflin, 2000.

———. *George B. McClellan: The Young Napoleon.* New York: Ticknor & Fields, 1988.

———. *Landscape Turned Red: The Battle of Antietam.* New Haven: Ticknor & Fields, 1983.

———. *To the Gates of Richmond: The Peninsula Campaign.* New York: Ticknor & Fields, 1992.

Secrest, Meryle. *Shoot the Widow: Adventures of a Biographer in Search of Her Subject.* New York: Knopf, 2007.

Shurter, Edwin DuBois, ed. *Masterpieces of Modern Oratory.* Boston: Ginn & Company, 1906.

Sides, Hampton. *Blood and Thunder: An Epic of the American West.* New York: Doubleday, 2006.

Silber, Nina. *Daughters of the Union: Northern Women Fight the Civil War.* Cambridge, Mass.: Harvard University Press, 2005.

———. *Gender and the Sectional Conflict.* Chapel Hill: University of North Carolina Press, 2008.

Simon, John Y. "A Marriage Tested by War: Ulysses and Julia Grant." In *Intimate Strategies of the Civil War: Military Commanders and Their Wives,* edited by Carol K. Bleser and Lesley Gordon, 123–37. New York: Oxford University Press, 2001.

Simpson, Brooks D. *Ulysses S. Grant: Triumph over Adversity, 1822–1865.* Boston: Houghton Mifflin, 2000.

Smith, Jean Edward. *Grant.* New York: Simon & Schuster Paperbacks, 2001.

Stanton, Elizabeth Cady, Susan Brownell Anthony, et al. *History of Woman Suffrage, 1876–1885.* Rochester, N.Y.: Charles Mann, 1887.

Stone, Irving. *Immortal Wife, the Biographical Novel of Jessie Benton Frémont.* Garden City, N.Y.: Doubleday, Doran, 1944.

Summerscale, Kate. *The Suspicions of Mr. Whicher: A Shocking Murder and the Undoing of a Great Victorian Detective.* New York: Walker & Co., 2008.

Sword, Wiley. *Mountains Touched by Fire.* New York: St. Martin's Press, 1995.

Tarbell, Ida. *The Life of Abraham Lincoln.* Vol. II. New York: The Macmillan Company, 1910.

Titone, Nora. *My Thoughts Be Bloody: The Bitter Rivalry between Edwin and John Wilkes Booth That Led to an American Tragedy.* New York: Free Press, 2010.

Twain, Mark. *The Innocents Abroad.* New York: Library of America, 1984.

Varon, Elizabeth R. *We Mean to Be Counted: White Women & Politics in Antebellum Virginia.* Chapel Hill: University of North Carolina Press, 1998.

Wagner, Margaret E., Gary Gallagher, and Paul Finkelman, eds. *The Library of Congress Civil War Desk Reference.* New York: Simon & Schuster, 2002.

Waugh, Joan. *U. S. Grant: American Hero, American Myth.* Chapel Hill: University of North Carolina Press, 2009.

Waugh, John C. *The Class of 1846: From West Point to Appomattox: Stonewall Jackson, George McClellan, and Their Brothers.* New York: Warner Books, 1994.

———. *Lincoln and McClellan: The Troubled Partnership between a President and His General.* New York: Palgrave Macmillan, 2010.

———. *Reelecting Lincoln: The Battle for the 1864 Presidency.* New York: Crown Publishers, 1997.

Williams, T. Harry. *Lincoln & His Generals.* New York: Knopf, 1952.

———. *McClellan, Sherman, and Grant.* New Brunswick, N.J.: Rutgers University Press, 1962.

Wilson, Robert Mills, and Carl Clair. *They Also Served: Wives of Civil War Generals.* Philadelphia: Xlibris, 2006.

Winschel, Terrence J. *Vicksburg: Fall of the Confederate Gibraltar.* Abilene, Tex.: McWhiney Foundation Press, 1999.

Young, John Russell. *Around the World with General Grant.* Edited by Michael Fellman. Baltimore, Md.: Johns Hopkins University Press, 2002.

Periodicals

Barnes, John S. "With Lincoln from Washington to Richmond in 1865." *Appleton's Magazine,* January-June 1907, 516-42.

Cincinnati Commercial

Dana, Charles A. "Reminiscences of Men and Events of the Civil War." *McClure's Magazine,* November 1897, 561-671.

Deupree, J. G. "The Noxubee Squadron of the First Mississippi Cavalry, C.S.A., 1861-1865." Publications of the Mississippi Historical Society, Centenary Series, Vol. 2, 1918, 12-143.

Emerson, John. "Grant's Life in the West." *The Midland Monthly Magazine,* January-June 1896, 121-31.

Evening Star

Frémont, John Charles. "The Conquest of California." *The Century Magazine,* April 1891, 917-28.

Goodheart. Adam. "Women and Children First." *New York Times* Disunion Blog, February 4, 2011.

Harper's Weekly

Hooper, Candice Shy. "The Two Julias." *New York Times* Disunion blog, February 14, 2013.

Howe, Daniel Walker. "American Victorianism as a Culture." *American Quarterly,* December 1975, 507-32.

"Jessie Benton Frémont in Her Girlhood Days." *Press and Horticulturist* (Riverside, Calif., weekly newspaper), January 16, 1903, 3.

New York Times

Nicolay, John G., and John Hay. "Abraham Lincoln: A History." *Century Illustrated Monthly Magazine,* 1888, 35, 281-305, 353-416.

Punch magazine

Rafuse, Ethan. "Typhoid and Tumult: Lincoln's Response to General McClellan's Bout with Typhoid Fever during the Winter of 1861/1862." *The Journal of the Abraham Lincoln Association* 18, no. 2 (Summer 1997): 1-16.

"Reminiscences of General Frederick Dent Grant." *U. S. Grant Association Newsletter* 6, no. 3 (April 1969): 17-24.

Schenker, Carl A., Jr. "Ulysses in His Tent: Halleck, Grant, Sherman, and 'The Turning Point of the War.'" *Civil War History* 56, no. 2 (June 2010): 175-221.

Sears, Stephen W. "The Curious Case of General McClellan's Memoirs." *Civil War History* 34, no. 2 (1988): 101-14.

Steckel, Richard H. "The Age at Leaving Home in the United States, 1850-1860." *Social Science History* 20, no. 4 (Winter 1996): 507-32.

Tap, Bruce. "Amateurs at War: Abraham Lincoln and the Committee on the Conduct of the War." *Journal of the Abraham Lincoln Association* 23, no. 2 (Summer 2002): 1-18.

Varon, Elizabeth. "Gender History and Origins of the Civil War." *OAH Magazine of History* 25, no. 2 (April 2011): 19-23.

Washington Globe

Online Resources

Abraham Lincoln, Special War Order No. 1, January 31, 1862. http://www.presidency.ucsb.edu/ws/index.php?pid=69788#axzz1JYf1qliC.

"Airliewood." http://www.airliewood.com/History/civilwar.html.

"American President: Ulysses S. Grant. A Reference Page—Julia Grant." http://millercenter.org/president/grant/essays/firstlady/julia.

Behn, Richard. "Mr. Lincoln and Friends." Web site courtesy of the Lehrman Institute and the Lincoln Institute. http://www.mrlincolnandfriends.org/inside.asp?pageID=12&subjectID=11.

"Catharine Beecher." http://150.mansfield.edu/beecher.htm.

Death statistics for the nineteenth century. http://eh.net/encyclopedia/article/haines.demography.

"History of the Maryland Flag." Maryland Office of the Secretary of State. http://www.sos.state.md.us/services/flaghistory.htm.

"A History of U.S. Topographical Engineers, 1818–1863." http://www.topogs.org/History2.htm.

Inflation calculator. http://www.westegg.com/inflation/infl.cgi.

Journal of Commerce. "Why Lincoln Closed the JoC." http://www.joc.com/sites/default/files/joc_inc/history/p8.html.

Library of Congress. "Irish-Catholic Immigration to America." http://www.loc.gov/teachers/classroommaterials/presentationsandactivities/presentations/immigration/irish2.html.

Lincoln Log. http://www.thelincolnlog.org.

Manning, Chandra. "Civil War Letters." http://teachinghistory.org/best-practices/examples-of-historical-thinking/25048.

National Park Service Web sites:
Appomattox Manor. http://www.nps.gov/nr/travel/jamesriver/app.htm.
Battle of Chickasaw Bayou. http://www.nps.gov/hps/abpp/battles/ms003.htm.
Civil War death statistics. http://www.nps.gov/nr/travel/national_cemeteries/Death.html.

Nelly McClellan's grave. http://www.findagrave.com/cgi-binfg.cgi?page=gr&GRid=8215496.

SS *Crescent City* passenger list. http://www.sfgenealogy.com/californiabound/cb077.htm.

Steven L. Hoskin Historical Autographs. Letter from EES to S. Hurlburt. http://www.civilwar-autographs.com/search.php.

United States Mint. http://www.firstspousecoins.us/home/julia-grant-first-spouse-gold-coins/.

U.S. Army History. http://www.history.army.mil/html/faq/oaths.html.

U. S. Grant Homepage. http://www.granthomepage.com.

Weather:
www.accuweather.com/en/us/washington-dc/20006/september-weather/327659.
www.currentresults.com/Weather/US/humidity-city-september.php.

http://www.wyohistory.org/essays/right-choice-wrong-reasons-wyoming-women-win-right-vote.

Index

CIVIL WAR IN THE NORTH